Bernarr Rainbow on Music
Memoirs and Selected Writings

Bernarr Rainbow on Music
Memoirs and Selected Writings

With introductions by
Gordon Cox & Charles Plummeridge

GENERAL EDITOR OF THE SERIES: Peter Dickinson

THE BOYDELL PRESS

ISBN 978 1 84383 592 9

The Boydell Press is an imprint of Boydell & Brewer Ltd
PO Box 9, Woodbridge, Suffolk IP12 3DF, UK
and of Boydell & Brewer Inc.
668 Mt Hope Ave, Rochester, NY 14620, USA
website: www.boydellandbrewer.com

A catalogue record for this book is available from the British Library

The publisher has no responsibility for the continued existence
or accuracy of URLs for external or third-party internet websites
referred to in this book, and does not guarantee that any content
on such websites is, or will remain, accurate or appropriate.

This publication is printed on acid-free paper

Designed and typeset in Garamond Premier Pro by
David Roberts, Pershore, Worcestershire

Printed in Great Britain by
CPI Antony Rowe, Chippenham and Eastbourne

Contents

Plates

Contributors

Gordon Cox has written extensively on the history of music education, including most recently his co-edited book with Robin Stevens, *The Origins and Foundations of Music Education: Cross-Cultural Historical Studies of Music in Compulsory Schooling*. He is a member of the History Standing Committee of the International Society for Music Education (ISME).

Charles Plummeridge is Emeritus Reader at the Institute of Education, University of London. He lives in Norfolk where he is an organist and choral conductor. His publications include books and articles on music education. He has lectured in Europe, South East Asia, the Caribbean and Africa, and was recently Visiting Professor at the new University of Nicosia.

Peter Dickinson is Emeritus Professor of the Universities of Keele and London. There are several CDs of his music available and his books include studies of Lennox Berkeley, Aaron Copland, John Cage, Lord Berners and Samuel Barber. This is the third major Rainbow book he has edited, published with the support of the Bernarr Rainbow Trust.

General Editor's Foreword
and Acknowledgements

*B*ERNARR RAINBOW ON MUSIC: *Memoirs and Selected Writings* is the largest of the three books devoted to his writings. First came *Music in Educational Thought and Practice* (Boydell Press, 2006) in an enlarged second edition with a Foreword by Sir Peter Maxwell Davies, Master of the Queen's Music, and additional chapters by Gordon Cox bringing the study up to date. Then *Four Centuries of Music Teaching Manuals, 1518–1932* (Boydell Press, 2009) which provides Rainbow's prefaces to his Classic Texts in Music Education. In this present book I have assembled Rainbow's own memoir as well as the study he wrote of John Curwen. Those are followed by Gordon Cox's selection from Rainbow's published articles.

I must first acknowledge the courage of Bernarr Rainbow himself in writing his memoir at my suggestion when he was struggling with ill health in the year before he died. I thought the task might focus his mind at a difficult time and also provide answers when posterity enquired who this pioneer in the history of music education had been, when the Bernarr Rainbow Trust would be keeping his name and his work alive. I was delighted at the result, although I found that Rainbow felt unable to continue after 1972 when he left the College of St Mark and St John. Like some other colleges of education, Marjon, as it was widely known, felt the need to move out of London. Rainbow knew his research would be impossible from a base in distant Plymouth, so he moved to Gipsy Hill College, later within Kingston University, and went on with his work well into retirement – to our great benefit.

All his concerns appear in the contents of this book. Some issues remain topical. He lamented the inadequate and uneven preparation from Primary to Secondary education as it affected music – the problem is still with us. He attacked the instrumental culture which is too often substituted for singing in the Primary school and he lamented the retreat from teaching musical literacy – little change there. But, perhaps above all, he saw salvation in Tonic Sol-fa, investigating at great length and for many years all the conflicting techniques that have been employed. One can be forgiven for concluding that the complex systems adumbrated by some of the teaching specialists in their handbooks in previous centuries make conventional staff notation seem a brilliantly lucid invention. The crusade for Tonic Sol-fa is one battle that Rainbow has not won, but the stages in the campaign as he outlines them remain intriguing.

His career was ending at a time when popular culture began to accumulate prestige at the expense of classical music in school and elsewhere. We are now faced with the dominance of democratic culture through the media and the internet; the downgrading of music to an accompaniment for visual images; and the cult of the celebrity.

There is inevitably some overlapping in these articles because Rainbow was dealing with a slightly different readership on each occasion and at a different period.

When I cleared Rainbow's desk and prepared the house for sale in 1998 I found a piece of paper in shaky handwriting. On one side there was a note of a hospital appointment but on the other he had written:

Perfectability   Sandcastles

... and then I think, well, if that's all I've done, at least I enjoyed doing it – immensely.

It's not a bad epitaph, and his enjoyment emerges clearly from all the varied subjects represented in this collection. I have not provided biographical information beyond the notes I have added to *A Salute to Life*, since those details are in my introduction to *Music in Educational Thought and Practice*.

I am grateful to both Charles Plummeridge for his introduction to the memoir and to Gordon Cox for making his selection of writings which he also introduces. Both of them knew Rainbow. I appreciated talking to Christian Wilson, Rainbow's colleague at the College of St Mark and St John, about the context there. I have also had discussions with John Stephens about the current scene in music education and with Yvonne Lawton about the Curwen Institute. I spoke to Canon Colin Scott Dempster, the Chaplain at the College of St Mark and St John in Rainbow's last year, and I decided not to include Rainbow's derogatory remarks about the more popular approach to chapel music or the ways in which he thought the College's move was being negotiated; his memoir stopped abruptly anyway. Sarah Aitchison and her colleagues Katie Mooney and Rebecca Webster at the Institute of Education, University of London, have helped with photocopying. So did the Rev. Professor Anthony Kemp, Claire Kidwell at the library of Trinity College of Music and Elizabeth Fulton at the Incorporated Society of Musicians. I am grateful to my wife Bridget, one of Rainbow's students, for advice with all these publications.

It was a pleasure to deal with the publishers who allowed the Bernarr Rainbow Trust, as a charity, to reprint his articles without charge. I am especially grateful to David Roberts for extensive work preparing material from so many sources and for design, as well as the team at Boydell & Brewer where so much has been done for the writings of Bernarr Rainbow.

The sources of the contents of this book:

A Salute to Life is © the Bernarr Rainbow Trust.

John Curwen: A Short Critical Biography is reproduced by kind permission of Novello & Company Limited, London. It can still be obtained separately.

The portrait of John Curwen, National Portrait Gallery, London, is reproduced by kind permission. The original of the sketch of San Gimignano was kindly provided by Rainbow's valued neighbour Sheila Sutehall.

The photographs are © the Bernarr Rainbow Trust, except where otherwise indicated, and are now in the archive at the Institute of Education, University of London.

The articles listed in order of appearance:

'That Great Dust-heap Called History', *International Journal of Music Education*, o.s. vol. 20 no. 1 (1992), pp. 9–16 (by permission of Sage Publications Ltd)

'Historical Research', in *Some Approaches to Research in Music Education*, ed. A. E. Kemp (Reading: International Society for Music Education Research Commission, 1992), pp. 19–32 (© International Society for Music Education, www.isme.org; used by permission)

'Count Leo Tolstoy, Music Teacher', *Music Teacher*, August 1980, pp. 11–12 (© Bernarr Rainbow Trust; by permission of Rheingold Publishing)

'The Land with Music: Reality and Myth in Music Education', in *Research in Music Education: A Festschrift for Arnold Bentley*, ed. A. E. Kemp (Reading: International Society for Music Education, 1988), pp. 88–96; also in *Music in Educational Thought and Practice* (Aberystwyth: Boethius Press, 1989), pp. 342–54 (© Bernarr Rainbow Trust) (© Bernarr Rainbow Trust)

'The French Revolution and Music Teaching: A Bicentennial Review', *Music Teacher*, July 1989, pp. 26–7 (© Bernarr Rainbow Trust; by permission of Rheingold Publishing)

'An Excellency in Music', *Journal of Education*, vol. 8 no. 1056 (July 1957), pp. 292–5 (by permission of Elsevier Ltd)

'The Glass Harmonicon Rediscovered', *Music in Education*, January 1974, pp. 18–19 (by permission of Novello & Co.)

'The Miseries of Music Masters', *The Musical Times*, vol. 127 no. 1718 (April 1986), pp. 201–3 (by permission of Peter Phillips, *The Musical Times*)

'The Rise of Popular Music Education in Nineteenth-Century England', *Victorian Studies*, vol. 30 no. 1 (Autumn 1986), pp. 25–49 (by permission of Indiana University Press)

'Plato and Music Today', *Music Teacher*, December 1981, p. 12 (© Bernarr Rainbow Trust; by permission of Rheingold Publishing)

Onward from Butler: School Music, 1945–1985 (Coventry: The Curwen Institute, 1885); also in *Music in Educational Thought and Practice* (Aberystwyth: Boethius Press, 1989), pp. 342–54 (© Bernarr Rainbow Trust)

'Freedom and its Price', *British Journal of Music Education*, vol. 6 no. 2 (1989), pp. 193–203 (© Cambridge University Press; reproduced by permission)

'Some New Music Teaching Devices from France', *Music in Education*, September 1961, p. 119 (by permission of Novello & Co.)

'Curwen, Kodály and the Future', *Music Teacher*, December 1979, pp. 11–12 (© Bernarr Rainbow Trust; by permission of Rheingold Publishing)

'An Ear for Music', *Incorporated Society of Musicians Journal*, October 1980, pp. 15, 17, 18 (by permission, *ISM Journal*)

'The New Curwen Method: A Partnership of Ear, Eye and Voice' [3 parts], *Music Teacher*, May 1988, pp. 9–10; June 1988, pp. 19, 21; August 1988, pp. 15–16 (© Bernarr Rainbow Trust; by permission of Rheingold Publishing)

'Sol-fa as an Ethnic Link', *Music Teacher*, March 1982, p. 16 (© Bernarr Rainbow Trust; by permission of Rheingold Publishing)

'The Kodály Concept and its Pedigree', *British Journal of Music Education*, vol. 7 no. 3 (1990), pp. 197–203 (© Cambridge University Press; reproduced by permission)

'Cheironomy', *Music Teacher*, August 1979, pp. 19, 21 (© Bernarr Rainbow Trust; by permission of Rheingold Publishing)

'Victorian Street Music', *Trinity College of Music Magazine* [2 parts], Autumn, 1997, pp. 6–7; Summer 1998, pp. 16–17 (by permission of Trinity College of Music)

'The English Promenade Concert' [3 parts], *Trinity College of Music Magazine*, Summer 1995, pp. 24–5; Autumn 1995, pp. 26–7; Spring 1996, pp. 28–9 (by permission of Trinity College of Music)

'Thomas Helmore and the Anglican Plainsong Revival' [3 parts], *The Musical Times*, vol. 100 no. 1400 (October 1959), pp. 348–9; vol. 100 no. 1401 (November 1959), pp. 621–2; vol. 100 no. 1402 (December 1959), p. 683 (by permission of Peter Phillips, *The Musical Times*)

'Notes from Two French Organ Lofts', *The Musical Times*, vol. 102 no. 1423 (September 1961), p. 578 (by permission of Peter Phillips, *The Musical Times*)

'William Dyce', *The Musical Times*, vol. 105 no. 1462 (December 1964), pp. 900–1 (by permission of Peter Phillips, *The Musical Times*)

'Walmisley's Psychedelic Magnificat: a New Hypothesis?', in *English Church Music: A Collection of Essays* (Addington Palace, Croydon: Royal School of Church Music, 1980), pp. 19–24 (by permission of The Royal School of Church Music, 19 The Close, Salisbury, SP1 2EB)

'The Hymn-Singing American', *The Musical Times*, vol. 123 no. 1674 (August 1982), pp. 565–66 (by permission of Peter Phillips, *The Musical Times*)

'Charity Children: Singing for their Supper', *The Musical Times*, vol. 125 no. 1694 (April 1984), pp. 227–9 (by permission of Peter Phillips, *The Musical Times*)

'John Jebb (1805–1886) and the Choral Service', in *The World of Church Music*, ed. Lionel Dakers (Addington Palace, Croydon: Royal School of Church Music, 1986), pp. 69–80 (by permission of The Royal School of Church Music, 19 The Close, Salisbury, SP1 2EB)

'In Quires & Places Where They Sing: Some Historical Aspects of Anglican Church Music' [3 parts], *Choir & Organ*, vol. 3 no. 1 (February 1995), pp. 13–7; vol. 3 no. 2 (April 1995), pp. 16–19; vol. 3 no. 3 (June 1995), pp. 23–7 (© Rhinegold Publishing Ltd; reproduced by permission)

Review of R. M. Wilson, *Anglican Chant and Chanting in England, Scotland and America, 1660–1820*, in *Choir & Organ*, vol. 6 no. 2 (March/April 1998), pp. 67–8 (© Rhinegold Publishing Ltd; reproduced by permission)

PETER DICKINSON
Aldeburgh, May 2010

PART I

A Salute to Life

Introduction to 'A Salute to Life'

Charles Plummeridge

BERNARR RAINBOW was a prominent member of a group of forward-looking musicians and educationists who made a significant contribution to the growth of music in schools during the immediate post-war years. Through his pedagogical writings he influenced a large number of teachers, and as a researcher was a major figure in the establishment of music education as an academic field of study. A stimulating and often-provocative lecturer and an active member of numerous committees, he was well known and highly respected within the music education community. His memoirs are full of interest and wry humour, and help us to understand the thinking that informed his views and practices. They also provide some fascinating insights into a period of extensive educational development and far-reaching social change.

Rainbow's recollections of his early years reveal much about educational policy and provision in the 1920s as well as musical tuition in schools. At the elementary level, class singing featured as a regular component of the curriculum, and had done so since the nineteenth century, but there was little musical education for secondary pupils. Rainbow attended a reputable grammar school – Rutlish School, Merton – which was renowned for its academic standards but, as he relates, never regarded music as an integral part of a general education. This was by no means uncommon. In a famous report on the state of music in secondary schools at the beginning of the 1920s, Dr Arthur Somervell, HM Chief Inspector for Music, expressed disappointment over the limited provision for the subject within the curriculum.[1] Some years earlier, policy makers had drawn attention to the educational value of music and advised on classroom activities, but their ideals were often far removed from the reality of practice.[2]

Accordingly, for Rainbow and his fellow pupils there were no class music lessons, although he did enjoy taking part in the school's annual Gilbert and Sullivan productions and later produced these operas himself. However, like many of his contemporaries, he began as a church chorister. Where there was a good musical tradition, the boys performed an extensive repertoire and acquired a range of aural and reading skills that would provide an excellent

---

[1] Board of Education, *Report on Music Teaching in Secondary Schools*, Circular 1252 (London: HMSO, 1922). See also G. Cox, ed., *Sir Arthur Somervell on Music Education* (Woodbridge: Boydell Press, 2003).

[2] Board of Education, *Memoranda on Teaching and Organisation in Secondary Schools*, Music Circular 832 (London: HMSO, 1914).

grounding for more advanced studies. Rainbow's years as a chorister began a long and distinguished career as a church musician, and his experiences as a young organist and choirmaster clearly had an influence on his later decision to pursue a career in teaching.

On leaving school Rainbow first obtained employment in the Map Branch of HM Land Registry, but his main interests were always in music and the arts, and he became increasingly involved with local amateur choirs and dramatic societies. It was a full and satisfying life that might well have continued in much the same way had it not been for the outbreak of war.

Former colleagues say that Rainbow rarely talked about the war years, but it is apparent from the memoirs that had he not served in the armed forces his future would have been very different. His detailed and unusually lively accounts of army service convey something of his personal qualities. In spite of having to adapt to a very different environment with all its inevitable difficulties, discomforts and dangers, he quickly applied his resources to military situations. His intellectual and leadership skills were recognised by his superiors, he soon gained promotion, and eventually received a commission. Rainbow always sought some musical activity in the most unlikely circumstances and managed to further his studies even in the early years of the war.

As he describes so graphically, Rainbow was discharged from the army on medical grounds in 1944. Like thousands of others returning from the conflict he had to make decisions regarding his future. He did not want to return to the civil service, for he was really set on following a career as a professional musician. Following advice and support from his friend and mentor Leonard Blake[3] he successfully applied for the post of organist and choirmaster at High Wycombe Parish Church. There he was able to combine his church commitments with class and instrumental teaching at a local preparatory school. As he points out, the position of the church musician in the immediate post-war years was very different from what it is today. At this rather fashionable and well-to-do church with a large choir the organist was a respected local personality, received a good salary and had a certain social standing.

It was partly through his contacts in the church that Rainbow came to be appointed music master at the Royal Grammar School in High Wycombe. He had been granted qualified teacher status in 1946 by virtue of having obtained conservatoire diplomas in music and music teaching. These were the years following the McNair Report,[4] when government policy was to encourage music

[3] Leonard J. Blake: Director of Music at Worksop College, later at Malvern College, composer and church musician.

[4] Board of Education, *Teachers and Youth Leaders: Report of the Committee … to Consider the Supply and Recruitment and Training of Teachers* (London: HMSO, 1944).

and the arts in secondary schools. It was at High Wycombe that Rainbow formulated his ideas on class music teaching, which were to be elaborated and disseminated in publications over the next three decades, and put on concerts throughout the region as well as a highly successful annual festival.

In 1952 Rainbow's appointment as Director of Music at the College of St Mark and St John, Chelsea, marked the beginning of a period during which he amplified and publicised his views on teaching and furthered his interests in the historical study of music in social and educational contexts. The first edition of *Music in the Classroom,*[5] published in 1956, was recommended by music educators as one of the most convincing and useful guides to school music teaching. For Rainbow, music as a curriculum subject was class singing together with related aural activities and some musical appreciation, and he offers detailed advice on voice training, lesson planning, appropriate repertoire and classroom organisation. He believed that all children should be musically literate and learn the basics of music reading in the primary school. This would be achieved through the employment of tonic sol-fa, a system which he strongly advocated throughout his life. Rainbow's recommendations about the content and conduct of class lessons were in keeping with mainstream thinking and practice of the times. They were not especially original and the presentational style now seems quaintly prescriptive. But classroom teachers in the 1950s liked his straightforward approach and welcomed his ideas as a sound basis for practice.

The 1950s and 1960s were years of widespread educational expansion and curriculum innovation, with the introduction of new forms of organisation and different methods of music teaching. An examination of the second edition of *Music in the Classroom* indicates that whilst Rainbow remained convinced of the central importance of singing and the teaching of musical literacy, he had been prepared to move with the times. Recognising the need for change and the necessity of fresh ideas he made two significant staff appointments at St Mark and St John in the early 1960s. Peter Dickinson and George Self added a new dimension to the college's music department, which soon became known as one of the most enlightened and progressive in the country. In the new edition of *Music in the Classroom* Rainbow voices approval of the more recent emphasis on exploration and creativity. He also acknowledges that children and young people have interests in music beyond the classroom. Earlier, in the *Handbook for Music Teachers*, which he edited in 1968,[6] he is dismissive of 'the stream of commercial rubbish' that had become part of the musical landscape. By 1971 he seems to have adopted a more liberal stance, although he was

[5] B. Rainbow, *Music in the Classroom* (London: Heinemann, 1956; 2nd edn, 1971).

[6] B. Rainbow, ed., *Handbook for Music Teachers*, 2nd edition (London: Novello, 1968).

always committed to a form of musical education that reflected the classical tradition.

There have been many changes in the content and operation of the school music curriculum over the past fifty years, but singing and performance combined with guided listening and composition are still central activities. No doubt there are teachers who continue to emphasise the importance of musical literacy skills but not all would share this view. Whether there ever was a period when the majority of young children could read music fluently is questionable. Rainbow was always an admirer of John Curwen's methods and in 1978 became one of the founders of the Curwen Institute. Members of the organisation maintained that literacy skills should and could be promoted in primary schools and published the *New Curwen Method* to that end.[7] Rainbow, like Curwen and Kodály, always focused on the promotion of 'inner hearing' as the main aim of a musical education, and exercises in sol-fa were for that purpose. The reason for teaching literacy was not simply so that the pupil could 'translate' standard notation; the objective was the development of aural acuity. Some contemporary educators would agree with this aim, but not the method. Others argue that concentration on literacy skills is to focus on a narrow and limited view of music and musicianship. And there are those who maintain that Rainbow's seemingly traditional attitudes to musical values and educational practice are elitist. He was well aware of such observations and in the memoir he takes a mischievous delight in supporting elitist positions. This is because he had little time for those radical extremists who maintained, without justification, that anything of the past was unacceptable if it seemed to be contrary to their progressive ideas. In fact, it is readily apparent that he was far from being elitist and was fully committed to the principle of music education for all children and young people.

One of the most significant features of Rainbow's writings is the practical advice he gives on organisational factors and teacher–pupil relationships. He offers no grand theory or philosophy of music education but he knew about school life. For him, establishing and promoting music in a school was not simply a pedagogical matter. It also required an understanding of the politics of the school, the staff room and the curriculum, and how to form the right sort of working relationship not only with pupils but also with colleagues. This is an issue that is often strangely overlooked by many of those who write about school music teaching. Some observers will feel that Rainbow's advice now sounds rather old fashioned, but those who actually work in schools know that

---

[7] W. H. Swinburne, *The New Curwen Method*, book 1: *Tonic Sol-fa in Class* (London: Curwen Institute, 1980); book 2: *Notation: the First Steps in Sight-Reading* (London: Stainer & Bell, 1981); book 3: *Notation: Reading the Stave* (London: Stainer & Bell, 1984).

much of what he has to say about the running of a school music department is just as applicable today as it was fifty years ago.

As well as implementing and developing teacher education courses at St Mark and St John, Rainbow was also responsible for music in the college chapel where he reorganised the chapel music with his customary zeal and determination. The reputation of the choir added to college prestige and for many years Rainbow received strong support from the principal and senior staff, although he was unsympathetic towards attempts to widen the scope of chapel music in more popular directions in his last year. As somebody who subscribed to Tractarian principles, he was disturbed by any threat to a noble choral and liturgical tradition. Although he had no church post after leaving the College he retained a keen interest in church music and remained a supporter of the Anglican tradition, becoming President of the Campaign for the Defence of the Traditional Cathedral Choir.

His disquiet about the chapel music coincided with the decision to relocate St Mark and St John to Plymouth. Some of Rainbow's colleagues were unhappy with the plan, but for him it was entirely unacceptable. His working life had been in the London area; he was an active member of numerous committees, including the University Board of Studies for Music; and was fully engaged in research projects. He concluded that he would not be able to pursue his research work in the new location and secured a post at Gypsy Hill College, initially as post-graduate tutor. From 1973 until his retirement in 1979 he was Head of Music at the College, which became part of Kingston Polytechnic and eventually Kingston University.

Nowadays, Rainbow is best known for his historical writings. His research activities were initially prompted by the fact that two of his predecessors at St Mark and St John – John Hullah and Thomas Helmore – had both been national figures although their work at the college was largely forgotten. Rainbow discovered their writings and manuscripts and decided to pursue research at the University of Leicester, which led to master's and doctoral dissertations published as *The Land without Music*[8] and *The Choral Revival in the Anglican Church, 1839–1872*.[9] To some extent he devised his own research methods and tracked down original materials in markets and second hand bookshops. He built up an impressive personal library, some of which is now housed at the Institute of Education and King's College, London. During the 1970s he became the foremost authority on historical research in music education

---

[8] B. Rainbow, *The Land Without Music: Musical Education in England, 1800–1860, and its Continental Antecedents* (London: Novello, 1967; Aberystwyth: Boethius Press, 1991).

[9] B. Rainbow, *The Choral Revival in the Anglican Church, 1839–1872* (London: Barrie & Jenkins, 1970; Woodbridge: Boydell Press, 2001).

and outlined his methodology in his essay 'Historical Research', published in 1992.[10] For anybody about to embark on a historical investigation, or indeed any type of educational research, this essay should be essential background reading.

Rainbow's best-known work is probably *Music in Educational Thought and Practice*.[11] Originally published in 1989, the book deals with the growth of musical education in the United Kingdom and Europe over a period of some 2,500 years. Rainbow discusses the various theories regarding the value of music in schools and societies, and traces the many factors that have had a bearing on the evolution of musical studies. He was always intrigued by different methods of teaching and provides illuminating descriptions of the numerous, and sometimes obscure, schemes designed to help students acquire musical literacy. A revised second edition with a foreword by Sir Peter Maxwell Davies and additional material by Gordon Cox was published in 2006.

In his paper 'Onward from Butler; School Music, 1945–1985'[12] Rainbow reflects on changes in music teaching that occurred during his career. He complains of the neglect of singing and aural skills in school programmes and argues that there has been insufficient understanding of many modern innovations. Whilst not directly advocating any one approach to class music teaching he suggests that there is a need for a consensus over the content of the curriculum that in turn would provide the basis for greater continuity and progression. Rainbow was not alone in calling for consensus, and in many ways this was brought about by the establishment of the National Curriculum. One can only speculate on his reaction to central control of the music curriculum. His principles evolved during a period when teachers themselves were responsible for the design of their own programmes. It was a time of much more professional freedom and less direction from official bodies. He was always an independent thinker, and it is hard to imagine him responding positively to what he would probably have seen as invasive inspections and bureaucratic accountability.

Bernarr Rainbow's scholastic achievements have been internationally acknowledged and were recognised through the award of a DPhil at Leicester University (1992) and an honorary fellowship by Trinity College of Music (1995). People who knew him remember a charming and affable colleague who

[10] B. Rainbow, 'Historical Research', in *Some Approaches to Research in Music Education*, ed. A. E. Kemp (Reading: International Society for Music Education Research Commission, 1992). See pp. 158–67 below.

[11] B. Rainbow, *Music in Educational Thought and Practice: A Survey from 800 BC*, (Aberystwyth: Boethius Press, 1989); 2nd edition with Gordon Cox, foreword by Sir Peter Maxwell Davies (Woodbridge: Boydell Press, 2006).

[12] B. Rainbow, *Onward From Butler: School Music, 1945–1985* (London: Curwen Institute, 1985), also Appendix I in the 1st edition of *Music in Educational Thought and Practice*. See pp. 230–44 below.

encouraged others in their work and careers. Much of his professional success arose from his shrewd understanding of social situations and the politics of higher education. He knew the game and was astute at adopting strategies that were in the best interests of his colleagues and students. In 1996, with the help of Professor Peter Dickinson, he set up the Bernarr Rainbow Trust, a charity that provides financial support for a range of musical and educational projects. And it is through the Trust that much of Rainbow's highly original research and his many informative writings will be accessible to musicians and educationists both now and well into the future.

A Salute to Life:
Sketches Toward a Personal Memoir

'One's work should be a salute to life.' (Pablo Casals)[1]

'Everybody has his own theatre, in which he is manager, actor, prompter, playwright, scene-shifter, box-keeper, door-keeper, all in one, and audience into the bargain.' (Julius Hare)[2]

CHAPTER ONE

LET ME BEGIN with my very first recollection on the night of 19 July 1917. It was wartime; my father was serving with the army in Flanders and my mother had left what was considered the vulnerable coast of her native Norfolk, taking me to live with her sister at Rushden in Northamptonshire. I was a distinctly precocious, hyperactive two-year-old of a type then jocularly known as 'a handful'. And on that July night in 1917 I sleepily overheard my aunt describing the dread appearance of a German Zeppelin caught in searchlights directly above us on industrial England's first bombing raid. I promptly began screaming my head off and can still recall the nightmare figures her overwrought account summoned up in my childish imagination – of everyday objects turning into giant silver bubbles that went on growing alarmingly till they burst.

This is my first conscious recollection; and though evidently indelible, it luckily represents my only memory of the direct impact of World War I. Yet quite as fantasy-ridden in its way is the echo of a very different event a year earlier. Surrounded by a group of bemused relatives I was now being bathed by a Queen!

Though too young to remember this remarkable occasion myself, the event understandably became the subject of recurrent anecdote during my

---

[1] Pablo Casals (1876–1973), Spanish cellist. 'The only credit we can claim is for the use we make of the talent we are given. That is why I urge young musicians: "Don't be vain because you happen to have talent. You are not responsible for that; it was not of your doing. What you do with your talent is what matters. You must cherish this gift. Do not demean or waste what you have been given. Work – work constantly and nourish it." Of course the gift to be cherished most of all is that of life itself. One's work should be a salute to life.' *Joys and Sorrows: Reflections by Pablo Casals, as told to Albert E. Kahn* (New York: Simon & Schuster, 1970), chap. 1.

[2] Julius Hare (1795–1855), English theological writer. *Guesses at Truth by Two Brothers* (1827).

childhood and I can almost persuade myself I recall it happening. We, that is my mother and I, were staying at the time with my paternal grandparents at Dersingham on the outskirts of the Sandringham estate where my grandfather served as a member of the royal household. Away from the formalities of court life in London or Windsor it was not unusual at Sandringham for the Queen Mother, the unassuming, recently widowed Alexandra, to call unannounced at nearby homes of close personal servants for companionable conversation less rigid than her ladies-in-waiting might be expected to provide.[3] Among the houses she visited in this way was my grandfather's at Dersingham.

And so it happened that on this occasion as Her Majesty unexpectedly entered the room, I was being washed ready for bed in an enamel bath in front of the living-room fire. 'Oh,' cried the Queen, throwing up her hands in delight at this homely spectacle, 'do let me do that!'

Readers of a Freudian disposition may be disappointed to find my later recollections decidedly less ready subjects for psychoanalysis than either of those early incidents. But, to continue: by the age of three I was attending my first school. It was, in fact, a Dame School, an institution even then recognised as the anomalous survival of a former age.[4] But it was conveniently near my aunt's house in Rushden, and I have since – as a student of the history of education – come to prize having had that opportunity of experiencing the daily routine of a long vanished institution.

Admission to the school was fixed at four years of age. But as my mother (a certificated school teacher before her marriage) had already taught me to read, add up, and tell the time, after some debate with the two autocratic old ladies who ran it, I was admitted to the Farm House School, Rushden, at the irregularly early age of three.[5]

At lesson times I remember sitting with a dozen or so other little boys and girls around a large dining table while one of the proprietresses instructed us in such forgotten skills as 'Strokes and Pot-hooks'. This staple feature of the daily timetable involved inscribing on our slates row upon row of the diagonals (strokes) and s-shaped symbols (pothooks) deemed to form the basic structure of copper-plate handwriting. An ability to form these two essential shapes presentably formed an essential preliminary to learning cursive handwriting. The

---

[3] Queen Alexandra (1844–1925), Danish princess who married Albert Edward, Prince of Wales, later King Edward VII. She became Queen Consort during his reign (1901–10) and Queen Mother after he died.

[4] An ancient type of school usually run in the teacher's home where provision ranged from good primary teaching to what would now be regarded merely as day-care facilities.

[5] Nellie Rainbow, née Neal (1889–1965).

next stage involved making complete letters and then doing our best to reproduce the beautifully engraved aphorisms set out as models of calligraphy in our copy-books.

As I recall it, working on a slate was the most enjoyable part of these exercises. Each slated wooden frame had a tiny sponge attached to it on a short length of string. When this was moistened, the slate could be wiped clean after use and then presented a satisfyingly shiny black surface. This, alas, faded to a disappointing streaky grey as it dried. Meanwhile the squeaking slate pencil failed to make any impression while the surface remained wet. But all this remained largely a matter for speculation since both our martinet instructors insisted on slates being turned over promptly and discouraged attempts at didactic experiment on the wet side.

I cannot have remained more than a year or so at this Northamptonshire Dame School; and my next recollection finds us back with my grandparents in Norfolk – the Zeppelin raids now a thing of the past. It was at Dersingham a little later that, playing in the garden one day, I watched a soldier in uniform walk purposefully up the path and ran indoors at once to report this intrusion. The unknown interloper proved to be none other than my father, now back from France for good. An earlier surviving photograph taken about 1916 of him in uniform alongside my grandfather and me at Dersingham, shows that he had been on leave at least once before; but I have no memory of that occasion. And my failure to recognise him at the end of the war exposes the damage to our relationship that my father's long wartime absence from home had caused – an unhappy shortcoming that I have since come to realise was never to be fully overcome.

My father, born in 1888, was a journeyman cabinet-maker proud to recount the part he had played, during his apprenticeship with the renowned firm of John Thompson, in carving and assembling new choirstalls for Peterborough Cathedral.[6] In his early twenties he had gone on to secure a post on the permanent staff of craftsmen employed at Buckingham Palace. And on his discharge from the army in 1919 he returned to work there, my mother and I joining him to live perforce in cramped lodgings and a London overcrowded with the families of soldiers recently returned from overseas.

I was now to attend my first London County Council Infant School, in Ethelburga Street, near Battersea Park. It formed part of a typical three-storey Board School building (destroyed during World War II) with the Infants

[6] Ephraim James Rainbow (1888–1983). On his retirement as Curator of Pictures at Hampton Court, he was received by the Queen at Buckingham Palace on 26 February 1970.

Department suitably situated at ground-floor level. I remember little about it beyond the precise situation of my classroom and a clear picture of kindly Miss Kavanagh, our portly class teacher. She wore a favourite mauve-coloured knitted jumper, and one day brought a pet chameleon to school in a jar to show us. When she let it climb on to her jumper we were all suitably astonished to see it turn mauve, too.

For me, the only other at all memorable event at Ethelburga Street was the celebration of Empire Day. This took place annually on 24 May, Queen Victoria's birthday, and was marked by an assembly of the whole school in the flag-bedecked playground where we were addressed by the Mayor. We then all saluted the Union Flag and sang a long-rehearsed programme of suitably patriotic songs until a seasonal downpour drove us back to our classrooms to steam ourselves dry again.

By now I was six, and preparing to move up to the school's top floor, reverently known to us Infants as the 'Big Boys'. But just at this time my father announced he was buying a house of his own at Clapham Junction. And it was only after we moved to live there that I first really became aware of music as a source of rare pleasure.

My father had been a keen amateur musician since boyhood, first playing the cornet in uniformed local bands in rural Norfolk and later adopting the trumpet for more orthodox orchestral work. He had always secretly hoped I would become 'musical' too, and would sometimes take me to band practice with him. I enjoyed the splendid noise these players made, but was mystified by the varying sized pools of water to be seen alongside most of their chairs – only discovering later that this was not due to some physical disability but to tipping out their instruments.

Our arrival at Clapham Junction brought my father's hopes for my musical salvation nearer realisation when we found ourselves living next door to a husband and wife, Frank and Winifred Galpin, who were both versatile professional musicians – he, as singer, organist, cellist, private teacher, and the conductor of a local theatre orchestra; she, as an accomplished pianist who also played the double bass in the same orchestra.

Frank Galpin agreed to take me as a piano pupil; and the fact that, if he chose to, he could clearly hear me practising next door perhaps sharpened my efforts in that direction. For better or worse, I was quite soon rattling off little pieces from Smallwood's *Piano Tutor* with an assurance well beyond that of other children of my age.

A couple of years later I could play readily at sight, delighted my father by accompanying his solos, and was allowed to join with him and our indulgent neighbours to form a tolerable instrumental ensemble. Our repertoire comprised what were then called 'classics'. I remember being especially fond of a

Suite de pièces from Gounod's *Faust* [7] and found myself greatly enjoying our regular domestic concerts.

Soon after we had arrived at Clapham Junction I was taken for a voice test and admitted to the very competent surpliced choir at nearby St Mark's Church, Battersea Rise. Following the usual pattern there, before being admitted to the choir-stalls, probationer choristers spent their first services sitting alongside the organist. I found the experience an indelible one. Mr Stott amazed me as he manipulated the stops and piston buttons, played on three keyboards in turn with his hands and on what was evidently another with his feet. On the following Sunday I was almost disappointed to find I had to sit in the choir-stalls – but I now began at the age of seven to grow familiar with standard anthems and settings from the Anglican choral repertoire.

The vicar, Mr Mills, I saw was no singer and very aware of the fact. I would watch him as he tackled the opening versicle, 'O Lord, open thou our lips,' with a look of agonised appeal on his face, rocking himself backward and forward on his heels as he struggled to find the right notes. He was evidently a notable preacher and commanded a strong following on that account. Though most of his sermons passed over my head I can recall him referring topically to the marvels of Tutankhamen's tomb when it was discovered by Lord Carnarvon and Howard Carter in November 1922. It is difficult not to feel that a parson today with Mr Mills' general success but lack of musical awareness would be prone to curtail music's part in the church service. It is a tribute both to him and to the thinking of his day that the vicar at St Mark's made no such move.

At the Carol Service in the previous year I must record having sung my first treble solo. Two rather older boys made their debuts on the same occasion, and in the January number of the parish magazine Mr Stott laconically reported the event as 'a somewhat trying ordeal'. However, I preferred to remember it because in the vestry afterwards one of the choir-men presented me with a half-crown – which I subsequently regarded as my very first musical fee.

It is possible to claim that by the late 1920s a faint impression of the future pattern of my life and the direction my enthusiasms would take was beginning to emerge. I enjoyed going to school and, judging by the annual prizes for Progress and Good Conduct I received there, managed to satisfy my teachers. Honeywell Road School was widely recognised in the neighbourhood as superior to another school closer to hand. For that reason, after some negotiation I

[7] Charles Gounod (1818–93), *Faust* (1859).

was entered there. The school was in fact situated something over a half-mile away; but I walked there every morning, walked home for a midday meal and walked back to and from school again in the afternoon. This daily trek (something scarcely to be imagined in today's circumstances) was undertaken quite alone. Indeed, as an only child I was accustomed to being by myself and never felt at a loss on that account, happily entertaining myself with some flight of imagination or improvised game; and at home there was always a book or the piano to occupy me.

Observers, I was later to learn, thought me an odd, over-serious child: stand-offish and a 'loner', never seen kicking a football about or joining with the rest in noisy street games. Truth to tell, I was no good at ball games and unaware of either lacking or deliberately avoiding such pastimes and the company of those who enjoyed them.

Other critics declared me 'spoilt' – for my mother, with her teacher's instincts, devoted herself assiduously to my upbringing – answering seriously my endless questions, taking me to explore London's monuments, visiting the museums at South Kensington during school holidays, and generally seeing to it that I used my brains and kept myself respectably tidy. To suggest that she was simply spoiling me was unjust – for a boy of seven or eight who was allowed to take an unescorted two-mile walk back and forth to school each day – as I was – could hardly be regarded as 'spoilt'.

As to my precocious musical activities, detractors disposed to question the standard of tuition in piano technique I received or anxious to decry as unedifying the repertoire I was encouraged to adopt, should first familiarise themselves with the musical norms of those days.

There was very little opportunity for ordinary folk to hear music well performed at home. Regular broadcast programmes from the London station, 2LO, began in 1922; but for several years after that, reception was too uncertain to warrant the inclusion of musical items beyond a very occasional vocal or instrumental solo. Wisely, as things then stood, no attempt was made to broadcast orchestral music of any merit.

Middle-class homes such as ours relied for their domestic music on the individual efforts of members of the family, or more ambitiously, on occasional social gatherings ingenuously called 'musical evenings'. These involved inviting a few 'talented' acquaintances to come and perform a selection of well-tried instrumental solos or popular ballads to a circle of friends adept at expressing counterfeit enjoyment.

A piano, it is true, was a usual item of furniture in most middle-class homes; but, even when regularly used – at least for children's enforced practice – it seemed to represent a claim to respectability rather than serve an essentially musical purpose. In those days possession of a gramophone was a more reliable signal of a taste for music – albeit the quality of reproduction on early machines was extremely poor and the available selection of recorded items entirely determined by commercial considerations.

Conversely, outside the home, opportunities to hear what is now called 'live music' were much greater. In most towns there were professional instrumental ensembles galore. Every local theatre and cinema of any standing had its own orchestra. Some cinemas were just beginning to install elaborate Wurlitzer concert organs as well. The larger restaurants and tea-shops, then enjoying great popularity in established shopping centres, would employ at least a piano-trio to entertain their patrons. Brass or military bands played regularly in public gardens and parks; dance halls and skating rinks all had bands of their own. In addition, every community had its amateur choral society and many towns supported a modest amateur orchestra as well. Then there were numberless church and chapel choirs – the best of them attaining commendable standards within the bounds set by contemporary taste.

It was within those general areas that a corpus of music ranging from Ketèlbey's maudlin *In a Monastery Garden* to the bouncy ballet music of Delibes established itself.[8] And it was within those well-explored bounds that 'music lovers' generally, and young people rash enough to entertain ideas of a musical career, would settle their tastes. Not without justification, average aspirants to the music profession in those days regarded the concert platform, at national level or the metropolitan opera house, as the preserve of foreigners and the miraculously endowed. The cathedral organ loft seemed equally unattainable without long years as an articled pupil. Musical study at a national conservatory or university was something quite outside most young people's conception. Realists consequently set themselves more modest goals conformable with the situation as they knew it, equipping themselves meanwhile with a working repertoire to match.

By the time I was ten we had moved house yet again – this time even further out of central London to a newly developed estate at Merton Park, near Wimbledon. Just at this time work was under way at Wembley preparing for the British Empire Exhibition of 1924–5. Vast ferro-concrete buildings – a Palace of Engineering, Palace of Industry, Palace of Arts, and the like – were being erected adjoining the gigantic out-door sports and entertainment arena with a capacity of 120,000 which later became the present Wembley Stadium. An additional popular attraction was to be an Amusement Park offering all

---

[8] Albert Ketèlbey (1875–1959), English composer. *In a Monastery Garden* (1915) began a series of extremely popular pieces. Léo Delibes (1836–91), French composer primarily known for his ballet scores.

the side-shows, thrills and entertainments of a traditional fair on a mammoth scale.

When it was eventually opened in 1924 the Exhibition was always thronged with visitors – whole families as well as parties of schoolchildren daily filling it to overflowing. My parents and the Galpins took me there several times to ride on the scenic railway and roundabouts in the Amusement Park and explore the unusual exhibits on display – there was a memorable life-sized model of the Prince of Wales in Canadian butter; but I recall especially attending a pageant of some kind in the stadium which at that time contained a huge organ, voiced and adapted for open-air performance. It has long since been dismantled and is now generally forgotten; but I can remember the way in which the whole arena rang with the sound, and how thoroughly I envied the player conjuring it all up.

It was customary to use this organ to entertain the tens of thousands assembling to watch the regular displays and sporting events that took place in the arena and to encourage them to join in what was called 'Community Singing' under the direction of a white-clad and extremely acrobatic conductor. The lasting tradition of singing 'Abide with me' at cup finals arose from this practice, that particular hymn being proposed for the purpose by George V and the custom continuing long after the organ itself had been dismantled.

By this time I had been enrolled as a pupil at Merton C of E School and joined the choir at the adjoining parish church. The school was quite unlike the one I had grown used to at Honeywell Road. It was smaller, more intimate, rather old-fashioned, and strongly influenced by the foibles of a highly individual, not to say, eccentric headmaster. I had not previously been aware of any of my head teachers; but it was scarcely possible to be unaware of Mr Johnson. Something of his particularity revealed itself in the spats and detachable celluloid cuffs he favoured. The latter, as I saw for myself one day when called to his office, would be left standing upright on his desk when he was dealing with routine affairs. They were slipped up over his wrists and inside his jacket only when a parent or important visitor called upon him, or when he undertook one of his regular tours of inspection of the school. The hard core of pedantry in his make-up came to light in various ways, among them his flair for writing impressive inscriptions in the books presented as school prizes. Where the headmaster at Honeywell Road had written 'For Progress and Good Conduct' Mr Johnson preferred, 'For Good Work in Orthography'. I remember being taken aback at prize-day in 1925 to find I had done good work in this remarkable discipline, and rushed to the dictionary to find what it could possibly be.

At the same time, for all his idiosyncrasies Mr Johnson ran his school smoothly and had assembled an effective, dutiful staff. Of them I recall readily enough my likeable class teacher, Mr Barnes, responsible for teaching us the whole of our basic curriculum; Mr Salmon, who taught us drawing and pen-and-ink sketching – including how to differentiate between the foliage of oak, poplar and willow trees; and Mr Jordan, who took us for singing – and first unwittingly revealed to me the peculiar value of being able to play the piano *standing up!*

As a new but inquisitive member of the choir at St Mary's Church I soon noticed distinct differences separating it from St Mark's, Battersea Rise. I could not then have put those differences into words but the two buildings struck me as very unlike. Where St Mark's was a lofty, distinctly urban, brick-built structure with a post-Tractarian atmosphere, Merton Church was ancient, little altered by time, overtly evangelical, and still in essence a country church.[9] Fewer anthems and settings were sung here – though the choir was quite a substantial one and capable of putting on what was proudly known as a 'fully choral service' at festival times.

Mr Hyde, the organist, was a less impressive figure than Mr Stott. And the organ at Merton was a smaller instrument lacking the rows of stop-knobs and pistons that had so fascinated me at St Mark's. Yet Mr Hyde and his little two-manual tracker-action instrument were, in due course, to have considerable influence on my future.

A more immediate change in the pattern of my life, however, was to take place in the following year when I was nearing eleven. After no more than a few terms at Merton School the time came for me to sit for a scholarship at Rutlish, the local grammar school. The examination involved was far from an empty formality and included, I particularly recall, a personal interview held at the County Education Offices in Kingston. It was conducted in my case by a digni-fied elderly lady (no doubt a retired Inspector of Schools) who began by ques-tioning me searchingly on general knowledge topics. I was, of course, wear-ing my best suit for the interview and chanced to have a reproduction Albert watch-chain complete with an imitation seal slung across my waistcoat.

'Ah!' cried the lady after a while, 'and what is that you have there on your watch-chain?' It's for sealing letters,' I explained. 'You melt your sealing wax over a candle, drop it on the flap of the envelope and then press it down with the seal.' 'Oh,' she said, 'so that's how it's done. And what are those semi-precious stones on either side of it?' This, of course, was the critical question. Fortunately, however, native curiosity had already led me to go into the whole

---

[9] The Tractarians, also known as the Oxford Movement, emerged in the 1830s. They brought about a return to traditional values within High-Church Anglicanism and leant towards Rome.

matter with my mother long before, when I had first worn the watch-chain. 'On one side,' I said firmly, 'is a bloodstone; on the other, it's a cat's-eye.' The lady nodded and gave me a knowing smile. I knew then I had passed!

CHAPTER TWO

RUTLISH SCHOOL had been founded in the seventeenth century, was now highly regarded locally, and under the influence of E. A. A. Varnish, its current headmaster, had become noted for the transformation it rapidly effected and maintained upon the decorum and healthy self-respect of newly admitted pupils. In fact, with its encouragement of civilised behaviour both on and off the premises, its insistence on good standards of spoken English, and a unique custom of regularly drilling the whole school in speech training until cockney accents were eradicated, Rutlish could be counted (one rejoices to recall) a thoroughly élitist establishment. There was an annual intake of something under a hundred boys, most of them fee-paying and a handful with scholarships.

When our first term began, we discovered with varying degrees of surprise that we were to be taught by a wide range of masters, each sailing into the classroom in a weathered academic gown to introduce the mysteries of a different subject. About most of these men there was an intensity of purpose we had not found in our former teachers – about one or two there was an absent-minded inadequacy not previously encountered either. As we grew older and more confident we would become adept at tormenting masters whose grip on their specialisms (and their pupils) had lapsed. But during those first bewildering weeks we were too elated at finding ourselves admitted to this spruce, blazer-wearing, well-spoken company, too afraid of breaking accepted patterns of behaviour, too bemused by the array of different subjects requiring our attention, to consider anything but the demands of the immediate present.

Gradually a perspective established itself as hitherto unexplored subjects – Latin certainly the most singular of them – fell into place alongside more familiar ones. Bright eleven-year-olds revelled in the challenge this new cosmos presented. Yet as one moved up the school and that challenge relentlessly broadened, we found that brightness was no longer enough.

In my own case, while the excitement of making so many new discoveries was sufficient to carry me swimmingly through the classroom demands of life at Rutlish, it later became more difficult to penetrate the complexities certain subjects progressively introduced. Chemistry, for instance, lost its early charm for me when it became necessary to call water H_2O and carbon dioxide CO_2 and then do sums with these new names. Though cheerfully at home with the arts, I found the sciences regularly presented tiresome, but quite substantial obstacles.

Another disconcerting feature of grammar school life for a boy who had never delighted in ball games was the importance attached at Rutlish to cricket and, to the point of idolatry, to rugby. Half a day every week was devoted to these salubrious pursuits; and our rugby coach was a fierce little north-country science master who wasted no time on persuasion. Either you enjoyed the game and literally threw yourself into demonstrating the fact, or you were pilloried for idleness the whole time it went on. I became a regular candidate for this belittling regimen.

Nor was Physical Training a consistent romp. Sometimes one entered to find the gym redolent of leather and sweat: boxing was taking place. On such occasions Sergeant Hornigold, the caricature ex-army sergeant-major equipped with a tiny waxed moustache who was in charge of physical training, would enjoy organising serious bouts of fisticuffs between suitably capable boys. But when he felt it added piquancy to the proceedings he would arrange an encounter, by way of comic relief, between an able boxer and a clown with no pugilistic instincts. I was a regular choice to provide this entertainment. Leaving the gym afterwards with another bloody nose I planned (and later relished) secret revenge.

Another source of disaffection lay for me in the fact that, like every other grammar school for boys in those days, Rutlish made no provision at all for music teaching. There was not even a school choir. The prospectus named Claude Landi, LRAM, among the academic staff. But Mr Landi taught Modern Languages and I never heard him so much as mention music during my time at the school. Not until the passing of the 1944 Education Act was music admitted as a serious discipline to schools like Rutlish; and the absence of musical training during my secondary school years was to prove both disappointing and a handicap.

For reasons such as these, by my fourth year at Rutlish I began to find myself falling out of love with 'school'. There was still a great deal of satisfaction to be gained in the course of each day's programme. Certain tasks and activities retained their original hold; several of the masters gained a universal respect and admiration that was to earn them a permanent place in all our memories. But despite this, I realised that, to a larger extent than formerly, I was relying on out-of-school activities for gratification.

Paradoxically, this compensatory process began with a musical event organised by the school itself. Contradicting, as it were, the traditional embargo imposed on music in the school time-table, Rutlish produced each year a Gilbert and Sullivan opera. Rehearsals were held after school, starting in the autumn term, and the production followed in the spring. With no school choir to form a proving ground, singers were selected by a rough-and-ready process with applicants spread in extended order throughout the school hall. Then, as they sang together some well-known song remembered from primary school days, the masters responsible for producing and conducting the opera would walk around listening to each boy in turn. Those thought suitable received a tap on the shoulder and assembled afterwards as the coming year's principals and chorus. The orchestra, mustered later and conducted efficiently enough by the geography master, largely comprised friends and parents; the producer, evidently more subject to stressful happenings, varied from year to year.

New boys entered the school in September. By then it was too late to join rehearsals for the current production. But at the audition in the following year I was accepted and sang Lady Saphir in *Patience*.[10] After that I should have gone on to play Dame Hannah in *Ruddigore*, but my voice broke at the last minute; and I had to wait till I could sing baritone before appearing in *The Gondoliers* a couple of years later.

Another popular annual event in the school calendar was the Gym Show mounted by Sergeant Hornigold at a local hall. Rehearsals for this display took place in the periods normally devoted to Physical Training and comprised vaulting over the horse, various traditional exercises, and drills with dumb-bells and Indian clubs. These precious clubs were locked away and never used in the ordinary way, making their appearance only in the weeks immediately before the Gym Show. The class which was to wield them consequently needed extra preparation. As the display itself always took place with orchestral accompaniment, Hornigold decided that his Indian club exercises should be rehearsed to music. My pianistic leanings being well known at school he arranged for me to be excused from my normal lesson once a week to play for his club-wielders. All the exercises proved to be in waltz time. So, with my recent humiliation in the boxing ring very much in mind, I decided to introduce in my accompaniments an occasional passage in march time. As intended, this sent everything out of gear, and I had the delightful satisfaction of watching innocently as the class grinned approval and the wretched sergeant, unable to make out what was happening, stamped about the gym roaring his baffled rage.

But these diversions were only incidental. By now I had begun to find musical satisfaction outside school altogether. For some time I had been allowed to accept invitations to play the piano at amateur concerts in church halls locally.

[10] In 1928 a local newspaper (unidentified) reported: 'Rutlish Schoolboys' Fine Effort. Members of the Operatic and Dramatic Society of the Rutlish School added once more to their former signal triumphs by their fine performance of *Patience* ... an evening of exceptional interest and thorough enjoyment was spent by a large audience which included the Mayor and Mayoress and the Deputy Mayor.' The quintet in which Rainbow sang was a great success.

In deciding what I should play, I abandoned for the time being Haydn, Handel, Chopin, and Beethoven – who now owned my devotion. I chose instead to dazzle my uncritical audiences with showy pieces full of notes. Sinding's *Rustle of Spring* or Chaminade's *Autumn*, earned more ready applause.[11]

Thirty years later I was to meet socially a woman who had attended some of those concerts as a schoolgirl. As soon as she heard my name she fixed me with an accusing eye. 'I remember you,' she cried. 'You used to play the piano. I *hated* you. Because of you our parents made us all have piano lessons too.' And, indeed, several neighbours of ours now persuaded my parents to let me teach their young children to play the piano – evidently supposing that I possessed some magic power that I would pass on.

I was still in the church choir at this time, of course, and one of the choirmen had heard me play at an earlier concert. One evening, as the choir were robing for a mid-week Lenten service, it was realised that Mr Hyde, the organist, was not present. With the choir already lined up to enter the church, he had still not arrived. In the absence of anyone else to play for the service the choirman who had heard me play the piano suggested I should do it; and although I had never touched the organ before, the vicar agreed to let me try. My advocate came with me to the organ bench, knowledgeably switched on the blower, drew a few stops, and then sat with me until the time came for the first hymn. I duly played it. After the prayers and address he selected some different stops, I played the final hymn, and the ordeal was over.

That unexpected coup and Mr Hyde's remorse over his lapse – led to his giving me my first organ lessons. I could soon accompany choir practice and simple services with aplomb, and a couple of years later, when my treble voice had just broken and a daughter-church, St James's, Merton, was established, I became its first organist. With the help of friends a scratch choir was formed – including a handful of boys very little younger than I was. I used to go to take

---

[11] Christian Sinding (1856–1941), Norwegian composer: *Rustle of Spring*, op. 32, no. 3 (1896). Cécile Chaminade (1854–1944), French composer: *Automne*, Études de concert, op. 35, no. 2. On 20 October 1933 the *Wimbledon Borough News* reported: 'Mr Rainbow is a promising young pianist. He plays with an understanding and depth beyond his years and was particularly happy in the Beethoven items.' No further programme details. A year later there was more information. On 8 December 1934 the *Middlesex Chronicle* reported in some detail on Rainbow's recital with singer Irene Hurran. His solos (identified as in the review) were: Chopin – Waltzes op. 18, no. 7; op. 62, no. 2; op. 70, no. 2; Beethoven – Andante and Variations 1–4 from Sonata, op. 26; Bach – Prelude, English Suite III; Mendelssohn – *Lieder ohne Worte* nos. 14, 18 and 20; Brahms – Intermezzo, op. 118; Beethoven – Andante, Scherzo and Trio from Sonata, op. 28. Grieg – *Wedding Day*, op. 62, no. 6; Beethoven – Allegro, Minuet and Trio from Sonata, op. 49, no. 2; Chopin – Nocturnes, op. 32, no. 2; op. 35; Mazurka, op. 67, no. 3; Scherzo, op. 3. Rainbow played to 'a large gathering' at St Stephen's Hall, Hounslow, and his two encores were pieces of his own and Alec Rowley.

their choir practices with my school-cap hidden in my pocket; but they were not fooled, and the first few months of trying to control them were decidedly taxing. But I gradually got the hang of things – learning the job by doing it.[12]

At school, meanwhile, tension was growing over the approaching examinations for School Certificate now less than a year ahead. What was known as the 'matric bogey' equally haunted sixth-formers soon to be seeking university places. I entertained no such lofty aspiration; and certainly no one in this music-less school thought of sending a boy up to university to read Music. Had they done so, his chances of securing a place with no academic musical experience would have been negligible. At that time I had no concept of Harmony as an academic study and had never even heard of a triad. Asked what I wanted to do when I left school – that immemorial question – I always found it difficult to frame an answer. What *did* I want to do?

I have since come to the conclusion that I could not answer this question because I was in fact already doing in my spare time what I wanted to do in the future: be an organist and choirmaster, and teach music. The drawback was, of course, that this calling was not at present earning me a living, and as things stood, seemed unlikely to do so in the future. The solution, I supposed, was to get a salaried job doing something else, and continue with musical pursuits in my spare time.

As I wrestled impotently with this conundrum, a major change in my family's affairs suddenly presented itself. In 1931, after long service as a craftsman at Buckingham Palace, my father was unexpectedly appointed by the Lord Chamberlain to the post of Curator of Hampton Court Palace. The post was held under royal warrant and would involve residence in the Palace itself.[13]

This development threw existing arrangements into pleasurable confusion, for it involved leaving Merton Park as soon as the Curator's apartment – a large Tudor house forming one side of Master Carpenter's Court – was vacated and redecorated.[14] In the event the move did not take place until early in the following year. And by then it had been decided that since my performance

---

[12] In May 1928 a local newspaper (unidentified) reported under the heading Wimbledon Orchestra: 'Master Rainbow, son of the cornet player in the Wimbledon Orchestra, played the organ. This lad was the winner of a certificate at the RACS Musical Eisteddfod, held in 1927.'

[13] In 1514 Cardinal Wolsey rebuilt Hampton Court Palace on a grand scale and under Henry VIII it became a royal residence. In 1689 Sir Christopher Wren demolished much of the Tudor building to provide a new palace for William III and Mary II but in 1760 George III abandoned Hampton Court as a royal residence. As the site of the Chapel Royal, the court musical establishment where there have been continuous services for over 450 years, Hampton Court has been influential in the history of English church music.

[14] See plate 3.

in School Certificate seemed likely to commend me to a potential employer I should leave Rutlish at the end of the summer term and seek a suitable job. In my private estimation, 'suitable' here meant a job that gave me time, and left me enough energy, to follow my musical interests in the evenings.

It was chance – in the person of a friend of a friend of the family – that found me such a job in the Map Branch of HM Land Registry at Lincoln's Inn Fields. During my last year at Rutlish I had won the Louisa Bennett Art Prize with a portfolio of drawings, water-colours, and pen-and-ink sketches. Skill of that order was now seen as a recommendation for a would-be cartographer; and after an interview and test of penmanship I was appointed as a trainee 'mapping assistant' at the Land Registry with a salary of thirty shillings (£1. 50p) a week. Later, it appeared, in addition to map-making, the post involved training and experience in land-surveying, culminating in a qualifying examination conducted by the Civil Service Commissioners.

I decided to take all this as it came, meanwhile planning to draw on my minuscule wage to pay for weekly lessons in organ-playing, and harmony and counterpoint. My immature enquiries revealed that part-time students were accepted, and fees just about affordable, at the London College of Music, in Great Marlborough Street. So I enrolled there. This arrangement meant attending two early evening sessions at the College each week. Two other evenings were already partly occupied by my choir practices. The piano pupils I was now beginning to attract could be fitted in between those fixtures. This proved a workable, though demanding programme which I was more than content to adopt for several years.

With the move from school to drawing office the last remnants of my early reputation for unsociability faded. Though still able to withdraw within myself when occasion demanded, I now became positively gregarious. This transformation certainly took place because the mapping staff at the Land Registry at that time included a number of talented young people whose interests, like my own, really lay elsewhere.

Among an otherwise unremarkable assembly of some fifty or sixty draughtsmen and women tracers there were to be found frustrated painters, as yet unfulfilled writers, a number of trained singers, and several other talented individuals. All of them were consciously devoting the daytime to earning a wage that enabled them to exercise their talent when at leisure in the evenings. I set about pursuing their closer acquaintance and found it rather like joining a cultivated club.

Conversation across the drawing-boards when two of these birds of a feather took wing would fascinate less sophisticated colleagues quite as much as it exasperated boorish supervisors within earshot. A contemporary who joined the staff in 1936 has published his recollections of that time:

... Those Map people of the early days had personalities and characteristics that made them somehow 'different'. We were a peculiar lot ... They were able to discuss knowledgeably many topics that were out of my ken. Music and painting seemed an open book to them, to be chatted about in a light-hearted but rarefied atmosphere ... 'Gerry' Hardwick was one of a select group of talented artists who must have felt very frustrated at the limited scope for their talents in the Map Branch ... I am always amazed that such gifted and clever people remained in the Land Registry but I suppose one reason was that the Department was, most of the time, fun to work in and many of [Gerry's] colleagues, like Bernarr Rainbow, Ron Aynsley, Fred Terry, Doug King and others were also talented and knowledgeable. The erudite conversations of this group left us Philistines feeling like lesser mortals. They went off on holiday to far away places like Switzerland, quite outside the wildest dreams of the rest of us.[15]

Making appropriate allowance for the nostalgic generosity of those recollections, and bearing in mind that they relate to a time when at the age of twenty-one I was already an old hand with four years' service at the Land Registry, the picture they present is a recognisable one. With my schooldays far behind me, conversations with my sophisticated friends had nourished my budding enthusiasms and introduced me to aspects of the arts I had not previously encountered.

For instance, several of these colleagues with their friends from outside the Land Registry, used to visit Covent Garden during the Russian Ballet season, and I soon joined them. I took friends of my own along with me: notably Olive, the school-girl sweetheart of my chorister days at Merton who was to become my wife;[16] and Fred Cogman, a fellow Rutlishian with whom I used to nibble at the Beethoven violin sonatas.

Without doubt, the experience which was to exert the greatest aesthetic impact on me in those days was my introduction to the music of Stravinsky, as interpreted by the choreography of Nijinsky, and framed by the scenic art of Bakst.[17] It was in the gallery at Covent Garden with my new friends that this vital enlightenment took place.

To secure one of the remarkably cheap (but un-bookable) seats in the gallery at Covent Garden it was first necessary to buy a ticket as soon as the box office

---

[15] G. P. Bird, *Not the Civil Service* (private edn, 1994), *passim*. BR

[16] Olive Grace Still (1915–96). They were married at St Mary the Virgin, Merton Parish Church on 9 August 1941 before a large congregation. Two local papers referred to the wedding march and voluntary composed by the bridegroom, who wore army uniform.

[17] Vaslav Nijinsky (1890–1950), Russian choreographer of Stravinsky's *The Rite of Spring*. Léon Bakst (1866–1924), Russian painter and stage-designer. Both figures were prominent in the Ballets Russes of Sergei Diaghilev (1872–1929).

opened at lunch-time, then book a place in the queue by hiring a numbered stool. These stools were set out on the pavement, under formal supervision, to reserve places until one returned to claim them in the early evening. With Covent Garden so conveniently near the Land Registry the business of buying tickets and stools was usually done by one person on behalf of the rest. We tended to go as a group mainly for that reason. Our party in the gallery, seated *en famille* on their stools an hour or so before the doors were opened at Covent Garden, provided an entertaining prelude to the performance itself. Many of these extrovert enthusiasts would be dressed to impress, in garments no ordinary Londoner would have chosen to wear publicly in those ultra-conservative days. Some of the women would affect flowing robes of homespun, or equally voluminous gowns made up in the clashing colours to be seen later in the evening in Bakst's stage costumes. For a man it was enough to appear in an open-necked shirt and sandals to turn the heads of passers-by.

Additional entertainment was provided as we waited on our stools by buskers who worked the queues at all the West End theatres, as well as by unidentified individuals who made a nightly excursion round all the theatre queues for obscure reasons of their own. Among the most regular of these was a rather jaded young man in sandals who walked at just the right pace to keep his cloak and shoulder-length hair floating in air behind him. No night passed without his ritual appearance. He was said by some to be an exiled Russian prince; others insisted he was Isadora Duncan's young brother.[18] We never discovered the truth of the matter.

In due course our stools would be collected up and we were left to stand until the gallery doors were flung open. Thereupon what had been an orderly, if singular-looking queue was transformed into a herd of wild mountain goats as we fought our way up the stone stairs to secure favourite seats. Soon the curtain would rise and we would enter again the magic world conjured up by Diaghilev and his inspired collaborators ...

For me, those opportunities to savour the interplay between music, choreography, and visual art in such works as *Petrushka*, *The Firebird*, *The Three-cornered Hat*, and the *Polovtsian Dances,* both explained and justified what had hitherto been inexplicable (and rather intimidating) musical territory.[19]

Poor Mr Galpin, now long retired from active musical life, would fly into an extravagant rage at the mention of Stravinsky and still enjoyed recalling having first heard *Petrushka* on the 'wireless' with incredulous disgust. Remembering those execrations of his, I recognised that an important step in my own musical

[18] Isadora Duncan (1877–1927), American dancer prominent in the development of modern dance.

[19] Igor Stravinsky: *The Firebird* (1910); *Petrushka* (1911). Manuel de Falla: *The Three-Cornered Hat* (1919). Alexander Borodin: *Polovtsian Dances* (1890).

education had clearly been taken. For me, indeed, those Land Registry years came close to compensating for the university I had missed.

The Promenade Concerts under Henry Wood[20] at the Queen's Hall in Langham Place had already introduced me to many orchestral works – such as the symphonies of Haydn and Beethoven – previously known to me largely in piano transcription. I had also met there works by composers known hitherto only by name, and gained a fuller picture of others usually represented by a handful of over-familiar pieces. Dutiful study of Rosa Newmarch's programme notes helped set these discoveries in appropriate context.[21] The Proms provided a model training ground for students and young music-lovers, for whom it had long become a cachet to stand rather than sit. I always did so myself, and had two personal adventures there that should perhaps be recorded.

The first occurred during a Bach programme. By now I was in my early twenties, and standing behind a fair-headed young woman – a stranger – I had noticed soon after the violin concerto began a single long blonde hair trailing across her jumper. Being of a naturally meddlesome disposition I had to resist a temptation to remove it. Every so often it would catch my eye again and the temptation gradually became irresistible. Finally, midway through the slow movement I succumbed; and taking the end of the hair between thumb and finger I carefully drew it off. It was, of course, growing in her neck – but I was able to move discreetly away before the Adagio ended.

A second incident amounts to what some will consider a serious misdemeanour. Even in those pre-war days the 'Last Night of the Proms' had become a festive, uninhibited occasion. This time – about 1937 – overcome by exuberance, while the audience was making its way out I climbed up on to the conductor's rostrum and filched one of the cork-handled batons Henry Wood had been using. Stuffing it into my rolled umbrella, I smuggled it out of the hall. Until very recently it found an honoured place in a glass case in my study; but I have since presented it to one of our distinguished professors of music, whose advocacy I hope to rely upon when I come to stand before the judgment seat.[22]

I benefited as well from two other influences. The first was the appearance in 1935 of a revolutionary new series of books – the Penguins, published at sixpence (2½p) each and regularly appearing in groups of about half-a-dozen titles at a time. I recall first seeing them on the bookstall on Waterloo station

[20] Sir Henry Wood (1869–1944), started the Proms in 1895, knighted in 1911.

[21] Rosa Newmarch (1857–1940), pioneering authority on Russian and Czech music, official programme-note writer for the Queen's Hall Orchestra, 1908–27.

[22] This baton is now framed and displayed in the Bernarr Rainbow Room at Trinity College of Music (now Trinity Laban Conservatoire of Music and Dance), King Charles Court, Old Royal Naval College, Greenwich. This room was endowed by the Bernarr Rainbow Trust and opened on 19 October 2004.

one morning on my way to the Land Registry. For the next couple of years I bought (and read) every Penguin as soon as it came out. This development set me exploring bookshops generally and the second-hand bookshops in particular, introducing me to many important writers – Aldous Huxley, Virginia Woolf, Ernest Hemingway, Osbert Sitwell, E. M. Forster, Evelyn Waugh, and T. F. Powys, then attracting attention.

The second of these influences was, of course, the great theatrical revival associated with the names of John Gielgud, Laurence Olivier, Edith Evans, and Peggy Ashcroft. To have seen their performances in *Hamlet*, or *Romeo and Juliet*, for instance, was unforgettable and an experience that permanently altered one's estimation of the actor's trade, and increased serious interest in the theatre.[23]

My organ lessons, meanwhile, had gone well enough for me to be playing some of the more accessible Bach preludes and fugues, the Mendelssohn sonatas, and a selection of 'modern' pieces by Guilmant, Boëllmann, and the like.[24] Consequently, when I had caught up with 'paper work' I successfully entered the College diploma examinations and joined that category of amateur musician then admiringly described in popular circles as 'having his cap and gown'. The kudos of this achievement was, alas, to be short-lived.

My father had by this time made the acquaintance of the organist of the Chapel Royal at Hampton Court. Dr W. J. Phillips was a kindly, elderly man who had formerly been organist of that renowned Tractarian church, St Barnabas, Pimlico. Under his direction the chapel choir at Hampton Court maintained the high standards to which he had always been accustomed. I had not previously met him – my own Sunday duties preventing my attending services in the Palace. But at my father's invitation Dr Phillips agreed to come to tea one day and hear me play something on the piano.

He was sufficiently happy with what he heard to ask me about my current musical activities; but when I told him about the diploma examinations I had recently passed he greeted the news with carefully concealed disapprobation. The experience of taking those exams, he suggested, was not without value; but

---

[23] Rainbow says nothing about his own activities in local theatre. On 31 October 1937 he took an acting part and was responsible for 'production and setting' in the comedy *Tobias and the Angel* (1930) by James Bridie given by the Molesey Players Guild. Two local newspapers reported: 'Raphael, the Archangel, was played in an accomplished style by Mr Bernarr Rainbow' and 'Bernarr Rainbow was ideally suited for the part of the Archangel'. Before that, in 1933, when he was organist at St James's, Merton, Rainbow put on *The Story of the Nativity of Our Lord*, which ran for three nights, was witnessed by 'huge congregations' and the 'young organist of St James' was 'warmly congratulated on his conception of the biblical story' where he was responsible for the play, the music and the painted curtains.

[24] Félix Alexandre Guilmant (1837–1911); Léon Boëllmann (1862–97), almost certainly the popular *Suite gothique* (1895).

he thought it would be an advantage if I worked for a diploma more widely recognised in the profession. There was one he thought particularly suitable for someone in my position, covering 'Choir-training and Organ Accompaniment' it was offered by the highly reputable Guildhall School of Music. Would I like to consider preparing for that?[25]

CHAPTER THREE

D R PHILLIPS' kindly criticism and the challenge presented with it amounted to the first professional advice of any substance I had as yet received. Although secretly humiliated by what he had said I took his remarks very seriously, realising that as things stood I was risking a headstrong plunge into technical mediocrity. In the following year I entered successfully for the Guildhall diploma he had mentioned, and had already enrolled as a student at Trinity College of Music – a respected institution in central London where part-time students were accepted. My tutor for organ-playing was Maurice Vinden, and I began a course of study for the London BMus under Dr William Lovelock, a celebrated examinations coach.[26] I also took up the cello as second instrument – largely to help me in string-writing.

As at other universities in this country, in those days music degrees at London still bore the stamp of the nineteenth century. The principal emphasis was on Harmony, Counterpoint, and Orchestration, though there were also papers on Music History and 'set works'. An 'Exercise' – in this case an extended composition for chorus and orchestra – was also required. Music was first offered as a degree subject at London in 1879, and since that time the Professor had always been appointed to examine, not teach. Trinity College of Music, on the other hand had been recognised as a teaching centre for London degrees from the outset. I soon became aware of the increased demands made on me by my new tutors, and besides being stimulated to greater effort I began to develop a much needed sense of self-criticism,

This was a time of intense international upheaval. Many people had long regarded military confrontation with Germany as inevitable. That prediction was to be fulfilled when, on Sunday, 3 September 1939, the prime minister broadcast a declaration of war. Later that same morning, just as I was playing the opening hymn of the Sung Eucharist at St Andrew's, Wimbledon, we incredulously heard the sirens sound the first air-raid warning of the war. It

[25] Rainbow passed this diploma in 1940.

[26] Maurice Vinden (1894–1968), teacher of singing and organist at the fashionable London church, St Mark's, North Audley Street, from 1918 until his death fifty years later. William Lovelock (1899–1986), teacher, composer and writer of several music theory textbooks.

became my urgent duty to see the choirboys take shelter. They had not long done so, when the sirens sounded again – this time, an 'All Clear'. It had been a false alarm, but our former composure was lastingly shaken by that anti-climax.

By now women and children had been evacuated from London and men aged 19 to 41 were being called up for national service. Yet on the Franco-German border opposing armies faced one another for months in stalemate. Peace-feelers from Adolf Hitler that autumn were summarily rejected – to be followed by increased bombing raids on London and heavy losses among our shipping. Six months later the western front erupted, the German invasion of Norway and Denmark, Holland, Luxembourg, Belgium and France took place, and in August, 1940, an all-night raid on London heralded the 'Blitz'.

Government departments still based in London were now evacuated. The Land Registry and its staff were moved to Bournemouth. This put an end to my musical activities in London and I found myself stranded in an unfamiliar seaside town with no likelihood of their resumption.

I was not left to brood on this state of affairs for long. Before the end of the year I received my call-up papers, reported at a heavily bombed, window-less hall in Southampton for a very chilly medical examination, and was soon posted to an army training depot on Leicester race course.

When I arrived, it was snowing hard, there was no hot water in the wash places, and we were issued with straw and a palliasse to sleep on the floor of the deserted stables. Those first few days seemed both intolerable and unend-ing. We were issued with prickly uniforms, inflexible boots, armed with rifles, steel helmets, respirators, and a mass of unmanageable equipment; our time was shared between learning how to assemble and wear it all and by squad drill. We were also shown exactly how to blanco our webbing, polish our buttons and boots, and to march in step carrying all this paraphernalia. The regime was known, it appeared, as a Hardening Process.

A few days later we were marched down into the town itself and billeted in a row of derelict houses. There was not a stick of furniture in any of them; we again slept on the floor. But to my mind the greatest hardship was the lack of anywhere to sit down.

Not that there was much opportunity to do so. Our days were now filled with parades, arms drill, physical training, route marches, and firing on the rifle-range, interspersed with lectures on a variety of military topics recited from memory by NCOs with incomprehensible accents. The programme had been ingeniously planned to involve as many changes of dress as possible: at the end of a session of physical training wearing singlet and shorts we were to be on parade again in five minutes in full battle order. Lateness was rewarded with extra drills. The only advantage was that at the end of each exhausting day we had no difficulty in sleeping soundly – even if on straw.

In the course of an address by our commanding officer we were informed that the Royal Army Ordnance Corps, in which we now had the honour of serving, existed to provide the army as a whole with the resources necessary to perform its duties – from heavy artillery and weapons of all kinds to everyday items that every soldier needed. In due course, after our basic military training was completed, we would each be posted to a depot specialising in some particular branch of supply, and trained to handle the commodity it maintained and issued.

We were not told on what basis those postings would be decided or whether our experience in civilian life would have any bearing on them. But we had already decided among ourselves that of all the possible specialisms available, the one that stood out as presenting most danger to life and limb, the one at all costs to be avoided, was the maintenance and storage of ammunition. When our postings were eventually published it was therefore with a groan of mortification that I found all those whose names began with P, Q, or R (including me) were allocated to the Central Ammunition Depot at Bramley, in Hampshire.

CAD Bramley occupied a vast secret area screened by trees from surrounding roads. Spread across it stood a couple of dozen huge permanent warehouses carefully camouflaged and widely spaced from each other to avoid the risk of sympathetic explosion. They were connected by a full-gauge railway system linked in turn to the main line. Needless to say, smoking or even carrying cigarettes and matches was strictly banned; anyone entering the storage zone was subject to search at the gate. For inveterate smokers this was almost the worst feature of an ammunition posting. Our first tour of inspection of these monstrous sheds with their great stacks of bombs, shells, mines, mortars, fuses, and ammunition of all kinds was daunting. So was the first task we were allotted – to load a complete train standing alongside one of the sheds with boxes of hand-grenades. Most of us handled those boxes as if they contained crystal goblets – in spite of the bellowing NCOs chivvying us to 'Get A Move On!' When loading was at last completed we were marched off to a midday meal. An hour later we were marched back to a more remote part of the depot. There, alongside another shed stood what was recognisably the very same train we had loaded in the morning. We were now ordered to off-load it. This was apparently a frequent process at CAD Bramley, known as 'internal movement'.

Familiarity, they say, breeds contempt. In no time at all, our efforts sharpened by rage, we were tossing boxes of grenades off that train with something approaching nonchalance. Our first incidental lesson in the handling of explosives was over. We had learnt that until it is primed, a stored grenade is as stable as a toffee-apple.

After that practical introduction, elementary details of various types of stored ammunition were systematically explained to us. Shells, it appeared, were marked in colour to denote their function; a green ring round the nose meant armour-piercing; a red ring, tracer; a blue ring, incendiary; and so on. We learnt which kinds of explosive must be kept dry, which might be stacked in the open. These, and a host of similar facts were explained as we toured the sheds examining their contents. Then followed instruction in the simple accounting system in use – the way stock-tallies were kept and replenishments ordered from munitions factories. All this sometimes seemed boring; but it was a great improvement on loading and off-loading trains.

When the course was eventually over we were all posted to smaller units throughout the country. I was sent to an Ammunition Supply Depot in the Sherwood Forest.

24 ASD was situated in the wooded grounds of Clumber Park, the former home of the dukes of Newcastle. Conditions here resembled more closely those likely to be found in the field: ammunition was delivered and collected by lorry and stacked in small corrugated iron shelters hidden under trees among the bushes and undergrowth. Clumber House, the ancestral mansion, had long since been demolished, but the neglected mews buildings still remained; and it was in the stables there that Headquarters staff – to which I was attached – were billeted.

After the succession of postings and re-postings during those first months in the army it came as something of a solace to find oneself settled, at least temporarily. I was to be further cheered by events that soon followed. Church parades at Clumber were held in the Duke's private chapel still standing in the grounds.[27] It was built in the style of a French Gothic cathedral and had been erected by an earlier duke, evidently under strong Tractarian influence. To enter it for the first time was an extraordinary experience; the fine proportions belied its comparatively small scale.

As we clumped in on that first Sunday the lofty nave echoed our noisy army boots and I looked around at the surviving fitments with great interest. There, high above us, was the organ loft; but in one of the transepts at floor level stood a row of pedal-reed pipes. On that showing alone, this was evidently an instrument designed to match the grandeur of the rest of the building.

Settling into my seat I found myself trying to hypnotise the chaplain to come out from the vestry and say: 'Can anyone here play the organ?' While the thought was still in my mind he did just that. I shot up the chapel before he had finished speaking and found myself, glowing with delight, ushered up the lofty spiral staircase to the organ loft. Mysteriously, the organ was already switched on. Remembering my army boots – in which it was quite impossible to play – I

---

[27] The Chapel of St Mary the Virgin was built between 1886 and 1889, and has a 180 ft spire.

hastily took them off and played (most uncomfortably) in my socks. It was an altogether remarkable occasion.

Afterwards, when I had played them all out of the chapel I stayed behind to discover more of the situation. I now met an old man, part caretaker, part verger, who held the keys of the chapel. He explained that he had started the bellows for me while I was climbing the stairs, and said it had been good to hear the organ played again after so long. If I cared to I could come and practise sometimes. He then showed me how to turn on the Heath Robinson water-pump at the foot of the stairs that filled the bellows. I left in something of a daze, feeling that I had surely landed on my feet at Clumber.

During the next fortnight I sent home for my old 'organ' shoes and went in to play the organ a couple of times in the evenings. Though the reeds had long been untuned and were unusable, the rest of the instrument seemed in good order and sounded even finer now that the chapel was empty. Coming away afterwards I realised that, though I knew how to start the bellows, I had not found out how to turn the water-pump off. But after five minutes' fiddling with it in a growing puddle I succeeded.

Cheered by this turn of events, I recalled Dr Phillips' advice and decided to work when off duty for another musical qualification. Circumstances ruled out instrumental performance, but I found the Royal College of Music offered a diploma in Teaching Musical History and Appreciation' and sent for a syllabus and some past papers.

And then the bubble burst. It was announced in Orders that we were to fall in for church parade half-an-hour earlier on the following Sunday. The chapel was declared out-of-bounds forthwith. The Duke's London house had been bombed, and all the surviving furniture was being sent to Clumber to be stored in the chapel. Church parades would be held in future at Worksop College, a couple of miles away. This seemed highly unfortunate news to me. However, my disappointment was short-lived. The chaplain, it appeared, had been in touch with Worksop College and had arranged for me to meet the Director of Music who would 'show me over the organ.'

Although I had not met him previously Leonard Blake was to play an important part later in shaping my career. When he greeted me for the first time at the College I saw a short, highly-strung man in early middle age whose tense manner masked a genial nature. He asked about the situation at Clumber and about my musical background as we made our way to the college chapel.

Worksop is a school of the Woodard foundation. As such it attaches considerable importance to religious observance, and the chapel is a spacious building laid out collegiate fashion with a serviceable organ in a west gallery. Leonard Blake demonstrated its capabilities, then signalled me on to the organ bench to try my hand, discreetly making his way down to sit in the choir stalls while I did so. He was doing his best to put me at my ease; but I knew I was under examination and made my extemporisation short, then went down to rejoin him. 'Well,' he said, 'what did you think of it?' I made some suitable reply. Then he went on, 'Perhaps you'd like to stay for a cup of tea?' After that (and I was reminded of my scholarship interview long ago) I knew I had passed muster.

Over tea, joined by his wife, we chatted about the organ in Clumber chapel and I was soon telling him about my plan to prepare for an ARCM by working at past papers. Blake said that if I would welcome it, he would be glad to 'look over' my workings. Perhaps we could then meet and discuss my answers over a cup of tea? And Sunday by Sunday, while I was still at 24 ASD, that is what we did. Such kindness demands to be recorded.[28]

Just as I was beginning to find myself recognised in the unit as 'the chap who plays for church parade' I was charged with the duty of playing in the unit dance band the Entertainments Officer was now forming. This was by no means an unwelcome or unfamiliar task. I had often played in an amateur dance band side by side with my duties as organist at Merton and found it relaxing and worth while. On the lighter side, too, the programme of a concert given in Worksop at that time includes the strange item, 'Corporal Rainbow Entertains'. I think this must have been the occasion when I guyed a feature of arms drill known as 'weapon-stripping'. This involved systematically taking a Bren gun apart while describing potential faults in firing and their cure, using the jargon of a training manual. The gun was then re-assembled and fired. I parodied the process under the title 'piano-stripping' by taking the entire action out of an upright piano with a similar commentary. After putting it all back I then played the Chopin 'Military' Polonaise. With a 'difficult' audience largely of servicemen this went down well enough.

It was at this time that Corps troops generally began to be aware of the existence of a General named Montgomery. A controversial and outspoken figure, he was to defeat Rommel at El Alamein and play a key role in the invasion of Italy and Normandy. But at this earlier stage of the war he was best known for his insistence on making every man serving with the army – whatever his specialism – a fighting soldier with the necessary military skills and efficiency. Corps troops, of course, were particularly assailable on such grounds; and units such as ours at Clumber fell to mounting extra parades, exercises, and route marches. Men who had spent the day humping ammunition did not welcome these extra duties; but they were tolerated with the wartime soldiers' inveterate complaint about being 'browned-off'.

This drive toward greater military efficiency came just as the question of

---

[28] Surprisingly, in view of his military duties, Rainbow passed this diploma in 1941.

my applying for a commission was first being discussed. It was decided that in such circumstances my chances of being accepted for officer-training would be enhanced if I first attended a Battle School. Battle Schools were then very new institutions and the subject of much rumour. They were said to make physical demands beyond the capacity of all but the most valiant; to tax stamina to breaking point; and (heaven preserve us) to fire live ammunition at men who were already at risk on assault courses of fiendish toughness. Like many army rumours, this contained elements of truth but was grossly exaggerated. A fit man with sufficient determination was certainly able to meet the demands made at Battle School. It was true that live ammunition was fired there; but it was on fixed lines – which meant that unless a man stood up when supposed to be crawling on his stomach, or veered off course instead of advancing straight forward, he would not be hit. Nevertheless, I cannot deny that when my posting came through, I left for the Battle School at Penmaenmawr in North Wales with some trepidation.

The course began rather ominously with several night exercises in which groups of two or three individuals had to locate distant sites from map references and make their way to them across open country among the foothills of Snowdon in complete darkness. Apart from the disappearance of a few untalented map-readers among us, who had to await the coming of daylight before finding their way home, these exercises went encouragingly well. The next test was more demanding. We were set to paddle across Lake Ogwen in small canvas boats, wearing battle order. On reaching the further bank we had to charge full tilt through a smoke screen and up a distinctly steep mountainside, urged on now by machine-gun fire reminiscent of those earlier rumours. This experience was exhausting, but a quick head-count showed no one had been drowned or shot.

After breakfast next morning, while everyone else was preparing for another day's trial, I was called to the Orderly Room and spent a few anxious minutes wondering what misdemeanour had brought me there. 'Ah,' said the adjutant when he arrived, 'we see from your records you draw maps. The colonel wants a special map of the Snowdon area. Is that the sort of thing you can do?' I assured him warmly that it was; and spent the rest of the course preparing the largest, most colourful – and most time-consuming – map imaginable. The colonel was pleased, and so was I.

When I returned to Clumber, intact and surprisingly spry, everyone wanted to know what it had been like at the Battle School. My replies were distinctly circumspect. But Destiny was not to be deprived of her prize so easily. In due course the forms and reports that follow a serviceman's every move caught up with me. The secret was out, and I was posted to a second Battle School – this time in Lincolnshire.

I knew I could not expect to escape so lightly this time. Added to that, I had been promoted to sergeant immediately before being posted; and that, I told myself, surely bore some hidden significance. My destination was Sutton-on-Sea, a tiny deserted coastal resort; and there, joined by a small contingent who had travelled on the same train, I was billeted in an empty seaside bungalow and put on guard duty until the main body of troops arrived.

What we found ourselves guarding was a series of mysterious structures resembling large vertical wire mattresses held aloft on pylons and facing sea-wards. Referred to only by the code name CDCHL, they made a constant humming sound and occasionally swung round eerily to face another direction. We had never heard of 'radar', of course, and did not know that the code name stood for Coastal Defence Command High Link. We would speculate anxiously on what we were guarding – for it was disconcerting to pace up and down on sentry duty at night on a beach open to seaborne invasion with those mysterious robots humming and swinging overhead.

A few days later the rest of the contingent arrived and we found ourselves attached to a company of the Gloucesters for the duration of the course. We were now moved to the grounds of a large country house a few miles inland. As we marched in we could see a couple of obstacle courses laid out under the trees. They resembled others we had met before; though these looked far more demanding. However, one lay-out situated in an open meadow was quite unfamiliar. It comprised long narrow, shallow trenches a foot deep, and aroused considerable speculation. Later, we found ourselves lying face upward in those trenches as a tank was driven across a few inches above our noses. It was a dramatic and portentous introduction to the course as a whole.

Although, simply stated, most of the demands made upon us at this Battle School were just very much more severe versions of challenges we had met in our earlier training, the central feature of the programme was a hundred-mile forced march occupying three days and nights. News of this event was deliberately leaked at an early stage to raise tension, But precise details were given only when platoon commanders and their sergeants were briefed. At that meeting I found – with secret alarm – that, although only a recently-promoted sergeant, I was to be made acting-commander of one platoon myself.

Our orders were clear. Each platoon would work independently, and we had to march throughout the day to reach a given map reference point by a given time that night. A truck would await us there containing uncooked rations for the next twenty-four hours. If we were late or mistook the map reference the truck would not wait; and we should lose our rations. The men had to manage with the kit they carried and cook their own meals in their mess tins, They must sleep wherever they could find cover. Each man would carry a single blanket. If it rained he must make do with his gas-cape. Platoon commanders were reminded of their responsibility for the men under them; they must use initiative to ensure that things went smoothly.

The next day each platoon commander was given his map reference and set off urgently with his men towards it. My confidence rallied as the morning went well, and we could afford time for a reasonable break while everyone ate his midday rations. Not long after we had resumed our march pandemonium broke out as we were showered with thunder-flashes and ambushed by 'enemies' hidden along the roadside. Thereupon, umpires with arm-bands appeared and declared we had been wiped out. My platoon accepted all this with cold disdain – merely withdrawing to settle along the roadside and declare they were browned-off. I began feckless argument with the umpires, but they just called their band of assailants together and drove off smiling smugly.

We resumed our march and reached the rallying point in time to collect rations, conjure up something in the way of a meal, and then settle down unenthusiastically for what sleep we could summon, It was not an enjoyable night. And I was simply not prepared to be messed about like this. I had been told to use my initiative on the men's behalf and that was what I proposed to do. With our rations that evening I had received the next day's map reference. I saw from the map that besides the obvious road there was another way of reaching it by country lanes. We would go that way instead.

When the platoon was formed up in the morning I told them what I proposed to do, and we set off again. The morning passed uneventfully, we had our break and resumed our march. There was still no ambush in the afternoon and we envisaged the umpires and their raiding party waiting impatiently by the main road for us to arrive. The platoon enjoyed that.

At the rendezvous point that evening the umpires soon arrived to protest about my changing the route. Where had I got to – and why? It was not difficult to dismiss their complaints by reminding them that the instructions given to platoon commanders at the briefing required them to use their initiative. Besides that, I had another arrow in my quiver.

When we arrived that evening at the village crossroads indicated by our map reference, I had sought out the vicar, told him about our previous night spent in the open, and got his permission for the men to sleep in the village hall. We had a much better night as a result and the men cleared the place up gratefully in the morning. That day we saw nothing at all of the umpires and their band of highwaymen; and on the following night arrived back in our billets, tired but quite cheerful. I heard no objections from the Orderly Room about what I had done as acting-platoon commander – indeed, gossip had it that official response had been amused approval.

On my return to 24 ASD I soon heard that a favourable report had been received from Battle School, and that I was now to be posted to pre-OCTU – the sorting house for those proceeding to an Officer Cadet Training Unit. After making my goodbyes – particularly warmly to the Blakes – I set off for Wrotham in Kent, where the unit was housed.

The atmosphere here was very different from previous postings. At mealtimes, for instance, we sat at separate tables in groups of five with a resident 'host'. The cynics said he was on the look-out for those who ate their peas with a knife or blew their noses on the table-napkins. He was certainly noticing our table manners and conversational aptitudes. We found a bar in the mess; but felt that what we ordered and the way we drank it were being observed. Most of the senior 'indoor' staff were clearly psychologists-in-uniform. They called us in turn for interview and tested our responses with flash-cards, asked us to define our main loves and hates, to describe our proudest achievements, or sat us down in front of a cinema screen to write narratives about the pictures projected on it.

The 'outdoor' staff were all sergeants who tested us individually on our knowledge of a comprehensive range of practical military skills. Weaknesses or inexperience in any area meant staying on at Wrotham for corrective training. I had to take two courses – in driving a heavy truck, and a motorcycle. These were completed in a few days and I was off to OCTU.

The training unit for Ordnance officers was at Foremark Hall, near Derby. Once again, army rumours made it a centre of harsh discipline, severe physical demands, and taxing mental pressures. In comparison with Battle School it was none of those things; but the impression of being under constant observation we had sensed at pre-OCTU lingered on here, and left us at first feeling very exposed. We now took down our badges of rank and wore white cap bands instead. As officer-cadets we were required, of course, to jump through the usual hoops – squad drill, physical training, weapon training, and the rest. It was especially interesting now to see how our NCO instructors, confronted with virtually rank-less trainees, enjoyed combining insolence with deference – addressing us as 'Gentlemen', but not failing to threaten violent reprisal if they detected any lack of application. We had to pretend not to notice.

Our training in the regimental duties awaiting us was conducted by senior officers. We worked our way with them through niceties of taking parades, inspecting guards, publishing Orders – even of supervising kitchen duties and the best ways of cutting up meat in bulk. Training in specialist areas would follow when we were posted to our units. Meanwhile we sometimes acted out the officer's role by addressing fellow cadets on selected topics or by giving 'lecturettes' on past experiences.

From time to time during all this we would become aware that one of our number was no longer with us. Inadequacy earned the ignominious signal, 'Returned to Unit' in mid-course. There would be no failures at the end of the course, and we were eventually told – as if confidentially – that there was a rural branch of a London tailor in nearby Repton where we could order our uniforms. We then walked there, cock-a-hoop across the fields, to be measured; and returned a week later to collect the precious garments. Finally, our next postings were published. With some sense of anti-climax I found I was to go back to CAD Bramley.

CHAPTER FOUR

SEEN FROM AN OFFICER'S POINT OF VIEW, once-familiar Bramley now appeared very different. The great sheds, the railway lines, the permanent barracks, were all still there; but now one discovered the comparative calm of the Officers' Mess and the luxury of quarters where a shared batman cleaned one's boots and made the bed. Time was divided between more advanced practical instruction inside the depot; supervisory duties under the watchful and experienced eye of an elderly warrant officer; and technical instruction by senior officers on details of the care and maintenance of various types of ammunition under active service conditions. There was, one found, a very great deal still to be learnt.

There was also more leisure time in the evenings. But apart from recurring duty as Orderly Officer there was little to fill it. I did not care for an evening spent in the Mess and rather reverted to the withdrawn role of my boyhood. At one stage in the search for something to do I went so far as to the write the first chapter of a novel sitting on my bed of an evening. It was heavily influenced by my recent reading and began:

> Peering through the concentric obstacles of a bottle-glass window, Ursula Trent thought she detected movement in the far corner of the room ...

It never got further than a first chapter and I cannot now remember what it was to have been about.

I stopped work on it when I discovered that although no concert was ever held while I was at Bramley there was in fact a large concert hall containing a grand piano in good order. I would spend an occasional solitary spell there playing it; and one evening a captain I had not previously met came in and introduced himself. He was a good baritone and we used to practice together. I wrote a setting of Christina Rossetti's 'Remember me,' for him – of which I was not at all ashamed; but it has long since disappeared.[29]

---

[29] Christina Rossetti (1830–94). 'Remember me when I am gone away' from *Goblin Market and Other Poems* (1862), frequently heard at funerals.

On the whole, life at Bramley struck me as extremely boring. This, how-ever, had the effect of heightening any incident approaching the dramatic. One night going the rounds of the ammunition area as Orderly Officer I came upon a sentry asleep at his post. Technically this was, of course, a mortal offence; my sergeant, a regular soldier, agreed the man must be charged, and a formal report on the matter was filed with the Orderly Room. The incident weighed very heavily on my conscience. I felt very far from willing to see the man shot. But when the court martial took place the army's ancient wisdom revealed itself. The prisoner's regimental number had been 'accidentally' entered incor-rectly on the charge sheet, and the case was promptly dismissed. There was no doubt in any of our minds that the wretched fellow would never repeat his offence.

Another departure from routine came with the introduction of an activ-ity, unknown to most of us raw subalterns, called a TEWT. In full, this was a Tactical Exercise without Troops in which officers of all ranks were assembled to consider and discuss some recently developed military tactic or future enter-prise, purely from a theoretical viewpoint. The example I remember best was a TEWT on 'Ammunition Supply in a Seaborne Invasion', held not long after I had settled in at Bramley.

The title speaks clearly enough for itself. But what can adequately be sum-marised in those few words actually amounts to a highly complex operation. Consequently, three speakers had been chosen to introduce the discussion, each dealing with a single aspect. The first would summarise initial selection and assembly of ammunition; the second, its transfer to sea-going vessels; and the third, beach-landing and subsequent procedures.

On the day a draft programme for this TEWT was published I was button-holed in the Mess by a very senior officer who would not normally have spo-ken to a novice like me. He told me that I had been selected to introduce the beach-landing stage of the TEWT. I looked at him in disbelief. My OCTU lecturettes, he added slyly, had been well spoken of.

The prospect of addressing the assembled senior ranks of CAD Bramley on a topic within their own specialism was no less than alarming. But once I began to seek material on which to base my remarks it became clear that few of my audience were in a position to know much about landing ammunition on an enemy coast. I raked through training manuals and more recent supple-ments, looking principally for data on 'Invasion'. I found realistic mention of the wisdom of selecting a beach with a sandy bottom, and the importance of making stacked ammunition available on landing craft in the order it would be needed. By a stroke of serendipity, I also came across details of a newly-created detachment known as a 'Forward Ammunition Section' whose job it was to set up ammunition stores in forward areas ready for use when the guns moved up. I confess to thinking of an FAS at the time as the most uninviting posting imaginable; but examination of its role and structure greatly helped me draw the necessary picture of supply in a beach-head situation.

Drawing up an acceptable discourse from the material I had assembled proved quite an enjoyable task. I should have enjoyed it less had I known my apparent 'grasp of the subject' would find me put in charge of a Forward Ammunition Section later.

After a few months at Bramley I received an overseas posting. For security reasons, ultimate destinations were never disclosed; but at the pre-embarkation centre I was issued with tropical kit – a displeasing assortment of khaki-drill and a pith helmet – which in itself suggested a Far East location.

I travelled throughout the night to an unknown embarkation port on a train crammed with troops and their kit, in blacked-out carriages blue with cigarette smoke. The more hardened among us managed fitful sleep as we were shunted back and forth during an air raid. But as daylight grew, this or that landmark was recognised, and eventually we emerged from a long tunnel on what was distinguishably the quayside at Liverpool.

The men who now poured off the train were painfully formed up into sections and companies and prepared to board the troopship (whose name I fear I have forgotten) moored alongside. Decks and companion-ways were soon jammed with men weighed down with kitbags and rifles struggling to find their allotted places. After a couple of hours' chaos things settled down. Then, with a great sense of anti-climax came an urgent call to hand in all tropical kit. It had been issued only to mislead enemy agents. We were not, it seemed, bound for the Far East after all.

Officers' quarters on the boat occupied two main decks. Cabins designed for two passengers now contained six bunks, but the dining-room remained as luxuriously furnished as it had been when the boat carried affluent passengers on world cruises. The waiters were still the original white-gloved Lascars and we were called to meals by a discreet gong. After the rigours of wartime England this was a striking change.

It became much more than that when one took duty as Orderly Officer and went below to inspect the men's quarters on the troop-decks. There, they were crammed into holes and corners, eating and sleeping in squalor – and when the going grew rough, awash with vomit. I had, then as now, no political allegiances, but I cannot recall ever feeling so ashamed as when I first witnessed that spectacle of gross inequity and the amazing docility of its victims.

The troopship headed first for Greenock, where we joined other boats to form part of a convoy, then made out to sea. Now sailing north-west and soon joined by marshalling destroyers the wags among us declared we were off to invade Iceland; but during the next twelve days – no less – the changing position of the sun showed us turning south and roughly following the coastline of America down to a point where re-crossing the Atlantic brought us in line with Morocco. There we turned north again and came to the Straits of Gibraltar, as someone put it, 'by the back door'.

These manœuvres, designed to take us out of easy range of both U-boats and bombers, proved successful. For although from time to time some emergency made our escorting destroyers dash about like sheepdogs while the entire convoy made a diagonal change of course, we arrived at the entrance to the Mediterranean intact.

I have come across a brief account of the events that followed, doubtless written to fill up a boring evening after I arrived at my destination. Its authenticity justifies inserting it here:

The New Ararat

My first sight of Africa after fifteen days afloat came just as dusk was falling. There, directly ahead of us, where veteran sailors had been pointing out landmarks to each other for half an hour or more while landsmen could only see clouds on the horizon, a high mass of rock with a lighthouse at its foot gradually took definite shape. The news rapidly spread amongst the men on board and very soon the rails were full of eager seekers for the phenomenon – land.

Of course we all said it was Gibraltar – but the patient mariners, not without ill-concealed patronage, explained that we shouldn't see The Rock until much later. As always we seemed to be moving annoyingly slowly and before the headland had grown appreciably nearer daylight had quite gone. Then suddenly on the starboard side appeared the lights of a town – the first street-lighting I had seen for four years – and on the portside the coast of Spain could just be distinguished as the moon came up. As the Straits grew narrower the lights of Tangier seemed absurdly close; it seemed that a very short swim indeed would bring one to all the strange brilliance of a town at peace.

Suddenly an orange light appeared on the portside, and a tiny Spanish fishing- boat carrying a naphtha flare bobbed past, the occasion of ribald comments from the hundreds of troops lining the decks, and hearty shouts of 'Put that something light out' from men who had been sternly warned that the glow of a cigarette on deck by night might lead to torpedoing and the loss of thousands of lives.

I did not stay on deck to see Gibraltar. It grew increasingly cold and although at one time a distant line of flares could be seen ahead on what appeared to be the summit of The Rock it seemed unlikely that we should reach it for a considerable time.

Just before I went below I heard some very young subalterns singing 'Greensleeves' under the stars on the Promenade Deck and the song seemed to me to be the very quintessence of England. I spent an ecstatic, melancholy ten minutes musing alone in the cold before I went back to my crowded cabin.

Next morning we were well into the Mediterranean. The sea was disappointingly grey and choppy, and all along the starboard skyline stretched the barbaric mountains of North Africa.

Speculation about our destination now broke out again; but it was soon dispelled when we turned into the harbour of Algiers and prepared to disembark.

Algiers was a surprise. I had seen the white-washed Kasbah from the boat, and it fitted in with my concept of an African town. But when we landed and found ourselves in the streets of what looked like a modern European town with the sophisticated Aletti Hotel dominating the waterfront, I had for the first time to adjust the narrow conception of foreign lands my background and schooling had implanted.

I was posted to the Command Ammunition Depot situated just south of Algiers and given charge of a storage area whose corrugated iron shelters were scattered throughout an orange grove, then in full fruit. It was very like Clumber transposed to another climate. My duties resembled those I had in England; my evenings, however, were not quite as dull – for Algiers itself was reasonably accessible.

There was a limited black-out, but the central square outside the Post Office was always lit by a single powerful electric light which could be switched off in emergency. The Aletti Hotel was the recognised place for officers to meet 'for tea'. I went there once but felt no urge to repeat the experience. Instead of serving tea (which was quite unavailable) one was given an unglazed terra-cotta beaker of harsh Algerian wine, and a couple of unappetising biscuits.

Where 'sight-seeing' was concerned, the Mufti of Algiers had given special dispensation for conducted parties to visit the ancient Mosque by the quayside. I joined a party going there one evening. To avoid being molested for desecrating the building unbelievers had to walk on a narrow uncarpeted strip of the flagstone floor specially provided for the purpose. The interior seemed to me far less impressive than the outside; and I was further alienated by the guide's tale of a devout Moslem who was taken ill there. For involuntarily vomiting on the floor and defiling the mosque he was immediately beheaded, by order of the civil court. Particularly after that anecdote I found myself preferring to admire the exterior with its tower and dome, and the bronze statue of the Duc d'Orléans silhouetted against its white-washed walls.

Though free of many of the restrictions of wartime London, there were marked limits to what one could safely do in Algiers. The trams still ran regularly, but they were out of bounds to military personnel for fear of rampaging louse-borne typhus. The ancient Kasbah was likewise out of bounds – assassination was regarded as a real feasibility in its narrow alleys and 'houses of ill-repute'. Local legend had it that a group of American GIs had defied the ban, and gone in disguised as women in yashmaks. There were various accounts of what happened to them as a result, and no one seemed anxious to repeat the adventure.

Soon after my arrival I had been referred to the Entertainments Officer at HQ in Algiers and met Lionel Salter[30] there who invited me to organise a series of gramophone recitals for troops in surrounding areas. A few days later when I called in to discuss this further I passed a tiny, unhappy-looking man – clearly a foreigner – sitting crouched in the corridor outside the Entertainment Officer's room. 'Did you see that little guy?' he asked as soon as I entered. 'That's Pouishnoff,' he went on.[31] 'He's supposed to be giving a piano recital tonight; but he says the piano won't do ... I know! You'll have to play instead.' In the circumstances there was no alternative; and I did. That was the only occasion, however, on which I can claim to have deputised for an international concert pianist.

Such off-duty pranks apart, life in the Depot itself was pretty humdrum. Yet even there an occasional diversion occurred. As I have mentioned, my area was sited in orange groves, and it was customary to keep the Mess supplied with the fruit – an unknown luxury in England at that time – by purchasing oranges in bulk direct from the Arab who owned the groves. The Mess Caterer told me as soon as I arrived that it would be my duty to handle this, and a few days later he asked me to buy the usual quantity, pay for it, and he would reimburse me

Next day when I bought the oranges with due ceremony, using my very rusty French, I mistook the figure mentioned as the price and paid ten times what I should. The owner took the largish sum without question. When I handed over the hamper of oranges that evening the Mess Secretary indignantly refused to pay more than the proper price. I must pay for my own stupidity.

The next day when I arrived in my area still smarting about this I spotted a little procession coming. It was the owner with a couple of veiled wives and

[30] Lionel Salter (1914–2000), versatile keyboard player, conductor and writer, on the staff of the BBC from 1948–74.

[31] Leff Pouishnoff (1891–1959), Ukranian-born pianist who settled in England in the 1920s.

a scattering of their children. They approached with great dignity, the owner bowed and addressed me earnestly. He had spent a wakeful night, he said. When I gave him the money yesterday he 'thought he was mad', and said nothing. But he now saw I had mistaken the price he asked. He next produced from his *jellabah* a fistful of notes, handed them to me, bowed solemnly again, and followed by his family withdrew, leaving me speechless. Once again I had to adjust my narrow view of life in foreign lands.

It was now wintertime; and just as the weather suddenly turned wet and stormy I received an urgent posting to Italy where our Fifth and Eighth Armies were slowly fighting their way towards Rome. I was to replace an officer due to return to England in preparation for the Second Front. Travel documents were hastily drawn up and I was rushed to Maison Blanche airport to fly to Naples.

At the airport I found there were no flights to Italy. The Mediterranean was too storm-ridden. I went back the next day with the same result. I must go by boat, they said. At the port the authorities were quite as definite. There were no boats. The Mediterranean was impossibly rough. I could go on the first crossing available. The following day I was summoned to board a long, narrow troopship bound for Taranto, on Italy's heel. From there I must make my own way to Naples by train.

As soon as the boat left harbour it was clear that we faced an exceptionally violent crossing. More to the point, when Orders were published I found I was down as 'Officer of the Watch' for some part of the night. To begin with, we skirted the coast of Algeria and as darkness fell made across toward Pantelleria. By now the boat was rocking and reeling in every direction at once: it was impossible not to feel ill. But I was due to start my watch shortly, and must not allow myself to be sick. As we rolled and pitched our way past Sicily and I took over from my predecessor on deck I was silently repeating, *à la* Mme Coué, 'I won't be sick, I won't be sick.' And I wasn't – until I went below when my watch was over.

Next day we disembarked in the harbour at Taranto. I went urgently to report my arrival and explain that I should have been in Naples long before this. 'That's a pity,' they said in the ESO's office. 'There's only one train a week to Naples – and it left yesterday. Your best bet is to beg a lift from the Yanks. They are always running Jeep convoys to Naples and will probably take you along with them.

And that is what happened. We left the following morning in a convoy of four Jeeps and a couple of trucks, travelling along the coastal road past Bari and Barletta. And when we stopped for a midday break the Americans casually lifted their cars' bonnets, took out cans of stew they had slung behind the radiators, and we all had a hot lunch. That evening we reached Foggia, and they apologised for not being allowed to put me up at their camp. They would pick me up in the morning, but now dropped me at the so-called Officers' Transit Hotel.

This proved to be a small requisitioned suburban hotel which was already full by the time we got there. But the Italian civilian manager said I should be found a bed for the night in the new annexe across the road. Meanwhile I could get something to eat at a condittore round the corner.

After I had eaten a large, unidentifiable, but magnificently coloured fish I was taken across to the Annexe where an elderly, unamiable-looking Italian was waiting to show me my room. The whole place seemed deserted; I was to be the only resident, and I certainly did not take to this chap. At that stage of the war the loyalty of many Italians was distinctly questionable, I decided to sleep with my revolver under the pillow.

Sure enough, when I had not long been in bed I heard a creak on the stairs and footsteps cautiously approaching my room. As I grasped my revolver the door slowly opened and my unlikeable Italian's head appeared. Did I want a *signorina*, he asked.

Early next morning I left with the Americans for the mountainous journey across the Apennines to Naples. Parts of the rocky countryside were under deep snow, and we passed several communities of cave-dwellers who survived each winter up there shoeless and in rags. Although their feet were literally blue with cold these people evidently preferred their way of life to the relative comfort of the plains not many miles distant.

Late that evening we skirted the foothills of Vesuvius and arrived in Naples. I was deposited with all my kit at another Transit Hotel. The generosity of the Americans had saved me five days' delay waiting for the train at Taranto. Settling into my room I decided (quite improperly) that I deserved at least one day to myself to look round fabled Naples before I reported to Command HQ on the Riviera di Chiaia.

After breakfast next morning I booked in for another night, saw my kit locked away, and set out on foot to explore. Simply following my nose, I found close to the harbour the Castel Nuovo, Palazzo Reale, and the San Carlo Opera House. Crossing the road in search of something to eat I saw a street sign: Via Chiaia. Sight of this familiar name reminded me that I must eventually report to an address on the Riviera di Chiaia. I would go and search it out – so as to know just where I had to report tomorrow – or the next day, perhaps ...

The Riviera di Chiaia is a long esplanade flanked by gardens and an aquarium. As I made my way along it, looking for the building where I must report, a window was thrown open and I heard my name shouted. It was an officer I had known at Bramley. 'We're all waiting for you,' he shouted. 'Where on earth have you been?' He ushered me inside while I explained what had held me up. 'You'd better come and see the colonel,' he said.

Half an hour later I was being driven by the colonel himself in his Jeep to pick up my kit. We then drove hot-foot to Capua, an ancient Roman town some twenty miles north of Naples where my new unit awaited my arrival. It was, the colonel confided expressionlessly, a Forward Ammunition Section.

CHAPTER FIVE

No. 2 FORWARD AMMUNITION SECTION was 'resting' and we found its twenty or so men, their sergeant, and the captain I was to relieve billeted in a large house untouched by the bombing that had wiped out much of Capua. The colonel introduced me, issued a few instructions, and promptly drove back to Naples. The necessary formalities of handing over carried out next day proved a simple business with such a small detachment; and that evening the men held a Farewell Party for their former CO. The acting-cook had rustled up a notable meal and bought enough local grappa to knock many of us out by bedtime. In the relaxed atmosphere I found these men quietly proud of having advanced with the 8th Army through Egypt, Libya, and Tunisia, before taking part in the invasion of Italy. It was a humbling experience, I felt, to be put in charge of them.

Once my predecessor had left next morning, and while we waited for a posting back to an active role, I took the opportunity to explore something of Capua itself. It was the main crossing point over the River Voltumo – consequently its bridge and the approaches to it had been very heavily bombed and shelled. The great ninth-century cathedral was completely destroyed, but I found an imposing church in one of the squares and ventured inside. On the wall above the high altar a little balcony supported a dignified row of diapason pipes. Looking around the church I could see no other part of the organ or its console. However, in the sacristy I caught sight of a priest carrying out some sacerdotal task and decided to introduce myself to him as an English organist, and ask him to show me the organ. Having as yet little or no Italian, I recklessly thought of trying something simple in Latin. How, I wondered, should one say, 'Good afternoon,' in Latin?

When I entered the sacristy he looked up, a shade startled by this martial intrusion. 'Pax vobiscum,' I began. He made the appropriate reply, though casting a covert glance at the revolver on my belt. 'In Anglia,' I explained, 'pulsator organorum sum. Organum hie videre volo.' Surprisingly, he understood me, and putting down the chasuble he had been folding, beckoned me to follow while he led the way behind the high altar. There stood a tiny ramshackle harmonium. The pipes above our heads were just dummies ... We were both, I think, somewhat embarrassed by the incident. But I bowed my thanks and made my escape.

Our Movement Order now came through. We were to move another twenty-five miles forward and establish a depot at the abandoned railway station at Cellole-Fasani. This, I saw from the map, was close to the River Garigliano, an obstacle still being vigorously contested with the Germans.

When we arrived at our new position we found the whole area deserted and the station an isolated, building-less halt. Cellole and Fasani, after which it was named, were two adjacent villages; but there was only a small empty house near the station, and that became our HQ. Any idea of expecting ammunition deliveries from the railway was soon scotched – the whole line had been systematically destroyed: the wooden sleepers were all snapped in half, the rails dynamited into short lengths. This, we learned later, was the work of a special railway engine equipped to space out the explosives and gouge out each sleeper as it slowly advanced. Most of the Italian rail system had been put out of action in this way.

A preliminary inspection of our allocated area showed that deliveries by road could be marshalled readily enough in the station approach, and useful storage areas found among the shrubbery along adjoining minor roads. But first our equipment must be unloaded and the men billeted. Not far away, on rising ground, we found a modest farmhouse big enough to accommodate us all. While bedding and equipment were unloaded here, the sergeant and I clambered up on to a nearby mound for a broader view of the area. To the north – and surprisingly close – was the Garigliano. On its farther bank the ground rose steadily, and even as we watched we could see smoke-screens being laid as our troops cautiously advanced across it against German defences. It was at once absorbing and unreal – too theatrical, one felt, to be genuine. Of course, as we should discover later, while we gazed thoughtfully at this scene from our vantage point we were being observed far less speculatively through German field – glasses from the opposite side of the river.

During the rest of that day suitably sheltered sites for individual stacks were located and levelled. A despatch rider then appeared with details of the first deliveries of ammunition that would arrive early tomorrow. With this advance information it was easier to plan realistically for its reception. Already the general layout of the depot was taking shape. But it now grew too dark to continue working outside, and we withdrew to the farmhouse to settle in, have a meal, and get a good night's sleep in preparation for tomorrow.

Punctually at midnight the first shells began to land close by. At first I found myself wondering what was causing the din. Everyone else will have known only too well. But these men, being what they were, gave no sign of perturbation. So it was only slowly that I realised that we were being shelled. They were falling in twos and threes, with a sizeable pause between. I lay very still in my bed, with all my danger signals firmly switched off, consciously waiting for the next clutch to arrive. After a quarter of an hour the shelling stopped.

In the morning the sergeant greeted me with a quizzical expression, but said nothing about the shelling. 'Come and look at this, Sir,' he said, and led me to the farmhouse door. The flagstone paving outside had disappeared leaving a ragged hole. 'That was a near one!' he declared.

Our position was certainly pinpointed; and while the Germans might not know our precise function they were bound to keep us under observation. That being so, the regular arrival, loading, and off-loading of trucks – whatever their contents – would invite further shelling. The morning's delivery of ammunition must be halted at once. I sent our driver off before breakfast with an urgent report stating that the site was under observation and shell-fire, and advising cancellation. He arrived in time to stop delivery. Later that day we received another Movement Order: we were to dismantle the site and withdraw to Carinola, a small town only two or three miles back, but separated from the Garigliano by Mount Massico. There, the *podestà* was ordered to find us billets and we settled in, nursing our misgivings over this anticlimax. A few days later No. 2 FAS was recalled to UK and I was posted to the Command Ammunition Depot at nearby Teano. So ended my extended but ultimately fruitless flirtation with Forward Ammunition Sections. As if to demonstrate the Pathetic Fallacy, the weather now worsened suddenly, and the countryside was soon under deep snow.

The commanding officer at Teano was a figure from fiction – the 'mad major' who inflicts on his subordinates unpalatable tasks and unnecessary discomforts designed to 'keep them up to scratch'. His most reprehensible policy was to scorn the use of billets and insist on permanently quartering his unit under canvas. To make matters worse in present circumstances, the tents in use had originally been supplied during the North African campaign, and were designed to keep off the sun – certainly not to shelter from rain or snow.

On arriving at this CAD I was therefore astonished to see a tented camp, with its Orderly Room and Mess in two marquees more suited to a garden fête than a snowbound battle zone. The major and I took instant dislike to each other, and after a few chilly exchanges (in both senses of the word) I was shown to my saturated tent. That night and subsequently, undressing for bed meant taking off my boots and scrambling under the blankets in full uniform. It was abominable.

Next day I was shown round the depot – its only remarkable feature was the use of locally recruited Italian civilians to load and offload the ammunition – and allocated an extensive wooded storage area to administer. My HQ was a rambling farmhouse with two main rooms. I occupied one, with a corporal who kept the records; the other housed a dozen or so of the wives and

womenfolk of the Italian work-force, who spent their time cooking and clear-
ing up after the midday meals they prepared from rations we provided. The
noise these peasant women managed to make as they carried out their chores
was astounding. From my dictionary I learned a few objurgations – *Basta!* –
Silencio! – *Zitto!* – but such protests went literally unheard.

Once a week I met all these Italians when they assembled to collect their
wages on Pay Parade. It was conducted formally – a civilian parody of an old
military procedure in which each man came up to my table and received his
due under the eye of a sergeant and corporal.

There was another occasion, however, when I had to meet them – to explain
that, for whatever reason, their daily bread ration had not been delivered, and
they would be issued with flour instead. I was not sure how this news would
go down with so volatile an audience, and had spent a while anxiously probing
through my dictionary to make sure I said the right thing in as few words as
possible. The motto theme must be 'Flour instead of bread, today', and I arrived
hopefully at 'Farina invece pane, oggi' to cover the matter. Fortunately my anxiety was misplaced. The announcement was not only understood but greeted
with an audible murmur of approbation – they would prefer flour because the
women could make from it their favourite local pasta. And as soon as I had
withdrawn I saw them select a couple of the filthy old oil drums used as rubbish
bins, set the women to scrubbing them out, and then adopt them as cauldrons
in which to cook the local speciality.

It was only such incidents that provided relief to the boredom and discom-
fort of life at Teano. The evenings spent in the Mess marquee were an affront.
There were, admittedly, a couple of oil stoves there which warmed a small area;
but the major's entrance immediately lowered the temperature again by heralding interminable 'shop' and awkward confrontations if his views were questioned. On the other hand, it was impossible to think of sitting in one's icy and
waterlogged tent.

It reached a stage when I dreaded going to bed – in blankets that had by
now become saturated. And before long the results of regularly sleeping in a
thoroughly wet bed made themselves obvious: it became painful to bend, and
walking grew noticeably difficult. I saw the Medical Officer about this – and
he gave me a packet of aspirin. In due course, when I could hardly get about I
reported to the nearest Field Hospital. There they took things more seriously
and I was sent off to a base hospital at Barletta, on the Adriatic coast.

A week spent there in a dry bed had me feeling distinctly better – though I
was not yet allowed to walk. I was in a ward with about a dozen other casualties
– varying from a severely wounded Scot who was virtually encased in rigid plas-
ter, to a Greek soldier, in the next bed to mine, with a leg wound. Conversation
was made fitful by language; but we all found rusty French something of a

lingua franca. I recall trying to find a common topic for a chat with my Greek neighbour, and coming up with (of all things!) an Ancient Greek musical term I had picked up from Dr Burney.[32] 'What,' I asked him, 'does *proslamba-nomenos* mean?'[33] He looked at me dubiously and got me to repeat the question. After a few moments' thought he explained that it meant a charwoman, or someone who helped with the housework. It is a nice point. That absurd flight of pedantry on my part came, as it happens, shortly after my other neighbour, a Londoner, had said to me, accusingly, over breakfast one morning, 'You're a teacher, aren't you.' Cautiously I replied, 'What makes you think that?' 'Oh,' he said, 'you've been giving us all a music lesson half the night.' I had never been accused of talking in my sleep before.

An unexpected diversion while I was in hospital at Barletta came with the visit of a touring opera company. Sponsored by ENSA, it comprised an all-Italian cast, and their performance of *Rigoletto*[34] took place in the town's main theatre/opera house, a building large enough to accommodate an audience of both troops and local inhabitants. Walking-wounded from the hospital were invited, and someone agreed to push me round the corner that evening in a wheel-chair.

It was a full house, but the singers were all elderly and well past their prime. There was no scenery, make-up, or stage-lighting, and the costumes were stock 'period' garments that clearly served for general use, whatever the opera might be. The performance itself was, I'm afraid, quite indifferent. One unforgettable feature was provided by the prompter who sat gesturing and mouthing in full view of the audience at a card-table on the stage, his score illuminated by a domestic reading-lamp. For all these shortcomings, however, everyone enjoyed the evening; and when the audience poured out into the street afterwards all the Italians were giving repeat performances of their favourite numbers – frustrated opera-singers the lot of them!

Another more private diversion was the belated discovery on my part of Tobias Smollett.[35] Among a batch of old books distributed in the ward by the Red Cross I came across a copy of *Humphrey Clinker*, relished reading it for the first time, and Smollett promptly became a life-long friend. I was soon sit-

---

[32] Charles Burney (1726–1814), author of *A General History of Music from the Earliest Ages to the Present Period, to which is prefixed, a Dissertation on the Music of the Ancients* (1776) and many other writings.

[33] Apparently it refers to the lowest note in the Ancient Greek musical gamut, but is not mentioned by Rainbow in *Music in Educational Thought and Practice*.

[34] ENSA (Entertainments National Services Association), set up in 1939 with government support to entertain the troops during World War II. Guiseppe Verdi: *Rigoletto* (1851).

[35] Tobias Smollet (1721–71), Scottish-born novelist: *The Expedition of Humphrey Clinker* (1771).

▲ 1 Aged three at Rushden

◄ 2 Aged eleven at Merton Park

► 3 The Rainbow apartment at Hampton Court from 1931

▲ 4 With his parents

◄ 5 Rainbow's father,
   E. J. Rainbow (1888–1983)

6 In army uniform

7 OCTU Royal Army Ordnance Corps, 1942; Rainbow stands in the back row, far right.

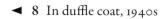
◄ 8 In duffle coat, 1940s

▲
► **9, 10** Olive Rainbow (1915–96)

▲ **11** The Royal Grammar School, High Wycombe, 1940s
▼ **12** St Mark's College, Chelsea, 1847

13, 14 Choir practice at High Wycombe

▲ **15** Bach's Toccata and Fugue in D Minor at High Wycombe

▼ **16** At the console of a large organ

▲ **17** Receiving the D Litt at the University of Leicester, 1992

◀ **18** In the garden at Richmond, 1996

▼ **19** Sketch from a visit to Italy, 1997

ting up in bed with a writing-pad busily parodying his characteristic litanies of displeasure with a diatribe of my own on the subject of military hospitals.

What with the clashing of bed-pans, probing of thermometers, constant changing of bandages, incessant remaking of beds ... And then one morning the doctor arrived on his rounds clutching my X-ray negatives. After fingering and manipulating my spine awhile, he could be seen making up his mind. 'I'm transferring you to Naples,' he said. 'Put him on the train this afternoon,' he added to the ward orderly.

I arrived in Naples by hospital train on the evening of 18 March 1944, and found myself installed in the dockside hospital on Via Amerigo Vespucci. It was a huge building, very typical of fascist architectural ideals, and through the tall windows opposite my bed in a top-floor ward there was a spectacular view of Vesuvius in the distance.

Next morning at about 5 a.m. I was awakened by my bed shaking violently. I suspected a bombing raid – there had been a severe one a few nights earlier – and looked rather blearily out of the window for any tell-tale puffs of anti-aircraft fire. Instead, the whole sky was a-boil with white cloud eerily resembling a gigantic cauliflower in slow motion. So that was it! Vesuvius was in eruption. It was the most awesome and hair-raising sight imaginable.

By now occupants of the other beds in the ward had become aware of what was happening. Everyone had some theory as to what to expect. But in fact the great bulging, solid-seeming cloud continued to hang palpitating across the sky, spreading throughout the day as far as one could see. Intrepid visitors to the hospital arrived in great excitement to regale the staff with tales of showers of hot ash burning holes in their clothes or setting their would-be protective umbrellas on fire as they walked about Naples. And then, as darkness fell, incandescent streams of lava could be seen steadily advancing down the mountainside, setting trees and houses in their path suddenly ablaze amid lightning flashes and bursts of molten rock thrown up from the crater itself.

The following morning the sky had ceased to boil, for the time being. There was a sullen fog and ash was still falling, covering the streets with a half-inch carpet of grey. Many of the Neapolitans, already panic-stricken by the recent air-raid casualties, were now frantic. And it was amid that atmosphere of fear and hysteria that I was stretchered on to a hospital ship in the docks and incredulously told I was on my way home.

As we sailed away from Naples our path took us beneath the great cloud of ash still hanging overhead. Showers of it constantly fell on deck. Not all of it was powdery, and the ward orderlies would bring specimens down for us as souvenirs, resembling small cubes of black sugar. We were not allowed on deck to witness this phenomenon for ourselves. I still have my sample.

Next day we were out of sight of land and it was strange to feel that it was only the huge red cross painted on our upper work that gave to this uncamouflaged white ship its uncertain chance of survival. Our first, and only, port of call was Gibraltar where we anchored in an inner harbour while the necessary shore visits took place and supplies were loaded. Casualties were still not allowed on deck, but from what could be seen through portholes there was little to attract us about this fabled Rock.

I remember nothing of the rest of our voyage except that it was much briefer than when we had come out; and that those of us who could were now allowed to don uniform again and try to find our feet. Eventually we put into Avonmouth, and there was a small gathering of civilians to greet us and see us onto the waiting train. Our destination, we learned, was Birmingham. During the journey, from conversations with those conducting us and from the newspapers handed round we learnt for the first time of the of the Allied landings at Anzio, the continuing stalemate at Cassino, the renewal of heavy raids on London, and the start of daylight reprisal raids on Berlin. But it was not altogether easy to take in the implications of all this news. For many it was sufficient to find themselves back home in one piece. And for me, I shall confess, perhaps the most memorable event in that journey was the sight of clumps of real English primroses in flower beside the track. Robert Browning, I thought: 'Oh, to be in England, now that April's there ...'

At the hospital in Birmingham where I was admitted, new tests and X-rays were carried out. I now learnt that through living in those wet conditions in Italy I had developed a condition known as spondylitis, which brought about spinal rigidity and required a recently-devised treatment known as 'deep X-ray'. As I lived in London, I would be referred to St Thomas's Hospital, which would make arrangements accordingly. Meanwhile, after a course of spinal manipulation, as soon as I could get about again I could go home. 'Home' at that time meant Hampton Court. I had been married in 1941, but since then had lived only where the army chose to put me. I must soon arrange things differently; but for the present it was a question of dealing with matters as they arose from day to day.

In due course I was summoned to report at St Thomas's Hospital and return weekly. There, each time I went I received a massive dose of deep X-ray on a ink-outlined area of my back. At length I was discharged – the treatment was still experimental at that stage and over-exposure regarded as, at least, risky. Besides, I was now walking more easily – at least with a stick.

The most pressing of the unresolved questions now confronting me was that of establishing a career. Every other decision depended upon it. Was I to return to the humdrum existence at the Land Registry – now being dispersed to various regional branches throughout the country – or should I take the bold step of seeking a musical career? I decided that the person best equipped and most likely to be willing to advise me wisely was Leonard Blake. During our long conversations over exam scripts and those Sunday teas at Worksop he had come to know my abilities, failings, and aspirations; he had, in any case, invited me to get in touch with him when I left the army.

I wrote quite briefly, outlining recent events and asking whether he thought it merely foolhardy for me to seek a professional appointment as organist and teacher. After being away so long my keyboard technique had, of course, suffered; but I was arranging to take a concentrated refresher course at Trinity College and looked forward to regaining it. He replied at once, saying that he was making a few enquiries about the current situation and would advise me accordingly in due course.

A few days later I received a letter from Hubert Crook, the organist of High Wycombe parish church, to say that circumstances made it necessary for him to find a deputy to play for services and take choir practices for two weeks during his unavoidable absence next month. He had been given my name, and wondered if I would be interested in the post. If so, perhaps we could meet to discuss it further. I replied at once, saying I would like to be considered.

I had never previously met Hubert Crook, though his name was somehow familiar. When he now met me in London he disclosed that he had been asked by Sir Sydney Nicholson, Director of the School of English Church Music (now the Royal School of Church Music)[36] to help run a choristers' course at Durham Cathedral. This would take him away from Wycombe for a fortnight, and he had no regular deputy. As we talked I recalled Crook's reputation as a gifted, dedicated choir-trainer and was little surprised when he went on to reveal that the choir at Wycombe mustered no less than forty boys and sixteen men. There was a longstanding musical tradition at the church extending back well into the last century; and the organ was a recently rebuilt three-manual Willis. Any doubts I may have had about the project had now disappeared and Crook, fortunately, seemed to favour my coming. It was arranged that I should go down to High Wycombe to see things for myself. He was always to be found in the church on such-and-such a day giving organ lessons. If I came in the late afternoon he would show me round, explain things more fully, and I could try the organ.

I so well remember coming down the hill from Beaconsfield that day in the bus, and seeing for the first time High Wycombe spreading along the valley in front of me. There in the middle rose the ample tower of what must be the parish church. When we reached the town itself the scale and dignity of the

[36] Sir Sydney Nicholson (1875–1947) founded the School of English Church Music in 1928. He was reported in the *Bucks Free Press* on 1 November 1948: 'If asked to name six choirs in England which carried out the traditions of the School, the High Wycombe Parish Church Choir would be one of them.'

building showed why this church was known as 'the cathedral of Bucks'.[37] And when I entered and saw the spacious choir-stalls and the organ console with its generous array of stop knobs I was overwhelmed by the size of the task I was undertaking. But undertake it I would!

Hubert Crook could not have been more patient and helpful. He outlined the musical policy at the church, showed me the music library, and introduced me to the vicar – an old-time, unaggressive Evangelical, deeply committed to preserving the traditions of the place, not least its music. Crook had even found boarding accommodation for me and took me round to meet the landlady. It was arranged that I would arrive on the Monday – and thus have the whole week to get used to the organ besides taking the choir practices. Finally, he disclosed that it was at Sir Sydney Nicholson's suggestion that he had got in touch with me; and that Sir Sydney had learned about me from a trusted ally – Leonard Blake.

I was to find those two critical weeks at High Wycombe at once a heavy strain and an unthought-of delight. It was essential, if I was to achieve a worthwhile result, that the choir – and particularly the boys – should take to me. I must confess to playing my cards artfully in that respect. I was still a serving soldier; and I went to Wycombe in uniform – as entitled to. The boys responded to this – but so, I thought, did the men. That battle at least was won. The Sunday services went well, too. And when Crook returned he and I were both relieved and pleased to learn that my efforts had been regarded on all sides as successful.

As a result, Crook now disclosed to me that he was about to be appointed Chief Commissioner to the SECM – Nicholson's assistant, that is; and as a result he was regretfully obliged to leave High Wycombe for good. It had been agreed that since my deputising in his absence had met with general approval I was to be offered the post as his successor. The salary was to be £250 p.a. – five times the average for a parish church at that time. There was also a teaching connection.

A prompt decision was now called for. My demobilisation leave had still a month to run, but I was unlikely to find a more inviting appointment than High Wycombe represented before then – if at all. The salary offered did not promise affluence; but it was enough to live on in those days. In any case, the teaching connection mentioned included part-time teaching in a Prep school.[38] This would provide something of a boost; and if it was necessary I was prepared to increase the number of private piano and organ pupils I taught. Most critically, once my formal discharge from the army came through, I should be obliged to return to the Land Registry unless I had already found another post

---

[37] Rainbow wrote *High Wycombe Parish Church: An Illustrated Guide* (1946); another edition with a similar text but with many advertisements added appeared in 1958.

[38] Oakend Preparatory School, Gerrards Cross, 1944–5.

and formally presented my resignation. All these matters were discussed and re-discussed at home, but the decision was always the same: the decision must be mine alone. Whatever it was, I could rest assured of support and encouragement in carrying it out.

I wrote at once to Hubert Crook, accepting the appointment; to the Land Registry, submitting my resignation; and to Leonard Blake, telling what I had decided and thanking him deeply for what he had done.[39]

CHAPTER SIX

RATHER THEN RECITE a string of superlatives to describe my first weeks at High Wycombe I shall just say that I was amazed each day to find myself actually experiencing what had formerly been the substance of a nebulous and improbable dream. Nor was it to be my onerous task to create a choir from scratch – the choir I was to be responsible for was already in existence; my task (in some ways a more difficult one) was to maintain it. I was not content, however, merely to duplicate what Hubert Crook had done, and introduced techniques of my own. The full choir rehearsed once a week and there were two boys' practices each at 4.30, immediately after school. Close attention was given in them to rehearsing psalms and hymns as well as anthems and settings. Where the boys were concerned I adopted several clear aims from the outset. Although spacious, the parish church was disappointingly unresonant. This made the restrained, ethereal, cathedral treble voice inappropriate there; and it became my aim to show the boys how to project their voices – rather than simply sing louder or adopt what was known in those days as the 'choristers' hoot'. Practices always began with vocal exercises, and here I introduced 'singing to the thumb'. This involved holding out one arm with the fist clenched and the thumb raised; and then, in the vowel-based exercises that followed, consciously directing the voice at that thumb. We found that, besides being satisfactorily unorthodox, this worked splendidly: instead of bottling up the sound they sang into the building. My second aim was to develop vocal agility and articulation – two qualities I consider closely related and readily responsive to drill. A third, more considerable task was to train these boys to read the music

---

[39] Rainbow's first organ recital after his appointment was reviewed (unidentified source) by H.C. – obviously Hubert Crook. The programme, given on 8 July 1945, included an early Prelude in G and the Toccata and Fugue in D minor by Bach – 'This ever-popular work has suffered so much at the hands (and feet!) from modern speeding that one was grateful to Mr Rainbow for adopting a speed at which the music, and not the performer, was the dominant interest'; the *Largo* from Dvořák's *New World Symphony* – 'a perfectly legitimate concession to popular taste'; Walton's arrangement of the Passion Chorale; the Trumpet Tune by Jeremiah Clarke and the first movement of Handel's Concerto in B♭.

which was consistently made available in their hymnals, psalters and sheet music. There are those who maintain that so long as musical notation is regularly provided, singers learn to interpret it. I did not subscribe to that opinion, believing that there was an essential intermediate stage to the process. I therefore made it a point of principle never to play over a chant before practising a psalm. Instead, I played just the first chord (thus establishing not only pitch but tonality) and then waited as the boys raised their hands to show they recognised the tune on the page – and, more to the point, were prepared to sing it. I then picked the boy who was to do so. This became a regular, and distinctly popular, feature of the boys' practices, and encouraged even the youngest probationers to look at the notes on the page and come to interpret them.

As compared with the boys I felt that the potential of the *men's* section of the choir had not been fully explored, and took to holding short extra sessions with them after the full practices when the boys had gone. This, I found, not only enabled us to iron out difficulties, treat appropriate passages more sensitively, and correct actual mistakes, but boosted morale to a surprisingly beneficial extent.

Altogether, I found taking those choir practices a most satisfying experience; and I felt I had the fullest co-operation of all concerned in them. The vicar unfailingly attended the full practices, and I would draw up a draft of each month's music list – with seasonal hymns, the set psalms, and an anthem and setting at every service – and submit them for his approval before sending them on to the printer. Meanwhile, my playing was improving noticeably with regular practice. The people I met were friendly, and about Wycombe then there was still something of the character of a nineteenth-century country town where I was The New Organist – someone to be greeted in the High Street, or congratulated after a service when the anthem had gone well. I also began to make a circle of musical acquaintances who were to play an important part in future developments.

At the prep school where I taught for two days a week my duties were limited to taking class-singing and giving some thirty-six individual piano lessons each week. To add variety to the singing lessons I introduced percussion-band work, and this feature – then regarded as distinctly novel – enjoyed the approval of the children and their joint headmistresses. In a word, there was an inspiriting feeling of challenge about every day's activities – a feeling sharpened by Hubert Crook's recent disclosure that, unknown to me, there had been a rival candidate for the post of organist – an older, highly qualified and experienced applicant with the backing of several influential figures. But Sydney Nicholson, who was acting as referee for the appointment, declared in his characteristically outspoken manner that Wycombe deserved a man with a Future, not one with a Past. I felt I had emphatically to live up to that estimate.

I was also aware of another challenging presence – that of a quasi-legendary predecessor of mine named George Frederick Andrews (the significance of those fore-names is inescapable). He had been appointed as a young man in the 1890s and remained at Wycombe throughout his life, during which time some of the older men now in the choir had been his choristers. They loved to relate tales of his exploits, and there was no doubt that in his day Andrews' influence had been considerable.[40]

Another figure from the past – but this time still very much alive – was Ralph Coles, the elderly Parish Clerk. Ill-tempered and perverse, he was said to hold his office by freehold and was thus regarded as unassailable. A man of great energy, always bustling about the church in his notably squeaky boots, he was also Captain of the Belfry besides acting as Verger. Hubert Crook had no time for him and returned his incivility with a brusqueness of his own. But his position as Parish Clerk gave to Coles a special importance in the organist's affairs – for he it was who made all the arrangements for weddings and funerals, including whether the organist's services should be engaged; and that consideration could seriously affect the organist's income. In my own case this was not a matter to be ignored, and I was always careful to treat Coles with pronounced tongue-in-cheek courtesy. As a result the number of weddings and funerals 'with music' at the parish church increased phenomenally – on a Saturday in June one year I played no less than eleven weddings – and the choirboys, engaged at a shilling a head on these occasions, equally welcomed this run of good fortune.

If there was a snag in those early days at Wycombe, it was the lack of suitable living accommodation. In the absence of an alternative I had returned to the lodgings that Crook found for me when I first stayed in the town; but whereas the landlady had originally enjoyed entertaining me – as surrogate for the son she had lost in a fatal accident not long before – now that Olive joined me the atmosphere became very different. We were rescued by a curate at the parish church, the Rev. Leonard Cowie, who told me of a forthcoming vacancy in the boarding house where he was living; and we moved there instead. Besides holding a curacy at the parish church Leonard Cowie also taught History at Wycombe's Royal Grammar School; and though the fact was never mentioned

[40] Interestingly enough, I have come across evidence that both G. F. Andrews and E. C. Bairstow (1874–1946) were pupils of Sir Frederick Bridge (1844–1924) at Westminster Abbey; and that both were invited to take the post of organist at High Wycombe. Bairstow describes the situation in these terms in his unfinished autobiography: 'Bridge was anxious that I should go to High Wycombe, where his brother-in-law had a school. I went to spy out the land (on a wet day) and thought the place would turn out to be a backwater. In fact another pupil who took the post instead of me stayed for many years and died there.' F. Jackson, *Blessed City: The Life and Works of Edward C. Bairstow, 1874–1946* (York: William Sessions, 1996), p. 30. BR.

at the time, I have always suspected that he had a hand in a turn of events that now followed.[41]

A few months after I had come to Wycombe I received a message from the Headmaster of the Royal Grammar School, E. R. Tucker, asking me to call on him. When I arrived he came to the door of his study holding a book in one hand, his finger marking the place where he had apparently just stopped reading. He greeted me and said that though we had not yet met he was aware of the work I had been doing since my arrival in the town. He then went on to apologise for having forgotten, when he asked me to call on him, that he was due to attend a governors' meeting forthwith. But, to put matters briefly, he wanted me to take on some teaching at the school. Thinking he was referring to music teaching I said I should like that. 'Well, now,' he went on, 'why not start at once?' He opened the book in his hand and passed it to me. 'I should be taking 3b for Latin. Here's where they've got. Let me take you along.'

There was no opportunity to voice my reservations, and I speechlessly followed him along the corridor, frantically working out what I should first say to the waiting class. The Headmaster opened the door and put his head in. 'This is Mr Rainbow,' he said. 'He will be taking you for Latin.'

The boys were already giving me that special, probing look they reserve for new teachers. How far, they were wondering, can we go with this one? But during that short anxious walk down the corridor I had managed to light on something unexpected to start on. 'Tell me,' I said brightly, 'how would you order a taxi, in Latin?' There was a shocked silence. I had knocked them for six, as the saying goes. We then had a short skirmish on the subject of taxis in ancient Rome and settled for 'chariot-without-horses', before returning to the substance of their textbooks. I never had any trouble with form 3b after that. I was also given junior forms to take in English and History; and enjoyed the experience. Together with the work I was already doing in the Prep school at Gerrards Cross, this filled all my weekdays – and reduced my financial worries.

It would be culpable to allow this incident to present E. R. Tucker as an inefficient, irresponsible headmaster. Far from that, under him the Royal Grammar School had achieved and maintained the highest standards. But it must not be forgotten that this was wartime; many of the younger teachers were serving in the forces, several women teachers had been appointed temporarily 'to hold the fort', and recruitment was minimal. It must be remembered, too, that the 1944 Education Act had just introduced sundry reforms in secondary education – among them the introduction of music teaching in boys' grammar schools, with the particular proviso that suitably qualified local organists should be appointed as members of staff. Holders of reputable music diplomas

---

[41] The Rev. Dr Leonard W. Cowie (1919–2004) was a historian who wrote many books and was on the staff at the College of S. Mark and S. John with Rainbow.

(I already held two) were now to be accorded 'qualified teacher' status, to that end.

Indeed, subsequent events confirm that Tucker planned to appoint a music master as the Act proposed – but that, music being a subject where indifferent teaching quickly leads to disorder, he wanted to test my ability to control classes of grammar-school boys (as against supposedly docile voluntary choristers) before offering me the post. He was, in other words, repeating the sort of trial run I had undergone during that fortnight's 'deputising' before being offered the post at the parish church.

At the end of that experimental term spent teaching English, Latin, and History, I was, in fact, offered the post of music master at the Royal Grammar School. It was revealing to find that, at a school founded in 1562, I was to be the first ever to hold the post. I now had to resign at Gerrards Cross; but was able to do so with little misgiving in the circumstances. More to the point, I draw up a realistic and attainable music syllabus for boys aged from eleven to eighteen.

The 'backbone' of the music course I intended was to be class singing. Supplementing it, and arising from it, were to be basic introductions to listening and using musical notation. From the outset I was determined to rid music of any suggestion that, where boys were concerned, it was 'just something you grew out of when your voice broke'. To that end, I planned a sixth-form course, beginning in the first year with baritone and simple part-singing, using light-hearted traditional songs of the type made familiar at the time in the widely popular programmes broadcast by the BBC male-voice chorus. Published sets of these songs were available, and using them helped familiarise the use of notation and thus prepare for the addition of tenor and bass parts to an SATB school choir. Once established the policy worked well. We indeed had become a 'singing school'.

Walking our dog one evening Olive met a couple of RGS boys. After touching their caps politely as they passed, one of them said to the other while still within earshot, 'I bet that dog has to sing.' Such remarks are telling. An ironic catch-phrase to match was sometimes heard in the staff common room when things had got out of hand: 'Too much music in this school!' Said as it was with a grin, it was something of a tribute. The official *History of the Royal Grammar School, High Wycombe* put it more formally:

> When B. J. G. Rainbow, invalided out of the army ... came to teach music in 1944, something of a revolution took place. His single-minded purpose was to involve as many people as possible in music; so his concerts gave much less scope to the competent solo performer than to the choirs, orchestras and groups of well or ill assorted musicians. He came to terms with the master in charge of rugby football, and many of the heftiest

athletes sang in the choir and the Gilbert and Sullivan operas which, with help from other masters, he started to produce in 1947. They have, with occasional intervals, been successfully produced ever since. The interest in music in the school has been maintained by his successors with operas, oratorios and frequent concerts of one sort or another.[42]

From modest beginnings it was possible to develop a worthwhile programme of musical activity throughout the school. Before long there was a Music Society, a Madrigal Choir, a Senior and a Junior Choir, an Operatic Society, a Recorder Club – all of them meeting outside normal time-table hours, but all of them loyally supported. Needless to say, at first there was no equipment specifically available for music teaching. When I began to introduce the concept of 'listening' I took along my own 'wind-up' gramophone and records. But as our musical reputation grew, and the county music adviser came to see what was going on, help in the form of an assistant music master, several visiting instrumental teachers, and the provision of an occasional orchestral instrument toward the establishment of a school orchestra was no small encouragement. The next step was the introduction of 'music sets' to enable boys who wished to do so to prepare for 'O' and 'A' levels. Before my stint at High Wycombe was over we had the satisfaction of securing an Open Scholarship in Music at the University of Durham.[43]

There were further developments, too, at the parish church. To celebrate the end of the war in 1945 I circulated in advance all the choral organisations in the district – both secular and church-based – inviting them to join in rehearsals for a combined performance of *Messiah*. Twenty-eight local choirs and musical organisations agreed to take part, and I set about recruiting an orchestra for the occasion. Several of the local amateur musicians whose acquaintance I had already made contacted their friends and a very serviceable orchestra resulted. The eventual performance in the parish church was well attended and enthusiastically received.[44]

Encouraged by this response I invited singers who were interested to form

[42] L. J. Ashford and C. M. Howarth, *The History of the Royal Grammar School, High Wycombe, 1562–1969* (High Wycombe, 1962), p. 96. BR.

[43] John Wilks (1948), composer and conductor, later known as an authority on steam locomotives.

[44] *Messiah*, 30 June 1945, High Wycombe Choral Union and Orchestra at the Parish Church. The local press said: 'the work was beautifully sung by both the choir and soloists and the balance and blend of the choir was excellent'. Rainbow's father was the solo trumpeter, as he had been in Rainbow's earlier performances such as with the Wimbledon Special Choir at St Andrew's Church on 25 April 1939, when both father and son were highly commended in the local press. *Messiah* opened the week-long High Wycombe Festival on 9 June 1947 which included an organ recital by Rainbow and Mendelssohn's *Hymn of Praise*.

a High Wycombe Choral Union which would meet regularly to rehearse and perform together. At the same time I asked the string players involved to form a permanent High Wycombe String Orchestra rehearsing weekly in the Grammar School, rent free in return for playing at school functions.[45] Further, with the town and neighbourhood supporting so many choral and instrumental groups, I suggested organising an annual musical festival based on the parish church and lasting a week, in which individual bodies would each present a concert or recital. The idea was welcomed, a committee formed, and the first of these festivals was presented in June, 1947.[46] It included a chamber concert by a local string quartet, a programme by the local Orpheus Male Voice Choir, an organ recital, a concert by the High Wycombe Oratorio Choir, a concert by my new String Orchestra (with Denis Stevens[47] as soloist in the Bach A minor violin concerto); the week concluding with Festal Evensong in the parish church. This was to become an established annual event throughout my time at Wycombe.

It will hardly be necessary to remark that organising and running so many different activities at church and school – not to mention the demands of my private piano and organ pupils – was both stressful and time-consuming. But I regarded all these things as forming part of that previously unfocused vision of 'what I want to do when I leave school'; and their realisation somehow restored the energy spent in bringing them about. Suffice to say that I found the labour much more than worthwhile.

My lack of leisure now meant abandoning my intention to resume work at Trinity College for the London BMus. But this did not mean I neglected musical study. I was helped in that direction in a highly improbable way. On market days, Wycombe High Street was lined with stalls selling the usual domestic

---

This festival was visited by Hubert Foss who was reported in the Bucks Free Press on 31 October: 'If 1,000 other towns would follow the example of High Wycombe, then English music would be vitally alive again as it was in the days of Queen Elizabeth I.' It was in this festival that Rainbow appeared prominently as composer when Bessie Tucker played the first movement of his Piano Concerto in C minor. Rainbow played it himself at the Royal Grammar School and he also wrote incidental music for play productions there. These scores are in the Bernarr Rainbow Archive at the Institute of Education, University of London.

[45] During Rainbow's tenure dramatic productions included the following Gilbert and Sullivan operas: *The Pirates of Penzance*, *The Mikado*, *The Gondoliers* and *HMS Pinafore*.

[46] Rainbow is describing the second festival: local papers reviewed the 'new festival' in June 1946, where a harpsichord was heard in the Parish Church 'for the first time since the eighteenth century' in Bach's Concerto in D minor and four Scarlatti sonatas.

[47] Denis Stevens (1922–2004) attended the Royal Grammar School, High Wycombe, before Oxford and war service. He was initially a professional violinist, then an influential musicologist and university lecturer.

supplies; but amongst them I came across one selling books. The elderly sales-man was clearly a foreigner, possibly an expatriate German, and a scholar. The books he offered for sale were not the usual second-hand relics, but mainly new copies of new editions, many of them published in America. He had a well-stocked section on music; and there I came across P. H. Lang's *Music in Western Civilisation*, first published in New York in 1941 and hitherto quite unknown to me. When the stallholder identified my field interest he made a point of add-ing to his future stock volumes he thought would interest me. It was from this humble source that I gradually built up a nucleus of books by Gustave Reese, Oliver Strunk, Donald Grout, Manfred Bukofzer, Karl Geiringer, and others, to supplement the standard works already on my shelves. At this time, too, to keep myself up to scratch. I took the Trinity College diploma in 'Class Music Teaching'.[48]

My scholarly bookseller was only one of many notable acquaintances I made. The organ console at the parish church was at floor level in the south choir aisle and in many ways all too accessible. Visitors, strangers, and sightseers apart – who came and breathed down my neck while I was trying to practise during the week – there were several members of the congregation who liked to come round from time to time as I played the final voluntary on a Sunday. Sometimes, as with an elderly blind organist whose wife led him there, it was to find out what I was playing and to share past experiences. Sometimes, as with lonely old Miss Rolph, it was just to find someone to talk to about her recent trip to Brighton – where she liked to go, as she innocently put it, 'to be picked up'. Sometimes it was the delightfully eccentric Mr Salisbury, an amateur organ-builder, to tell me of the latest stop he was adding to an instru-ment that was already advancing from the drawing room up the stairs of his large Edwardian house. More than once it was an odd chap who was writing an oratorio that Handel was dictating to him. But most often it was Major Vernon, who was a dog-fancier enamoured of the organ in an entirely unreal-istic and uninformed way. He would dismiss as worthless the instrument his neighbour, Mr Salisbury, was endlessly enlarging in his house, but refer to his own harmonium as 'my organ in the library'. I never quite got the measure of Major Vernon. One bumped into him in the street, always accompanied by a wire-haired terrier called Percy that stood and shivered violently while his master insisted every time we met that I must come to have lunch with him at the Kennel Club. This invitation was so often repeated that one day, during the school holidays, I accepted it. The Club was just off Piccadilly, Major Vernon was there to meet me in the hall, and we went straight into the dining room. A half-dozen elderly canine enthusiasts were sadly enjoying their lunch until the

[48] LTCL in 1946.

major interrupted with, 'Let me introduce Mr Rainbow, the great organist.' They all regarded me icily, with deep, incredulous loathing. No one said a word, and they resumed their meal. This was what might be called the Snub Direct; and I cannot say I enjoyed that long-threatened luncheon.

Among more distinguished encounters, however, I met Edmund Rubbra, who lived at nearby Speen.[49] I tried to persuade him to write something 'accessible' for performance at our new Musical Festival. But he could not agree that the demands made by many of his existing works were too great for modest amateur choirs, and I was unsuccessful. By that time I already knew his wife, Antoinette, who played the fiddle on the first desk of my string orchestra. Later I also met Gerald Finzi, who came to conduct a performance of his *Dies Natalis* in the 1952 Festival.[50] At the same concert Rubbra was the soloist in the Bloch Concerto Grosso.[51]

Another distinguished musician was Denis Stevens, then playing in the Philharmonia while conducting the research into early music that was to establish his name. He had been a boy at the Royal Grammar School before the war, but in the absence of a music course at the school, E. R. Tucker had arranged external coaching for him, enabling Stevens to go on to Jesus College, Oxford, in 1940. He was delighted to find the school had made good that early shortcoming and subsequently gave me warm support.

In another development, early in 1952, I was invited to put into rehearsal a series of performances of Benjamin Britten's *Let's Make an Opera* to be mounted jointly by the Gerrards Cross Community Association and the Royal Grammar School. First produced at Aldeburgh in 1949, this miniature had not then been widely played by the amateurs and children for whom it was designed. The present proposal was set in train by the Zanders, a gifted family living in Gerrards Cross.[52] The elder son, Michael, was a sixth-former at RGS High Wycombe and became a celebrated lawyer. His ten-year-old brother, Benjamin, has since become an equally distinguished orchestral conductor in the USA. While still a child, Benjy Zander had been a pupil, first of Britten himself, then of Imogen Holst. And the performance now proposed would see him cast as the Little Sweep, the central figure of the opera. The other children's parts were to be played by hand-picked boys and girls from

---

[49] Edmund Rubbra (1901–86): Rainbow refers to Rubbra's first wife, Antoinette Chaplin.

[50] Gerald Finzi (1901–56): *Dies Natalis* (1940).

[51] Ernest Bloch (1888–1959): Concerto Grosso no. 1 (1925).

[52] Michael Zander (1932–); Benjamin Zander (1939–) as a gifted boy was befriended by Britten in 1950 who looked at his scores. (See *Letters from a Life: Selected Letters of Benjamin Britten*, vol. 3: *1946–51* (London: Faber & Faber, 2004), pp. 597–8). As a cellist Zander worked with Cassals, then moved to the United States where he began a distinguished career as conductor. He spent twenty-eight seasons with the Boston Philharmonic and is on the faculty of the New England Conservatoire; his recordings,

Wycombe and Gerrards Cross; the adults were local semi-professionals, and there were to be three performances in each town in the following July. The music had been written with amateurs in mind, but I was interested to see how the youngsters took to it more readily than their elders. The performances went well and everyone on both sides of the footlights seemed to enjoy them.

By 1952, as I believe these representative activities indicate, my work at Wycombe could be counted at least fruitful. Yet, as can so easily happen in parochially based musical matters, with the retirement of the vicar who had appointed me, a successor now arrived who quickly showed an aversion to choral services and plainly regarded the Musical Festival as an improper invasion of priestly territory. A coldly ambitious man, he was not at pains to conceal his opinion that I had been allowed to play too active a part in the church's activities. His priorities were made clear in his public statement that the sermon, not the altar, was the central feature of divine service.

Although one would think of 1952 as being far too early to expect to find the slap-happy attitude toward the ordering of services that often prevails today, this man was given to introducing novelties into them, supposedly the fruit of inspiration. He would end a sermon by announcing a hymn different from that in the printed service sheets, and complain if the tune in the *Revised Ancient & Modern Hymnal* was not the old favourite he was expecting. At another time he would announce in the vestry that instead of Evensong we would have a procession around the church while he blessed the font, or delivered a homily on the significance of the pulpit. On Good Friday we found the chancel arch blocked by a large cinema screen on which torrid illustrations of the events leading up to the crucifixion would be projected. The planned, approved, and rehearsed service was scrapped without warning. Instead, we had an extemporaneous commentary on these illustrations interspersed with allusive hymns.

Then, one day came the ultimatum that in future anthems and settings were

especially of Mahler, have been acclaimed; and he also has an international career as a lecturer. Britten knew what Rainbow was doing. In 1950 the Musical Festival (affiliated to the High Wycombe Arts' Association] took place on seven evenings, 19–25 June. The programme book named Sir George Dyson as President and there was a Preface from the thirty-six-year-old composer:

> It is no accident that our best British music has been written for small ensembles. The great Tudor and Jacobean composers, Purcell and Blow, and even Arne and Boyce wrote music for the intimate occasion. Though we use Crystal Palace and Albert Hall for our Handel Festivals and Promenade seasons, these monstrous sheds do not produce the happiest results. The Private Concert Hall and the Parish Church are more successful. With us the bigger is seldom the better.
>
> Most of the music in this Festival was written for such occasions, and it is in this direction that I would like such Festivals to proceed.
>
> I wish the High Wycombe Festival a very happy future.

to be sung only once a month; a congregational service was to be regarded as the norm. As compared with the halcyon days of the recent past all these setbacks eventually became unacceptable; and in spite of the satisfaction I still found in my work at the grammar school I had grown increasingly restless. What finally tipped the scales was an advertised vacancy in the *Times Educational Supplement* seeking to appoint a Director of Music at the country's prime institution for training teachers – the College of S. Mark & S. John, Chelsea. The duties were twofold: to train and educate teachers of music in schools, and to restore the music of the College Chapel to standards that had prevailed there in former times. It had never been my custom to study vacancies announced in the press; but here, it seemed, was a post uncannily combining under the same roof my two principal enthusiasms. It would be culpable not to follow it up.

And now I came to think of it, I knew something of this institution already. It was situated in the King's Road, Chelsea, and visible from a passing bus. Two of my former teachers at Merton school had been trained there. So had a cousin of mine, now teaching in Surrey. Yet more recently – good heavens! – Dr Leonard Cowie, the former curate and a colleague of mine at Wycombe, had left to take up a lectureship there. I must get in touch with him and investigate further.

In response to my enquiry Cowie invited me to call on him at the College and be shown round. Meanwhile I had received details of the appointment, learned of Thomas Helmore's connection with the newly founded institution in the 1840s, and discovered from *Grove's Dictionary* the important (but now largely forgotten) work he had done there.[53] All these factors strengthened my instinctive feeling that this was a job I was cut out for. I applied for it, was interviewed, and appointed.

Leaving High Wycombe was a wrench. I had spent eight enjoyable, fulfilling, and instructive years there. Only later was I to realise that I could not have maintained the pace of life I had set myself there, indefinitely. To have remained – and soon been obliged to take things more easily – would have heralded decline.

---

[53] Thomas Helmore (1811–90) was appointed Vice-Principal and Precentor at St Mark's College, Chelsea in 1842 and became Master of the Children of the Chapel Royal in 1846, retaining the post of Precentor at St Mark's until 1877. He successfully introduced plainsong into congregational services and raised standards in sung services. See Rainbow's own article in *The New Grove Dictionary of Music and Musicians*, 2nd edn (London: Macmillan, 2001).

CHAPTER SEVEN

I REALISED that the post I had accepted at Chelsea involved snags as well as opportunities; and that to begin with, the snags predominated. At the initial interview, for instance, all six of us on the short list had exchanged glances of dismay on discovering the neglected state of the chapel organ and been further disconcerted at not being invited to inspect the music department's accommodation and equipment. Nor could we discuss departmental issues with the previous head of music who had recently died, it appeared. In spite of these inauspicious signals I still felt that this was a job I was cut out for; and during the long vacation after accepting it I paid several visits to Chelsea to find out more for myself. The results were not encouraging. The students themselves ran the chapel choir and one of them played the organ. My predecessor had been a string player not made responsible for the chapel music. I also found that music lectures were given in an uninviting basement room – ostensibly to minimise disturbing other lectures; that there was a single visiting piano teacher, and that students took turns to practise on the music room's solitary piano. My discoveries so far had only served to reveal music's low standing in the College.

On the other hand, the terms of the advertisement had expressed a desire to raise existing standards; and the Principal, Howard Cooksey, had explicitly introduced the title Director of Music – an unprecedented innovation in a training college – to emphasise the importance to be attached to the improvement of music in the College Chapel. I remained convinced that given due support I could bring about the necessary reforms.

During those early visits to the College I deliberately made the acquaintance of two members of staff who would clearly be influential in the future policy I had begun to formulate. The first was, of course, the Chaplain. David Worth was a dedicated, wise, and tolerant priest, an exact opposite to the parson I had fled Wycombe to escape. He was, moreover, more aware of the early history of the College than most of his colleagues, and had evidently drawn Principal Cooksey's attention to the unique and widespread celebrity the chapel music had originally enjoyed a century earlier. I could not suppose that such a man would disapprove of my intentions.

The second critically influential figure was the Bursar. He not only held the purse-strings but was in some ways to be regarded as an *éminence grise* capable of swaying the Principal's decisions and policy. As an overt High Churchman, Charles Freeman took more interest in the administration of the college chapel than others of his calling might be expected to do; but he was dogmatic, and irascible. I thought of him, I'm afraid, as a more sophisticated version of Ralph Coles, the equally peremptory parish clerk at High Wycombe, and as calling for much the same buttered words and smooth tactics.

I also took pains to make myself more conversant with the College's historical background. Apparently it owed its complex name – the College of S. Mark & S. John, Chelsea, – to the amalgamation of two earlier teacher-training institutions, St John's College, Battersea, founded in 1840 by that educational pioneer, James Kay-Shuttleworth, and S. Mark's College, Chelsea, founded in the following year by the National Society, a Church of England educational body.[54] (The abbreviation of 'Saint' as 'S.' at Chelsea was a Tractarian foible revealing the College's High Church stance under the principalship of the Rev. Derwent Coleridge, son of the poet.)[55] My further investigations showed that in both colleges considerable importance had originally been attached to teaching a new method of 'learning to sing from notes' introduced in 1840 by John Hullah,[56] who was consequently engaged to teach there. At S. Mark's that basic musical instruction was supplemented by forming and training a choir for the college chapel which should become a nationwide model for churches seeking to introduce surpliced choirs of their own – as Tractarian reformers were then advocating. To that end, the Rev. Thomas Helmore, a former priest-vicar at Lichfield Cathedral, was appointed joint vice-principal and precentor. He trained the choir which soon became noted. Both Hullah and Helmore – jointly my first predecessors – had thus acquired national celebrity. I promised myself I would investigate their activities further. Meanwhile, they presented a challenge I would not fail to respond to.

When term began and I first met my students in their basement quarters I did not conceal from them my dissatisfaction with such insalubrious accommodation; but otherwise confined myself for the time being to urging the practical advantages of their joining the chapel choir, and then pressed on with teaching the syllabus already established by the Institute of Education at London University for all thirty constituent training colleges in its area. My first active attempts at reform I had decided to direct toward the chapel choir.

On weekdays, it appeared, there was a morning 'assembly' in chapel with a hymn; on Sundays, Sung Eucharist with the choir (all men, of course) in cassocks and surplices. The same musical setting was always used. On learning

---

[54] Sir James Kay-Shuttleworth (1804–77).

[55] Derwent Coleridge (1800–83), third child of Samuel Taylor Coleridge, first Principal of St Marks' College, 1841–64.

[56] John Hullah (1812–84), teacher and composer, appointed to St John's, Battersea in 1840, whose influence nationally helped to secure a place for music in schools. See John Hullah, *Wilhem's Method of Teaching Singing* (1842), ed. B. Rainbow, Classic Texts in Music Education vol. 7 (Kilkenny: Boethius Press, [1983]); John Curwen and John Hullah, *School Music Abroad (1879–1901)*, ed. B. Rainbow, Classic Texts in Music Education vol. 15 (Clifden: Boethius Press, [1985]); Bernarr Rainbow, *Four Centuries of Music Teaching Manuals, 1518–1932* (Woodbridge: Boydell Press, 2009); and Rainbow's article in *The New Grove Dictionary of Music and Musicians*, 2nd edn.

that in future I should be rehearsing and accompanying them myself some former members of the choir and the student-organist were somewhat disgruntled. But this was the start of a new academic year; and there was no shortage of students present when I went to take my first choir practice. We sang through the distinctly pedestrian male-voice setting regularly used for the Sunday celebrations (I have forgotten now who wrote it) and it proved very easy to enliven what had formerly been an accurate but lifeless performance. I then rehearsed the choir in a deliberately formal manner of entering and leaving the choir-stalls – maintaining that a robed choir that just sauntered into their places lost an opportunity to add to the dignity and reverence of a service. The improvement in both music and decorum noticeable on the following Sunday was the subject of favourable comment – not least, I was glad to note, by the Principal, the Chaplain, and the Bursar.

In response I cautiously began to air ideas for further improvement of the chapel music. Repetition week by week of the same music for the Eucharist was an unacceptable policy. The repertory urgently needed widening; and, bearing in mind Thomas Helmore's pioneer activity in this field, the College should also revive what had once been a precious feature of the college chapel services – the singing of the psalms in English to plainchant. That the practice had not in fact been allowed to die out entirely was shown by the survival in chapel of copies of an early edition of Helmore's *Manual of Plainsong*. But these were in very poor condition besides failing to represent modern views on the practice. I recommended the adoption of J. H. Arnold's 1951 revision.

At this stage I did not mention the ramshackle state of the organ, but it was a matter causing me considerable concern. When the tuner had paid his regular visit just before term began I climbed up with him to examine the interior of the instrument for myself. Things were even worse than I had suspected. Wear was weakening the leather of the bellows and stiffening the tracker-action, and inspection showed that two ranks of pipes had quite recently been added – very amateurishly – resulting in fluctuating wind-pressures. Two of the old reed stops were so worn as to be virtually untunable. I decided that the best way of making these shortcomings known was to give an organ recital, dividing the programme into two sections. The first half would consist of a modest selection of typical recital items, the second would be announced as a 'Demonstration of the Organ' in which I could shock the audience with a display of the instrument's failings. They were unlikely to become aware of them in the ordinary way – for no conscientious organist would use the offending stops at service time. The success of this stratagem was unquestionable.

An organ recital in the college chapel was not an event likely to attract large numbers; but there was a respectable attendance from the student body and, as the result of careful soliciting, the audience also included the Principal, the Chaplain, and the Bursar. Without the need for further pleading I soon heard that an Appeal was to be launched to rebuild the chapel organ and I was invited to consult suitable organ-builders for tenders.

My response was to persuade Hubert Crook to act as consultant, and to discuss with him a suitable specification. I favoured an instrument possessing characteristics of the Willis at High Wycombe – particularly the 'cathedral' Swell section owing much of its richness to a versatile 16' chorus reed.[57] Crook agreed, and together we drew up the specification of a rebuild converting the present two-manual tracker into a three-manual electric instrument with detached console. Positioning the console at floor-level would release space in the organ loft for the extra pipe-work and wind-chests involved. This draft scheme was submitted to three leading builders for their comments and estimates. The most reasonable tender was returned by Willis together with several advantageous modifications; and the Organ Appeal was now launched to raise what seemed to many a very large sum.

It was typical of Howard Cooksey to insist on personally signing every one of the hundreds of circular letters sent out as a result to former students and other potential donors. The son of a missionary, he had inherited a measure of evangelical zeal that showed itself in many ways. His championship of the reform of the choir and the rebuilding of the organ were two examples. Another was the appearance in the current College time-table (a document Cooksey always drew up himself) of a new feature – a full period for all first-year students devoted to 'hymn practice'. This was to take place in the chapel, and I was made responsible for conducting it. I will confess that I found this a most unwelcome task – not least because many of the students concerned had just completed two years' military service under the National Service Act of 1948 and were mature, experienced adults not to be treated like raw ex-school-boys. I considered weekly sessions of compulsory hymn-singing likely to be counter-productive.

On taking the first of those hymn practices I shared my feelings openly with the students concerned, and told them that I proposed to detain them only so long as it took to satisfy myself that they were familiar with the hymns to be sung at the following week's morning assemblies. Ignoring well-known items I then helped them with any less familiar tunes and sent them away once the result justified it. We had usually finished in a quarter of an hour. And then, after two or three of these sessions, the Principal came across unannounced to see how we were getting on. With masterly timing he arrived just as I had

---

[57] English organ building firm started by Henry Willis in 1845 and flourishing to the present day as Henry Willis & Sons. The large organ at St Paul's Cathedral was built in 1872.

released the hundred or so students involved and narrowly escaped being trodden underfoot as they poured out upon him in the porch.

I watched this near-inundation take place with considerable dismay, and hastened to explain the circumstances. Cooksey's understandable indignation gradually faded as I made the point about the National Servicemen; and I pressed boldly on with another proposal I had been nurturing. If he would allow me to use the period concerned for what might be called 'General Music' I was prepared to guarantee that the students would sing in chapel. In John Hullah's day, I reminded him, every student at S. Mark's College received a full course of basic musical training. It seemed regrettable that the majority of their successors today would leave College to teach in schools without receiving any musical instruction at all. I hoped he would agree to give the suggestion a trial, and allow General Music to take place in the main lecture theatre, rather than the chapel. If a problem arose with hymn-singing in the future I would deal with it during this period. With some reluctance Cooksey agreed – though when the amended time table appeared I found myself due to meet the first-year students at 9.00 a.m. on Monday mornings – hardly the most stimulating hour of the week for aesthetic pursuits.

For their own part the students seemed happy enough with the new arrangement. When I met them for the first session I outlined my bargain with the Principal, emphasised the experimental nature of the course, and said its continuance depended upon their co-operation.

What they had seen announced on the time-table as General Music, I went on to explain, would comprise a series of informal weekly lectures in which I would be talking about the nature of music and illustrating some of its characteristics with musical examples. It seemed regrettable that a teacher of any subject should appear to his young pupils to scorn music – having had no chance to find out more about it. What was more, if he was a good teacher his pupils might be encouraged to follow his example and shrug off music themselves. At least for those reasons I welcomed the opportunity of speaking to them on the subject. Besides, I thought they might even find it interesting.

The substance of the General Music course at Chelsea was in fact an elaboration and extension of the deliberately light-hearted lessons I had evolved to interest the sixth form at High Wycombe. That approach had worked well there; it was to do so, with regular revision, at Chelsea. Full attendance at General Music lectures was consistent over the years – a compliment no experienced lecturer will underestimate.

The introduction of the General Music course marked my first attempt to introduce innovation in the lecture programme at Chelsea. As things stood, there were already two established music courses there, each following a syllabus laid down by London University Institute of Education and representing post-war thinking on the education and training of teachers. It was not enough, the argument ran, to spoon-feed potential teachers with the methodology of teaching this or that subject. Student teachers should be educated, as well as trained. Every student must therefore select a Main and a Subsidiary study. If music were chosen as a Main study it would be pursued at a serious level for the student's personal benefit – whether or not it was to be taught in schools subsequently. At Subsidiary level it would be studied less thoroughly but the course would examine ways of teaching it in schools. Over all, however, it was emphasised that teaching skills were best acquired in the classroom during teaching practice.

I was not happy to find Main music students deprived of formal guidance in teaching methods – simply on the grounds that some of them might not want to teach music. Teaching music involved too many different skills for a few supervised lessons in schools to cover them. But the regulations were inflexible; and it was in order to get round this problem that during that first year at Chelsea I wrote my first book, *Music in the Classroom*. I was disappointed to find that continuing post-war paper rationing delayed its publication until 1956, but to some extent mollified by a review of it in the *Times Educational Supplement* that began:

> What an excellent book this is. The reader puts it down, feeling no doubt whatever that he would have enjoyed being in Mr Rainbow's music classes, and that they would have had the qualities which make the book: purpose and pace, and a rare combination of thoroughness with a light touch and a spark of humour ...[58]

I offer no apology for quoting that passage. It brings to the reader an opinion other than my own as to how far my efforts were proving successful. For that matter, *Music in the Classroom* was to enjoy a long run before going into a second and extensively revised edition fourteen years later.

Early in 1953, by which time the Chapel Choir had reached a good standard of competence, the repertory had been enlarged, and choral evensong (employing the revised *Manual of Plainsong*, settings of the canticles and an anthem) had become a regular weekly feature at Chelsea, I requested a formal advisory visitation from the Royal School of Church Music, to which the choir was now affiliated. Nicholson himself was now no longer alive, but Hubert Crook came in his capacity as Chief Commissioner. He attended the regular choir practice and remained to Evensong after dinner, complimenting the choir afterwards on its dignified and competent rendering of the service. A few weeks later I received a letter from the RSCM to say that the choir of St Paul's Cathedral

---

[58] *Times Educational Supplement*, 15 February 1957.

was undertaking an extensive North American tour during the whole of the coming Michaelmas term. The RSCM was taking steps to provide alternative choral arrangements for the cathedral services during their absence and wondered if the College chapel choir would be prepared to sing Evensong at the cathedral each Tuesday and Thursday throughout the term.

Needless to say, the Principal was delighted by this invitation. I must accept it at once, he declared. Meanwhile he set about redrafting the timetable to make the choir's absence from College on two afternoons a week possible. The Bursar's response was almost equally enthusiastic, particularly when he discovered that St Paul's would cover the cost of hiring a coach for the journeys. From this point onward his estimate of the music department's standing began to rise, a new lecture room was made available and I was given a more spacious study next door to the Chaplain's on the first floor main corridor.

The choir were understandably proud of the compliment the RSCM's invitation paid them; and, for my own part, gratification was mingled with awareness of the heavy responsibility this compliment carried with it. Other considerations apart, the male-voice repertory was far from extensive and included several compositions I should not be happy to adopt. I set to work urgently to locate additional items which we might use at the cathedral. At the British Museum Library I came upon several sixteenth-century pieces not available in print, edited (and in some cases, translated) them and approached various publishers to see if they would be interested in bringing them out. Several motets and canticle settings were accepted and Novello in particular helpfully agreed to publish six of them in time for us to sing in the autumn at St Paul's. Among these was a remarkable plainchant and fauxbourdon setting that I virtually stumbled upon in the Museum Library and which is now in regular use in many of our major cathedrals.[59]

In due course I had also to familiarise myself with the organ at St Paul's; and during the summer vacation I was given some very useful advice and a demonstration of what to do and what not to do by one of the sub-organists. Without such informed guidance, accompanying a service sympathetically on this organ would hardly have been possible. Sections of the instrument were installed in widely different parts of the building. There was a tuba mirabilis at the summit of the dome. Balance was very difficult to gauge. So remote were some of the pedal stops that it was impossible to hear them at all at the

---

[59] The six Novello publications were: *Domine, non sum dignus, Miserere mei, Domine,* and *O vos omnes* by Vittoria; *Laetentur coeli* by Hassler; Magnificat and Nunc Dimittis by Morley; and Magnificat and Nunc Dimittis IV and VI (all 1955). In the same year Stainer & Bell published 'Hodie natus est' by Orlando di Lasso and 'Confitemini Domino' by Constantini.

keyboard. The player sat hidden inside the north organ case enclosed in what seemed like a very large wardrobe high above the choir and completely out of touch with everything going on in the body of the building – unless one picked up the telephone alongside the console. There were, however, two tiny openable panels – one giving a distant view of the high altar, the other revealing the remote west door of the cathedral – and by squinting between the row of dummy organ pipes behind one's back it was possible to see something of the choir-stalls.

Left alone to practise in the cathedral after it was closed for the night with the astonishing machine Father Willis and his successors had built was at once thrilling and humbling. The echoing resonance under the dome was such that if a single staccato chord was played, the sound was left hovering about the building for ten long seconds before it finally died away. Contrary to expectation, it was not tempting to explore the organ's more extravagant features – the banks of tubas and trombones requiring their own separate bellows, the fanfare trumpets under the dome, and the earth-shaking 32' pedal stops. It was a sufficient task to concentrate upon specifications that would not drown the choir; I was careful to keep within the limits recommended to me, mainly using the stop-groupings already set on the pistons by those whose experience had shown them how to adjust to the cathedral's extraordinary acoustic.

In the event, the choir rose to the occasion splendidly; all the services went well. I took no liberties in accompanying them, and eventually grew used to playing 'by faith' up there in my Grinling Gibbons eyrie.[60] I learned, for instance, that a sound like a prolonged sneeze was caused by the Dean's Verger drawing back the curtain in the south choir aisle. This heralded the entry of clergy and choir – at which point I would add the Swell reeds and lend a touch of solemn pomp to the procession into the choir-stalls. For unaccompanied motets and anthems I came down from the organ loft to conduct, and felt (as I have always done) that, musically speaking, it was these *a cappella* items that came off best in those exceptionally resonant surroundings. At the end of the term Dean Matthews complimented the choir not only on their singing, but on their dignified and reverent manner in the choir-stalls. Every member of the choir received a signed parchment especially designed to record the occasion. We were invited to sing again at the cathedral in future. And for many years after that past and present members of the choir returned to Chelsea during the summer vacation to sing services for a week while the cathedral choir was on holiday.

Another event that took place in 1953 was a formal visit to Chelsea by Bernard

[60] The unique carved woodwork of the choir stalls is by Grinling Gibbons (1648–1721).

Shore, H.M. Staff Inspector in Music.[61] It was as well that he approved of the work he saw in the music department, for his visit proved not to be the routine inspection I had imagined. Under the 1944 Education Act a recognised music diploma had been accepted as an adequate initial qualification for entrants to teaching. I had in fact myself been appointed at RGS High Wycombe on the strength of that regulation. Experience had soon shown, however, that many of those admitted in this way lacked teaching skill. A subsequent attempt on the part of the colleges of music to correct this weakness by introducing a graduate diploma course incorporating methodology still failed to produce satisfactory teachers and was soon abandoned. Another new scheme for training diploma-holders was now to be introduced under which a small number of training colleges selected by the Inspectorate would run one-year 'post-diploma' courses introducing educational principles, studying music teaching skills, and providing supervised practice in schools. Successful students would qualify for a teaching certificate. As a result of Bernard Shore's visit S. Mark and S. John was one of the colleges selected to run such a course.

This addition to the teaching load within the department justified the appointment of a second music lecturer who joined us early in the following year[62] – by which time the rebuilt organ was in use, the chapel itself had been refurbished, a newly equipped music lecture room and half-a-dozen practice rooms complete with pianos had been provided and several visiting instrumental teachers appointed. Expansion of this order did not pass unnoticed by my colleagues. And while in somewhat similar circumstances at High Wycombe the response within the staff room had been that semi-jocular cry, 'Too much music in this school', at Chelsea the aftermath was much less tolerant.

I was to discover later that collectively the staff at S. Mark and S. John bore an unenviable reputation elsewhere for being difficult. Indeed, early in my first term I became aware of a state of Cold War existing between many of my colleagues and the Principal – though it was not until later that the reason for this became clear. When the College had reopened in 1945 Michael Roberts, a noted intellectual, a poet and ex-schoolmaster, was appointed principal.[63] Also a disillusioned former communist now convinced of the importance of

[61] Bernard Shore (1896–1985), prominent English viola player, Staff Inspector for Schools, 1948–59.

[62] Christian Wilson (1920–), on the staff of the College, 1956–73, including periods as Vice-Principal and Acting Principal.

[63] Michael Roberts (1902–48), also editor of influential anthologies including the *Faber Book of Modern Verse* (1936). See *A Portrait of Michael Roberts*, ed. T. W. Eason and R. Hamilton (Chelsea: College of S. Mark & S. John, 1949); also Andrew Roberts, 'Michael Roberts and a College in Chelsea', *Changing English*, vol. 10 no. 2 (October 2001), pp. 156–62.

Christian philosophy, Roberts yet preferred an enquiring mind to dull acceptance; and if the best candidate for a tutorial post happened to be an agnostic in
general sympathy with the aims of the College, Roberts appointed him. When
he died suddenly after only three years at Chelsea the staff he had appointed,
some of them strongly left-wing, were desolated.

The successor now appointed by the National Society was Howard Cooksey,
a man of very different calibre whose evangelical zeal, inherited as we have seen
from his missionary father, led him to view his task at Chelsea as cleansing this
Church College from the taint of Communism. What was more, he inadvis-
edly addressed the staff in precisely those terms at their first meeting. He was
never to be forgiven for that solecism.

Even after discounting the mutinous disposition of a large faction within
the staff there often remained in the Senior Common Room at Chelsea a distinguishably caustic edge to dialogue that would have been regarded elsewhere
as a matter for straightforward discussion. Staff meetings and, above all, meetings of the Academic Board chaired by the Principal, easily became jousting
matches. And I began to suppose that at least something of the brief but bitter
exchanges that sometimes took place consciously imitated what was thought
to be the characteristic High Table malice of Oxbridge dons – this was after all
the heyday of F. R. Leavis.[64]

I was not, then, too surprised to be buttonholed during my first term by
one of the scientists who wanted to know at what intellectual level I proposed
to establish the Main music course. When I outlined what I intended he pat-
ted my arm. 'Oh, good,' he said. 'I was afraid it would just be the *Bluebells
of Scotland* and all that.' Much of the patronising arrogance bandied about
came from the scientists. Another of them took to questioning individual
first-year students on the content of my General Music lectures – and then
belittling them. I found it best to appear unruffled by these unprofessional
skirmishes.

Howard Cooksey, hounded by such dedicated opponents, was not in a
position to ignore their attacks; and when, after enduring them for some six
years, he received an invitation from the Ministry to take up the principalship of a new training college for Malaysian students he resigned the post at
Chelsea with an almost audible sigh of relief. I had reason to be grateful to
him insofar as his personal aspirations for the College Chapel had benefited
my own situation so advantageously; but I could only regard his departure as
a merciful deliverance. He was succeeded by Alex Evans, a former HMI who
had previously taught at Bedales and now brought the enlightened stance of

[64] F. R. Leavis (1895–1978), Cambridge-based literary critic who interpreted modernist
writers and was capable of trenchant denunciations.

an informed devotee of the arts to the post of Principal.[65] He was neither a religious enthusiast nor a party politician; and the Michael Roberts faction was at least able to soften its aggressive behaviour.

While it was for the Inspectorate to decide which colleges should mount the forthcoming post-diploma courses, deciding their syllabuses, and supervising the admission and examination of candidates remained the responsibility of local Institutes of Education. The thirty or so constituent colleges of the London University Institute covered an area extending as far afield as Canterbury and Brighton. To maintain contact and promote discussion between them each college sent a representative to a series of Standing Subcommittees, one for each academic discipline, meeting on a termly basis at the Senate House in Russell Square. In that way such matters as syllabus content, examination procedures and the appointment of external examiners could be mutually agreed.

When I attended my first meeting of the Standing Subcommittee in Music I was struck by the preponderance of women present. This, I soon realised, was due to the fact that in the recent past most training colleges had been devoted to producing primary teachers, largely young women whose tutors were former primary teachers now in middle age. With the raising of the school-leaving age and the advent of secondary education for all, this situation was rapidly changing. More men were entering teaching, and the limited content of the primary music curriculum – what my arrogant colleague had called '*The Bluebells of Scotland*, and all that' – was no longer sufficient equipment for a successful teacher of music. The academic content of teaching-certificate courses demanded considerable strengthening to equip secondary teachers adequately

After attending a few more meetings I sensed that resistance to change was very strong in this subcommittee. The same chairman, Mabel Chamberlain, and the same external examiners, Ernest Read and Thornton Lofthouse,[66] had been reappointed annually for many years. All had given valued service; but they were unlikely to press for the radical changes that circumstances had now begun to demand. Not until there was a sufficient influx of new blood into this subcommittee was that situation likely to change. Meanwhile, the deliberations necessary to drawing up a syllabus and examination procedures for

---

[65] Alfred Alexander Evans, known as Alex (1905–2002). As Principal of the College, 1955–65, he supported the creative arts and appointed the poets Thomas Blackburn and John Heath-Stubbs. He published *Contemporary: an Anthology of the Poetry of our Time, 1940–64* (1965) and left the College to be chief executive of the Association of Teachers in Colleges and University Departments of Education.

[66] Ernest Read (1879–1965) started an enterprising movement founding youth orchestras in London and elsewhere, later named after him, and pioneered concerts for children; Thornton Lofthouse (1895–1974), harpsichordist, Director of Music at Westminster School and then Reading University.

the forthcoming post-diploma course were astutely referred to a working party largely comprising lecturers from the handful of colleges concerned. They, at least, aware that they had been specially selected to run the course, would see to it that realistically demanding goals were set.

CHAPTER EIGHT

WHEN ONE'S PROFESSIONAL PREDECESSORS are found to have been established national figures in their day it is natural to speculate about their activities and way of life, to wonder how far they were able to attain the goals they set themselves, and to compare their circumstances with those of today. Having indulged in such fancies where John Hullah and Thomas Helmore were concerned, I found myself becoming convinced that, even at the distance of a century and a half since their pioneer work at S. Mark's had begun, it should be possible to replace speculation with something more tangible. Both men had published extensively and their contemporaries had written about them. A modestly serious investigation with published evidence as its starting point should help build up portraits of them more substantial than the cardboard figures embalmed in the first edition of *Grove's Dictionary*. Such an enterprise, I decided, would make a rewarding spare time pursuit – for I now found myself with what had been an unknown luxury at High Wycombe, a half-day a week free from time-tabled commitments.

I began to use some of this leisure to explore London's suburban second-hand bookshops and, often more rewardingly, her junk shops. In those early days, before the tyranny of the traffic warden and the parking meter, I would set out from Chelsea after lunch and follow my nose until I spotted books, or bookshelves. If the books were in boxes marked 6d, I would rub my hands and rake my way through them, often to light upon some unknown music manual or outmoded hymnal. If the bookshelves were standing empty on the pavement outside some ramshackle shop among old chairs, coal-scuttles and towel-rails, so much the better! The books they had originally contained were probably to be found in a heap inside the shop awaiting the dustman's next call. I came across several copies of Hullah's *Manual* (1841) and Helmore's *Psalter Noted* (1849) and *Hymnal Noted* (1851) in just such heaps.

In time I had mapped out a circuit linking shops that carried large stocks deserving regular visits and covering an area from Streatham to Notting Hill. Several of them had shelves from floor to ceiling packed with unsorted books; and here, after first checking the spines I would sometimes indulge in a reckless *sortes Virgiliana,* picking on a volume at a time at random and flicking over the pages in search of musical references. More than once something relevant resulted. I also discovered the stalls at Portobello Road, the book barrows in

Farringdon Road and, much further afield, the specialist dealers of Oxford, Winchester, and Brighton.

From the fruits of these excursions I began to stack my own shelves with an apparently haphazard collection of shabby volumes. Some of them related directly to Hullah or Helmore, others concerned some aspect of music's application to an educational or religious context. Some of the early hymnals and many of the still earlier collections of metrical psalms, I unexpectedly found, were relevant to both categories – for they contained special Prefaces designed to explain the mysteries of musical notation to humbler church-goers.

Reviewing this growing hotchpotch, it became clear that although, with industry and patience, the life and work of Hullah and Helmore individually could be recorded readily enough – and I had by now come upon contemporary biographies of both men – assessment of their separate achievements must depend not only upon detailed examination of what they had done but on thorough familiarity with the conditions they inherited when their careers began. In Hullah's case this meant investigating the state of music teaching in schools before 1840; in Helmore's, an examination was necessary of changing attitudes toward choral worship in England over the centuries. I began to widen the areas of my search accordingly, seeking out specific titles now, rather than relying on chance, and having recourse to the Reading Room of the British Museum rather than the stalls of Portobello Road to locate source material.

Where Helmore's work was concerned it was disappointing to find so little first-hand evidence of his activities surviving within the College itself. His life-size portrait in oils still occupied an honoured place in the Senior Common Room; but none of its members seemed to know much about him. I could find nothing tangible to support what I had read about his activities at Chelsea – until my hunt for evidence took me to a little-used basement store room. There, I was astonished to find a bound but worn copy of the College Chapel music lists for the year 1849. Written in Helmore's own hand the book revealed a breadth of repertory no less than astonishing for that time. At those daily services, it appeared, works by Tallis, Byrd, Gibbons, Palestrina, Victoria, Marenzio, and the like, were sung unaccompanied as a matter of routine – works seldom or never heard even in our cathedrals during the musical doldrums then still prevailing in England.

This discovery opened my eyes to Helmore's historic achievement at Chelsea. But there was still much to investigate before a full picture of the joint scope of Helmore's and Hullah's work could be revealed. During the next five years I assembled (and digested) sufficient material to map out the territory concerned in considerable detail, recording now not only contemporary achievement but influential statements of opinion on music's place in worship or in popular education

It was at this stage, in 1957, that I unexpectedly received copies of the first volumes of Fiske and Dobbs' *Oxford School Music Books* to review for the *Journal of Education*.[67] In my opinion those carefully contrived and remarkably comprehensive manuals represented a major milestone in the post-war development of music in schools. Accordingly, I drafted a substantial review-article which set them against the background of the vicissitudes I had identified in popular music education in England over the past three centuries.

Boris Ford, then the youthful editor of the *Journal of Education*, decided that my historical survey of a previously unexplored topic warranted publication in its own right. It appeared under the title, 'An Excellency in Music', in July 1957,[68] detached from the detailed review of the *Oxford School Music Books* which was now included separately in the appropriate section of the journal. That article represented the first summary of my as yet incomplete investigation into the history of popular music education to be published. Two years later, in 1959, I had assembled sufficient material on Thomas Helmore to form three successive articles in the *Musical Times* outlining details of his pioneer contribution to the Anglican choral revival.[69]

An enterprise that had been started merely out of sentimental curiosity had now begun to take on the character of a substantial research project. To appreciate both Hullah's and Helmore's achievements it would be necessary to investigate the impelling forces that prompted them. The views of the early Tractarians on music in worship which had motivated Helmore proved to be readily accessible. On the other hand, the continental origins of Hullah's widely adopted method of teaching music demanded more complex investigation. I had tackled something of the situation in France already and was currently working on a translation of J. J. Rousseau's views on the subject.

Rousseau's *Écrits sur la musique*[70] was then little known among musicians in this country, had not yet been translated, and was only available in the original French in expensive editions of his *Complete Works*. I had never managed to run to earth a second-hand copy – until one day in the exclusive furniture department at Peter Jones in Sloane Square, unable through habit to pass a

[67] Roger Fiske and J. P. B. Dobbs, *The Oxford School Music Books*, books 1–3 (London: Oxford University Press, 1954), book 4 (London: Oxford University Press, 1961).

[68] *Journal of Education*, July 1957, pp. 292–5. See pp. 189–92.

[69] 'Thomas Helmore and the Anglican Plainsong Revival'; 'Thomas Helmore and the Mystery of *Veni Emmanuel*'; 'Thomas Helmore and the Revival of Carol Singing', *Musical Times*, vol. 100 nos. 1400–2 (October–December 1959). See pp. 319–24 below.

[70] See Jean-Jacques Rousseau, *Project Concerning New Symbols for Music (1742)*, ed. B. Rainbow, Classic Texts in Music Education vol. 1 (Kilkenny: Boethius Press, [1982]).

bookcase uninspected, I came upon an elderly leather-bound set of Rousseau's *Works* on display among other volumes to enhance an expensive bookcase. Assuming my most naive manner, and singling the most junior salesman in sight, I explained that I was not thinking of buying the bookcase in question, but 'one of those old French books' it contained was just what I had long been looking for. I took down the volume containing *Écrits sur la musique* from the shelf. I wondered if I might buy that. The young salesman's expertise was clearly limited to furniture. He didn't see why not, he said. I handed him five shillings and came away clutching my prize. Half an hour later I was back in College making a start on translating *Projet concernant de nouveaux signes pour la musique, lu par l'auteur à l'Académie des Sciences, le 22 aôut 1742.*

As if prompted by that encouraging turn of events an opportunity now arose for me to investigate matters in France itself. A longstanding connection existed between S. Mark and S. John and the École Normale at Versailles. Every year resident students from either college studying French or English respectively would exchange visits for ten days or so. A tutor always accompanied them, though his duties and responsibilities were nominal. I volunteered to go, and the offer was accepted. All I had to do, I was told, was to be available in case of need, and to reply to welcoming toasts by the mayor of Versailles and the Principal of the École Normale.

When seated at a desk with a dictionary alongside, my French was adequate. To make a speech on a formal occasion in France was another matter; and I painstakingly wrote out what I proposed to say, had it checked for linguistic gaffes, and committed it to memory before setting off across the Channel. It was not a recklessly lengthy harangue, but I thought I had struck the right note – thanking M. le Maire for his welcome, then paying homage to Versailles as a celebrated seat of European culture and adding suitably fulsome references to Louis XIV and 'La Gloire'.

On our first morning at Versailles we were conducted to the Hôtel de Ville, up the marble stairs and into the sumptuous *salle des fêtes* where wine was being served. The mayor then entered wearing his tricolour sash, shook hands liberally, and began his speech of welcome. I listened in growing panic as he began to recite the very speech I had prepared – but as it were in reverse. To most visitors, he declared, Versailles represented the cradle of European culture, the home of Louis XIV, and a bastion of La Gloire. He wished to point out that, however true those remarks might be about the Palace we could see through the windows, we were now on the other side of those gilt railings down the road; and Versailles itself, as opposed to the Palace it adjoined, was essentially a modern town looking to the future rather than to the past, etc., etc. As I listened to him demolishing my precious rhetoric I was desperately adapting the reply I had prepared for use at the École Normale later that day; and so, in due course I found myself thanking him, apologising for my halting French, but trusting that the old proverb, 'Quand le cœur est plein il faut que les lévres s'ouvre'[71] might prove my salvation. It was an altogether nerve-wracking business; but at least I could claim not to have been left speechless!

Back at the École Normale my hopes of finding surviving evidence of nineteenth-century practice in the library were disappointed. The teaching staff proved every bit as scornful of the past as their partisan mayor could wish. I did, however, have opportunity to see some interesting music lessons in a local school, and found them entirely devoted to singing and sight-reading from hand signals – though not those of either Kodály or Curwen.

Shortly before I left Chelsea for this French excursion Henry Willis had brought a visitor to inspect the new organ at Chelsea. I told him I was shortly going to France and looked forward to hearing again the highly individual sound of the organ at Notre Dame. He promptly gave me letters of introduction to Pierre Cochereau, organist at Notre Dame, and Marcel Dupré, at Saint-Sulpice.[72] As a result, on the first Sunday at Versailles, accompanied by the serving English *assistant* there, I set out for Paris in good time for High Mass at Notre Dame. When I showed my letter to a *bedeau* at the cathedral he explained that M. Cochereau was away in America, but led us up to the organ loft nonetheless. It was a large bare, shadowy gallery the width of the nave and considerably higher than its counterpart in English cathedrals. The deputising organist was already playing and several young people, presumably pupils, stood watching. Let me quote from an account of the incident I wrote for the *Musical Times* on my return:

> The maître presides – that is the only apposite term – at a detached Cavaillé-Coll console, raised on a substantial tiered tribune, so as to face the high altar and command full view of the vista towards the east. In the remote chancel the mass proceeds – the plainsong sung by men's voices accompanied by the altar-organ, the polyphonic settings sung by an unaccompanied choir of boys and men. The first organ interludes occur during the Credo. This is sung to plainsong but divided at the paragraphs by pungent modal outbursts of extemporised, deliberately 'primitive' organ music from the west end. These were played during my visit largely on manual reeds at 16', 8', and 4' – a registration which seemed thick to English ears, but which filled the cathedral with a pageantry of sound –and as each ended the choir instantly took up the plainsong at their conductor's signal. At other times during the mass the great organ played further interludes – while the celebrant was officiating at the altar, and

---

[71] E. T. A. Hoffman (1776–1822), German author influential in the Romantic movement.
[72] Pierre Cocherau (1924–84); Marcel Dupré (1886–1971).

during the communion of the people ... At the conclusion of the mass, as the priest's procession left the high altar, the organ burst into a final extemporisation. This seemed at first a typical toccata in the French manner, with a busy repetitive figure on the manuals, to which the pedal reeds were added ostinato fashion. But it quickly developed into something quite extravagantly unorthodox, with daring discordant embellishments and several glissandi from top to bottom of the pedal-board. In another, smaller building it might have sounded merely cacophonous, but here it seemed no more than daring. One was reminded curiously of the bold primitive brilliance of the illuminations of Froissart's Chronicle.[73]

On the following Sunday I made my way to Saint-Sulpice. Rivalling Notre Dame in size but classical rather than gothic, this church is recognised as the cathedral of the aristocratic Fauxbourg Saint-Germain. As before, the organ was already playing when I was taken up to the organ loft, but the scene that greeted me there was totally unexpected. The large organ-gallery was brightly lit, quite full of mainly elderly, impeccably dressed members of upper-class society, and in general effect resembled nothing so much as a well-attended, fashionable garden party. As each couple entered they made their way across to the organ console on its tribune where Marcel Dupré would spare one hand from his extemporised prelude to reach over and shake hands while exchanging civilities with them. As far as one could tell, these constant interruptions made no difference at all to his playing which matched the rococo elegance of the architecture with corresponding musical suavity. A noble, near-motionless figure at the console, Dupré surveyed the drama at the altar dispassionately. All the organ music at this service seemed to be extemporised and reflected that response.

There was no robed choir at Saint-Sulpice. The mass was sung in unison rather tentatively by a minority of the congregation to the overanxious conducting of a priest stationed distractingly on the chancel steps. It was difficult not to feel that the social gathering being held simultaneously upstairs in the organ loft had very little connection with what was going on in the body of the church below. Nothing could have been more different from the immediacy of the service I had attended the week before at Notre Dame. I presented my letter of introduction to the Maître afterwards. He had clearly met far too many people already that morning, and after an unconvincing exchange of mutual expressions of delight I came away bearing his formal greetings to Henry Willis. Yet, it had been enlightening to see him at the console; and had achieved nothing

---

[73] 'Notes from Two French Organ Lofts', *Musical Times*, vol. 102 no. 1423 (September 1961); see pp. 325–6 below. The Chronicles of Jean Froissart are a contemporary account of the background and onset of the Hundred Years' War from 1322 to 1400.

else during that Versailles trip, the opportunity to experience so intimately those two diametrically opposed musical treatments of High Mass would have sufficiently justified the journey.

Nor was I unduly disappointed to have found no evidence at Versailles of earlier methods of teaching music in French schools. Indeed, the implication was that I was better informed on the subject than my French counterparts themselves. For by this time my investigations had not only involved translating Rousseau's observations on music teaching – as we have seen – but also my providing an English version of Loys Bourgeois's highly relevant *Le Droict chemin de musique* published in 1550 – a copy of which I had come across in a continental facsimile edition.[74] This translation, together with a substantial historical and expository introduction, I had recently submitted successfully for a Fellowship diploma at Trinity College of Music.[75] These two excursions into historical aspects of continental methodology exemplified the broadening that had taken place in my research since I first began in 1952 to trace John Hullah's work as a teacher.

Early in the 1960s London University Institute of Education announced the establishment of a post-graduate music course for potential teachers. I was short-listed to run it. At the interview I saw that one of the interviewing panel had inserted a large cross against the qualifications listed on my application form. I was not a university graduate; and I was not appointed. When I recounted the incident to the new Vice-Principal at Chelsea, Dr Hugh Pollard,[76] he realised that it rankled, and forthwith contacted the University of Leicester urging my admission to work for a Master's degree in educational research. I was called for interview by Professor G. H. Bantock,[77] who sent to Trinity College for the Bourgeois dissertation I had submitted for the Fellowship there, and accepted me on the strength of it. My proposed research topic, an extension of the investigation I had already completed on John Hullah, was to be 'Musical Education in England, 1800–1860, and its continental antecedents'. Bantock would supervise it himself.

As had been the case with Dr Phillips in the '30s, Leonard Blake and Sir Sidney Nicholson in the '40s, now in the '60s I owed a further step in my career

---

[74] See Loys Bourgeois, *The Direct Road to Music* (*Le droict chemin de musique, 1550*), ed. B. Rainbow, Classic Texts in Music Education vol. 4 (Kilkenny: Boethius Press, [1982]).

[75] FTCL (Research in Music), 1961.

[76] Dr Hugh M. Pollard, Vice-Principal, St Mark and St John, 1960–3. See Peter Dickinson, 'Hugh Pollard: Founding Principal of St. Martin's College, Lancaster' [obituary], *Independent*, 13 April 2005; William Etherington and Alan Bennett, 'Hugh Pollard: Christian Educationist who founded a College' [obituary], *Guardian*, 9 May 2005.

[77] G. H. Bantock (1914–), writer and educational philosopher.

to the generosity of a sponsor – Hugh Pollard. I talked over with him the way in which I hoped to treat my topic and welcomed with gratitude his offer to read and comment upon each section before it was submitted. Bantock had already allowed me to write my thesis in a style suitable for publication – though he thought publication unlikely for so recondite a subject. The minimum period of part-time study before submitting for MEd at Leicester was two years, and attendance at the university was required three times a term. As the bulk of the research involved was already completed I intended to write up two chapters a term; and that proved manageable – so long as I devoted an average of an hour a day, usually before breakfast, to the task. My eventual external examiner was Dr W. L. Sumner, and after what was an uneventful *viva voce* examination he regretted not being able to let me know the result; but he wondered if I had yet decided on a follow-up subject for a PhD. Once again, as at that scholarship examination long ago, I then knew I had passed. I received the degree in July, 1964, and my thesis was published by Novello in 1967 under the title *The Land without Music*.[78]

By that time I had almost completed the statutory three years of part-time work on my PhD thesis. This was a study of the origins of the surpliced parochial choir, entitled *The Choral Revival in the Anglican Church, 1839–1872*, and represented the completion of my investigation into the circumstances surrounding Thomas Helmore's work at Chelsea. The external examiner on this occasion was Professor Ivor Keys[79] who expressed great interest in my topic and hoped I would find a publisher for a thesis already framed for publication. Knowing from this remark that my thesis had been accepted I sent home and to College a cryptic telegram: 'James, 1. 9'. Turning to the Epistle indicated the recipients found the indicated passage read, 'Let the brother of low degree rejoice that he is exalted', and celebrated accordingly. I received the degree in July, 1968, and *The Choral Revival* was published by Barrie & Jenkins in their series 'Studies in Church Music' in 1970.[80]

Throughout the whole of this period I was also directly concerned with another substantial publication. At a meeting of the Standing Subcommittee in Music in February, 1959, I had proposed the preparation and publication of an advisory Handbook for Music Teachers on lines similar to the Institute's pioneer *Handbook for Geography Teachers*. The proposal was well received and a group of members was appointed to draw up a draft outline. The resulting recommendation, submitted to the Subcommittee in September, 1960, was that while the Music Handbook should follow the general pattern of its pred-

---

[78] Now Boydell Press.

[79] Ivor Keys (1910–95), organist, Professor at Belfast, Nottingham and Birmingham universities, dedicated teacher. See *The Times*, 17 July 1995.

[80] Reprinted by Boydell Press, 1991.

ecessor, greater attention must be paid in it to the wide variety of skills called for in music teaching. The approval of the Academic Board of the Institute of Education was now obtained for publication; and as the person responsible for suggesting the Handbook in the first place, I was (hardly surprisingly) appointed its General Editor. The task this imposed was a heavy one, and even with the assistance of colleagues who sub-edited the reviews, and that of the secretarial staff in the Institute's Publications Office, it was not until 1964 that the *Handbook for Music Teachers* was eventually published. It then enjoyed wide circulation justifying a second, revised and enlarged edition four years later.

This second edition of the *Handbook* contained a challenging Foreword by Thurston Dart, the newly appointed King Edward Professor of Music at the University of London.[81] I had first known this distinguished musician as Bobby Dart, when he was head chorister at the Chapel Royal, Hampton Court, in the thirties, but had not met him again since then. However, it was by referring back to that early acquaintance that I was fortunately able to persuade him to contribute a foreword.

Some months later I asked to meet him again to discuss another matter. By now, the amount of source material I had assembled relating to the historical development of music in education ranged from Ancient Greek and Cretan times, covered most western cultures, and could be regarded as comprehensive. It was, moreover, unique. With Oliver Strunk's classic *Source Readings in Music History* in mind, I sought Professor Dart's advice on the viability of compiling a Source Book from this material. He showed encouraging interest in the idea and I began to annotate and file the material chronologically. But without more time at my disposal – and there were no such luxuries as photocopying devices, word-processors, and periods of sabbatical leave at S. Mark and S. John in those days – progress was inevitably intermittent and slow.

In addition, several further publishing ventures had surfaced at about this time. I was commissioned to write articles on 'Degrees in Music' and 'Musical Education in Britain' for the *International Cyclopedia of Music and Musicians,* published in New York and London in 1966; and to contribute sundry musical entries for the SCM *Dictionary of Liturgy and Worship* published in 1971. Meanwhile occasional articles of mine began to appear in the *Musical Times, Music in Education*, and *Music Teacher.*

I confess to having found all this activity stimulating rather than taxing. But it should not be supposed that this quota of what might be called extramural activity was undertaken because my departmental responsibilities had been reduced. On the contrary, the expansion of teacher-training that took

---

[81] (Robert) Thurston Dart (1921–71), prominent musicologist, performer and teacher.

place during this decade greatly increased the number of courses the Music Department was called upon to provide and made my duties and responsibilities that much greater. A year's professional training was now made compulsory for music graduates as well as diploma-holders, the basic course of education and training for teaching was extended from two to three years; and for those preparing jointly for the London BA and a teaching certificate it became four years. The resulting increase in the number of students on the roll was reflected in the additional number undertaking teaching practice and requiring supervision in schools. All these extra demands made the appointment of further staff in the department essential.

It will hardly be necessary here to enlarge upon the upheavals that characterised so many aspects of national life in the 1960s. As post-war austerity at length gave way to new-found affluence, the psychedelic American dream challenged native realism, and long-standing social conventions were assailed by what we grudgingly learned to call 'popular culture'. For present purposes our concern lies with the impact such exuberantly liberalising trends exerted upon young people's musical preferences, and the gulf that separated the music they met in school from what they came across in the world outside. Nor was it only in the field of 'popular' music that the discrepancy showed itself. Many teachers were not conversant with the musical idioms favoured by contemporary composers and consequently preferred not to introduce their pupils to music they found unsympathetic themselves.

These were matters that demanded the attention of those like myself responsible for planning and running courses to equip a new generation of teachers of music in schools. Until now, established teachers of my generation, recalling their own childhood, had tended to regard youthful musical enthusiasms as indiscretions to be grown out of; as trifling, harmless pranks not meriting serious attention in school. Similarly, those of us who had grown too set in our ways to warm to revolutionary compositional techniques saw no need to excuse ourselves if we avoided introducing anything approaching *avant-garde* works to our pupils. There was, after all, plenty of other music available. Faced with this impasse I found myself remembering dear old Mr Galpin and his inflexible loathing for Stravinsky. Better not try to encourage the blind to lead the blind.

But now, with the current opportunity of appointing additional members of staff, a bold answer to a hitherto insoluble problem seemed to present itself. Instead of reduplicating the type of lecturer already on the strength – for instance, the safe exam coach, good at teaching harmony and counterpoint, or the music historian fascinated by the past – we could afford to appoint a forward-looking musician capable of enlarging and widening the range of expertise within the department. At least, we were in a position to take that daring step, provided the post attracted a suitable applicant. After all, not every talented, forward-looking music graduate would welcome a post in teacher-training.

Another issue relating to the future appointment of staff was to surface after a subsequent conversation I had with Reg Rennoldson, the most cordial member of the ILEA music inspectorate. Describing the current situation in the London area he mentioned some interesting experimental teaching he had seen going on at the large Comprehensive School at Holloway. There, despite a general lack of music-reading skills average classes of children were taking part in concerted musical performance organised on aleatory lines. The teacher responsible for this adventurous work, George Self, made it part of his aim to familiarise children with the 'flavour' of contemporary music in a way he felt traditional preliminaries failed to achieve. I thought that George Self might welcome a post in teacher-training.

There was one strong reservation in my mind as to the wisdom of encouraging the introduction of 'contemporary' attitudes into the curriculum. Such a move could well add to the student's resources; but it must not be allowed to do so at the expense of traditional approaches offering the beginner an essentially realistic challenge. By analogy, whatever adventurous exercises a teacher of English might provide for the edification of sixth-formers, who would seriously consider starting in the primary school with excerpts from James Joyce? This point must be appreciated by new members of staff.

In due course it was encouraging to find that applicants for the first advertised vacancy included an outstanding candidate. Peter Dickinson had been organ scholar at Queens' College, Cambridge, then studied on a scholarship at the Juilliard School in New York where he had met and been influenced by Cage and Varèse.[82] He offered just the qualities I was seeking and joined the department in 1962, forthwith starting classes in experimental composition and improvisation that soon began to disperse lingering cobwebs.[83] Two years later George Self also joined us and my earlier vision of a department equipped to deal with both traditional and progressive teaching methods was to a large extent realised.[84]

News of these developments was not slow to reach other teacher-training institutions, and reactions ranged from exasperated, but unspoken disapproval to watchful curiosity. One of my opposite numbers remarked cautiously, 'What

---

[82] Edgard Varèse (1883–1965); John Cage (1912–92).

[83] For an account of this see Peter Dickinson, 'Music for Today', *Music in Education*, May/June 1965.

[84] See George Self, *New Sounds in Class* (London: Universal Edition, 1967); *Lessons in Listening: Aural Adventure* (London: Novello & Co., 1969); also 'Holloway', 'Silverthorne' and 'Nukada' in *Music for Young Players* (London: Universal Edition, 1967–8).

interesting appointments you have been making!' Repercussions extended much further afield; and within a year I had been invited to contribute an article on 'Modern Attitudes in School Music' to the Australian *Education News*. In it I described what Peter Dickinson and George Self were doing at Chelsea, and concluded that watching young people at work under their direction demonstrated the value of such work to the music lessons of today's children. I had been astonished to watch blasé adolescents with no previous musical inclinations at work with their whole attention concentrated on their performance. The sound of the music they performed was far removed from the usual run of school music. It reminded us, and more to the point, it reminded them, of what they were used to hearing as an accompaniment to television epics of space travel and similar high adventure; and it belonged unmistakably to the age they lived in. This article was reprinted in the *Australian Journal of Music Education* in 1966.[85]

An account of these ramifications written by Peter Dickinson thirty years later when he had become successively professor of music at Keele University and Goldsmiths College, University of London, supplies a participant's view:

> I joined Rainbow's Music Department at the College of S. Mark and S. John, in 1962. Even after three years in New York, I found myself in a lively intellectual environment. As with Wilfrid Mellers' Department at York, Music Education was at the cutting edge of the challenge of the 1960s. At that time Rainbow, who had been a collector for years, had a magnificent research library ... But, apart from his own research, he had other abilities which his headship of the Department brought into play. He was a generous enabler, able to sense contributions to new ideas in musical education which could be made by younger people. After appointing me, he took on George Self, who joined the contemporary music in schools debate at the same time as Peter Maxwell Davies and David Bedford. Thirty years later these ideas about creativity in school music are now built into the school curriculum – to the extent that there is a danger of losing the basics of Western music, as Rainbow himself foresaw.[86]

The expansion that had brought extra staff to S. Mark and S. John saw a general increase in staffing levels at other colleges, and this in turn brought new blood to the Standing Subcommittee in Music at the Institute of Education.

---

[85] See also Bernarr Rainbow, 'Music Education, Yesterday, Today & Tomorrow: A British Perspective', in *Music Education: International Viewpoints: A Symposium in Honour of Emeritus Professor Sir Frank Callaway*, ed. Martin Comte, ASME Series no. 3 (Melbourne: Australian Society for Music Education, 1994), pp. 152–9.

[86] Peter Dickinson, 'Bernarr Rainbow at 80', *Choir & Organ*, vol. 2 no. 5 (October 1994), p. 30.

As a result, a drive to appoint new External Examiners was now successful and with the retirement of Mabel Chamberlain I was honoured to be elected to succeed her as Chairman.

CHAPTER NINE

D ESPITE THE SOCIAL TURMOIL that typified the 1960s, in many ways this had been for me a Golden Decade. At a personal level, during those ten years my initial curiosity over Hullah and Helmore had matured into a serious research project at doctoral level. On that basis I had published two definitive texts. In College, I had received a Principal Lecturership, and the expanded music department now provided special one-year courses for post-graduates, diploma-holders, and seconded teachers, as well as standard three- and four-year courses for undergraduates and students preparing for teaching qualifications at main or subsidiary level. On the practical side the department now enjoyed the services of visiting piano, organ, string and wind teachers. The chapel music embraced weekly choral Evensong and Compline, with Sung Eucharist at major festivals; and the Advent Carol Service and annual liturgical performance of Victoria's austere *Passion* were noted features in the College calendar. The choir sang annually at St Paul's and Southwark cathedrals, and services broadcast from the College Chapel on radio and television had given rise to correspondence from listeners commending the wider use of plainchant for the prose psalms. The former custom of the whole College singing 'Non nobis, Domine' in canon after dinner had been revived. Regular concerts and recitals took place, and besides such domestic performances visits from notable contemporaries to speak and play in College were frequently arranged.

I suggested to Peter Dickinson that he should discuss with the poet, Thomas Blackburn of the English Department, the possibility of their collaborating to produce a joint work. The first result was two male-voice anthems, *Mark* and *John*, written for the ATB chapel choir, followed by *The Judas Tree*, a musical drama employing five actors, two tenors as narrators, a thirty-voice SATB chorus, an orchestra of strings, brass and mixed percussion, and organ. First performed in 1965 by students under a student conductor in the College Chapel it was then given successively at the Edinburgh Festival, Liverpool Cathedral and elsewhere.[87]

[87] *The Judas Tree*, produced by James Smyth, conducted by Brian Wilson, at the College of St Mark and St John, 27, 28, 29 May 1965, and 18–19 November: 'Compelling Drama of Judas', *The Times*, 28 May 1965; 'Heaven and Hell within', *Times Educational Supplement*, 4 June 1965; David Cairns, 'The Judas Tree', *Financial Times*, 1 June 1965; Dramatic Impact of The Judas Tree, *Daily Telegraph*, 22 November 1965. At the Edinburgh Festival Fringe, 6–11 September 1965: 'Play that assaults the Mind: powerful religious Drama', *Scotsman*, 7 September 1965; 'Judas in an Evening

It is pleasant to recall that all these activities took place at a time when an aesthetically sophisticated Principal, Alex Evans, was at Chelsea to give them his approval and support. That circumstance was also reflected in the provision at this time of entirely new premises for the music department comprising two lecture rooms, a wing of practice rooms, adequate storage facilities and appropriate equipment.

In comparison the 1970s were to have a different flavour. By now another, less discriminating Principal had taken the place of Alex Evans; Dickinson and Self had moved on to run departments of their own elsewhere. Their specialisms were commendably taken up by Michael Burnett and Brian Dennis respectively, enabling work in the department to continue healthily. But in spite of a justifiable sense of continuity, I personally became aware of sundry new influences brought to bear – some of them encouraging, others, less so. On the positive side I was invited to speak on 'Music and the Anglican Revival' at the Victoria and Albert Museum as one of a series of lectures illustrating the *Exhibition of Victorian Church Art* being held there for three months from November, 1971. Shortly afterwards I also read a paper on 'The Nineteenth-century Choral Revival' at the annual conference of the Victorian Society held at Selwyn College, Cambridge. This latter event led to a somewhat disconcerting encounter.

Arriving at Selwyn rather earlier than intended I was received by a young don and shown into a junior common room where a man in shirtsleeves was wrestling to fit up a coffee urn for our use. We went across to watch and my escort told him who I was. 'Delighted to meet you,' he said, 'and I enjoyed your little book.' This flummoxed me completely and I muttered some reply. At which he went on, 'You brought Thomas Helmore and J. M. Neale to life for me. They had always been cardboard figures before.' I thanked him for this unexpected tribute and realised that the 'little book' in question must be my published PhD thesis. Who might this shirt-sleeved pundit be, I wondered. He had at last, I now saw, got the urn working. As we moved away with our

Suit', *Evening News* 7 September 1965; Godfrey Hutchinson, ' The Judas Tree', *Music in Education*, 1965, p. 283, and 'The Tree grows in Edinburgh', *Music and Musicians*, November 1965, 39–40. At Liverpool Cathedral, 21 November: Benedict Nightingale, 'The Judas Tree at Liverpool', *Guardian*, 22 November 1965, 'Ill wind rustles Judas Tree', *Liverpool Daily Post*, 22 November 1965. The New Opera Company, Guildhall, Cambridge, 19 March, and Southwark Cathedral, 13–14 April 1967: 'Judas as a necessary Evil', *The Times*, 14 April 1967; Noel Goodwin, 'Muddled but expressive', *Guardian* 14 April 1967. In the USA: 'Judas Tree powerful, impressively done', *Evening Star* [Washington DC], 24 March, 1967; 'Judas Tree is a powerful triumph', *Washington Post*, 24 March 1967; Irving Lowens, 'Current Chronicle: Washington', *Musical Quarterly*, vol. 53 (July 1967), 400–2. See also Peter Dickinson, 'A Note on The Judas Tree', *Musical Times*, vol. 8 no. 1490 (April 1967), pp. 323–25. Vocal score and text, Novello.

coffee my friendly don gave me a sidelong grin. 'You mustn't mind the Vice-Chancellor,' he said. 'You see, he probably read your book before breakfast one morning.' My apparent handyman had been that formidable scholar, the Master of Selwyn, Owen Chadwick, himself![88]

Early in the 1970s I first learnt that an entirely new twenty-volume version of Grove's monumental *Dictionary of Music and Musicians* was being prepared when I received an invitation to write some forty articles, biographical notices, and factual entries for it, drawing upon my recent studies. This, of course, was a challenging task but one to be welcomed as capable of setting a seal of authority upon my work. It was, moreover, to prove consolatory at a time when all I had set out to achieve at S. Mark and S. John seemed, almost overnight, to be placed at risk.

EDITOR'S NOTE

All footnotes, apart from those initialed BR, have been added to clarify references in the text. Documents and photographs providing some of this detail are now with the Bernarr Rainbow Archive at the library of the Institute of Education, University of London.

---

[88] Owen Chadwick (1916–), Master of Selwyn College, 1965–83; Vice-Chancellor of Cambridge University, 1969–71.

PART II

John Curwen

Portrait of John Curwen by William Gush, *c.* 1857.
By permission of the National Portrait Gallery

John Curwen: A Short Critical Biography
[1980]

Here is a man six feet high, and you are angry because he is not seven.

Samuel Johnson

PREFACE

T HE OBVIOUS SOURCE from which to trace John Curwen's career is the *Memorials of John Curwen* which his son published soon after his father's death in 1880. Careful study of that book, however, reveals that it incorporates a number of independent but mutually contradictory recollections, written after a lapse of many years and under the emotional influence of their subject's recent death. Moreover, John Spencer Curwen himself sometimes understandably softens, even omits, details which might present a picture of his widely respected father in a less than favourable light.

By widening the range of enquiry to include John Curwen's own writings and a few other sources it has proved possible to compile a more objective account. Bur since this book offers nothing more than a straightforwardly readable narrative, footnotes referring the reader to source materials have been consistently omitted. All the sources consulted appear in the appended Bibliography.

B.R.

I PRELUDE (1816–41)

In some ways John Curwen might be said to have had greatness thrust upon him. Celebrated as a young man for his remarkable skill as a teacher, he turned to the special field of music teaching only at the request of his fellows and with great misgiving. Yet the method which he evolved during the rest of a long career was to spread throughout the world and to gain for him an acknowledged place in the history of musical education. In the centenary year of his death, and at a time when the lasting worth of John Curwen's principles has been demonstrated to the world afresh in the schools of Hungary, a new appraisal of the life and work of this discerning and dedicated pioneer seems a fitting tribute.

John Curwen was born on 14 November 1816 at Heckmondwike, then an undeveloped Yorkshire village largely given over to blanket-weaving on handlooms. His father, the Revd Spedding Curwen, was nonconformist minister of the Independent Chapel; his mother, Mary Curwen, a teacher. The professional attributes of both parents were later to reappear combined in their son.

In 1817 Spedding Curwen was appointed to a new pastorate at Cottingham, near Hull. There, John Curwen reached an age to go to his first school and his younger brother, Tom, was born. But after only five years, when John was six years old, his mother died, and his father decided to seek another situation – this time in London where he became minister of the Barbican Chapel. John and his younger brother were now sent to boarding school at Ham, in Surrey.[1] Finally, in 1828, the motherless family moved to Frome, in Somerset, where Spedding Curwen was made minister of Zion Chapel, remaining there for the next eleven years.

While at Frome, John Curwen began to show determination to succeed at school. With the purposeful seriousness which so often marks the boyhood of outstanding figures in the nineteenth century, he was seldom satisfied unless he gained the top place in his class, and had soon firmly resolved to follow his father as a nonconformist minister. This meant preparing himself for several further years of study upon leaving school.

England at that time maintained two ancient universities, both of which required of students and staff alike an oath of allegiance to the Church of England. Neither Oxford nor Cambridge would confer degrees upon nonconformists. On that account, to provide for students unwilling to subscribe to Anglican articles of belief, during the seventeenth and eighteenth centuries an increasing number of Dissenting Academies had been established in many parts of the country. In the best of them an education at least comparable to anything then offered by either Oxford or Cambridge was provided. It was at one of these, a college established for the education and training of Independent ministers at Wymondley in Hertfordshire, that John Curwen secured a place late in 1832.

Whatever educational benefits it may have afforded, Wymondley College was in its own way quite as narrowly sectarian as either Oxford or Cambridge. And during his first weeks there, John Curwen's youthful diary began to show him as given to religious introspection verging on the unhealthy. But within a few months of his arrival a fortunate development took place. A new university, imposing no religious tests on its members, had been founded in London in 1827. Later to be known as University College, London, the new institution admitted its first students in 1828; and in 1833 Wymondley College was

---

[1] It is tempting to suppose that this may have been the school established at Ham by J. P. Greaves, Pestalozzi's disciple, at just that time. Such a circumstance would help to explain John Curwen's later enthusiasm for Pestalozzian methods. But there is no evidence to justify such a claim.

transferred to London to enable its students to attend the university classes in classics and mathematics, while continuing to study divinity under their own tutors. This was in every way a gain. The students were now able to mix with the larger life of a non-sectarian institution and gain both in tolerance and culture.

John Curwen was often to look back with pleasure to the six years he spent as a student. Only sixteen years old when he first went to Wymondley, during those formative years he was to develop pronounced traits of character which remained with him throughout life. Fellow students noted his honour, methodical ways and invincible tenacity, and were impressed particularly by his intense interest in teaching children. This inheritance from his mother showed itself most clearly in the voluntary work which he undertook at the Barbican Sunday School in his father's former parish. This was not a Sunday School in the modern sense of the term – devoted exclusively to elementary moral and scriptural teaching – but one established for the general education of children obliged to work on weekdays and thus deprived of attendance at day schools.

From 1834 John Curwen taught regularly at the Barbican school, developing there his 'Look and Say' method of teaching reading. Instead of teaching children to read by spelling out words letter by letter, Curwen encouraged them to read short words as a whole. With a tray of movable letters on his lap, he would arrange simple words to form a short sentence. More difficult words were divided into syllables before being joined together. During the next forty years this method was to be 'rediscovered and practised by innumerable teachers'; but John Curwen was already using it in 1834. It provides an interesting example of his instinctive ability to analyse the processes of instruction, an instinct which he was to supplement by enthusiastic study of the writings of the progressive teachers of his day.

Later in life, John Curwen was to acknowledge how much and how deeply he was indebted to Pestalozzi. But his first guides in forming those radical notions of teaching which were to form the basis of all his work were David Stow, Elizabeth Mayo, Horace Grant and Jacob Abbott.

David Stow's Normal Seminary in Glasgow was an institution for training teachers, famous during the 1830s for its progressive outlook and interesting teaching methods. In his book, *The Training System*, Stow outlined those methods, drawing a sharp distinction between instruction and education, and insisting that teachers must interest their pupils if a desire for self-improvement was to result. He advised that this should be done by 'picturing-out' the main features of a topic, and illustrated the process in a series of classroom dialogues between teacher and pupils. Deeply impressed by Stow's theories, Curwen later travelled to Scotland to meet him and gain closer acquaintance with his work.

Elizabeth Mayo's book *Lessons on Objects* provided examples of teaching according to the principles of Pestalozzi in which the pupil was trained to exercise his own senses – an aspect of teaching which had not hitherto been appreciated in Britain. The author's brother, the Revd Charles Mayo, had returned to England in 1822 after spending three years teaching at Yverdun under Pestalozzi's general direction. His sister's book was intended to supplement the lectures which Mayo gave to interest his fellow countrymen in Pestalozzi's pedagogical principles. In 1836 the Mayos were to be jointly instrumental in founding the Home and Colonial Infant School Society in Gray's Inn Road, London, an institution with a Model School and a 'training establishment' for Infant teachers. Curwen was later to be invited to teach there, but it was from Elizabeth Mayo's book that he gained his first acquaintance with Pestalozzian principles.

The third writer who influenced John Curwen at this time was Horace Grant, whose *Arithmetic* was prefaced by a discourse on general teaching principles based upon observation of the young mind. 'Children ought not to be perpetually harassed with dry questions'. Grant wrote. 'The grand object is to cause them to exert their minds with pleasure, and for this a lively conversation is the most effectual means.' When teaching Geography, the teacher was advised not to begin with some remote land, but to start with the geography of the children's own district – 'the street and the roads leading to it: their parish, its roads and rivers: thence the county, and thence the country, interesting them in what is about them before going on to what is beyond them'. When it came to the teaching of Arithmetic itself, Curwen followed Grant's advice by using beans, peas, shells and wooden bricks for the children to use in adding, subtracting, multiplying and dividing, so as to develop truer ideas of number before attempting to learn the tables. Such ideas were later to become commonplace; but this was by no means the case in the 1830s.

John Curwen's fourth mentor was Jacob Abbott, the progressive American teacher of the Mount Vernon Academy at Boston, USA. In his book, *The Teacher*, Abbott emphasised that the art of guiding the pupil on the path of discovery formed the true basis of teaching. Before doing this successfully the teacher must first take the subject to pieces in his own mind, and then decide how to give it, piece by piece, to his pupils. His book presented a series of classroom dialogues, meticulously worked out, demonstrating this principle. *The Teacher* exerted the greatest influence upon Curwen, who later wrote, 'In studying again Mr Abbott's book, after thirty-six years, I am astonished and delighted to find how much I owe to him, and I can see how one page after another in his book has had a long trail of results in my own preparation and my own teachings'.

From such sources as these, then, during his student days John Curwen augmented his own natural gifts as a teacher. From such authors, too, he developed an interest in the workings of the mind – a topic known in those days as Mental Philosophy which, he declared, became his favourite study. In such circumstances it is not surprising to find repeated references, in the reminiscences of those who knew him, to his remarkable powers as a teacher, even at this early stage of his career. Indeed, at his death more than forty years later, there were to be instances of elderly folk anxious to relate details of Sunday school lessons which he had given to them in childhood and which they vowed still remained fresh in their memory.

In 1838 his studies and preparation for the ministry completed, John Curwen was appointed assistant minister at the Independent Chapel at Basingstoke, Hants, at a salary of fifty pounds a year. It seems clear, from what we already know of him, that a decision to open a little school for boys at his lodgings was not designed merely to supplement that meagre stipend. He began, moreover, to teach from time to time in the local Sunday school, and an account, written many years afterwards by one of the children present, sums up the impact that his visits made upon them:

> Whenever he entered our school the faces of both teachers and scholars lighted up with unusual pleasure. One had only to see him with young people, and one felt to be in the presence of a man who lived for children, and who, by every word and look, won their love and gave them instruction and delight. His manner of communicating thoughts and ideas was perfectly unique. I shall never forget …

Many similar accounts might be presented, each bearing witness to John Curwen's remarkable powers in addressing children.

But, for the purpose of this account, the Sunday School at Basingstoke assumes particular importance for another reason – it was to be the scene of John Curwen's first serious attempt to teach children to sing. This task, he admitted, was undertaken 'chiefly with the design of making them love the Sunday School'. There was as yet no wider educational or aesthetic aim. Indeed, at that point in his career Curwen knew hardly more about music than the children themselves. The incident acquires special interest because of its unexpected sequel a few years later.

For those first singing lessons Curwen assembled all 200 children of the Sunday school. He stood on a platform in the middle of the room and the children stood around the walls. With no instrument to guide the singing, Curwen was obliged to rely on his own voice both to pattern and control the mass of children's voices. The louder they sang, the louder he was obliged to sing. In desperation he called in the assistance of a second teacher, when their united efforts managed to give a firm lead. In this way many new tunes were taught; but only at the expense of two sore throats.

In an attempt to widen the children's musical experience, Curwen called in a young member of his congregation to teach the rudiments of music to them. But for all their new acquaintance with crotchets and quavers, flats and sharps, the children seemed to gain little in the way of practical ability. Meanwhile, Curwen began to battle his way through an old-fashioned music primer in an attempt to unravel its mysteries for himself. To be able to read a simple hymn tune became the height of his musical ambition. But no amount of theoretical study seemed to increase his ability to recognise a tune on the page. Disappointed by these setbacks, Curwen had to be content with continuing the singing class on the basis of rote-learning. Soon afterwards his brief ministry at Basingstoke came to an end.

However, before he left Basingstoke another event took place which made John Curwen's name more widely known among teachers in this country. This was the publication of a story book which he had written for children, entitled *The History of Nelly Vanner*. A deliberately simple account of incidents in the daily life of a little girl, it was written from the point of view of a child, and in language which a child could easily understand. Immediately successful – it was to pass through fourteen editions – the little book quickly brought Curwen to the notice of a wide circle of those interested in progressive teaching; and, as a result, he soon found himself invited to address meetings and conferences of teachers, outlining his views upon the educational approach to young children. It was through such contacts that the next, as yet unforeseen, phase of his work came about.

II CHALLENGE (1841–4)

The three short years that John Curwen spent at Basingstoke were sufficient to reveal that this young man's true vocation lay in teaching. His firmly held religious beliefs, sincere concern for the poor and unfortunate, his responsible handling of pastoral duties, and a natural charm of manner that made for happy relations with his flock, all ensured Curwen's ready acceptance as a minister. But few members of his congregation will have failed to note their pastor's special abilities as a teacher, the growing number of his invitations to lecture elsewhere on educational matters, or the fact that, when at home, many of his chapel sermons were chiefly addressed to the children present. As yet, however, the calls upon him as minister and teacher were sufficiently compatible and complementary to cause no perplexity.

In 1841 John Curwen left Basingstoke to take up a new post as co-pastor at the Independent Chapel at Stowmarket, in Suffolk. Once again he received a warm welcome from both adults and children among his congregation, and the personal pattern of his pastoral activity was quickly resumed. But at Stowmarket Curwen found himself more and more involved in educational matters. Invitations to lecture on general teaching methods increasingly came his way; and in an attempt to fulfil the separate roles of minister and teacher he formed the habit of rising at six to devote the first two hours of the day to educational study and writing so that his pastoral duties should not suffer.

In the autumn of 1841 Curwen undertook an extensive tour of Yorkshire to address meetings of Sunday School teachers at Leeds, Hull and many parts of the West Riding. During this tour his health began to suffer. A severe attack of palpitations was an alarming sign of the self-imposed strain under which he was working. And the death of his fiancee at this time was a further tax on his never robust constitution. But in spite of all these portents, while Curwen was at Hull he received a challenge which circumstances made it impossible for him to refuse. At the conference which he was addressing there, the state of congregational singing was discussed at some length. The subject was a topical one. At that time the rival singing classes of Hullah and Mainzer were newly established in the capital and attracting large attendances and general public interest. Impressed by John Curwen's grasp of educational matters as shown in his recent address, the conference chairman promptly commissioned him to undertake a review of available methods of teaching singing, and to recommend 'some simple method to the churches which should enable all to sing with ease and propriety'.

Aware of his own musical shortcomings, John Curwen received that charge with considerable misgiving. But it seemed to him a solemn pledge and he returned to Stowmarket resolved to carry it out. Following the failure of his own earlier attempt to conduct a singing class at Basingstoke he had appealed, both to his brother and to former fellow students, for guidance. In response, and shortly before leaving Basingstoke, he had received from an old friend at college, Andrew Reed, a copy of a book outlining a new method of teaching music to children. Reed had been appointed minister of an Independent Chapel at Norwich, and found there that something of a stir had been caused locally by the excellent singing of a children's choir in one of the city's churches. The book, he explained, outlined the method employed in training those children. On receiving it Curwen had given the book little more than a baffled glance at the time. But now he turned to it again for more serious consideration.

From John Curwen's point of view the book's distinctly unappealing title made it seem highly relevant to his needs. It was called *A Scheme for Rendering Psalmody Congregational*, and although published anonymously, proved to have been written by the daughter of a Norwich parson at whose church the celebrated children's choir regularly sang. Curwen's own account of what he discovered there speaks for itself:

> I soon found that the old methods of teaching [music] had deceived me with the shell of knowledge instead of giving me its kernel. The *thing* music, I perceived to be very different from its names and signs. I found it much more simple and easy in itself, and incomparably more beautiful than the explanation of the signs of the old notation, with which elementary books are commonly filled. I had easily mastered them all, and had also studied a 'first book' on harmony, but I seemed to know nothing of music till then. I now saw that Miss Glover's plan was to teach, first, the simple and beautiful *thing*, music, and to delay the introduction to the ordinary antiquated mode of writing it, until the pupil had obtained a mastery of the thing itself. Her method was, beyond all controversy, more deeply established on the principles of the science than any other, and, by giving it a fair trial on myself, and on a little child who lived in the same house, I became convinced that it was also the most simple of all – the most easy to teach, and the most easy to learn. The methods of teaching which are truest to the nature of the thing taught, and the least artificial, are always the most successful. In the course of a fortnight, I found myself, *mirabile dictu*, actually at the height of my previous ambition, being able to 'make out' a psalm-tune from the notes, and to pitch it myself! It was the untying of the tongue – the opening of a new world of pleasure ...

That rhapsodic response, from an experienced teacher with John Curwen's acute educational insight, leaves little room for doubting his conviction that he had stumbled upon a valid solution to the problems facing the musical beginner. It also reveals that he had studied other books than Sarah Glover's. And we know, from other sources, that he had worked away at the old-established musical grammar of Dr Callcott and even travelled to London to attend John Hullah's Singing School in Exeter Hall. Yet it was the Norwich schoolmistress's book that had most impressed John Curwen.

❊ ❊ ❊

Sarah Glover's *Scheme for Rendering Psalmody Congregational* outlined a method evolved empirically over a period of some twenty years before its first publication in 1835. While it would be inappropriate to attempt a full account of her work in these brief pages, its main features must necessarily be explained.[2]

---

[2] A full description of Sarah Glover's work is contained in the present author's book, *The Land without Music* (London: Novello, 1967) which comprises a detailed study of the reintroduction of music teaching in English schools during the nineteenth century.

At a time when most teachers in this country insisted upon memorising and catechising, Sarah Glover rejected mere fact-cramming as the basis of instruction. In her view, all theory not immediately connected with practice should be omitted. Children should be taught music as they learned to speak – by deducing theory from practice, rather than the reverse. She therefore began by teaching the class to sing the notes of the common chord to the traditional sol-fa names, gradually building up from there all the degrees of the major scale. Children were next exercised in pitching notes from a vertical chart bearing the initial letters of each of the sol-fa syllables of the scale as a preliminary form of notation. To avoid a duplication between the initials *of Sol* and *Si*, she had renamed the seventh degree *Te. Do* always represented the keynote.

Once familiar with this basic material, the children learned to sing simple tunes printed in her sol-fa notation, the rhythm being shown by means of bar lines and a system of punctuation marks. An example will help to clarify the situation:

All Miss Glover's lessons were conducted without instrumental accompaniment, pitch being established before each exercise by means of a small dulcimer with glass resonators. This device, adopted for its cheapness and simplicity, she dubbed a Glass Harmonicon. A coded symbol *(Column O* on the example above) indicated to the teacher or monitor the position of the keynote to be sounded on the harmonicon. At a very early stage in her lessons, two-part singing was introduced – a step made possible only by the children's growing ability to sing from notes, but one which automatically developed their musical competence and sensitivity. Canons and rounds also formed a regular part of their classroom repertoire. All elementary lessons employed only sol-fa notation;

staff notation was not introduced until complete assurance in pitching notes
had been achieved.

Such, in outline, was the system of teaching children to sing from notes
which had so captivated John Curwen and enabled him to read a tune from
the page for the first time, meanwhile testing its potential value in schools by
teaching the system to a little girl. Full of his discovery, Curwen began to subject Sarah Glover's system to the same careful analysis which he had formerly
given to the methods of Stow, Mayo, Grant and Abbott before adapting them
to his own purposes. As a result of that examination he identified a number of
details which seemed to call for modification. First among these, and indicating Curwen's eye for practical considerations, was the adoption of small letters
instead of capitals. This, and the use of only such signs and marks as were likely
to be found in sufficient numbers in a local printer's stock, was designed to
enable schools and churches to produce their own music copies cheaply. He
also wanted a more varied repertoire than Miss Glover's hymns, rounds and
canons, and a full course of progressive lessons for teachers to employ.

Perhaps the simplest way of outlining Curwen's modifications is to provide
a version of the same tune in either notation. Here is the hymn tune *Abridge*
(usually sung to 'Be thou my guardian') written, first, in Miss Glover's version,
then in Curwen's. The neater and more compact appearance of the latter is
immediately obvious:

NORWICH SOL-FA VERSION

COLUMN U.

{.D· | Ś .— .Ď | Ď .T́) .L̀ | Ś .F) .M | M .R) .M }

{|L̀ .— .Ś | Ś .— .tu | Ś .— .ŚI | M .F) .L̀ | Ś .— .Ś }

{|L̀ .T́) .Ď | Ď .T́) .Ś | Ď .M) .Ś | F .M) .R | D .— }

TONIC SOL-FA VERSION

Key E♭

{:d | s :— :d' | d' :t :l | s :f :m | m :r :m }

{| l :— :s | s :— :tu | s :— :s | m :f :l | s :— :s }

{| l :t :d' | d' :t :s | d' :m :s | f :m :r | d :— ||

Curwen states the key, instead of using the *Column* code, employs small letters
instead of using capitals, separates beats by colons; indicates slurs by horizontal
lines instead of brackets. He had not at that early stage yet introduced the chromatic note name *fe* to represent the sharpened fourth in a modulation.

Such minor revisions apart – all of them based upon practical considerations

– Curwen's ideal system followed Miss Glover's in general outline. He now began to prepare a series of model lessons and a children's hymnal employing the notation as he had amended it.

Only when he had been carried so far on that first wave of enthusiasm as to forward both lessons and hymnal to the printer did it occur to John Curwen to seek Miss Glover's approval for the modifications which he had made. In a humble letter which he addressed to her on 4 October 1841, he explained his precipitate actions as best he could, outlining the minor changes which he had made to her notation. 'I shall be anxious till I hear from you,' he concluded: 'if indeed I may presume to ask such a favour from one to whom I am unknown.'

A successful if not celebrated teacher then in her mid-fifties, Sarah Glover was emphatically not prepared to accept the modifications which this eager young man attempted to thrust upon her. Indeed, for the next twenty years she was to resist Curwen's attempts to persuade her to do so. In such circumstances, perhaps only a triumph of diplomacy on the part of Curwen's friend, the Revd Andrew Reed, can explain how, shortly after the receipt of that letter, Miss Glover invited John Curwen to visit her school in Norwich.

The two days which Curwen spent at Norwich confirmed his belief in the basic worth of Sarah Glover's system. Indeed, he was astonished at what he found. Entering Black Boy Yard, where the school stood, he could already hear soft, cultivated singing voices such as he had never heard from schoolchildren before.

> As I opened the door [he afterwards wrote] I saw a little girl pointing to syllables on a diagram, singing as she pointed. Stepping in, I saw that she had in front of her a gallery of children who were following her pointing and singing the syllables with her. I had never been able to get anything like it in all my two years work![3]

Afterwards he watched the older children at work under Miss Glover's own direction as they sang their hymns, songs, rounds and canons – the last of these in as many as eight parts, though one class comprised only twenty children. On the following day Curwen returned to the school to see Miss Glover teaching the minor scale – firmly based on *la* as the tonic – to a select group of children. Finally, he saw the way in which the oldest children were introduced, step by step, to the use of staff notation. His friend declared him 'riveted by the astonishing results produced.' However, nothing he had seen persuaded Curwen to abandon the amendments which he had already decided to make to the detail of Miss Glover's notation. The residual task of developing a complete scheme of teaching music on that basis was to occupy what spare time he could find.

---

[3] A fuller account, published in 1842, is given in the Appendix, pp. 134–6 below.

Back in Stowmarket once again, John Curwen resumed his dual responsibilities. An additional self-imposed task was now the editing and compilation of the *Independent Magazine*, an educational periodical largely written by himself, which included articles on methods of teaching various subjects in Sunday Schools. The first issue appeared in January 1842, and included not only an account of Curwen's 'Look and Say' method of teaching reading but the first of a series of model music lessons introducing his modified version of Sarah Glover's system. There can be little doubt that it was the extra strain imposed by this further undertaking that finally broke Curwen's health, already giving warning signs during the previous tour. After only eighteen months at Stowmarket, he was obliged to resign his pastorate, going to live quietly with his father at Reading until his health was restored.

Freed from ministerial duty at Reading John Curwen devoted himself to perfecting his system of teaching music. And since Miss Glover was unwilling to accept the proposed changes in her 'Norwich Sol-fa' method, he gave to his own system the name 'Tonic Sol-fa', to emphasise its relevance to any key. At Reading he completed and published at his own expense an account of the new method, *Singing for Schools and Congregations*, which appeared in June 1843. In the preface Curwen, clearly aware of the debt which his system owed to her, paid unreserved tribute to Sarah Glover for providing the foundations upon which his own method was based. In all his subsequent publications he never failed to acknowledge that debt.

Singing for Schools and Congregations was to be the forerunner of many revised versions of Curwen's system. At a later stage in this account the modifications which Curwen introduced in an attempt to perfect the system will be enumerated and discussed. And it is significant that almost as soon as the book appeared he began to test its content on an experimental class of children. In October 1843, he called together some seventy children from the Sunday Schools of Reading for the purpose. It is a bitter comment on the social conditions of the day that the class could meet only at eight in the evening because many of the children did not leave work until then, but it was a further tribute to John Curwen's charisma that he was able to attract so many children under such conditions on two evenings in the week. From the journal which he kept to record the progress of these classes it is possible to trace his growing awareness that the beginner could be helped far more than even Sarah Glover had realised.

Typical of John Curwen's insight into the beginner's difficulties was his realisation at this time that we sing at sight by recalling the 'character' of individual notes in the scale rather than by simply calculating intervals. After describing in his journal some of the mistakes made by the children in pitching intervals, he went on to state his belief that the difficulty did not arise from the mere distance of the notes from one another, but from their relative position in the key. A fourth in one part of the scale, he found, was harder to pitch than another fourth elsewhere. Having formed this theory he began to seek for confirmation in whatever treatises he could lay hands on. Eventually he came across Jue de Berneval's recent book *Music Simplified*; in which a distinct character was attributed to each degree of the scale. Fortified by that concept, Curwen promptly incorporated into his method that deliberate study of the 'mental effects' of the degrees of the scale which later formed an essential element in the Tonic Sol-fa method.

The incident serves to demonstrate that Curwen was not so much trying to 'invent' a new method of teaching music to beginners, as to analyse existing difficulties, then seek such proffered remedies as he could locate in the work of others. As a solution to each new problem was found, he incorporated it with due acknowledgment into the system already founded upon the work of Sarah Glover. That deliberate process of analysis and synthesis was already in operation during the year's convalescence which he spent at Reading. It was to continue throughout his life.

III ACTION (1844–62)

Early in 1844 John Curwen had sufficiently recovered in health to resume ministerial duty. Accepting a new pastorate at Plaistow, then still a rural village some five miles from London, he soon won the affection of the local people, infecting them with his own enthusiasm. The chapel was redecorated, the Sunday School revived; Tonic Sol-fa classes were started. There was no day school, but Curwen quickly found guarantors for one. By midsummer it was opened. For the time being he was content to set aside musical matters. There now seemed no great urgency: his first definitive Tonic Sol-fa book was published, and already the Home and Colonial Model School had adopted it for the training of teachers. This was an encouraging development – for in other training institutions for teachers the government-sponsored 'Hullah' system held sway, and Curwen knew that his own system was unlikely to reach schools through their agency.

A year after arriving in Plaistow John Curwen married Mary Thompson, the daughter of a Manchester cotton manufacturer. They had first met in 1842 when Curwen was lecturing in Manchester and her father had taken the chair for the occasion. Mary's parents were dismayed by the slender means of their daughter's suitor, and at first refused consent to the marriage. But now, at the age of twenty-eight, Curwen was receiving an annual stipend of £160, and whatever reservations Mary's parents may have had, the wedding was approved.

Thereafter John Curwen and his wife were content to make Plaistow their permanent home.

Reviewing his life at Plaistow in those early days John Curwen was later to outline the way in which its planned course was unsettled:

> As a young minister I had – first, my church: second, my Sunday school; and third, my day school. All these came before my duty to music. I was even so jealous of myself that I would not learn the piano, lest I should be tempted to waste time. But looking back, I see that I have been gradually forced, sometimes by strong encouragements, sometimes by misfortune, and more often by the sharp stimulus of opposition, to put music in the front.

For the first four years at Plaistow Curwen's established priorities were maintained. Although music was allotted only the fourth place there, what spare time he could find was given to revising his earlier book. By 1848 a new edition was ready for publication. But no publisher would entertain it. Curwen and his wife agreed to risk all their combined savings to bring it out themselves – though Mary Curwen had little interest in Tonic Sol-fa and vowed that the book would never pay. It appeared later in the same year with the new title, *A Grammar of Vocal Music*, and bearing formal acknowledgment to Miss Glover on its title page. Almost at once the first of the many misfortunes to which Curwen later referred took place.

The secretary of the Home and Colonial School Society wrote reluctantly to inform Curwen that its teacher training institution was passing into Government hands. This meant that the 'Hullah' system of teaching music must in future be adopted there, and that Curwen had lost his only formal contact with music teaching in schools generally. Likening himself to Jonah, Curwen declared that he needed this sudden plunge into the cold waters of rejection to awaken him to a new sense of his mission. The necessary time must be spared from other duties to enable him to publicise his work.

For the next six years John Curwen conducted a personal campaign to make Tonic Sol-fa more widely known. With direct access to the day schools closed to him, he directed his attention instead to meetings of Sunday School teachers, the clergy, mission and temperance workers, and evening classes for adults anxious for 'self-improvement' – that now unfashionable Victorian virtue. His successful work in this last field was to give rise to an unexpected boost to his efforts. In 1851 he was approached by John Cassell, a leading advocate of adult self-education. Encouraged by the success of a series of French lessons published in the magazine *The Working Man's Friend*, Cassell had decided to publish *The Popular Educator*; a weekly magazine costing a penny a copy and 'conveying a large amount of information on all subjects coming within the limits of what may be called an ordinary education'. It was to contain serialised articles on Ancient History, Architecture, Arithmetic, English, Latin, French, German, Geometry, Natural History and Physiology. John Curwen was invited to add to these topics a series of articles on Music.

Cassell's *Popular Educator* enjoyed an enormous circulation, carrying Curwen's exposition of Tonic Sol-fa into thousands of homes. That his lessons were carefully studied is obvious from enquiries raised in the correspondence columns of the magazine, ranging from an anxious letter from a boy worried about his breaking voice to the expostulations of 'Professor of Music', exasperated by Curwen's omission of clefs and key signatures from his early exercises. To the latter Curwen pointed out that these omissions were 'to prevent the pupil attempting to learn too many things at once ... If our correspondent will be patient for a few weeks, he shall be gratified in seeing clefs and time signatures, and flats and sharps gathering in all their ominous dignity at the beginning of the staff.' Other less petulant enquirers were sometimes answered in the course of subsequent articles.

The appearance of John Curwen's first musical article in the *Popular Educator*, on 10 April 1852, marked a welcome upward trend in his affairs. In 1853 he began regular public lectures at Crosby Hall in central London. They were attended by many educationists and called wider attention to his work. In the following autumn four further large meetings of solfaists were held in Finsbury Chapel, Moorfields, at which Curwen spoke and a choir of 150 pupils sang. By this time it was estimated that 2,000 pupils in London and an equal number in the provinces were following his published lessons. Three years later those numbers had multiplied to an astonishing 20,000.

These were encouraging developments. But the growing claims upon his time and energy made by the Tonic Sol-fa movement now began to tell on Curwen. In 1855 a lecturing tour in Scotland taxed him further, making him realise that he could not continue as minister at Plaistow. In November he felt obliged to tender his resignation, explaining that a new chapel was needed and he could not enter upon this fresh responsibility. That announcement caused great concern among the chapel folk, who managed to persuade him to postpone his resignation and to take a long holiday instead.

In April 1856 John Curwen thus travelled with his family to a German spa where he took a month's course of treatment, next spending a further six months at a village near Heidelberg. As his health steadily returned Curwen began to take new interest in his surroundings. The letters which he wrote to his friends and followers in England at that time were later published as *Sketches in Nassau*, a volume sold to raise funds for the new chapel at Plaistow. From it we learn not only of Curwen's delight in the beauties of the countryside, but also of his deep interest in the musical customs of the Germans. There are long descriptions of the congregational singing in various towns and villages. All the children, he found, had regular singing lessons at school. 'No wonder', he declared, 'everyone can sing in Germany!' On one occasion when visiting Wiesbaden he suddenly heard the sound of men's voices singing in parts inside a nearby house. This proved to be, not an organised concert as he had expected, but a group of shoemakers at their daily work. 'Why should not English shoe-makers rejoice in such harmony as this? They soon shall', Curwen wrote.

It was perhaps that incident which prompted John Curwen to investigate the teaching of Harmony while in Germany. As we have already seen, at an early stage of his career he had made a study of Dr Callcott's treatise. But a combination of chance and dogged enquiry now placed in his hands the man-uscript of an unpublished book on Harmony jointly compiled by Josef and Anton Gersbach, teachers in the Normal School at Karlsruhe. Both men had died before the work was published, and Curwen had bought the manuscript from the surviving widow:

> I obtained [he wrote] two months ago, a very valuable manuscript work, the joint production of two brothers, which had cost these highly edu-cated men – thorough educationists as well as musicians – many years of thought and practical testing. It teaches the elements of harmony and composition, not by dogmatic instruction, but by making the pupil con-struct for himself little musical sentences, which are constantly increasing in difficulty and beauty as he goes on ... Even A. B. Marx's great work does not, in the first volume at least, equal Gersbach.

Adolf Bernard Marx's authoritative *Allgemeine Musiklehre*, published while Professor of Music at Berlin University, had first appeared in English trans-lation as the *Universal School of Music* so recently as 1853. Curwen's casual reference to this substantial treatise provides a useful indication of the ambi-tious level which his own musical studies had now reached. His comparison of Marx's book with the Gersbach manuscript, didactically considered, reveals the same objectively analytical approach as he had adopted early in his career when assessing the works of Sarah Glover and his first educational mentors.

At a later stage of this biography, when the development of the Tonic Sol-fa system itself is examined, something of the width and adventurousness of John Curwen's musical reading will be more fully revealed. Meanwhile, his account of the discovery and purchase of the Gersbach manuscript again dem-onstrates Curwen's constant search for teaching materials and ideas. That same alert quest had already led him to assemble, while ostensibly recuperating in Germany, various published collections of popular songs suitable for use in his own classes. Moreover, during the brief visit to Switzerland which ended his holiday, Curwen purchased a copy of Nägeli's *Gesangbildungslehre*, a book then scarcely known in England, which represented the first attempt to apply Pestalozzi's general principles to the teaching of music. All these acquisitions were soon to contribute to the evolution of John Curwen's ideal system.

In the autumn of 1856 Curwen returned refreshed and invigorated to take up his duties at Plaistow. Foremost among these, in his view, was the building of a new chapel. The little village of 1844, when he had first come to Plaistow, had now become part of London's dockland, with rows of terraced dwellings to house the labourers in the shipyards and factories which were springing up along the Thames just over a mile away. This influx of newcomers presented Curwen with a double problem – although a new building to seat something approaching a thousand worshippers was now needed, the gentry and well-to-do who might otherwise have contributed generously to its cost had left the district for more rural surroundings. Curwen threw his new energy into the task of fund-raising, and by 1860 the necessary sum of £3,000 had been raised and the new church was opened.

While that strenuous campaign went ahead, the Tonic Sol-fa movement continued its steady growth. The year 1857 was to witness two major events which attracted the widest public attention. The most vigorous and enterprising among Curwen's disciples had now formed themselves into a Tonic Sol-fa Association. This body decided to hold a Juvenile Choral Meeting by mustering a thousand of their pupils at the Exeter Hall in the Strand – then the largest of London's assembly halls. The event took place in June before a capacity audience. That successful occasion encouraged the Association to undertake a yet more ambitious venture: a concert by no less than 3,000 children in the vast arena of the Crystal Palace, now newly erected on a suburban hilltop at Sydenham.

The result was a triumph exceeding the hopes of even its most optimistic supporters. On 3 September London Bridge Station was besieged from an early hour by an enormous crowd determined to reach Sydenham. Extra trains were hastily summoned, but even then hundreds were disappointed. On the following day every newspaper carried notices of the event at the Crystal Palace and the astonishing scenes which had preceded it. Even the august *Times* felt obliged to record the event in its first public acknowledgment of the existence of Tonic Sol-fa:

> Something like 30,000 people were attracted yesterday to the Crystal Palace, by an entertainment of a peculiar and interesting nature. No doubt most of our readers who now and then give a thought to music, have heard of the 'Tonic Sol-fa Association' although, probably, the majority of them have not the least idea of what it means ... Not to enter further, however, into a dry discussion, we may state that the 'Tonic Sol-fa'

has been taught in a large number of schools, and is spreading all over the United Kingdom. Its influence in London and the vicinities may be understood from the fact that, yesterday, a performance was given at the Crystal Palace, in the Handel Festival orchestra, by between 2000 and 3000 children, boys and girls, from various schools, in which the system has been taught ... The effect was striking, in some degree recalling the meetings of the charity children at St Paul's Cathedral, but with respect to the precision with which the indications of the conductor's stick was obeyed, it was far more remarkable ...

Another newspaper observed that it was left for an almost unknown institution to draw a larger concourse of persons than had ever been attracted in this country to listen to a musical performance. Demands on every side called for a repetition of the concert. But Curwen was firm. Except for the children themselves, he declared, everyone concerned with the concert was worn out. As for the children, too much exhibition was not good for them.

After that triumphant demonstration, the Tonic Sol-fa movement could no longer be described as 'an almost unknown institution'. Curwen was delighted to find public attention so dramatically drawn to his work. Yet he was not without misgivings about one feature of the Crystal Palace concert. Many of the children who took part, it appeared, had been taught the music by rote. In Curwen's eyes, that marked a negative step. His own mind was so concentrated on developing in children the ability to read music that teaching singing by rote seemed to him almost heretical. He was not alone, of course, in that view. The impulse prompting all the nineteenth-century pioneers of popular musical education had been toward the development of musical literacy – often at the expense of the quality of the music sung. It thus seemed to John Curwen that to encourage children to sing what they could not read 'was as much an educational injury as it would be to pass a boy on from addition and subtraction at once to decimals'.

That this was a fallacious view, and that singing and sight reading are in fact complementary, needs little debate today. But John Curwen, perhaps hitherto presented in these pages as a paragon of wisdom, was both a man of his times and possessed of that inflexibility of purpose that verges upon stubbornness. The Crystal Palace success seemed to him 'won by a compromise of thorough educational truthfulness'. He refused to support the Tonic Sol-fa Association in the promotion of similar events in the future.

✳ ✳ ✳

That early disagreement between Curwen and some of his most eager and ambitious teachers led him to believe that a large part of his mission must now be the more thorough training of the teachers, in whose hands the future of the movement lay. A scheme began to form in his mind to establish a central college for the purpose. But as a first step, in December 1857, he called together a small group of his followers for a trial course in harmonic analysis – essential in transcribing advanced sol-fa.

Since his return from Germany Curwen had been studying the Gersbach manuscript and other Harmony manuals with a view to writing a text book on harmonic analysis for solfaists. His progress, frequently interrupted by other calls upon his time, had been slow. But now, just as he had formerly tried out Sarah Glover's *Scheme* upon the little girl in his lodgings, he tested the material he had drafted upon half a dozen of his most proficient teachers, assembled at Christmas in Plaistow for the purpose.

The experiment proved to raise as many problems as it solved. Only after another four years' patient work was Curwen able to publish his *How to Observe Harmony* (1861), a book designed to 'promote a more correct singing and a higher enjoyment of music'. It incorporated the results of an analysis of every chord in Palestrina's *Pope Marcellus Mass*, Handel's *Messiah*, Haydn's *Creation* and Mendelssohn's *Elijah*. That painstaking and improbable exercise had been carried out under Curwen's supervision by one of the teachers who had taken part in the experimental class at Christmas 1857. On that basis the new book examined cadences, chord progressions and modulation. To assist isolated students in working through the book's exercises, Curwen introduced what have been claimed to be the first 'correspondence classes' – an idea soon to be widely adopted by other institutions.

Another sequel to Curwen's stay in Germany was the publication in 1861 of *Songs and Tunes for Education*, a book incorporating material which he had collected abroad. In its preface Curwen emphasised that his aim had been to provide songs which might be made 'a mighty moral agent for developing and elevating the feelings and sentiments of children'. It would have been easier, he remarked, to put together a number of pretty pieces to delight the children: but that would not have satisfied the editor's desire. There, once again, Curwen showed himself to be a man of his time. Indeed, one of the original arguments which had gained a place for music lessons in schools at all, during the nineteenth century, had been the moral benefits arising from the words of well chosen songs.

On the other hand, it is possible to deduce from his preface that Curwen had a further aim in view when compiling *Songs and Tunes for Education*. In a letter written only a few months before that book was compiled he had referred to 'pretty Crystal Palace tunes, which may be drilled into the children, instead of the children being trained up to them'. His use of the phrase 'pretty pieces' in the preface of the new book indicates that Curwen had deliberately chosen for it songs suitable for practice in sight reading rather than singing by rote. The Crystal Palace incident, it seems, still rankled.

IV STRUGGLE (1862–74)

From the viewpoint of his contemporaries John Curwen's future in 1862 must have appeared secure. He was now forty-six years of age, an established public figure and the father of a family – the oldest boy, John Spencer Curwen, now fifteen years old, and soon to become a pupil at the Royal Academy of Music. His home life was happy, his wife and children gladly joining in the clerical work involved in running the Tonic Sol-fa administration – if only at the level of envelope addressing. With the appointment of a co-pastor at Plaistow, some of the weight of pastoral duty was now taken from Curwen's shoulders. He was thus able to undertake extended visits to Ireland and Scotland in that year to promote the teaching of Tonic Sol-fa further. And by then the estimated number of his pupils amounted to no less than 141,000. His goal seemed reached.

In fact, several years of crisis lay ahead. One major setback was the continuing unreliability of Curwen's health. In recent years illness had interrupted his work on several occasions, obliging him to convalesce at the seaside during the winter of 1858, only a year after his return from Germany. And now, the effect of the long, anxious struggle to establish Tonic Sol-fa began to weaken his powers of concentration. Curwen found himself unable to mount the pulpit without misgiving, to take up his pen without faltering. His future seemed to him far from secure.

At exactly which point during the next two years Curwen finally decided that he must abandon his ministry it is not now possible to tell. But it is perhaps significant that during 1862 he began to set up a printing press at Plaistow in order to publish Tonic Sol-fa texts and scores. The period in which printers generally had refused to print Sol-fa notation had now passed; but Curwen had always experienced difficulty in persuading them to conform with the precise requirements of letter-notation. By 1863 the press was established in a nearby cottage. It was soon to print all the publications of the movement.

At the close of 1864, after twenty-one years of his pastorate there, John Curwen finally resigned from the ministry. His own account of the circumstances makes further speculation unnecessary:

> With the help of my wife's property and the profits which, after twenty years, the Sol-fa publications were bringing in I was able to live. But it was a poor life merely to live and do nothing. Well, I could not give lectures;

I could not write books; for a long time I could scarcely write a letter; but I could look after the machinery, look after details of printing, stereotyping, and binding, and so in this dark season of my eclipse I took to business. I have sometimes been blamed for this by those who think that 'once a minister always a minister.' ... But a man must serve as he can. If he is shut out from the highest offices he must be glad to take a humbler post.

The difficult decision over his resignation taken, John Curwen moved to a new house a mile outside Plaistow, the daily walk to his new press providing him with the systematic exercise he would not otherwise have taken. He felt 'much benefited by the change' and, freed from many of his former responsibilities, began slowly to recover once again.

That immediate crisis overcome, John Curwen entered a new phase of his life. It was to be a period which saw the implementation of a major change of policy destined to affect the fortunes of Tonic Sol-fa in what must then have seemed the remote, barely conceivable, future. The consequences of that change during the twentieth century justify a careful review of the circumstances.

Hitherto, and from the earliest period of his musical work, Curwen had always firmly related sol-fa to staff notation. In his earliest publications the position of *doh* on the staff was customarily indicated by means of a square notehead, enabling the pupil to calculate the other degrees of the scale visually. Here are two examples from the *Pupil's Manual:*

The use of this square notehead made clefs and key signatures unnecessary in elementary exercises – a circumstance which had so annoyed 'Professor of Music' in the correspondence columns of the *Popular Educator*.

From that beginning Curwen's lessons, particularly those designed for children, consistently integrated sol-fa and staff notations. The original *Pupil's Manual* thus contained such mnemonics as 'The keynote in sharp signatures is always the note above the last sharp.' In his *Grammar of Vocal Music*, a book designed for adult use, Curwen also dealt fully with staff notation. But there he introduced the subject in an Appendix 'so arranged that it may be commenced at any stage of the pupil's progress.'

That distinction reflected Curwen's realisation that pupils of different ages required different treatment – a theory which he was anxious to stress to his followers:

I believe that the infant must be taught to sing in one way, the elder child in another, and the adult in another ..., that, in schools it is best to follow Pestalozzi – to analyse, elementarise, and develop as faithfully and closely as possible – but that in teaching a Popular Adult Class, with a brief course of lessons, you will be obliged to dogmatize ...

But whether they were adults or children, all Curwen's early pupils were expected to develop familiarity with staff notation at some point in their course. Those who wished to obtain a certificate of proficiency by passing one of the more advanced grade examinations were required to demonstrate a knowledge of both sol-fa and staff.

In later times, when Tonic Sol-fa notation was frequently attacked by professional musicians, his most loyal supporters would often point out that Curwen urged his pupils to learn both notations. What they failed to mention was at least as important – his reason for doing so, and the fact that, at the period now under review, *he changed his mind*. On a matter so often made the subject of disagreement – even in our own time – the most reliable evidence will be John Curwen's own words, given in para. 669 of his *Teacher's Manual*:

The Staff Notation was in the earlier stages of our movement made an essential in the Intermediate and Advanced Certificates. This was for the sake of psalmody. So few books of psalmody were printed in any but the Staff Notation at that time that this was our only way of making the certificate helpful for psalmody. In March, 1863, however, so large a portion of the best known psalm-tune books were already published in the new notation that a change was made. The established notation requirements were made optional.

When we recall the circumstances which first led John Curwen to evolve his method of teaching music, that change of policy becomes more understandable from his point of view. He had been commissioned to find a 'simple' way of enabling humble chapelgoers to read the tunes of their hymns. Now that the unquestionable popularity of Tonic Sol-fa had eventually led many publishers to produce hymnals in that notation, Curwen no longer felt obliged to insist that staff notation be compulsorily studied. He was aware that many of his followers, both teachers and pupils, undertook that study unwillingly.

Moreover, hymnals printed in Tonic Sol-fa proved to be much less costly than those employing staff notation and were thus brought within the reach of the poor. The same consideration applied to other musical scores. And now that Curwen had set up his own press, the publication of an extended repertoire printed in sol-fa had become feasible. Tonic Sol-fa, in Curwen's eyes, was the New Notation. The Old Notation, he declared, could take care of itself.

Consequently, after March 1863, staff notation was no longer to form a compulsory part of class lessons. Those pupils who wished to do so were encouraged to study it at home, by transcribing sol-fa exercises into staff. Not a few took the trouble to do so, receiving an endorsement to that effect on any certificates gained at grade examinations. But the main stream of Tonic Sol-fa teaching now followed a path of deliberate isolation – with consequences that were not at first obvious. Curwen's conviction that sol-fa notation was able to exist in its own right alongside staff notation was so strong at this stage that he devoted considerable time during the 1860s to the preparation of instrumental instruction books based on its use. Their short-lived existence provided the first portent that a false step had been taken.

The flaw that hindsight enables us to detect was far from apparent to Curwen and his followers. Indeed, during the 1860s the Tonic Sol-fa movement advanced still farther, under its banner 'Easy, Cheap and True'. By 1863 the number of pupils had risen to 186,000 in Britain, and the movement was beginning to spread overseas. In Australia, Tonic Sol-fa was adopted by the governments of New South Wales, Southern Australia and Victoria for use in schools, while classes had begun in New Zealand, Canada and South Africa. Elsewhere, missionaries had introduced it to converts in India, Madagascar and the South Sea Islands. Curwen's reaction to this news provides us with a further example of his remarkable musical insight.

Missionaries in oriental countries, Curwen declared, must realise that the music of eastern nations was not confined to the major and minor scales. They must 'expect to find tunes based upon ray or me, or soh as the keynote'. Instead of neglecting this indigenous music they should adapt it to religious purposes – as Luther had done. Missionaries should make a study of native music, not attempt to introduce a style of music foreign to the people. They should be careful, too, not to contradict the natural rhythms of a language when supplying translations of hymns for native use. Particularly in oriental lands, they must realise that harmony was unfamiliar, and not try to force it upon the people. Instead, 'full use should be made of their old musical modes'.

These observations reveal John Curwen's practical wisdom at a time when few orthodox musicians in Britain would have been aware of the need to cater for exotic musical tastes in other lands. They also serve to contradict the view that Tonic Sol-fa was only designed for use with diatonic music – an opinion still expressed in some quarters and directly contradicted here in John Curwen's own words.

On the other hand, the news that Tonic Sol-fa had been formally adopted in the schools of several Australian states served only to arouse Curwen's indignation that so different a situation prevailed in the schools of his own land. There, the government-sponsored Hullah system was the only one to obtain official approval – even though many practising teachers were by now employing the Tonic Sol-fa method which they had learned independently. More to the point, teachers in training were obliged to adopt the Hullah system during their courses and were examined in it before gaining their certificates. Once appointed to schools, many of them found that their training was of little use to them in the classroom. Curwen raised the matter formally with the Education Department, and after long debate it was agreed in 1869 that examination papers for students in training colleges should be set in both staff and sol-fa notations.

The longstanding feud between the Hullah and Curwen factions in teaching music was not one of personal rivalry between the respective leaders, nor was it, as might appear, merely one between staff and sol-fa notations. Although Hullah employed staff notation consistently throughout his lessons, the names given to the notes were those of French sol-fa, the accepted alphabetical note names were never employed. That situation was made yet more idiosyncratic because the sol-fa names were permanently attached to the key of C. Thus, *do* was always C, *re* was always D, etc. Curwen had always rejected this 'fixed' use of sol-fa as fundamentally confusing. Long before the time now under review he had been proved right by the consistent failure of Hullah's child pupils to maintain progress once keys other than C were introduced.

The agreement to admit alternative Tonic Sol-fa notation in training college examinations somewhat appeased Curwen. But when the first set of papers under the new regulations appeared they were found to contain errors in sol-fa notation. This exasperating situation was to continue for a number of years. But meanwhile a new development took place which soon made possible the formal introduction of Tonic Sol-fa in schools generally. Under W. E. Forster's Education Act of 1870, School Boards were set up with local powers to build new schools and supervise their teaching programmes. Where music was concerned many of the local Boards approved the introduction of Tonic Sol-fa. In London itself, that decision was considerably influenced by the teachers' own opinions. The situation was described by John Evans, Inspector of Music to the London Board, in his first report:

> I have now visited all the schools – most of them twice, and many three times. In seventeen schools I found singing was not taught at all ... In seventy-eight schools the children were only taught to sing a few hymns or school songs by ear. Five schools had just begun teaching by the Tonic Sol-fa method. In one the children were being well taught to sing by notes on that method, and had made good progress. The Tonic Sol-fa

method is the only one used in any of the schools where the children are taught to sing by notes ... All the teachers prefer to teach by the Tonic Sol-fa method. Most of them were of opinion that it would be of no use to attempt to teach their children to read music by any other method ... Most of the teachers were anxious that teachers' classes might be opened, that they may have an opportunity of learning it more thoroughly ... I have succeeded in organising three Teachers' classes.

John Curwen was soon gratified to find Her Majesty's Inspectors for schools 'united in almost a chorus of praise for the Tonic Sol-fa method.' By 1871 the total number of pupils employing it was estimated at 315,000. Central government's continuing refusal to admit the system in training colleges was consequently made the subject of a Memorial to the Privy Council in 1874. When that approach was rejected Curwen made the confident claim that public outcry would eventually oblige colleges to meet the demonstrable needs of the schools. And indeed, by 1877, training colleges in Edinburgh, Glasgow, Bangor, Homerton, Hammersmith and Westminster had already adopted Tonic Sol-fa for the training of teachers. Other colleges were soon to follow suit.

During the years that witnessed the struggle to obtain official recognition for Tonic Sol-fa in schools, John Curwen continued in his efforts to perfect the system. For several years he worked on rewriting the original *Standard Course* (1861), the new version appearing in 1872. Among novel features which it contained was the series of 'Time Names' introduced in France by Aimé Paris as the *Langue des Durées* and then forming a regular part of the Galin–Paris–Chevé system. After first learning of the French device Curwen had made several experimental modifications to the names employed; but he eventually decided to adopt them as they stood following years of well-tested use in France, though anglicising them as *taa, taatai, tafatefe,* etc.

A second innovation in the *New Standard Course* was the 'Hand Signs' used to denote the degrees of the scale. These must be considered one of Curwen's most valuable and indestructible contributions to the class music teacher's resources. Widely adopted subsequently, the Hand Signs were evolved for two reasons. First, because they represent visually the different 'character' of each degree, secondly, because they enable the teacher to work facing his pupils. Curwen devised them after watching some of his most capable followers at work with their classes. Unlike many other features of the Tonic Sol-fa method, the Hand Signs were entirely original. And since attempts have sometimes been made to attribute them to sources other than Curwen, it is appropriate to preserve his own account of their origin:

The first occasion on which the manual signs were employed was at Ruthin, in Wales, where I had to address an audience of Welshmen, but few of whom knew English. I found, however, that, through the manual signs, I could speak to them, and make them discourse sweet music to me.

The Hand Signs were first announced in the *Tonic Sol-fa Reporter*, the movement's magazine since 1851, in 1870. Many years later, as we shall see, the sign for *fah* was altered to accommodate chromatic alteration more readily, but apart from that advantageous modification, Curwen's original Hand Signs for the degrees of the major scale have remained in use.

Another of Curwen's pursuits at this time was the preparation of a new edition of his *How to Observe Harmony*. The original version of that book had appeared in 1861 to afford a brief introduction to harmonic analysis. Within ten years some eight hundred students had satisfactorily worked their way through its exercises. In 1866 William Euing founded a music lectureship at Anderson's College, Glasgow, urging John Curwen to be its first holder. He agreed to deliver only the first term's lectures, living at Glasgow for the purpose during the winter of 1866–7 and lecturing twice a week. That experience, and the studies which he undertook to fulfil the role, next led to Curwen's arranging frequent consultations with G. A. Macfarren, then Professor of Music at Cambridge University, whose writings he had studied and who seemed to him 'the deepest and clearest thinker of harmony'. All these events contributed toward the publication of a new and much enlarged edition *of How to Observe Harmony* in 1872.

The appearance of Helmholtz's German treatise *On the Sensations of Tone* in 1863, had at once attracted Curwen's notice as a man now deeply interested in music's theoretical aspects. After studying the book with fascinated attention he at once presented a brief summary of its content in the *Tonic Sol-fa Reporter*, pursuing the subject further by attending a course of lectures on Acoustics at University College, London. Following that initiation, he began to prepare a book which should bring the results of his own studies to his followers in the Tonic Sol-fa movement. The result was *Musical Statics*, a book which appeared in 1874, two years before A. J. Ellis's English translation of Helmholtz's *Die Lehre von den Tonempfindungen* was published. Curwen intended his book to form the first part of a larger, comprehensive work embracing all branches of musical study. But that task was still uncompleted at his death.

Throughout all this time Curwen was frequently called upon to address audiences of supporters in many parts of Britain. But perhaps the most memorable public occasion so far came when he was invited, in August 1873, to act as one of the judges at the Welsh National Eisteddfod. During the ceremonies which opened the meeting Curwen learned that 'the literary brotherhood of Wales acknowledges my musical writings and musical activities and would be pleased to confer on me a title.' Thus it was that John Curwen later found himself standing bareheaded before the presiding Druid to receive the title *Dyrwent Pencerdd* – a tribute which he modestly hoped his followers would see as the formal recognition by the Welsh nation of the work of Tonic Solfaists throughout the world.

In the following year he was to receive another tribute, of a different kind but equally sincere, from his English supporters. In December 1874, the Exeter Hall, London, – the scene of one of the movement's first triumphs – was again filled with Tonic Solfaists, this time to see their hero receive a national testimonial. He was presented with a life-size portrait in oils and a purse containing £200. Sitting, or rather standing, for the portrait at the artist's Hampstead studio had been a taxing experience which Curwen accepted as his own contribution to the success of the occasion. The purse he had already decided to donate toward the realisation of a long cherished ideal – the foundation of a Tonic Sol-fa College.

V ACHIEVEMENT (1874–80)

The last years of John Curwen's life were dominated by his resolve to establish a college for the training of Tonic Sol-fa teachers. The idea had been in his mind ever since the first Crystal Palace concert in 1857 and had prompted that first gathering of Harmony students at Plaistow the following Christmas. In 1864 he took the project a stage further by announcing in the *Tonic Sol-fa Reporter* that his chief attention would in future be devoted to the improvement of the movement's teachers rather than to propagation of the method itself. The formation of a 'Tonic Sol-fa School', concerned with training and examining teachers of music, was now announced. As a temporary measure classes were held in the printing offices at Plaistow.

Ten years later, when addressing the audience assembled in the Exeter Hall for the presentation of his testimonial in 1874, Curwen affirmed his ambition to establish a permanent college. A campaign to raise £5,000 for the purpose was launched; and, as we have seen, the purse he then received from his followers was promptly devoted to that cause. While fund raising continued, often disappointingly, Curwen applied himself to writing an appropriate text book, his *Teacher's Manual of the Art of Teaching as applied to Music*. Published in 1875, that book was the first of its kind in the language. In many ways it must be considered his major work, summing up the educational principles upon which his own teaching had been based and deserving a distinctive place in the annals of educational literature.

John Spencer Curwen declared that his father's *Teacher's Manual* was written *con amore*. A young man's heart, he observed, stirred within the veteran's as he remembered his own early experience as a teacher, his fondness for teaching and talking with children, his study of Stow and Abbott. And indeed, even today the reader will find himself impressed by John Curwen's exposition of general educational principles, illustrated by excerpts from the writing of his mentors from Abbott to Spencer. Here is no jargon-ridden theorising, but the earnest common sense of an experienced and dedicated teacher.

The *Teacher's Manual* comprises almost 400 closely printed pages. The opening section, nearly a quarter of its length, is devoted to principles common to the teaching of all subjects. Next follows detailed application of those principles to the teaching of music. Developments in the Tonic Sol-fa method over a period of thirty years are next described, so as to illustrate ways in which careful analysis and planning of procedures can improve methods of teaching. Finally, there is an encyclopaedic section offering practical guidance on every aspect of teaching singing and note reading. Although now dated, much of the book remains valuable.

The *Teacher's Manual* completed, the as yet unbuilt Tonic Sol-fa College was incorporated in June 1875. Its administration was to be in the hands of a Council whose elected members must represent certain prescribed occupations – teachers, ministers of religion, merchants, mechanics, etc. – a policy adopted to prevent a monopoly of interest passing to any one class. By 1879 sufficient funds had at last been raised to start building on a site purchased at Forest Gate. On 14 May John Curwen laid a foundation stone there, inscribed to the memory of Sarah Glover, who had died in 1867. This was a symbolic act to record permanently her place as foundress of the movement. In July a completed wing of the new college was formally declared open and the first students assembled for the annual summer school subsequently held there for many years.

The opening of the Tonic Sol-fa College provided a more appropriate headquarters for the movement and seemed to John Curwen to set the seal of permanence upon his work. But less than a year of life remained for him to enjoy that achievement. Once again his health, severely taxed by his nationwide travels to raise money for the college, began to fail. Any unusual exertion left him short of breath, and now, the death of his brother and serious illness of his wife further reduced his powers of resistance. During the summer he lectured each day at the college on the art of teaching. Again in the following winter he taught each week at the Saturday classes held for London students. But though he was careful to walk slowly, and now never ventured to climb a hill on foot, his breathing troubled him seriously. His wife's death, in January 1880, utterly broke his spirit, and though Curwen tried to continue his duties as leader of the Tonic Sol-fa movement, his followers were struck by his enfeebled condition.

At length, persuaded that without the strength to work he no longer wished to live, John Curwen died on 26 May 1880, at the age of sixty-four.

Before following the fortunes of the movement during the century after its founder's death, we must not fail to notice the violent criticisms levelled against Tonic Sol-fa by John Curwen's professional contemporaries. Almost all those noisy objections were against the form of notation employed, though some were directed against Curwen personally as a musically ignorant interloper. Both criticisms call for comment.

The social and philanthropic circumstances which led to the exclusive use of sol-fa notation in Curwen's later publications have already been remarked. From a purely musical viewpoint there is little doubt that his eventual decision to curtail the use of staff notation was a regrettable one. Unfortunately, their dislike of his unorthodox notation prevented Curwen's most vocal critics from examining his methods of teaching. Disgusted by his notation, the professional musician of the day failed to discover the educational advantages that made Curwen's manner of training the ear far in advance of the methods then customary.

A generation after Curwen's death, however, blind condemnation of Tonic Sol-fa was less pronounced. Many eminent musicians had learned from experience that in spite of its unappetising notation Tonic Sol-fa laid secure musical foundations. Misgivings over the notation itself remained, but results had now shown the value of Curwen's practical methods, and his more ambitious pupils were in any case equipping themselves to use orthodox notation. The professors of music at both Oxford and Cambridge at that time were each prepared to announce publicly their approval of Tonic Sol-fa as a basic form of musical training – especially for use in schools.

His critics' unworthy picture of John Curwen as musically ignorant must not remain unchallenged. The briefest enquiry will produce a truer estimate. There is no doubt that when he first undertook his imposed mission to find a simple way of teaching music to humble chapelgoers Curwen knew very little about the subject. So much he admitted at the time. But what he did possess then was a twofold gift that many cultivated musicians lack – the natural equipment of a teacher, and the ability to assume a child's curiosity in learning. From that beginning, Curwen went on to develop true intellectual curiosity leading to a patient study and analysis of music and the resources for teaching it which lasted throughout his life. Few of his critics will have been at such pains to equip themselves to *teach* music. Most of them had been content to leave the task in schools unattempted.

The width of Curwen's musical reading, even at that early stage of his career when he produced his first substantial text book, the *Grammar of Vocal Music*, may cause surprise. By assembling only the titles which are actually cited in its pages, a catalogue sufficient to refute the charge of musical ignorance is readily provided:[4]

J. Callcott, *Musical Grammar* (1806)*

E. Jue de Berneval, *Music Simplified* (1832)*

W. Bryce, *Rational Introduction to Music* (1845)

J. Mainzer, *Music and Education* (1848) [CTME 12]

S. Glover, *Scheme for Rendering Psalmody Congregational* (1835) [CTME 5]

C. Burney, *General History of Music* (1789)

W. E. Hickson, *The Singing Master* (1836) [CTME 10]

M. B. Wilhem, *Méthode de lecture musicale* (1839)

J. Hullah, *Wilhem's Method of Teaching Singing* (1842) [CTME 7]

J. J. Waite, *The Hallelujah* (1842)

A. Wallbridge [A. W. Lunn], *Sequential System of Notation* (1843)

J. Turle and E. Taylor, *The Singing Book* (1846)*

G. F. Graham, *Theory and Practice of Musical Composition* (1838)

C. Dawson, *Analysis of Musical Composition* (n.d.)

J. Hamilton, *Catechism of Counterpoint etc. ...* (1837)

A. J. Reicha, *Traité de melodie* (1814)

G. Hogarth, *Memoirs of the Musical Drama* (1839)

P. Thompson, *Instruction to my Daughter for Playing on the Enharmonic Guitar*

J. Goss, *Introduction to Harmony and Thoroughbass* (1833)

G. Weber, *Versuch einer geordneten Theorie* (1815) [trans. 1846]

F. Oakeley, *Laudes Diurnae* (1843)

J. Hullah, *Grammar of Vocal Music* (1844)

R. Druett, ed., *The Parish Choir* (1848–50)

J. A. Latrobe, *The Music of the Church* (1831)

W. Crotch, *Specimens of Various Styles of Music* (1806)

W. Crotch, *Elements of Musical Composition* (1812) [CTME 16]

Something of the adventurousness of John Curwen's later musical enquiries has already been suggested when describing some of the new features which he added from time to time to his teaching methods. The youthful

---

[4] In the following list, items that were issued in the Classic Texts in Music Education series are shown with their series numbers in brackets. In addition, Rainbow wrote prefaces to items marked with an asterisk; these are published in *Four Centuries of Music Teaching Manuals, 1518–1932* (Woodbridge: Boydell Press, 2009). Ed.

discovery of Sarah Glover's *Scheme* had prompted a lifelong quest for further enlightenment.

The meticulous care with which John Curwen always acknowledged his indebtedness to Sarah Glover as the originator of Tonic Sol-fa should not lead us to suppose that he was a plagiarist. In the matter of nomenclature alone there were considerable differences between Norwich Sol-fa and Tonic Sol-fa. Where chromatic notation is concerned, those differences are perhaps best revealed by setting out the notes of a single octave side by side in each notation:

	NORWICH SOL-FA				TONIC SOL-FA	
♭	♮	♯		♭	♮	♯
	DO				DOH	
	TE				TE	
Tow		Loy		ta		le
	LAH				LAH	
Low		Soy		la		se
	SOLE				SOH	
Sow		Foy				fe
	FAH				FAH	
	ME				ME	
Mow		Roy		ma		re
	RA				RAY	
Row		Doy		ra		de
	DO				DOH	

Curwen's spelling of the diatonic note names was less ambiguous and his inflected syllables more singable than the original Norwich versions. A difference still greater was to occur over the notation of modulation.

Sarah Glover marked the point at which modulation took place by changing the name of the syllable immediately before the transition, by way of warning. A simple modulation to the dominant key was introduced by the syllable *tu* (as in the tune *Abridge* in Chapter II [pp. 100–7] above). More extreme modulations called for a bevy of other new note names, among them such unattractive vocables as *moze, baw, cole, gah* and *daze*. In his early *Grammar of Vocal Music* (1848) Curwen adopted the same general policy (*tu* appears in his version of *Abridge* above); but his own new syllables, *fi, ne, nu, ni, ge* and *ke*, however strange they may now appear, were less cumbersome than their predecessors. Moreover, Curwen finally concluded that his existing chromatic note names sufficed to indicate modulation, and with the publication of the *Standard Course* in 1861, the 'warning' syllables were permanently dropped.

The change was first announced in a footnote, dated 1859, in the *Grammar*. But, in practice, ever since 1843 Curwen had indicated simple modulation by means of a 'bridge-tone'. Like many other features of Tonic Sol-fa, this device was 'borrowed' from another source. The Revd J. J. Waite, a fellow Independent minister already known to Curwen for his energetic efforts to develop congregational singing, employed numerals rather than sol-fa notation for his lessons. Waite's proposal for indicating modulation was to allot to the new tonic a double name representing its relative position in both the old and new keys. An example will show Waite's recommendation and the adaptation which Curwen made of it:

Waite:	Five	one	seven	six	five	fiv-'one	seven	one
Curwen:	soh	doh'	te	lah	soh	s-doh	te,	doh

As with every other 'borrowed' device incorporated into Tonic Sol-fa, Curwen was careful to acknowledge the source from which the bridge-tone was taken. Indeed, his writings constantly refer to the works of others from whom he has adopted one or another tested device. By assembling here some outstanding examples of his acknowledged indebtedness to other teachers the scale of his activities as an agent of synthesis, rather than as the 'inventor' of a method, will be more fully revealed.

Apart from his own inherited gifts, the inspiration for much of John Curwen's teaching was provided by Pestalozzi. Although Curwen's first awareness of the Swiss educational reformer's precepts came from the writings of his disciples in Britain, rather than from the master himself, Curwen quickly became familiar with Pestalozzi's basic tenets: the easy before the difficult; the concrete before the abstract; teach one thing at a time; the thing before the sign; let each step arise from what has gone before; allow intelligence to assist mechanical skill. These were precepts which coloured all Curwen's own teaching and methodising. He in turn commended them to his followers.

From Sarah Glover, Curwen learned the use of the sol-fa initials as a preliminary form of notation, the superiority of a movable *doh*, and the possibility of developing instinctive recognition of relative pitch through controlled exercise. Jue de Berneval's *Music Simplified* introduced Curwen to the theory of the 'mental effects' of each degree of the scale, and gave him the square-headed note to represent the position of the tonic on the staff. Nägeli's *Gesangbildungslehre*, first made known to Curwen by the visiting American teacher, Lowell Mason, suggested that the study of rhythm and pitch was best conducted separately. Some ideas on the teaching of dynamic markings were also drawn from that book. The Revd J. J. Waite not only provided the principle of the 'bridge-tone' but also introduced Curwen to Rousseau's scheme for a simplified form of notation.

From Aimé Paris came the *Langue des Durées*, which Curwen anglicised as the 'French Time-Names'. The publications of W. E. Hickson, Joseph Mainzer, B. C. Natorp, C. A. Zeller, Lowell Mason and others were the acknowledged sources of many of Curwen's singing exercises, part-songs and vocal pieces. The Gersbach brothers provided the stimulus for his first essay in harmonic analysis, an enterprise which led to deeper study of Bernard Marx and English writers from Crotch to Macfarren. For his published chapters on Voice Production and Elocution Curwen drew upon Waldmann, Reismann, Nauenburg, Garcia, Sabilla Novello and many others. By analysing his writings more thoroughly, the list might be extended indefinitely. But even in its present incomplete state, it serves to demonstrate the thoroughness and determination that John Curwen brought to the creation of the Tonic Sol-fa method.

VI SEQUEL (1880–1980)

Upon the death of his father, John Spencer Curwen continued and developed his work. Now in his early thirties, although originally intended for the ministry like his father and grandfather, he had become a student at the Royal Academy of Music on leaving school, and had shared in the running of the printing press at Plaistow since its inception. Under his direction and that of his own sons, while maintaining its original function by publishing Tonic Sol-fa scores, the firm of J. Curwen and Sons was to extend its range, eventually becoming noted for the publication of many vocal works by younger contemporary British composers.

With John Spencer Curwen at its head the Tonic Sol-fa movement continued to flourish. One of his innovations was the establishment of England's first competitive musical festival, at Stratford in 1882, on something of the lines of a Welsh Eisteddfod. The idea of a gathering of amateur English musicians on that pattern had been in his father's mind when he had been made a bard in Wales in 1873. Its realisation now fell to his son. John Spencer Curwen also completed some of his father's unfinished books, including *How to Read Music* (1881), and was responsible for revised editions of various earlier texts such as the *New Standard Course* (1901).

By the turn of the century Tonic Sol-fa had become established on a worldwide basis. Apart from the British colonies, the system flourished in the mission field in outposts as remote as Fiji, Japan, Burma and China. And now, the remarkable sight singing of elementary schoolchildren in Britain had begun to attract the notice of educationists in other European countries.

In the Spring of 1897 Count Giuseppe Franchi-Verney della Valetta was appointed to enquire into the teaching of music in French and English schools on behalf of the Italian Ministry of Public Instruction. On his return to Italy his report was issued by the Italian government. From it we learn that he was struck by the absence in England of the state-dominated syllabus imposed in French schools. The enthusiasm and interest shown by the teachers also impressed him. Unlike their Italian counterparts, who tolerated music in schools without encouraging it, English teachers 'fostered it with diligent assiduity'.

After witnessing Tonic Sol-fa lessons at a school in Hampstead, the Count declared that it would be difficult to exaggerate his surprise at what was achieved:

> The results of this system [he went on] which, as I have said, appeared to me perfectly astounding, made me keenly desirous of studying it carefully; but my stay in London had already been too prolonged and I was therefore unable to make further investigations.

Before compiling his report, Count Verney corresponded with John Spencer Curwen who volunteered to provide full details of Tonic Sol-fa 'which has been tried with the most satisfactory results in other countries of Europe and was the subject of keen interest on the part of the late lamented Professor Roberts who had proposed to introduce it, at any rate experimentally, into our Italian schools'.

Elsewhere in his report, however, Franchi-Verney confessed that though the English did not surpass the Italians in musical aptitude, they excelled in system, in discipline and willingness to co-operate. He therefore felt obliged to conclude that methods which worked satisfactorily in England would be doomed to failure in his own country.

He might well have added that an obstacle quite as great was the adoption in Italy of the 'fixed *do*' nomenclature. There, as in France, the introduction of Tonic Sol-fa must cause confusion to the beginner – since the notes of the scale of C were already given the names *do, re, mi, fa, sol,* etc. To avoid that ambiguity, teaching on the tonic principle in France relied upon numerals for denoting the degrees of the scale: a system originating with Rousseau and continued by the Galin–Paris–Chevé Association. Thus, in effect, although Chevé used numerals and Curwen employed movable sol-fa, their systems were closely parallel – sufficiently so for John Spencer Curwen to declare, 'Chevé and Tonic Sol-fa are brother and sister. Whatever arguments are used for or against either apply to both. The existence and the extension of both movements at the present day (1901) is a proof of the universally felt need of approaching the staff notation through an enlightening medium.'

It was consequently in countries where fixed sol-fa was not adopted that

Tonic Sol-fa offered most advantage. It was soon to be introduced in adaptations in German-speaking Switzerland, Flemish-speaking Belgium, and in Poland. But the first important continental version of Tonic Sol-fa had already been introduced in Germany under the name *Tonika Do*, in 1897.

Over the centuries the excellence of music teaching in German schools had become legendary. Yet, during the nineteenth century, song teaching by rote had taken the place of the systematic music lessons of the past, particularly in urban schools. Although John Curwen had found music teaching in country schools impressive while in Germany in 1856, the formal visit which John Hullah made in 1878 to report on the state of school music in Germany revealed the decline which had by then taken place. The legend had become a myth, and Hullah's *Report* on the situation later provoked Hermann Kretzschmar, Director of the Berlin High School of Music, to publish his *Musikalische Zeitfragen* (1903) describing the straits in which music teaching was found at the turn of the century.

The publication of Kretzschmar's challenging document is usually taken to mark the beginning of a drive to reform music teaching in German schools. But, in fact, a personal effort in that direction was made earlier by Agnes Hundoegger, a teacher who had experienced the results of Tonic Sol-fa teaching in England and decided to introduce it in her own country. From 1897 she set out to adapt Curwen's method to suit the needs of German schools under the title *Tonika Do*. She retained all the principal features of the system, including Curwen's Hand Signs, but introduced one significant modification. Instead of notating rhythm by means of punctuation marks, Hundoegger employed the symbols first proposed by Rousseau, grouping quavers and semi-quavers under horizontal lines similar to tails of orthodox notes:

By 1909 *Tonika Do* was sufficiently established in Germany to justify the formation of a *Tonika Do* League and the establishment of a publishing company. On the death of Agnes Hundoegger in 1926 the movement was taken over by Maria Leo; then by Dora Gotzmann (died 1939) and Elisabeth Noack. Widely used in German schools, the system was regularly revised – but without losing any further features of Curwen's Tonic Sol-fa. The eighth revised edition of the *Lehrweise nach Tonika Do*, prepared by Maria Leo and published in 1942, was almost entirely destroyed by bombing attacks over Berlin and Leipzig. It was followed by a ninth edition in 1951, revised by Dr Elisabeth Noack whose preface outlines the history of the movement up to that point. In that preface reference is made to Sarah Glover's part in the evolution of Tonic Sol-fa: but, strangely, the name of the originator is incorrectly given as John *Spencer* Curwen. That readily detectable error, unimportant though it appears, will assume greater significance later in this survey.

A much later instance of the adaptation of Tonic Sol-fa for use in a continental country occurred in the case of Hungary. During several visits to England beginning in 1927 Zoltán Kodály was made aware of the 'highly developed singing' (his own words) found in the elementary schools of this country. The situation particularly interested him because at that time he was pondering on plans to reform the teaching of music in the schools of his own land by stressing the use of hitherto neglected national folksong and encouraging the development of musical literacy. The material for the first of those aims was already available through his own researches and those of Béla Bartók, a basis for the second now presented itself through his discovery of John Curwen's Tonic Sol-fa.

Official opposition prevented formal acceptance of Kodály's plans for national reform in Hungary until 1945. But during the 1930s, with the co-operation of his pupils and former pupils, he was already developing suitable materials and methods on the lines argued in his manifesto. *Children's Choirs* (1929). Between 1937 and 1943 various collections of songs and exercises were published, including his *Bicinia Hungarica* and *Songs for Schools*. Throughout all this time Tonic Sol-fa provided the basis of his recommended method of teaching – but with certain important modifications.

The first of these concerned notation. Instead of using the system of letters and punctuation marks (which Curwen favoured for its cheapness) Kodály took the *Tonika Do* version derived from Rousseau to its logical conclusion by combining note stems and tails with sol-fa initials in his early lessons:

At the same early stage he related sol-fa symbols to a clefless stave, as Curwen had originally done, marking the place of *doh* with its initial letter rather than a square note head:

Kodály's second modification was to Curwen's Hand Signs. Although minimal, the changes he made were important ones, introducing distinct practical advantages.

It will be seen, from Curwen's original chart (below), that his own sign for *te* was an upward pointing finger. To indicate *ta*, the flattened seventh, Kodály chose to point that finger downward – a clear pictorial representation. But since Curwen had already employed the downward pointing finger to represent *fah*, Kodály introduced in its place a new sign, the closed fist with downward pointing thumb. The sharpened fourth, *fe*, was then indicated by turning the thumb upwards. Similarly, *soh* was sharpened to *se* by again raising the thumb. The simplicity and increased representational value of these modifications are their own justification.

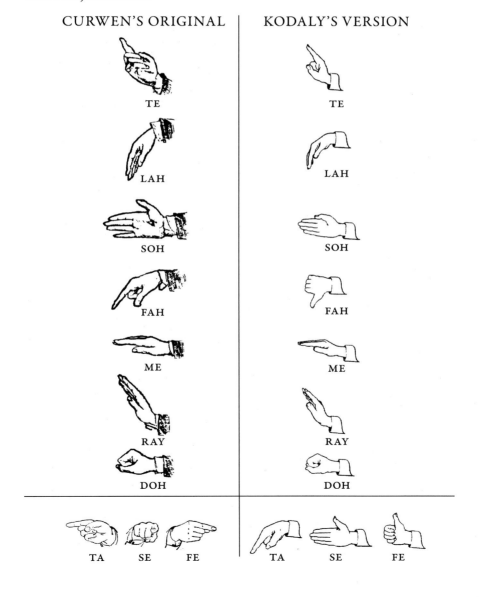

CURWEN'S ORIGINAL	KODALY'S VERSION
TE	TE
LAH	LAH
SOH	SOH
FAH	FAH
ME	ME
RAY	RAY
DOH	DOH
TA SE FE	TA SE FE

Apart from these two modifications to purely *visual* details of Tonic Sol-fa, Kodály adopted the system to an extent that left Curwen's teaching principles intact. That he chose to emphasise the pentatonic scale in his early teaching stages was due to the strong pentatonic element present in the national folk-song of Hungary.

In a Foreword to the first English version of his *Choral Method* Zoltán Kodály wrote:

> I am now pleased to return to the English what I learned from them, and was able to adapt to our needs in Hungary.

The parent body in England, the Tonic Sol-fa Association, has acknowledged that gracious tribute and reciprocated by adopting Kodály's modifications as unquestionably beneficial. In doing so, they have in mind John Curwen's own words: 'Those who have known me longest have found me ever ready to adopt improvements.' Had he been alive to do so, Curwen would surely have conceded that the need for letter notation had now passed, and that the new Hand Signs for *fah, fe, se* and *ta* were logically justified.

On the other hand, John Curwen would have been less than gratified by some more recent accounts of the origins of the Kodály Method. Notably, in that connection, mention must be made of the definitive *Musical Education in Hungary* (1966) edited by Frigyes Sándor. There, in the chapter on Sol-fa Teaching contributed by Erzsébet Szőnyi, Curwen's Hand Signs are attributed to Fritz Jöde, the author of the treatise *Musikalische Jugendkultur* published in 1918. Since, in the same chapter, the originator of Tonic Sol-fa itself is said to be John *Spencer* Curwen, it is apparent that these claims have been based upon familiarity with the *Lehrweise nach Tonika Do* (where the same misattribution occurs) rather than with John Curwen's own publications.

It seems appropriate, in presenting a fresh account of the life and work of John Curwen, to draw attention to such incorrect statements – not only in the interest of historical accuracy, but because they were given currency at a time when John Curwen's unique contribution to musical education was less appreciated in his own country than he deserved. It is ironical to find that at the very time when Kodály was making Tonic Sol-fa the basis of a drive to develop musical literacy in his own country, the system was being allowed to lapse into a decline in England. The reasons for that decline are complex and call for comment.

Well within living memory in Britain it was not unusual to find members of choral societies and church choirs who had learned Tonic Sol-fa without troubling to master the use of staff notation. As a result they could take part only when scores printed in their customary notation were made available. Fellow choristers brought up on more orthodox lines treated this foible as a mark of inferiority. In this way Tonic Sol-fa suffered a serious loss of esteem, the term itself becoming synonymous with a 'peculiar' form of notation, rather than with a proven method of training in aural perception.

A new generation of school teachers at this time, drawn from families where the possession of a piano had now become a token of respectability, often started their musical lives as modest pianists. Lacking a vocalist's outlook, and automatically prejudiced against Tonic Sol-fa, they were only too ready to neglect teaching it in schools. The broadening of the school music curriculum which took place during the thirties and forties provided an excuse for doing so. A new vogue for percussion bands, bamboo pipes and recorders, however meritorious in other ways, was now allowed to separate note reading from aural perception, often to supplant rather than complement singing. The advent of the classroom gramophone further reduced the limited lesson time available while calling for little technical expertise on the teacher's part.

The amazing growth in the scope of music teaching in our schools since 1960 has had the unfortunate result of endangering the fine tradition of choral singing and squeezing aural training out of the curriculum in all too many instances. That these changes took place against the shadowy background of such social manifestations as the rise of 'mass culture', 'élitism', and 'radical chic' considerably increased their impact.[5]

Understandably then, as news of Kodály's successful reform of music teaching in Hungary began to filter through in the sixties, teachers who had grown alarmed by the *nostalgie de la boue* which seemed to dominate popular musical taste, looked to him for salvation. Here, it seemed, was a man who offered a comprehensive scheme of musical training from nursery school to conservatoire which had transformed musical education in his own country. It sprang, they learned, from a new teaching technique known as 'relative sol-fa'.

Unacquainted with Tonic Sol-fa in their own schooldays, some hopeful readers of English versions of Kodály's Method failed to recognise the English origins of 'relative sol-fa'. Moreover, they were not to know that the thorough scheme of musical training which followed the early stages of that Method depended for its nationwide success on a state-controlled educational system quite as rigidly regimented as that under the *Code Napoleon*.

It is beyond the scope of this short survey to debate the merits of state-controlled educational systems, in music or elsewhere. But we recognise that a rigidly imposed curriculum would be unacceptable to teachers in this country, whatever theoretical advantages might be claimed for it. That being so, no matter how wistfully we may regard the musical achievements of Hungarian

[5] The known case of a London headmaster who disbanded his school choir as an undesirably élitist activity deserves to be recorded here. One wonders if the football team was abolished, for the same reason.

schools, we must evolve our own solutions. And the lesson to be learned from Kodály is that we have underestimated and neglected in Curwen's work an important part of our national heritage in musical education.

Once that fact is accepted, a start can be made toward making good the lack which at present weakens the structure of school music in Britain: a common core of systematic guidance in aural perception. In spite of the adventurous and successful work carried out in many schools, a child who moves from one school to another is liable to face disruption of his musical experience. One school tends to concentrate upon an aspect of music making not found in another. There is seldom a common element to link the music programme in different schools.

But since every kind of musical experience depends upon the ear, the true basis of all fruitful music teaching is aural training. Its general revival seems desirable, to act as a common denominator in school music which would both complement the wide range of activity at present found in different schools and also provide continuity for pupils moving between them. A start might be made by developing closer contact between individual secondary schools and the primary schools that feed them. Recent local experiments have shown that class teachers in primary schools welcome liaison of this kind, while their secondary colleagues look forward to future intakes who have learned to use their ears and voices intelligently and can read simple tunes.

The principles upon which Tonic Sol-fa is based supply a remarkably efficient, proven means of developing aural perception at primary school level. The Curwen centenary year seems to offer an appropriate occasion to press for the restoration of his work to its neglected place in the music curriculum. No acknowledgment of John Curwen's endeavours could be more fitting. Some tribute is certainly his due.

April, 1979

APPENDIX: A VISIT TO MISS GLOVER'S SCHOOL

John Curwen's own account published in the *Independent Magazine*, 1842, p. 240

This is an infant school at Norwich. It does not differ in its general aspect and arrangements from other infant schools. The daily employments of the children, their average age, and their appearance, correspond with what may be seen in most schools of a similar kind. But in one thing they are remarkably distinguished from all other schools that we have ever seen. These little children conduct their singing exercises with so much facility and delight, and, at the same time, with such accuracy both of time and tune, as to fill with astonishment all who hear them. Our readers will readily believe that this must be the case, when we tell them that, in the course of our visit, we heard the children sing canons in four, six and even in eight parts, with great precision and beauty of execution. This was done from notes, without any instrument to lead them, and only in one case did the voices flatten, and in that case only by half-a-tone. To those who have been accustomed to the singing of young children, this will appear indeed astonishing, but we shall astonish them still more when we say, that the training which has produced such results does not occupy more than two hours in the week! – a length of time not greater than is given to singing exercises in every infant school in the land! Whence, then, arises the difference? From this cause – that, while in other schools, the time is loosely spent without plan or design, in Miss Glover's school the time is husbanded by a carefully arranged method. But this is not sufficient to explain all: it is necessary to add, that the method itself contains *more of true science*; and *less of technicality*; then any other method now taught in England.

We will first describe the system as we saw it in operation, and then examine briefly its principles.

As we entered the room, the soft and regulated tone, and the sweet blending of the voices, such as to take not the ear by force, but steal on the senses as by some magic spell, assured us that music, real music, with all its subduing power, dwelt there.

On the gallery were seated all the younger children, with heads erect and shoulders back, singing (with the Sol-fa syllables), and as they sung, eagerly looking towards an upright board which stood at a little distance from the foot of the gallery. On this board were printed one above the other the initial letters of the Sol-fa syllables, showing much shorter distances between *Me* and *Fah* and between *Te* and *Do* (the third and fourth, and seventh and eighth *of the scale*; for in this method *Do* is always the key-tone) than between the other notes. This *Musical Ladder*, as it is styled, corresponds with what we call the Modulator. By the side of the 'Ladder' stood a little monitor with a wand in her hand. She was pointing to the notes as the children sang them. The very movement of her wand was musical. She also held in charge with her other hand, a little infant, the youngest in the school, who could scarcely stand, but who nevertheless could sing. The children are taught to sing in this way, looking at the exact intervals as depicted on the Musical Ladder, until they enter the higher class of the school. This may be in the course of six months, or in a much shorter time. We did not observe any distinct classification for the singing lessons; they are taken as part of the ordinary routine of the school. The children are thus rendered perfectly familiar with *an accurate pictorial representation of interval*; indeed they must carry a musical ladder in their mind's eye wherever they go, and by the correct association of mind thus established, they are well prepared for the next stage in their advancement.

This we had an opportunity of examining in another part of the room, where stood a class of twenty – the elder children in the school – having in their left hand the 'Sol-fa Tune Book', and in their right, short wands for the purpose of beating time.

The tune books were supported on a small instrument in the shape of a cross, with the longest bar extending beyond the book to the right-hand. Upon this projecting part of the 'book-holder', as soon as the tune began, the loud beats of the measure were pretty sharply struck, while the soft beats were indicated by gentle touches of the wand on their left arm.

Miss Glover, the lady from whose invention and zealous patronage all these results have sprung, and whose Christian solicitude for the better interests of the children thus taught we have been thankful to witness, with a courtesy which we cannot too gratefully acknowledge, kindly exhibited to us every part of the method. The plan of procedure was in this wise: – Supposing them about to sing the 14th canon, which is in eight parts, the teacher steps into the middle of the circle and announces 'fourteenth canon.' Immediately eight children hold up their wands, dividing the class into equal portions, so that each child may know which leader she is to follow. The chord of the keytone is then struck on a glass harmonicon, which is placed in the room for the purpose, and the canon begins. When the first division has sung the first measure, the monitor of the next division, giving a glance at those under her, which means 'follow me,' takes up the strain, beating time upon the book-holder and her arm. The rest of the division marked the time by *touching* with their wands the accent marks in their books. Thus round the class the growing harmony proceeds, until it swells out in the fullest chorus. Turning round we observed that the children on the gallery, by the help of a monitor and the musical ladder, were joining in the melody. Several pieces with words were also sung very beautifully, and on the following day Miss Glover very kindly exhibited to us, with a select class, her method of teaching the minor scale, and the manner in which the more advanced children were introduced, by easy steps, to the correct use of the old notation.

BIBLIOGRAPHY

A. Principal works of John Curwen on Tonic Sol-fa

The History of Nelly Vanner (London, 1840)

The Child's Own Hymn Book (London, 1841)

The Independent Magazine (London, 1842)

Singing for Schools and Congregations (London, 1843) [CTME 14]

Grammar of Vocal Music (London, 1848)

Pupil's Manual (London, 1849)

The Tonic Sol-fa Reporter (London), editor from 1851

Songs and Tunes for Education (London, 1861)

Standard Course (London, 1861)

How to Observe Harmony (London, 1861, revised 1872)

New Standard Course (London, 1872)

Musical Statics (London, 1874)

Teacher's Manual (London, 1875)

Tonic Sol-fa Primer (London, 1878)

Musical Theory (London, 1879)

B. Other sources

Beatty, H. M., *Brief History of Education* (London, 1922)

Brocklehurst, B., *Response to Music* (London, 1971)

Cassell, J., ed., *Popular Educator* (London, 1852)

Corben, P., 'Sarah Glover's Solfa Harmonicon', *MIE*, December, 1978

Crowest, F. J., *Phases of Musical England* (London, 1881)

Curwen, J. S., *Memorials of John Curwen* (London, 1882)

—— *School Music Abroad* (London, 1901) [CTME 15]

Franchi-Verney, G., 'Music in England', *School Music Review*, November, 1897

Fuller-Maitland, J. A., 'Tonic Sol-fa: pro and con', *Musical Quarterly* 7 (1921), pp. 68–72

Glover, S., *Scheme for Rendering Psalmody Congregational* (Norwich and London, 1835) [CTME 5]

—— *Sol-fa Tune Book* (Norwich and London, 1839) [CTME 5]

—— *Norwich Guide to Sol-faing* (Norwich and London, 1845)

Hullah, F., *Life of John Hullah* (London, 1882)

Hullah, J., *Wilhem's Method of Teaching Singing* (London, 1842) [CTME 7]

—— *Time and Tune in the Elementary School* (London, 1875)

Hundoegger, A., *Lehrweise nach Tonika Do*, revised E. Noack (Lippstadt, 1951)

Jue de Berneval, E., *Music Simplified* (London, 1831)

Kretzschmar, H., *Musikalische Zeitfragen* (Leipzig, 1903)

Lavignac, A., and L. de la Laurencie, ed., *Encyclopédie de la musique* (Paris, 1925–30)

McNaught, W. G., 'History and Uses of the Sol-fa Syllables', *Proceedings of the Royal Musical Association* 19 (1893), pp. 35–51

—— 'Psychology of Sight Singing', *Proceedings of the Royal Musical Association* 26 (1900), pp. 35–55

Mainzer, J., *Singing for the Million* (London, 1841) [CTME 9]

—— *Music and Education* (London and Edinburgh, 1848) [CTME 11]

Marr, R. A., *Music for the People* (Edinburgh and Glasgow, 1889)

Marx, A. B., *Universal School of Music*, trans. A. H. Wehrhan (London and Leipzig, 1853)

—— *General Musical Instruction*, trans. G. Macirone (London, 1854)

Nägeli, H. G., *Die Pestalozzische Gesangbildungslehre* (Zurich, 1809)

Phillips, W. R., *Dictionary of the Tonic Sol-fa System* (London, 1903)

Pollard, H. M., *Pioneers of Popular Education* (London, 1956)

Rainbow, B., *The Land without Music* (London, 1967)

—— 'The Glass Harmonicon Rediscovered', *Music in Education*, January 1974, pp. 18–19 [see pp. 193–5 below]

—— 'Curwen, Kodály and the Future', *Music Teacher*, December 1979, pp. 11–12 [see pp. 259–62 below]

—— 'The Sol-fa Story', *Guardian*, 15 January 1980

Sándor, F., *Musical Education in Hungary* (London, 1966)

Scholes, P., *The Mirror of Music* (London, 1947)

Simmons, J. *New University* (Leicester, 1958)

Simpson, K., ed., *Some Great Music Educators* (London, 1976)

Szőnyi, E., *Music Reading and Writing* (London, 1974)

Taylor, S., *A System of Sight-Singing* (London and New York, 1890)

UNESCO, *Music in Education* (Paris, 1955)

Venables, L. C., *School Teacher's Music Guide* (London, 1911)

Watkins Shaw, H., 'The Musical Teaching of John Curwen', *Proceedings of the Royal Musical Association* 77 (1950), pp. 17–26

Whittaker, W. G., *Collected Essays* (London, 1940)

Young, P. M., ed., *Kodály's Choral Method* (London, 1963–7)

– Newspapers and Journals –

Norwich Mercury, 26 April 1879

The Times, 4 September 1857

PART III

Selected Writings

Introduction
Gordon Cox

T HIS SELECTION OF THE WRITINGS of Bernarr Rainbow focuses chiefly upon his two principal research fields, the history of music educa-tion and the history of Anglican church music. He felt himself drawn to these subjects on his appointment as Director of Music at the College of St Mark and St John where two of his predecessors, John Hullah and Thomas Helmore, had made significant advances respectively within the teaching of music in schools and the development of music within the church. Hullah, later to be appointed Her Majesty's Inspector (HMI) for music in training colleges, had been responsible in the 1840s for the musical training of the students; Helmore organised the daily chapel services, in which the students were expected to play a full vocal part. The achievements of both men were to become an impor-tant feature of Rainbow's investigations, and resulted in his vivid histories of nineteenth-century music education and church music.[1]

Although Rainbow's preoccupation with music in schools and churches is the chief focus of this compilation, I have also included some of his writings about the musical life of London, in which he moves towards assembling a social history of music-making in the capital.

Rainbow's writings on music education form the most substantial part of his output, and consolidate his position as 'the key figure in the creation of music education history as a serious field of study in this country'.[2] I have organised them according to themes rather than chronological appearance.

In 'Reflections on Historical Research in Music Education' the two articles provide insights into his motivation and practice as a historian of music educa-tion. Rainbow sets forth his credo in 'That Great Dustheap called "History"'. Here he allies himself with G. M. Trevelyan's romantic view of the poetry of history, and of history as a form of literature. The two key words Rainbow uses in opposition are 'civilisation' and 'liberalism'. Rather than being overly con-cerned with establishing points of change, he was more in sympathy with the continuity of ideas and practice. In the succeeding article, 'Historical Research', he maintains the notion of history as a form of literature, and provides a

---

[1] B. Rainbow, *The Land without Music: Musical Education in England, 1800–1860 & its Continental Antecedents* (London: Novello, 1967; R/Woodbridge: Boydell Press, 2001); *The Choral Revival in the Anglican Church, 1839–1872* (London: Barrie & Jenkins, 1970; R/Woodbridge: Boydell Press 1991).

[2] V. Gammon, Review of *Sir Arthur Somervell on Music Education, British Journal of Music Education*, vol. 21 no. 2 (2004), p. 229.

straightforward no-nonsense guide to students interested in pursuing historically based questions, and advice about selecting a topic. His listing of standard works published in Britain and elsewhere presents an excellent starting point for researchers new to the field.[3]

In 'School Music Abroad' I have grouped together three articles which illustrate what I consider to be one of Rainbow's main strengths, his ability to work across national boundaries with an impressive range of sources. This is demonstrated in the selection of his forty-five *Classic Texts in Music Education*, which include such notable continental authors as Agricola, Berneval, Bourgeois, Chevé, Fétis, Galin, Hauptmann, Kollman, Kretzschmar, Mainzer, A. B. Marx, Nägeli, Pepusch, Rhau and Rousseau.[4] Something of this breadth of vision is apparent in the three articles presented here: the experience of Tolstoy in teaching music; the lasting musical influence of two of the true sons of the French Revolution, Bernard Sarrette and Guillaume Bocquillon Wilhem; and a survey of the history of music education in Germany with some cautionary warnings about throwing away musical achievements through laxity and would-be populism.

In 'Music Education in Nineteenth-Century England' Rainbow is on his favourite ground. Here can be found his first research-based article, 'An Excellency in Music', in which he brings to life the pioneers of music education in England during this period including John Curwen, Sarah Glover, John Hullah and Joseph Mainzer. This was the germ of Rainbow's masterly study, *The Land without Music*. In a later article Rainbow recounts his exciting discovery of Sarah Glover's rather intriguing teaching device, the glass harmonicum. It was Rainbow in *The Land without Music* who first paid Glover serious attention, placing her in the lineage of such distinguished eighteenth-century women writers and educationalists as Maria Edgeworth, Hannah More and Elizabeth Fry. Almost thirty years after 'An Excellency in Music' Rainbow offers an impressive wide-ranging account of 'The Rise of Popular Music Education in Nineteenth-Century England'. He considers the importance of the Education Bill of 1839, and in particular the central significance of James Kay, the Secretary of the Committee of Council on Education. It was Kay who enlisted, for good or ill, the musical help of John Hullah. By the end of Rainbow's survey, music had found its place not only in elementary schools,

---

[3] For a more recent survey of the field of music education history, see G. Cox, 'Transforming Research in Music Education History', in *MENC Handbook of Research Methodologies*, ed. R. Colwell (New York: Oxford University Press, 2006), pp. 73–94.

[4] To date, twenty-one of these *Classic Texts in Music Education* have been published. Rainbow's introductions to all forty-five texts are published in B. Rainbow, *Four Centuries of Music Teaching Manuals* (Woodbridge: Boydell Press, 2009).

but also in the less discussed middle-class contexts of independent secondary schools for boys and high schools for girls. This leads him to discuss the various interpretations placed on the content of the music lesson in relation to the social class of children attending these varieties of schools.

In these three articles the figure of John Curwen looms large. He clearly took pride of place in Rainbow's work, and it is appropriate that his fine critical biography of the man appears in this volume right after Rainbow's own autobiography. In his important recent book on the Tonic Sol-fa Movement, *Music and Victorian Philanthropy*, Charles Edward McGuire praises Rainbow for his 'admirable job of capturing the essence of the man'.[5] Many of the points Rainbow makes about Curwen are re-emphasised by McGuire but with a fresh interpretation stemming from the notion of philanthropy. McGuire's stance is worth considering as it may suggest fresh ways of looking at the Tonic Sol-fa Movement, a study pioneered by Rainbow. McGuire highlights three of the underlying factors which facilitated its rise: the expansion of Nonconformity in the nineteenth century, a distrust of centralised government intervention, and the rise of cheap information dissemination. The language used to promote the system was that of dissenting evangelical philanthropy. Belief in the power of music meant it could be harnessed on behalf of the moral reform of Victorian society. In all this, education was crucial. For McGuire, although Sarah Glover may have created the system of Tonic Sol-fa, it was Curwen's opportunism that would create 'briefly a musical and moral empire'.[6] These same arguments were also put forward in allying Tonic Sol-fa with the temperance movement and missionary endeavour.[7] More critically, McGuire points out that although Curwen and other Tonic Sol-fa enthusiasts believed that women could lead the way to moral perfectionism, nevertheless femininity had to be controlled and contained within traditional domestic contexts. For such reasons Curwen preferred classes to concerts, as concerts could threaten female domesticity through the encouragement of female spectacle.

By choosing Victorian philanthropy as a lens through which to view the Tonic Sol-fa Movement, McGuire demonstrates the manifold possibilities available to music education historians to contribute to what Mary Hilton and Jill Shefrin call 'a new cultural history of education', in which education

---

[5] C. E. McGuire, *Music and Victorian Philanthropy: The Tonic Sol-fa Movement* (Cambridge: Cambridge University Press, 2009), p. 18.

[6] McGuire, *Music and Victorian Philanthropy*, p. 17.

[7] For recent studies of the alliance of the Tonic Sol-fa Movement with missionary endeavour, see J. E. Southcott & A. H.-C. Lee, 'Missionaries and Tonic Sol-fa Music Pedadogy in 19th-Century China', *International Journal of Music Education*, vol. 26 no. 3 (2007), pp. 213–28; R. S. Stevens, 'Tonic Sol-fa in Asia-Pacific Countries – The Missionary Legacy', *Asia-Pacific Journal for Arts Education*, vol. 59 no. 1 (2008), pp. 52–76.

is redefined as a cultural rather than a political, social or purely instructive practice, thus freeing the history of education from its traditional constraints of providing accounts of the history of schools and schooling.[8]

Rainbow concludes his consideration of 'Music Education in Nineteenth century England' by extending his gaze towards piano teaching, through investigating Pitman's *The Miseries of Musick Masters*. This provides him with the opportunity to explore the status of the old-style professional music masters who exercised a near monopoly of teaching the piano to the daughters of the well-to-do, but whose position was being threatened by the growing army of women anxious to seek in such work a respectable means of gaining income.

Rainbow wrote several commentaries on what he saw as the process of the disintegration of music education in twentieth-century Britain begun in the 1960s. He warns us to take seriously Plato's warnings about the harmful potential of the Dionysian element in music. In 'Onward from Butler: School Music, 1945–1985' he bemoans all the talk of 'creativity' and child-centredness, which in his view downgraded 'the basics', such as the teaching of musical notation. The same arguments permeate 'Freedom and its Price', whose title sums up much of Rainbow's preoccupations. He became disillusioned about music teaching that favoured an egalitarian approach to mass culture and an abandonment of vocal work in the classroom. Although his observations need to be taken seriously, they do reflect his tendency to look back to a golden age of sight-singing and hand signs, which in reality probably never existed. If we apply what John Tosh calls 'the fallacies of Golden Age history'[9] to Rainbow's commentaries, we can see that the problem is that their view of unrelieved decline does not consider the major structural changes that have been taking place in the musical lives and tastes of young people, and so there is a temptation to fall into a nostalgic mindset.

Finally in Rainbow's educational writings I include his observations on music teaching methods. With the rise of compulsory schooling from the end of the eighteenth century in Europe and beyond, there were great debates about the pedagogical pros and cons of the different methods of teaching children to sing: fixed doh, movable doh, cipher notation, singing by ear, singing by note etc.[10] Rainbow's articles on methods range from the ancient use of hand signs as a form of musical notation called *Cheironomy* to an account

---

[8] See M. Hilton and J. Shefrin (eds.), *Educating the Child in Enlightenment Britain: Beliefs, Cultures, Practices* (Aldershot: Ashgate, 2009), p. 4.

[9] J. Tosh, *Why History Matters* (Basingstoke: Palgrave Macmillan, 2008), pp. 88–90.

[10] For cross-cultural perspectives on music teaching methods in the nineteenth century see G. Cox and R. Stevens, eds., *The Origins and Foundations of Music Education: Cross-Cultural Historical Studies of Music in Compulsory Schooling* (London: Continuum, 2010).

of his visit to a junior school in France where he was impressed by the use of Chevais' *phonomimie* which Rainbow felt to be more effective than Curwen's hand signs. Rainbow's curiosity also extended to ways in which sol-fa might be of help 'in multi-racial classes' – after all, India and China had employed equivalent sol-fa systems in the third century BC.

John Paynter observed that Rainbow was 'principally concerned with the voice as the vehicle for musical education',[11] and indeed it is Rainbow's achievement to have charted the progress of solmisation in music teaching right from Guido d'Arezzo in the eleventh century, until John Curwen in the nineteenth. It was Rainbow's belief that Curwen's 'educational insights enabled him to achieve a synthesis of many of the best elements in [the] indigenous and continental systems of music teaching'.[12] In 'An Ear for Music' Rainbow argues that rather than regarding Curwen as a historical figure, he should be seen as a living force whose influence could revitalise music teaching today. Furthermore, as we read in 'The Kodály Concept and its pedigree', the basis of Zoltán Kodály's methods was his discovery of John Curwen's Tonic Sol-fa teaching. Rainbow then contrasts the remarkable development of Kodály's system in Hungary with the neglect of Curwen's methods in England. It was Rainbow's wish to revive the Tonic Sol-fa system. His account of 'The New Curwen Method' emphasises the partnership of ear, eye and voice. Rainbow was convinced that this was the way forward, but in rightful continuity with the past.

As an interlude between Rainbow's educational and ecclesiastical concerns, his articles on nineteenth-century musical life in London provide some welcome contrast, and demonstrate something of his versatility. In 'The English Promenade Concert' he engagingly contests the abiding impression that all such promenade concerts had their origin in France. Among the sources of evidence he utilises are two contrasted prints by Rowlandson and Debucourt. He develops this fascination with visual evidence in 'Victorian Street Music', in which he takes the drawing by George Cruikshank of a London crowd scene, including a collection of street musicians, as the basis of his study. Rainbow's use of the work of these artists to illustrate contemporary insights into musicians and music-making, has its parallel in Richard Leppert's book *Music and Image*,[13] based upon visual representations of music in eighteenth-century paintings, drawings and prints, including several of music lessons, and music teachers.

The final selections from Rainbow's writings focus upon church music.

[11] J. Paynter, Review of B. Rainbow with G. Cox, *Music in Educational Thought and Practice*, 2nd edition, *Music and Letters*, vol. 89 (2008), pp. 148–9.

[12] Rainbow, *The Land without Music*, p. 165.

[13] R. Leppert, *Music and Image: Domesticity, Ideology and Socio-Cultural Formation in Eighteenth-Century England* (Cambridge: Cambridge University Press, 1988).

Here we find him tackling subjects of considerable range, including studies of the musical influence of Thomas Helmore, his esteemed predecessor at the College of St Mark and St John. As Rainbow states, his discovery of Helmore's diary of the music sung daily in the college chapel in 1849 'revealed a breadth of repertoire no less than astonishing for that time'.[14] Three of Rainbow's key articles on Helmore are presented here, within the contexts of the Anglican Plainsong Revival and the revival of carol singing. His discovery of Helmore's diary prompted Rainbow to explore the Anglican Choral Revival, within the context of the rise of the Tractarian Movement. Amongst other things the Tractarians wanted to remedy was what they regarded as the Puritan influence on the Church of England, which had led to the neglect of music in church services. A key figure in this revival was T. A. Walmisley, Professor of Music at Cambridge. Intriguingly, Rainbow, in 'Walmisley's Psychedelic Magnificat', unravels the mystery of the effects of opium on Walmisley's process of composing his setting.

One of the results of Tractarian influence was the development of robed choirs in parish churches in the nineteenth century. Rainbow considers the contribution of John Jebb to this development, and terms him an influential godparent of the surpliced parochial choir. Rather different from the surpliced choir was the annual spectacle of the thousands of untrained voices of charity children, who gave performances at St Paul's Cathedral until 1870. Rainbow points out in 'Charity Children: Singing for their Supper' that the sheer volume of sound had become a new luxury, although he contrasts this magnificence with 'their raucous performance, Sunday by Sunday in their own churches'. An exception of course was 'the choral splendour' of the Foundling Hospital Chapel Choir, which in years past had been the centrepiece of Handel's professional musical performances, including *Messiah*.

What I find of particular interest are the connections hinted at between education, music and religion that suggest future possibilities for research. In his article 'In Quires and Places where they Sing' Rainbow points out that by the end of the seventeenth century it was being left to itinerant teachers of psalmody to travel the country to teach psalm tunes to congregations, and to finance themselves by selling their own compilations together with often plagiarised prefaces. It would be fascinating to discover more about these teachers. There are parallels in 'The Hymn-Singing American', in which Rainbow discusses the American singing schools which were designed to address the poor quality of congregational singing in eighteenth-century America. Like the English psalm-tune collections, tune books such as William Billings's *The New-England Psalm-Singer* became essential educational tools. There are

---

[14] Rainbow, *The Choral Revival in the Anglican Church*, p. xi.

clearly comparisons to be made here. But what also is notable is the possibility of extending educational history to encompass pre-nineteenth-century studies of the connections between education, music and religion.

We should remember that, in addition to his scholarly work, Rainbow was an activist, and committed to the causes of music education and church music. He refused to shut himself away in an ivory tower. He wanted to influence current practice, both in churches and in schools, albeit in a somewhat conservative and traditionalist fashion. In 1978 he founded the Curwen Institute, in honour of his educational hero John Curwen, in the hope that teachers might restore Curwen's neglected principles to their merited place in British schools. In 1996 Rainbow issued a warning against neglecting what he regarded as one of our greatest national musical assets, and became President of the Campaign for the Defence of the Traditional Cathedral Choir, an organisation formed to champion the ancient tradition of the all-male choir in cathedrals and similar choral foundations by resisting the introduction of women and girls into such choirs. In such ways he was convinced that history had a practical relevance in the present, and its lessons could be applied to contemporary concerns.

In reading the following selection of articles by Bernarr Rainbow the breadth and depth of his research will become apparent. Some will agree with his interpretations, others will disagree. But hopefully what will shine through is the sheer commitment, energy and integrity Rainbow brought to his task as a researcher and practitioner, whether in relation to music in church or to the teaching of music.

That Great Dust-heap Called 'History'[1]
[1992]

T HOSE OF US with an unfashionable interest in the history of music
education cannot resist a feeling of sympathy for Richard Knolles, headmaster of the Grammar School at Sandwich in Kent late in the sixteenth century. After spending many years compiling a *General Historie of the Turkes
from the beginning of that Nation* when it was eventually published in 1603 he
was disappointed at the lack of interest shown in his book. A century or so
later Dr Samuel Johnson (always a man to put his finger on a point) sonorously
explained that Knolles had only himself to blame – for choosing to investigate
'a subject about which none desired to be informed'.[2]

Today it is not just the history of the Turks, but historical studies generally
that are out of favour. Many people –a surprising number of teachers among
them – seem eager to make a boast of their scorn for the past. And now that
watching television has largely replaced reading, little more than the occasional
simplistic cameo offered by the media remains to extend the average man's
awareness of his roots. Misled by the resulting rag-bag of anecdotes and calami-
ties, many of the susceptible prefer to close their ears to yesterday's catalogue of
disasters for fear of damaging tomorrow's aspirations.

A blinkered existence of that sort is surely insufferable. We cannot isolate
ourselves in a time-vacuum. To defy the past and shrug off the experience of
our predecessors may seem to offer an invigorating challenge to the disaffected;
but when solidly pursued it condemns its devotees to learn only what painful experience teaches. Meanwhile, as Polybius neatly puts it, 'History matures
judgement painlessly.'

But there is another, less portentous aspect of historical resource: one that
allows us to share with our predecessors their aspirations and achievements. As
an historian of our own day has expressed the matter:

The poetry of history lies in the quasi-miraculous fact that once, on this
familiar spot of ground, walked other men and women, as actual as we
are today, thinking their own thoughts, swayed by their own passions,
but now all gone, one generation vanishing after another, gone as utterly
as we ourselves shall shortly be gone ...[3]

[1] A. Birrell, 'Carlyle', in *Obiter dicta* (1884).
[2] *Aubrey's Brief Lives*, ed. O. L. Dick (Harmondsworth: Penguin, 1962), p. 261.
[3] G. M. Trevelyan, *Autobiography of an Historian* (London: Longmans, Green, 1949),
  p. 29.

It is in that spirit, as members of one generation in a seemingly endless chain of human endeavour, that we sometimes find ourselves discovering how our predecessors dealt with some self-same problem that confronts us now. The experience may sometimes assist us in turn – by suggesting either what we should or should not do. It may even reveal that some newly introduced technique is not as novel as we supposed – indeed, that it has already been tried and failed. But the fruits of experience of this sort are not limited to such gainful discoveries. Less obvious but no less rewarding is the sense they provide of our belonging to an ageless but age-old fraternity: of recognising an affinity with others of our own trade whose purpose, no matter how much their circumstances may have differed, was at heart very like our own.

Of course, critics will not fail to object to so overtly 'romantic' an attitude as that flight of fancy depicts; but it was curiosity of just this apparently idle sort that earned acclamation from the eminent historian whose vision of 'the poetry of history' has just been cited. In the preface to his undoubted popular masterpiece, *English Social History*, G. M. Trevelyan had this to say: 'Disinterested intellectual curiosity is the life-blood of real civilisation.'[4] And in our own day, when many sober attributes of that elusive condition called civilisation seem distressingly at risk, access to its very life-blood represents an opportunity we can hardly afford to neglect. And yet, even in our own small field – the history of music education – once interest is stirred and investigation into the records of the past begins, all is not plain sailing.

For instance, recent debate in the UK on the planning of a National Curriculum in music has provided rich opportunity for well-intentioned writers to the newspapers to quote favourite passages from the ancient philosophers on music's power as an educational force. The extract found to occur most often in this correspondence has been one favoured by writers on the subject since the Renaissance. Unfortunately, it was evidently drawn originally from a shaky translation of *The Republic*, for in it Plato is made to claim that learning music exerts a most salutary effect on a pupil's morals.

Less gullible readers will wish to dispute that contention. Unsavoury incidents involving reprobate music-lovers readily came to mind: were not concentration camp tyrants often found to be lovers of Beethoven symphonies! Other recollections follow that deny a direct relationship between music and morals – Plato or not – and the value of Greek thought on musical education as a whole is put in question.

Yet what Plato actually said in that extract is not what has too often been reported. Inadequate translation has changed the whole significance of his remarks. The Greek term he used, *Mousikē*, must always be carefully related

---

[4] G. M. Trevelyan, *English Social History* (London: Longmans, Green, 1944), p. viii.

to its context before being translated simply by our word 'music'. *Mousikē* describes the whole territory of the Nine Muses and so embraces epic and lyric poetry, mime, tragedy, comedy, history, dancing, sacred song, and astronomy. Its meaning is much closer to our wider term 'culture' than to 'music' as such. It is true that each of the activities it covers (even astronomy) involved some 'musical' association or accompaniment; but the point Plato is making does not concern that. He is simply saying that a person whose education has introduced him to the wide field of cultural pursuits covered by the term *mousikē* will be notably better equipped to make moral judgements than one who remains ignorant of them.

Once that misunderstanding is removed, Book III of *The Republic* still contains a wealth of valid argument touching the educational role of music – in our sense of the term. And, we must stress, what emerges from it, far from amounting to blanket approval of the kind it is so comfortable to meet, is a warning against assuming that all types of music equally afford civilising influences on a child's education. Far from that, according to *The Republic* the element of self-indulgence reflected in unrestrained, excessively rhythmic, violent, or sensual music totally rules out their use with the young. As Plato expresses it, the restraint of Apollo must be made to banish the licentiousness of Marsyas and Dionysus.

While we may respect or even reject what has been said by wise predecessors we must still make today's decisions ourselves. No past exhortation deserves compliance just because it was made yesterday rather than today. Nor is it the design of the present paper to claim for thinkers and teachers of the past the right to prescribe how music is to be taught now in our schools. At the same time, a thoughtful review of earlier opinion on music's role in education is likely to set our minds turning on matters previously taken for granted. Similarly, a survey of past practice is bound to supply insights inviting us to pause and think again before coming to our own decisions.

For instance, the distinction Plato has just been found drawing between the staid music of Apollo as suitable, and the wild music of Marsyas and Dionysus as unsuitable in a child's musical upbringing loses nothing of its force when transferred to a modern context. And when a choice of repertoire next appears in doubt, although there is no shortage of present-day pundits at hand to advise us we may find it agreeable to have the benefit of Plato's counsel, too.

Present circumstances and current doubts on the content of music education urge us to sharpen our judgement. One fruitful way of doing this, we find, is by consulting past experience. A little time spent sampling the less-than-familiar annals of music education will test the reasonableness of that claim. To take one instance. Current practice in schools favours the use of pitched classroom instruments – partly because they help make music lessons more enjoyable, but also (in the opinion of some exponents) because they are thought to facilitate reading music from a score. Of course, that depends on what is meant by 'reading' music. To rely on an instrument to provide the sound of a written note instead of training the inner ear to supply it seems an inadequate interpretation of the term. Let us see what History has to say on this debatable point.

It is now more than half a century since the Hungarian composer Zoltán Kodály insisted that instrumental music-making should not begin until experience in sight-singing had developed the child's sense of relative pitch:

> A child should not be given an instrument before it can sing. The inner ear will develop only if his first notions of tone arise from his own singing. and are not associated with any external visual or motor conceptions.[5]

On another occasion Kodály was equally emphatic about the relative superiority of skilful singing as an activity even when compared with more advanced instrumental performance:

> If, through the reading of music, a child has reached the stage where he is able to sing a small masterpiece in two parts with another child, he has acquired a hundred times more music than if he thrashed the piano from sun-up to sun-down.[6]

However arresting and uncompromising these two typical statements of his may appear, outside the now somewhat isolated ranks of his followers very little notice seems to have been paid to Kodály's advice. No comparable figure today appears to have made such a challenging remark on the subject. Indeed, the noticeable lack of support among his fellows elsewhere in Europe – where we find his contemporary Carl Orff emphasising the value of instrumental work in schools at that very time – almost makes Kodály appear an isolated eccentric.

Yet historically speaking he is far from being alone in insisting on the wisdom of learning to sing from notes before learning to play an instrument. Well over a century earlier Pierre Galin was complaining in France that because of their faulty early training competent performers had to rely on their instruments to pick out the sound of an unknown melody from the score in front of them:

> Here you have a strange process [he wrote]: the sight of the written symbols causes the fingers to move, and the instrument produces the sound.

---

[5] F. Sándor, *Music Education in Hungary* (London: Barrie & Jenkins, 1966), p. 247.

[6] G. Russell-Smith, 'Zoltán Kodály', in *Some Great Music Educators*, ed. K. Simpson (London: Novello, 1976), p. 81.

But why does the sight of the symbols themselves convey nothing directly to the reader's mind?[7]

This surely resembles what medical men call 'a second opinion' on a vital matter. And a little further probing will reveal an even more forthright declaration of the same principle three hundred years earlier. The writer now is Martin Agricola, one of the very first to establish those excellent standards of teaching in the schools of Lutheran Germany that laid the foundations of her musical pre-eminence two centuries later.

In 1529 Agricola published an instrumental tutor, *Musica instrumentalis deudsch*. In it he set down his view of the importance of learning to sing at sight before learning to play an instrument. To emphasise his argument he expressed it in verse – so as to impress its substance on the memories of his readers. Here is an English paraphrase of what he wrote:

> It you want to equip yourself to play
> With artistry on flute or crumhorn,
> With finesse on serpent, pommer, or shawm.
> Always remember this:
> To master an instrument
> First learn to sing.
> For instruments follow the same path.
> And once you can sing at sight
> You can learn to play better in six weeks
> (Given due diligence)
> Than the keenest non-singer will
> After six months.[8]

Alas, over four hundred years later there are still armies of pianists and instrumentalists of all sorts who cannot recognise a simple tune from the page until they have played it. Clearly, instrumental performance alone – whether on a glockenspiel or a Bechstein grand – does not remedy the shortcoming.

To turn to another point. A recent report on music education in the UK [*c*. 1990] draws attention to an aspect of school music teaching that normally

---

[7] P. Galin, *Exposition d'une nouvelle méthode pour l'enseignement de la musique* (Paris: Perrotin, 1818); translated B. Rainbow as P. Galin, *Rationale for a New Way of Teaching Music*, CTME 8 (Kilkenny: Boethius Press, 1983), pp. 42–3.

[8] In the original these verses began: 'Wiltu ein recht Fundament begreiffen / Auff Flöten, Krumphörner, könstlich pfeiffen, / Und auff Zincken, Bomhart, Schalmeyn mit list, / So mercke das volgend zu aller frist ...' The paraphrase provided here first appeared in my preface to M. Agricola, *The Rudiments of Music*, trans. J. Trowell in *Four Centuries of Music Teaching Manuals, 1518–1932* (Woodbridge: Boydell Press, 2009), p. 19.

excites little attention: 'We have much evidence which indicates that achievements in music can be a powerful motivating influence in other areas of study.'
The report then goes on to mention the acknowledged and familiar overlaps
found to exist between music and such other curriculum areas as English,
History, Geography. However, no reference is made in it to the general sharp-
ening of interest and attention many believe results from well-conducted
musical training in its own right, and to the impact this can have on a child's
response to his growing intellectual needs. Modern research has paid some
attention to this phenomenon; but few will realise it was already arousing wondering comment in the very early days of popular education in the nineteenth
century.

In 1819 music lessons were first introduced as an experiment in a few of
the commune schools of Paris. Ten years later the Municipal Council drew
surprised attention to this unexpected result:

> Not only do these schools stand out from the rest for their good tone
> and success; but within these schools themselves, the children who have
> learned music stand out among their fellows as having greater powers of
> application, courtesy and good conduct.[9]

Then in England, at St Mark's Teacher Training College, Chelsea, a generation later a few boys from the practising school were very reluctantly released
from their ordinary lessons for an hour's practice with the chapel choir daily.
After a six-month trial period the College Principal was reported as saying 'the
boys of the choir, although they have had one hour a day less than the others in
their ordinary school-work, have so far shot ahead of them in everything, that
the difference is perfectly fearful.'[10]

Again, in 1847, the authorities of the Foundling Hospital in London were
persuaded to permit the formation of a wind band from among the pupils. As
time for rehearsal had to be drawn from ordinary school hours the band-boys'
performance in the examinations was carefully monitored. They regularly carried off 'a full proportion of the prizes awarded for scholastic pursuits'; and a
somewhat bewildered governing committee offered these rather long-winded
comments on the experiment:

> This success at school may be fairly attributed to the salutary effect of
> music upon the character of those boys receiving instruction in the art,
> which imparts a vivacity to their tempers, and, by its enlivening influence,
> renders the mental capacities more energetic and susceptible of receiving

---

[9] G. L. B. Wilhem, *Manuel musical* (Paris: Perrotin, 1841), pp. viiif., trans. BR.
[10] F. Helmore, *Memorials of the Revd Thomas Helmore* (London: Masters, 1891), p. 30.

general instruction than the faculties of the other boys attain who do not enjoy the advantage of musical tuition.[11]

A little later again, Matthew Arnold stressed in his inspector's report for 1861 that a singing lesson he heard while visiting a teacher-training college reminded him how often he had found music seemed to awaken and stimulate those taking part in it 'in a way in which no other part of their instruction can.' He went on:

> No doubt it is because of this capacity that the civilising power of music has always been famed so highly; for instruction civilises raw nature only so far as it delights and kindles it.[12]

The topic is one that offers much to interest teachers today – once they become aware of it.

A mass of historical evidence survives, of course, to record the immense variety of different methods, techniques and attitudes adopted over the ages to teach music in the schools of many lands. A handful of brief references and a few snippets from it in this paper would be inconclusive. Instead, a more leisurely, personal examination of this material win reveal to the serious researcher problems very like our own and expose the wisdom – or the folly – of the methods formerly adopted to solve them.

However, the merest glance at the literature of this vast territory will reveal the amazing growth of a discipline that itself began only as teaching singing by rote. The options subsequently made available to music teachers have since become so profuse that individual preference no longer seems an acceptable method of deciding a school's musical programme. Indeed, by 1937 that situation had already become sufficiently apparent for teachers to be told that priority should be given to singing and aural training. Other activities, they were warned, would develop satisfactorily only if this were done.[13]

As the range of musical activities continued to grow, the equipment required for its implementation naturally had to keep pace. Classrooms provided with nothing more than a monochord in the Middle Ages, and later supplied only with a pitch-pipe or tuning-fork at best, began late in the nineteenth century to acquire pianos.[14] In the present century gramophones and recordings, an occasional pianola or organ, books, charts and scores, a wide range of traditional

---

[11] J. Brownlow, *History & Design of the Foundling Hospital* (London: Warr, 1858), pp. 89f.

[12] Board of Education, *Reports* on *Elementary Schools* (London: HMSO, 1908), pp. 250–1.

[13] Board of Education, *Handbook of Suggestions for the Consideration of Teachers* (London: HMSO, 1937), p. 174.

[14] *Musical Times* (1890), pp. 339–40.

and novel percussion instruments, radio and television receivers, numberless patented teaching devices, bamboo pipes, recorders, and orchestral instruments of all kinds have successively been added.

Latterly, with the growth of information technology and electronic equipment, schools have been equipped to levels that would formerly have appeared unattainably prodigal;

> All primary schools now have computers among their resources, and some have items such as electronic keyboards. In secondary schools, equipment such as synthesisers, sound processors and multi-track tape recorders is also frequently available and ... can help pupils to enjoy their musical activities.[15]

Faced with that unprecedented abundance it is difficult for impassive observers not to question how far such lavishness has been matched, not just by enjoyment but by musical achievement.

In that connection, perhaps today's most common criticism of our schools is that many children fail to reach their potential – because they are insufficiently stretched. 'Stretching' schoolchildren involves setting them tasks just beyond their reach, then helping them to achieve them. But with music lessons 'stretching' is patently not encouraged. Instead, teachers are advised to make their starting point well within, rather than just beyond a pupil's capability. The argument runs that children can then 'build upon' existing ability. Unhappily, this policy usually perpetuates (besides seeming to authorise) familiarity with music of questionable value. It also runs directly counter to traditional injunctions demanding that 'children are taught nothing but the best'.[16]

When those two pioneers, Arthur Somervell and Cecil Sharp, offered that counsel as a prerequisite for choosing school-songs early in the twentieth century they knew that children's music experience then was often limited to the flamboyantly vulgar music-hall songs of the age. Both men were convinced that their influence was harmful and they were determined to outlaw them. 'Good music purifies, just as bad music vulgarises,' Sharp uncompromisingly declared.[17]

Twenty years or so later, and referring to an exactly similar state of affairs

---

[15] Department of Education and Science/Welsh Office, *Music for Ages 5 to 14; Proposals...* (London: HMSO 1991), p. 10.

[16] A. Somervell, 'The Basis of the Claim of Music in Education', *Proceedings of the Royal Musical Association* (1904–5), p. 164.

[17] C. Sharp, *English Folksong: Some Conclusions* (London: Oxford University Press, 1907), p. 635.

in his own country, Zoltán Kodály emphatically agreed with them when he wrote;

> Bad taste is infectious. While deplorable fashions may not be a serious matter, since ugly clothes do not injure health, bad taste in the arts cauterises susceptibility.[18]

It has become a political solecism today to talk about good or bad taste. But that quibble did not concern Plato when he dealt uncompromisingly with matters of taste in his own day. Within a decadent society, he observed, popular opinion assumes there is no such thing as right and wrong in music. The decisive factor becomes the level of pleasure given to the hearer, however uncouth he may be.[19] He could well have been speaking today.

Our problems, indeed, seem often to be old problems. But before looking to the past for light on them it is wise, once again, to distinguish between History and Hearsay.

The pages of History are interleaved with old yarns and travellers' tales that have gained such wide acceptance that it seldom occurs to anyone to challenge them. A classic instance concerns the long unquestioned belief in the permanent supremacy of school music in Germany. There is no doubt that the impulse given to the teaching of music in Lutheran schools at the Reformation made possible the remarkable musical culture that produced Schütz, Bach and Handel; yet it is unrealistic to suppose that this thrust would prove sufficiently durable to survive the centuries without renewal. We need only recall the complaints made by Bach himself, by his predecessor Johann Kuhnau and by their successors at Leipzig about the inadequate choral resources made available to them there to see how far Luther's intentions had subsequently been abandoned.

Yet foreign visitors to Germany throughout the nineteenth century were still recording their astonishment at the musical powers of the German schoolchild. Unaware of the lowered standards of music teaching in German schools caused by the changing policies of the past hundred years, their tributes really served only to emphasise the shortcomings of the schools of their own homelands. Toward the end of the century a less ingenuous observer was to follow them.

In 1879 John Hullah, then government Inspector of Music in English schools, was despatched on an official tour of continental schools to examine the prevailing state of music teaching there. After visiting Switzerland he had gone on to Germany with high expectations. These were soon shattered.

---

[18] Russell-Smith, 'Zoltán Kodály', p. 61.
[19] Plato, *The Laws*, III.

School singing in Germany, he found, was all done by ear, most of it was out of tune, vocal tone was harsh. Little musical theory was taught; it was thought impracticable to teach sight-singing; and in most classes an indifferently played violin was relied upon to instil song melodies into pupils' heads. Hullah wrote in his subsequent *Report*:

> The teachers, each occupied exclusively with his own class, seemed to have no common plan, and indeed no knowledge of what was being done or attempted in other classes.[20]

Summarising his findings, Hullah stated that in spite of their lengthy training most teachers of music in German schools were ineffective. The results of their teaching he described as 'the poorest conceivable'.[21]

The shock and outrage caused by Hullah's *Report* when it eventually reached Germany was later followed by reluctant realisation of the truth of his criticism and careful analysis of the faults it revealed.[22] The cumulative decline that had overcome German music teaching since the mid-eighteenth century was then found to be due to would-be liberalising policies that had substituted rote-singing of simple ditties and part-songs for systematic musical training begun at an early age. That shift had next misled parents into believing that thorough training was best reserved for 'musical' children and provided for them at home out of school hours.

Once Luther's original aim of training a singing congregation and choir for every church ceased to motivate music teaching in German schools the former concept of music education as systematically and universally applied from early childhood was also allowed to lapse. To reverse the decline that resulted – while at the same time re-establishing music as a worthwhile educational discipline in its own right – was a task that took much more than a generation's struggle to achieve.

Such a disaster, we are wise to recall, is prone to repeat itself elsewhere, given a similar loss of purpose coupled with maladroit attempts at liberalisation. Uncomfortable parallels suggest themselves between the disturbed and haphazard state of music teaching found in German schools during its decline in the nineteenth century and that prevailing elsewhere today. And there is a worryingly familiar ring about several of Hullah's criticisms – notably his references to teachers believing training in theory and sight-singing to be impracticable; and to every teacher going his own way with 'no common plan, and

---

[20] J. Hullah, *Report on Musical Instruction in Elementary Schools on the Continent* (London: Board of Education, 1879), p. 534; J. S. Curwen and J. Hullah, *School Music Abroad*, CTME 15 (Kilkenny: Boethius Press, 1965), p. 6.

[21] Hullah, *Report*, p. 546; Curwen and Hullah, *School Music Abroad*, p. 18.

[22] H. Kretzschmar, *Musikalisch Zeitfragen* (Leipzig: Peters, 1903), *passim*.

indeed no knowledge of what was being done or attempted in other classes'. Equally reminiscent of current thinking is the defeatists' view that only so-called 'musical' children should receive training – and that they should be taught outside ordinary lessons.

In recent times changed musical tastes have prompted attempts to 'liber-alise' music teaching in schools. Yet however necessary these may appear to have been, we question the wisdom of leaving teachers entirely free to decide the aim and content of their lessons. Especially for the less discerning among those teaching younger children, this policy endangers continuity and a sense of direction at the very stage when musical foundations should be carefully laid. At secondary level, and with 'difficult' classes lacking basic skills, the admission of haphazard methods encourages reliance on music's capacity to entertain rather than enlighten.

While there is growing unease in many quarters about this stage of affairs, elsewhere perhaps particularly among devotees of what might be called the Shop Window school of thought – an atmosphere of self-congratulation pre-vails, centred around the admitted success of a talented minority of young-sters who form the bands, orchestras and (to a much lesser extent) the choirs of certain schools. The achievements of these able pupils invariably receiving individual instrumental coaching – are most gratifying; but they must not be used to mask the failure and indifference of many of their fellows. And there is certainly as yet no generally acknowledged public awareness of the decline of music as a purposeful classroom discipline in schools.

The necessary reforms achieved in German schools early in the twentieth century were not half-measures. The similar reforms that circumstances seem to demand elsewhere today will need to be just as rigorous and prolonged. We find ourselves recalling that though History does not repeat itself, those who refuse to learn its lessons are condemned to live them out afresh. That, alas, is just what many of us seem to have been doing for far too long already.

Historical Research
[1992]

A SENSE OF HISTORY, we have come to realise, forms a treasured feature of all productive cultures. For all but the most reckless of innovators historical awareness points the way ahead while affording safeguards against damaging excess; for the less mettlesome it extends inspiration and prompts courage to meet the challenge of the future. The truth of those claims is apparent in all fields of creative endeavour.

While perhaps more strikingly demonstrated within the fine arts the advantages conferred on the practitioner by knowledge of past practice and doctrine are also found in most other creative pursuits. The craft of teaching stands high among them and systematic examination of past aims, methods, and achievements within it offers a correspondingly fruitful and rewarding field for serious research. It is usual in academic circles to refer to research of this calibre as designed 'to contribute to knowledge'. When conducted only at undergraduate level within an existing field of study, activity classed as research is customarily designed strictly for the student's own enlightenment. Though limited in scope, so long as it is honestly carried out and authentically reported, such modest research experience provides a desirable and useful preparation for later and more mature investigation. This in turn may at first be confined to circumscribed areas, the findings perhaps being published in the form of short articles or papers in appropriate journals.

More advanced and extended work at postgraduate levels will normally be conducted in more depth with greater rigour over a longer period of time and under the regular direction of an appointed supervisor. The contribution looked for now will be substantial, capable of influencing received opinion, and thence be 'deemed worthy of publication'.

PRELIMINARY CONSIDERATIONS

Those who undertake historical research in the field of music education at higher levels must not allow the report they prepare of their eventual findings to relapse into imprecise narrative. This is best avoided at the outset by deliberately focusing attention on discoverable aims and procedures; by relating findings to current circumstances at home or abroad; by estimating revealed achievements and failures comparatively; and by meticulously recording all the sources drawn upon.

To fulfil all those requirements advanced students will need to undertake considerable preliminary reading. They must first become sufficiently aware of the educational scene as a whole to form a realistic estimate of the potential place and role of music teaching within it. They should make themselves familiar with the relevant findings of other researchers in the field so as to set their own results in perspective, both regionally and historically. Moreover, unless they become thoroughly conversant with the state of existing research in the chosen area their eventual personal discoveries may prove to be already familiar to scholars elsewhere.

Carefully conducted but narrowly based research can founder through lack of background awareness. For instance, a student might attempt to investigate the influence of autocratic rule on educational policy as demonstrated in a particular regime. He or she would not find it too difficult to identify decrees uttered by Napoleon, for example, laying down ambitious programmes for the schools of France. But unless it was realised before closely examining and analysing those decrees that at the time in question there were too few competent teachers available in France to implement them their conclusions would be valueless.

Similarly a student might choose to examine the grandiose educational programmes introduced in Italy under Mussolini and then attempt to estimate their national impact. Before being able to reach a worthwhile conclusion he or she must have discovered that though elementary education in Italy had been made compulsory from six to fourteen at the time in question, most of the nation's children stopped attending school at the age of eleven.

SELECTING A TOPIC

The choice of a topic for research is not something to be undertaken hastily. If it is to prove fruitful the chosen subject should be one the investigator is prepared 'to live with' over the considerable period of time it requires to locate, assemble, and assess data and then submit the findings to rigorous testing before writing them up.

In practice the most fruitfully rewarding areas of research usually prove to have chosen themselves – because they arise from interests and enthusiasms already present and subsequently nourished in the minds of those undertaking them. In that respect it is hardly too fanciful to claim that historically based research amounts to a form of inspired curiosity wedded to determined scrutiny of a type more usually associated with the great detectives of fiction.

Some mention of the sort of research question usefully addressed by historical methods may prove helpful here. An investigation relevant where the future development of music education is being considered – perhaps in a developing country – might involve comparison of past and present arguments advanced to support or oppose the admission of music lessons to the school curriculum.

At other levels the desirable content of the music curriculum, the choice of methods adopted to teach its component parts, and the wisdom or otherwise of available assessment procedures, all provide illuminating and potentially beneficial fields for historical investigation. Other topics inviting scrutiny which suggest themselves include the impact of social change on the choice of repertory, the effect on school music teaching of changing attitudes toward religious observance, or a comparison of the results of national preference for teaching *relative* as opposed to *fixed* sol-fa.

Less extensive topics relating to music teaching in schools and covering a smaller time-scale might concern varying attitudes toward children who cannot sing in tune, the influence of radio and television on school music lessons, or the impact on lesson content of the recent marked growth of instrumental teaching within the curriculum.

Topics relating to music teaching in schools perhaps provide the most inviting field for practising teachers to pursue; but equally rewarding areas of study present themselves within the territories of conservatory teaching and home-based musical study – as undertaken by adults as well as children. Worthwhile findings produced after careful, well-authenticated research in these and many other areas can exert valuable influence where the modification and improvement of long standing procedures is being discussed. Indifferent practices often survive only because it occurs to no one to question them. Historical evaluation of procedures can aid improvement; it can equally justify the reinstatement of practices too hastily abandoned on questionable grounds.

At post-graduate level a programme of research must be capable of being studied to the depth required to justify the award of a higher degree. Here it is not just the student's intellectual ability that is in question. An equally decisive factor will be the likelihood of identifying and locating sufficient source material on which to base worthwhile enquiry.

Yet the student should not be discouraged too readily by an apparent shortage of suitable material. Diligent and patient investigators who acquire a feeling for tracking down source material will often find themselves developing something of the quality that Horace Walpole named 'serendipity' – *the faculty of making valuable discoveries by accident*. There is no shortage of anecdote on this subject among hardened researchers who enjoy telling how they found a critical report in a second-hand bookshop, or unexpectedly ran to earth an invaluable contemporary handwritten account in a basement lumber room.

Suffice to say that besides such inspired flukes an encouragingly large amount of material remains waiting to be extracted from surviving minute books, autobiographical memoirs, provincial and national newspapers and journals, library and college archives, government pronouncements, personal correspondence, and the like. Another invaluable source of historical information is to be found in outmoded textbooks. Long withdrawn from use in schools such books are not perhaps now so easily come by on second-hand bookstalls as was the case a generation or more ago; but they are still often to be found preserved in such specialist libraries as the Euing Collection at Glasgow University Library. An additional resource in this respect is the growing selection of such material at present being reproduced in facsimile in the series *Classic Texts in Music Education*.

COMPILING AN ACCOUNT

Earlier in this chapter regret was expressed that familiarity with the published results of research in music education remains regrettably thin among those it is intended to inform. It is difficult not to feel that much of the blame for this state of affairs rests with researchers themselves – for persistently framing their reports in such indigestible language.

It is not many years since Arnold Bentley first warned against the unnecessary use of 'jargon' in reporting research findings. Certain of the early research papers published in England at that time, dealing largely with the psychology of music and drawn up in many cases by non-musicians, seemed as uninviting to the practising music specialist as the arcane liturgy of some exclusive sect. The vogue since adopted in some quarters of affecting preposterous circumlocution when writing PhD theses and dissertations has done nothing to improve that situation.

It is greatly to be wished that this fashion be encouraged to lapse; and that what perhaps really amounts only to a candidate's anxiety to emphasise the intellectual respectability of his submission will cease to encourage the use of highfalutin' language when compiling it. Research findings in the history of music education fortunately require neither elaborate terminology nor prolixity for their expression. They can as readily be stated in everyday terms immediately accessible to those whom they are meant to influence. General agreement among examiners and candidates to dispense with pretentious verbosity would help ensure that published findings reached teachers at large – instead of seeming to be the jealously guarded preserve of an inward-looking coterie.

The wisdom of making the findings of historical research inviting and interesting to the ordinary reader cannot be overstressed. One area where inexperienced research students may find themselves in doubt concerns the incorporation in a thesis of extended passages drawn from earlier treatises. If simply quoted verbatim these can prove highly indigestible. It is a good policy in such cases to limit direct quotation to passages where some individual feature – an original turn of phrase or an idiosyncratic term – justifies this treatment. For the rest, it is best to paraphrase and condense as far as possible. But when this is done the precise source of the material itself must always be cited.

History, declared Carlyle, is the essence of innumerable biographies. It is the essential humanity implied in that remark that is so often and so strikingly lacking from much current thesis writing. The turgid nature of most dissertations has led to a general assumption that before research findings merit publication in book form they must be entirely rewritten. Why, one asks, not write in readily readable form to begin with?

A SUMMARY OF HISTORICAL RESEARCH
IN MUSIC EDUCATION

The different pace at which historically-based research in music education has developed in different countries is striking. It is possible to argue that the wide discrepancy found between the interest taken in research in neighbouring countries of Europe can to some extent be explained by differences of outlook and national temperament. However true that may be a complementary explanation also suggests itself.

The markedly different experience of formal music education enjoyed in each of those countries throughout the ages necessarily affects the occasion arising there for historical investigation. In German schools, for instance, systematic music teaching has flourished without interruption (despite some acknowledged lowering of standards during the 19th century) at least since Luther built upon medieval practice in the schools of the Reformation. Among her European neighbours no such long standing tradition is found. More usually the situation is one of long periods of neglect followed by sporadic though often energetic revival or reform.

That being so (and given the national temperament) in Germany there is no scarcity of historical discussion of music education. Elsewhere, however, it is more usually the introduction or re-introduction of music lessons in a country's schools that tends to spark off purposeful investigation of the scene in the past. Successive attempts to introduce music teaching in French, American, and English schools during the first half of the nineteenth century each produced isolated but important accounts of music teaching as it existed at home or abroad in former times. The situation in developing countries today suggests similar opportunities may arise there.

Against that background it would be invidious to attempt to draw up here a summary of each nation's contributions to historical research in what might readily be made to appear a league-table of achievement. To be compassable in a single chapter of the present book such a survey must inevitably be incomplete. It would consequently present individual countries with a misleading impression of their neighbours' activities while at the same time affording an inadequate picture of their own.

We have chosen instead to outline the situation that exists in the United Kingdom alone; and to do so by presenting a chronological list of representative articles and books published on the subject. In this way a realistic impression of the intermittent growth of research in this field in a single country – a pattern not unlikely to be found also elsewhere – can be recorded. The titles of some standard works published in other countries have then been added at the conclusion.

Starting in the 1840s with a handful of examples, early investigations in Britain accompanied and were stimulated by individual efforts to re-introduce music teaching in schools. Many of these investigations were conducted by the innovators themselves for their own guidance. Later in the century research specifically dealing with music education is rare; but incidental references to music teaching can be found tucked away in such classic treatises on the general educational scene as A. T. Drane's *Christian Schools and Scholars* (1867), A. F. Leach's *History of Winchester College* (1899) and *Educational Charters and Documents* (1911).

Attention returned to the subject when plans for post-war development led to the formal review of many aspects of national life during World War II. Educational reform and the need to make detailed plans for its implementation occupied an important place in that debate. The general mood of earnestness and need for action – in music education as elsewhere – stimulated some modest research into past practice and a second wave of publications dealing specifically with the history of music teaching in schools now began.

The first investigations concerned the medieval and renaissance periods – and perhaps strike an observer today as musicological exercises in escapism rather than attempts to reveal foundations on which to rebuild a modern scheme of music education. But the mood changed and strengthened as the centenary of the founding of *The Musical Times* in 1944 inspired the publication of Percy Scholes' remarkable two-volume digest of the musical progress of the nation. The *Mirror of Music*, as his study was called, gave pride of place in its pages to the singing-class movement of the 1840s – a movement whose activities *The Musical Times* itself had first been designed to record. One of Scholes' subsequent chapters traced the history and growth of 'Music in the Nation's Schools'.

Following the impetus provided by Percy Scholes' conspectus a few further articles on the subject began to appear. The first considerable texts then followed in the 1960s heralding a literature that has since shown signs of growing more substantial. It is from examination of all these publications – not

forgetting their often extensive bibliographies – and from such former journals as the *Tonic Sol-fa Reporter*, the *Musical Herald*, the *School Music Review*,
Music in Education, and the *Music Teacher*, that serious students will be able
to equip themselves with the necessary background material needed to pursue
research of the type and quality this chapter is designed to encourage.

SOME CONCLUSIONS

Research in music education may take the form of experimental or quantitative
analysis, philosophical enquiry or historical investigation. Most participants
today are attracted to work within the scientifically-based areas. That preponderance, so understandably in tune with the spirit of a technological age, has
perhaps been allowed to suggest too readily that research in music education is
only justified when it provides scientific answers to current problems.

The present chapter was invited with a suggestion from the editor that it
should describe the kinds of question which historical methods are most able
to address. That condition has been accepted and some answers supplied. Yet
it is desirable here to emphasise that it is also a function of historical research
– and one at least equally important in the opinion of many observers – to compile and furnish an accurate record of past events intended purely for present
enlightenment.

In this instance that course involves describing how and why former procedures were evolved that contributed toward laying the foundation of the
modern music curriculum. It also involves describing the aims, achievements
and failures of pioneer music teachers – all of them empirical rather than
theoretical endeavours and concerned with real schools replete with real children. The beneficial influence on present-day teachers of an awareness of their
predecessors' efforts to achieve what we have all in turn inherited should not
be underestimated. Indeed, many students and teachers whose temperament
leaves them untouched by the results of statistical research find themselves edified and inspired by discovering the emergent background of their craft. If for
no other reason than this, historical and scientific research are wisely to be
regarded as complementary.

But there must be a proviso. Scientific research carries its own implicit math-
ematical infallibility. Historical research deserves equal esteem only so far as
its findings prove equally reliable. For that to happen there can be no juggling
of material to fit predetermined conclusions; no omission of inconvenient or
uncomfortable data. Truth, not just meeting the routine academic requirements for the award of a degree, must be the investigator's goal. Ultimate findings satisfying those conditions deserve to be carefully written up with due

sense of pride. History, after all, has long and rightly been regarded as a form of literature.

A LIST OF BRITISH PUBLICATIONS

– *Part One: 1842–1900* –

Curwen, J., 'Introduction', in *Singing for Schools & Congregations: A Grammar of Vocal Music* (London: Curwen, 1848; R/1985 [CTME 14])

—— 'History and Statistics II', in *The Teacher's Manual of the Tonic Sol-fa Method* (London, 1875; R/1986 [CTME 19])

Hickson, W. E., 'Music, and the Committee of Council on Education', *Westminster Review*, vol. 37, no. 1 (January 1842), pp. 11ff.

Macfarren, C. A., *Addresses and Lectures* (London: Curwen, 1888).

Mainzer, J., *Music and Education* (Edinburgh: A. & C. Black; London: Longman, Brown and Green, 1848; R/1984 [CTME 12])

Marr, R., *Music for the People* (Edinburgh: Menzies, 1889)

– *Part Two: 1900–1992* –

Cant, S., 'Women Composers and the Music Curriculum', *British Journal of Music Education*, vol. 7 no. 1 (March 1990), pp. 5–14

Dobbs, J. P. B., *Three Pioneers of Sight-Singing in the 19th century* (Newcastle: Institute of Education, 1964)

Harris, D. G. T., 'Musical Education in Tudor Times', *Proceedings of the Royal Musical Association*, vol. 65 (1938)

Le Huray, P., 'The Teaching of Music in 16th-century England', *Music in Education*, March/April 1966

Rainbow, B., 'An Excellency in Musick', *The Journal of Education*, vol. 89, no. 1056 (July 1957) [see pp. 158–67 below]

—— 'The Historical and Philosophical Background of School Music Teaching', in *Handbook for Music Teachers* (London: Novello, 1964; R/1968)

—— *The Land without Music: Musical Education in England 1800–1860 & its Continental Antecedents* (London: Novello, 1967; R/1991)

—— *English Psalmody Prefaces: Popular Methods of Instruction, 1562–1835* (Kilkenny: Boethius, 1982 [CTME 2])

—— *Music in Educational Thought & Practice* (Aberystwyth: Boethius, 1991; Woodbridge: Boydell Press, 2006)

——*Music and the English Public School* (Aberystwyth: Boethius, 1991 [CTME 20])

Scholes, P. A., *The Mirror of Music*, 2 vols. (London: Novello, 1947)

Simpson, K., *Some Great Music Educators* (London: Novello, 1976)

Southcott, J. A., 'Music Education Pioneer – Dr Satis Naronna Barton Coleman', *British Journal of Music Education*, vol. 7 no. 2 (July 1990), pp. 123–32

Sternfield, F. W., 'Music in the Schools of the Reformation', *Musica Disciplina*, vol. 2 (1948)

Thompson, A. H., *Song Schools in the Middle Ages* (London, 1942)

See also the article 'Education in Music' in *The New Grove Dictionary of Music and Musicians*, ed. S. Sadie (London, 1980)

SOME STANDARD WORKS PUBLISHED ELSEWHERE

– United States of America –

Birge, E. B., *A History of Public School Music in the United States* (Philadelphia: Oliver Ditson, 1937)

Britton, A. P., 'Music Education: an American Speciality', in *One Hundred Years of Music in America*, ed. P. H. Lang (New York: G. Schirmer, 1961)

Keene, J. A., *A History of Music Education in the United States* (Hanover, NH: University Press of New England, 1982)

Tellstrom, A. T., *Music in American Education, Past and Present* (New York: Holt, Rinehart & Winston, 1971)

– Australia and New Zealand –

Bartle, G., *Music in Australian Schools* (Melbourne, 1968)

Bridges, D., 'Some Historical Backgrounds to Australian Music Education', *Australian Journal of Music Education* (1974)

Tait, M. J., *Music Education in New Zealand* (Hamilton, 1970)

– Canada –

Beckwith, J., 'Music Education', in *Encyclopedia Canadiana*, vol. 7 (Toronto, 1957)

Walter, A., 'The Growth of Music Education', in *Aspects of Music in Canada* (Toronto, 1969)

– *France* –

Chevais, M., 'L'enseignement musical a l'école', in *Encyclopédie de la musique*, ed. Lavignac et Laurencie (Paris, 1925)

Clarval, J. A., *L'Ancienne Maîtrise de Notre-Dame de Chartres du Ve siècle à la révolution* (Paris, 1899)

– *Germany* –

Abel-Struth, S., 'Materialien zur Entwicklung der Musikpädagogik als Wissenschaft', in *Musikpädagogik, Forschung und Lehre*, vol. 1, ed. S. Abel-Struth (Mainz, 1970)

——'Aktualität und Geschichtsbewußtsein in der Musikpadagogik', in *Musikpädagogik, Forschung und Lehre*, vol. 9, ed. S. Abel-Struth (Mainz, 1973)

Braun, G., *Die Schulmusikerziehung in Preussen von den Falkschen Bestimmungen bis zur Kestenberg-Reform* (Kassel and Basle, 1957)

Hopf, H., W. Heise, and S. Helms, *Lexikon der Musikpädagogik* (Regensburg: Gustav Bosse Verlag, 1984)

Kretzschmar, H., *Musikalische Zeitfragen* (Leipzig: Peters, 1903)

Schunemann, G., *Geschichte des Schulgesang unterrichts* (Berlin, 1913)

– *Switzerland* –

Cherbuliez, A. E., *Geschichte der Musikpädagogik in der Schweiz* (Zurich, 1944)

Count Leo Tolstoy: Music Teacher
[1980]

F EW OF THOSE who subscribed to the recent wave of enthusiasm for his first great novel *War and Peace* will have realised that only three years before its appearance in 1864 Leo Tolstoy was teaching music to peasant children just over 100 miles from Moscow. So improbable a situation invites further investigation.

Born at Yásnaya Polyána in the: province of Tula in 1828, Leo Tolstoy came of a family of Russian gentry dating from the 16th century. He received his first education from French tutors, going on to the University of Kazan in 1844. But scornful of academic learning, he made little effort to further his studies beyond reading the works of Rousseau, who influenced him strongly. On leaving the university in 1847 he returned to the family estate at Yásnaya Polyána with the intention of taking up farming; but his lack of practical ability in that direction led to failure and he left for Moscow, where he abandoned himself to the dissipation and inconsequence characteristic of young men of his class at that time. Yet he remained self-critical; and a few years later in a determined attempt to reform he volunteered for service in an artillery regiment. He was commissioned and served at the siege of Sebastopol in 1854. Three years later he resigned his commission and retired from the army to travel abroad in western Europe – an experience which deepened his disgust with the materialism of modern civilisation. Returning home in 1861, he settled again at Yásnaya Polyána where he determined to put into practice something of his own ideals.

Early in 1861 the Russian Emancipation Act gave to the serfs their freedom from feudal servitude. It was under those new social conditions that Tolstoy entered the next phase of his life. He first accepted a post as a magistrate, to settle disputes between emancipated serfs and their former masters; and next decided to open a school for the peasant children on his estate. He taught in the school himself, deciding his own curriculum and adopting a policy of encouraging 'natural' development rather than accepting 'artificial' standards imposed in schools elsewhere. It is not difficult to trace in that liberal attitude the influence of his earlier acquaintance with the writings of Rousseau. Nor will the inclusion of music lessons in his school programme contradict that impression.

Soon after starting the school in 1861, Tolstoy began to publish a journal designed to advance his educational ideas. Named *Yásnaya Polyána* after his estate, the paper included first-hand accounts of Tolstoy's own efforts in the classroom.[1] From them we may obtain an unexpected picture of the great novelist and philosopher, at the age of thirty-three, in the role of music teacher. We learn, too, that the children were allowed to come and go as they pleased; traditional disciplinary measures were abandoned and outdoor pursuits were encouraged. It was, in fact, during an excursion to take the children swimming that Tolstoy first decided to include music lessons in the curriculum. The story is a delightful one.

As the children and their teacher made their way back to the school from the river on that summer afternoon in 1861, one of the boys – a thickset youngster with the manner of an adult, an acknowledged ringleader among the rest – ran ahead and clambered up into the cart leading the way. Taking over the reins, he set his cap at an angle, spat out of the side of his mouth and began to sing a melancholy folksong with great feeling. When the other boys laughed at this performance, he shouted back at them in an assumed grown-up voice and went on with his song. Soon two other boys joined him in the cart and began to sing the chorus. Tolstoy observed that they were instinctively able to harmonise the tune, singing in thirds and sixths with the original singer. Before long, all the children were singing – though not with the same natural aptitude. Tolstoy decided to build upon that foundation.

When they got back to school the first singing lesson began. Tolstoy's gambit was an interesting one. Instead of starting with a melody, he introduced the children at once to singing in harmony. The class was divided into three and, using the French sol-fa names, he taught them to sing the chords, adding the bass line himself.

This was soon mastered; and before long the most able were passing from one part to another, having learned them all. 'Oh, we like this,' the children cried, 'It makes some thing shake in our ears! Let's do it again.' There was no stopping them. They sang their four chords in the classroom, in the garden, on the way home from school. Late at night they were still doing it. No one could relinquish this musical triumph.

The next day, following that happy overture, Tolstoy began teaching them to sing up the scale. The 'musical' children managed this without difficulty, though the weaker ones hardly got as far as the third. The notes were written upon the board using the C clef, but the children were taught to use the sol-fa names for the notes. After some half-dozen lessons, still much enjoyed by the class, the children had learned to sing a *Kyrie* and *Gloria* as well as a three-part song with piano accompaniment. Half of each lesson was spent in learning these things, the rest in vocal exercises which the children made up for them-

[1] The two articles concerned appeared in the issues for November/December 1862.

selves – *do–mi–ré–fa–mi–sol*, etc., or *do–mi–ré–do–ré–fa–mi–ré*, etc., and the like.

Before long, however, Tolstoy had become aware that staff notation was puzzling many of the weaker children and he decided to use numerals to represent the degrees of the scale. This proved a great help. Soon they were all able to pitch named intervals, calculating them in their minds from the figures. He found that they were particularly fond of fourths. *Fa*, the subdominant, captivated them with its strength; and they took to calling it 'the Giant'. *Do*, the tonic, they called 'the Crier'. Their next discovery was that each of these characterful notes was preceded in the scale by a semitone. From that, they went on to examine the make-up of the major and minor scales. The setting of the *Gloria* which they had already learned was in a minor key; and this allowed their ears to guide them in framing the scale itself.

When that stage was reached, some of the children found their music lessons less enjoyable; and under the system of free-discipline followed in the school, they were allowed to drift away. The rest went on to investigate sharps and flats; and at least two of the children made a hobby of writing down the tunes of songs they already knew, from memory. Soon, the idea was proposed that the class should surprise the rest of the village by singing in the church. They began to rehearse the music of the Mass and the Cherubic Hymn of Bortniánski. The children and their parents were enthusiastic about the project; and the performance of the music at the church was well received. But Tolstoy found himself regretting that in order to reach a satisfactory standard, choir practices had to be made compulsory, at the cost of some loss of enthusiasm among the children. 'I must confess,' he wrote, 'that I often felt sorry, watching some tiny Kiryúshka in his tattered peasant coat as he sang away at his part, only to be told to repeat it again and again until he lost patience.'

How far Tolstoy's own lack of conviction affected the children it is not easy to estimate. But there is no doubt that, after that first public appearance, the children lost much of their original enthusiasm. An attempt to get a choir together for the church the following Easter was successful only after much effort. And for Tolstoy, who felt that the children's enthusiasm for what they were doing was the paramount consideration, the singers began to acquire some of the characteristics of professional choristers. They sang well, but he thought their pleasure in singing was not spontaneous. Soon after that the project was dropped.

Before drawing too hasty a conclusion from that incident, we should note that the life of the school itself was to be all too brief. By 1864, Tolstoy's energies were diverted to the writing of *War and Peace*, which came out in instalments for the next five years, to be followed at regular intervals by his five other great novels. His flirtation with schoolmastering was at an end. While there is no doubt of the real nature of his fascination with the education of deprived children, one is left with the feeling that Tolstoy lacked the equipment of a teacher prepared to accept both the triumphs and failures of a lifelong career in a school. No doubt his own undisciplined youth demonstrated that shortcoming. And the reader will perhaps find himself wondering how far a child's enthusiasm for his studies should be allowed to decide his involvement in a curriculum; how far 'pleasure' equates with entertainment as opposed to achievement. These are matters which it is not intended to pontificate upon here.

But before leaving the story of Tolstoy's adventure as a teacher of music there are other matters mentioned in his account which deserve notice. For instance, he tells us that when he came to assess the progress made by his pupils after a few lessons, he realised that he was adopting a method of teaching music which he had first encountered during his foreign travels. While in Paris he had attended the classes given by Émile Chevé:

> I saw hundreds of horny-handed labourers sitting on benches under which lay the tools which they had just brought from their work, all singing from notes, all able to understand and enjoy the music in their hands. As I looked at these French workmen I could easily see in my mind's eye Russian peasants in their places ...

The classes conducted by Chevé in Paris during the late 1850s, while Tolstoy was there, had their first origins in the numeral notation proposed by Rousseau in 1742.[2] Although Rousseau's plan to employ numerals in place of staff notation was never adopted, long after his death the value of this method of representing pitch *to beginners* was recognised by Pierre Galin. In 1818 Galin published an account of experimental teaching based on numerals which had met with remarkable success in his native town, Bordeaux.[3] He next established himself as a teacher of music in Paris, where similar success soon resulted. But his constitution was not equal to the demands made upon it by his efforts to popularise his methods. He died prematurely in Paris in 1822, before his work was much more than begun.

Following Galin's death a number of his pupil-assistants attempted to continue his work – but with small success. They lacked his charisma and each added personal modifications to his method without improving its effectiveness. Interest in Galin's work gradually faded. Twenty years later, however, two of his original pupils, a brother and sister, Aimé and Nanine Paris, revived the

[2] K. Simpson, 'Jean Jacques Rousseau (1712–78)', *Music Teacher*, October/November 1967; reprinted in *Some Great Music Educators*, ed. K. Simpson (London: Novello, 1976), pp. 14–19.

[3] P. Galin, *Rationale for a New Way of Teaching Music (1818)*, CTME 8 (Kilkenny: Boethius Press, 1983).

Galin method, publishing in 1838 a *Méthode élémentaire de musique* as a definitive textbook. Upon Nanine's marriage to Émile Chevé, her husband took on the role of active publicity agent and principal teacher in the movement soon to be known as the Galin–Paris–Chevé Society.[4] It was Chevé who produced the revised *Méthode Elémentaire* in 1856 used in the class which Tolstoy had attended.

Tolstoy had been deeply impressed by the spectacle of 'five or six hundred men and women, some of them between forty and fifty years of age, all singing in perfect harmony and at sight whatever their teacher put before them.' Yet his deep dislike of 'formal' teaching caused him to reject using Chevé's *Méthode* as a means of instructing his own young pupils. He had not adopted it, he declared, simply because it *was* a Method. As such, it included many rules, exercises and teaching devices which Tolstoy believed to have no vital significance. Every teacher, he declared, fabricated such devices 'by the hundred' in the course of his daily task. It was his own preference to select from among Chevé's ideas those which seemed to simplify the learner's task at a particular stage. Among such considerations Tolstoy was particularly impressed by the following, which he recommended to the readers of his educational journal.

1. He had tried to teach staff notation for 'about ten lessons' before using numerals to represent Pitch. After a single lesson the children adopted them at once, asking him (in the uninhibited manner encouraged at Yásnaya Polyána) to employ them in future.

2. Chevé taught the pitch and rhythmic aspects of notation separately. Tolstoy had found that when children tapped out the rhythm of a passage before attempting to sing it, difficulties which previously seemed insuperable at once disappeared. Having but tried this approach, teachers would realise what torments their pupils might be spared.

3. Much of Chevé's success seemed to Tolstoy to depend upon his ability to make his lessons enjoyable and the subject popular. Music lessons conducted in the same pleasurable manner elsewhere would help to popularise music and arrest the decay of the art. It was not enough to concentrate on technique. Teaching must be done *musically*. Although 'young ladies' might be made to play demanding technical exercises, with the average child it was better not to teach at all than to teach music mechanically.

4. The aim of musical instruction must be to impart a knowledge of music without transferring personal limitations of musical taste.

4 K. Simpson, 'Pierre Galin (1786–1822), Aimé Paris (1798–1866) and Émile Chevé (1800–64)', *Music Teacher*, December 1967/January 1968; reprinted in *Some Great Music Educators*, pp. 20–7.

These and other observations upon pedagogical matters advanced in *Yásnaya Polyána* were based upon something like two years' practical experience in the classroom by an amateur who, though gifted with a remarkable mind, was by no means free from firmly held prejudices. Debate upon child-centred education, free-discipline in schools, and other theories toward which Tolstoy was reaching, still continues. It is not our intention to add to the pages already devoted to those discussions, here. But something further must be said about one aspect of Tolstoy's experience and consequent recommendations. This, it seems clear, was due to the French bias of his own early education – he had French tutors in childhood – and the continuing use of French in polite Russian society throughout much of his life.

With that cultural and linguistic background, Tolstoy naturally found himself most at his ease, during his foreign travels, in Paris. And it was there that he took advantage of the available opportunity to attend public singing classes. His own musical training, moreover, had been in the French tradition; to him the notes of the scale of C were named *do, ré, mi, fa, sol, la, si*. Those 'fixed' sol-fa names offered no assistance to a sight-singer reading a passage in other keys: the scale of B major ran *si, do, ré, mi, fa, sol, la*, despite its array of sharps. It was this idiosyncratic use of sol-fa in France that caused not only Chevé, but Paris, Galin and Rousseau before him, to employ numerals as an aid to sight reading.

What, one wonders, would have been the result, if Tolstoy had been fluent in English, had made London the scene of his investigation of popular singing classes, and had encountered the Tonic Sol-fa system which John Curwen[5] was even then bringing to thousands of amateur choralists? Perhaps, then, fewer of Tolstoy's little pupils would have drifted away from their music lessons once keys other than C were introduced ...

---

[5] Watkins Shaw, 'John Curwen (1616–80)', *Music Teacher*, March/April 1968; reprinted in *Some Great Music Educators*, pp. 30–42.

The Land With Music:
Reality and Myth in Music Education
[1988]

Reading maketh a full man ... Histories make men wise.

(Francis Bacon, 1597)

History is bunk.

(Henry Ford, 1919)

One of the benefits of a study of history is that it suggests that it is always possible to reverse, as Plato puts it, an apparently tendency towards decay, however late the hour. (Hugh Thomas, 1981)

ALTHOUGH the expression *Das Land ohne Musik* has never been traced to an early German source, there is no doubt that the unfavourable concept of England which it encapsulated was long familiar abroad.[1] Here at home during the nineteenth century, even those whom the slur most offended seldom paused to question the implicit notion of German musical supremacy which it carried. Few bother to challenge a truism.

'I have said very little about music in Germany,' wrote one author describing domestic conditions there, 'because we all know and admit that it reaches heights that no other nation can approach'.[2] That fulsome statement with its air of helpless adulation was published in 1908 and typified many others. Some vowed that musical ability among Germans was 'inborn'. Making that claim, another author painted a sentimental picture of the people's habits in 1876:

> Every German man and woman is born with the musical instinct; in many it grows to be a passion; in the poorest German villages you will be certain to find an admirable quartett ... Boys and girls the touching melodies of the mountains and woodlands ... Pious pilgrims passing across the lakes from shrine to shrine lift up their voices in song ... The soldier sings as he keels the regimental pot and pipe-clays his belt and breeches; the laundress sings amongst her suds ...[3]

[1] The precise phrase 'Das Land ohne Musik' was first used as the title of a book, published by Oscar A. H. Schmitz in 1914, with the subtitle 'Englische Gesellschaftsprobleme'. The book had remarkably little to say about music as such, using the title only as a general slur against English lack of *Kultur*. On the other hand, as early as 1840, Englishmen's unmusical reputation abroad was recorded as an established fact: 'Their dull ears and tuneless voices are now a proverb on the continent.' F. Oakeley, *The British Critic* 28 (1840), p. 374.

[2] A. Sidgwick, *Home Life in Germany* (London, 1908), p. 316.

[3] Anon., *German Home Life* (London, 1876), pp. 154–5.

In spite of its unctuous tone there is no doubting the truth of the incidents described in that encomium – many similar accounts have been recorded. What remains in doubt, however, is whether this love and understanding of music was 'inborn', and how far it would endure. Nor is this just a question of semantics. For while it was justifiable to maintain that the Germans had become a musical race, they had not always enjoyed that standing.

The earliest known reference linking the people known as Germans with any mention of music Is contained in the study of the race compiled by the Roman historian, Tacitus. In his *Germania*, written in AD 98 and recognised as verifiably just, Tacitus described his country's foes as valiant, austere and chaste; though when not at war given to indolence and gluttony. Drinking bouts lasting a day and a night were not unusual with them. He also told of their war chants. In times of battle, he wrote, to kindle courage while inspiring terror in their enemies they employed a kind of chant named *barritus* or elephant-roar, holding their shields against their mouths to make the sound more resonant and alarming. Sheer volume of sound, not vocal skill, was the aim: an army that roared the loudest was destined to be the winner.[4]

Six centuries later, as the belated conversion of Germany gathered strength and Christian song-schools were first established there by Bishop Boniface, John the Deacon described the difficulty of teaching the Germans Gregorian chant. Their rough voices,' he declared, 'roaring like thunder, are not capable of soft modulation; for their throats, hardened by drink, cannot execute with flexibility what a tender melody requires. Indeed, their voices give out tones similar to the rumbling of a baggage-wagon rolling down from a height.'[5]

Under Charlemagne (768–814) further schools were attached to every monastery and abbey, and with the passing of the Dark Ages came new centres of learning eventually to become universities. Music was now taught at all levels – from simple plainchant to a study of the writings of Boethius – and during the Middle Ages professional musical establishments were formed at the courts of German princes and in many towns. After this upsurge of musical activity among the Germans it is disconcerting to find Andreas Ornithoparcus in 1517 still echoing Tacitus:

> Every man lives after his own humour ... Hence it is that the English do carrol; the French sing; the Spaniards weep; the Italians that dwell about the coast of Janua caper with their voice, the other barke; but the Germans, which I am ashamed to utter, doe howle like wolves ... Germany nourisheth many cantors but few musicians. For very few, excepting those

[4] Tacitus, *On Britain and Germany*, trans. H. Mattingly (London, 1948), pp. 102–5.
[5] John the Deacon, *Life of St Gregory*, trans. in F. L. Ritter, *History of Music* (London, 1876), p. 23.

which are or have been in the chapels of princes, do truly know the art of singing. For those to whom this charge is given, do appoint for the government of the service, Youth Cantors, whom they choose by the shrillness of their voices, not for their cunning in that art, thinking that God is pleased with bellowing and braying.[6]

That forthright criticism from the pen of an able and respected musician was published just one year before Martin Luther signalled the Reformation; and it was In order to correct the situation which it described that he required every teacher in a Lutheran school to be musically proficient.[7]

It will scarcely be necessary to argue here that the prime stimulus for musical capability among successive generations of ordinary Germans was the systematic teaching provided in the schools of the Reformation. Daily periods of instruction conducted in every Lutheran school by teachers appointed only if they 'knew how to sing',[8] when added to weekly participation in church services under the direction of the same teachers, enabled theory and practice to develop side by side. Over the generations disciplined teaching guided by the music manuals specially written by Rhau (1517), Listenius (1533), Agricola (1539) and others, was to produce musical competence at a level sufficient to stimulate enjoyment.

But to suppose that, once prompted by the partnership of church and school to meet the needs of a particular era, such a pattern of teaching and experience must survive unshaken over the centuries would be foolhardy. Paul Henry Lang, while paying unreserved tribute to its cultural impact, was careful not to suggest that the influence of Lutheran musical training was limitless:

> Musical instruction in the Protestant *Gymnasia* and parochial schools was exemplary ... This active and well-directed musical life furnished the background for the incomparable musical culture of the Saxon-Thuringian provinces, a culture which produced Schütz, Bach, and Handel.[9]

It is not difficult to trace the erosive influences responsible for later fluctuations. The Thirty Years War (1618–48) damaged every sphere of art; musical establishments in church, court and town were all reduced in size. With peace came further destructive change. The growth of secular values, and the

---

[6] A. Ornithoparcus, *Micrologus* (1517), trans. J. Dowland (1609); quoted in J. Hawkins, *History of Music* (London, 1776; edn of 1853), vol. I, p. 313.

[7] M. Luther, *Colloquia Mensalia*, trans. H. Bell (London, 1652), p. 500.

[8] The German original of the passage translated by H. Bell (above) reads: 'Ein schulmeister muss singen können, sonst sehe ich ihn nicht an ...'

[9] P. H. Lang, *Music in Western Civilisation* (New York, 1941), p. 213.

puritanical Pietism designed to counter it, both damaged the status of music in the Lutheran church. As a result skilled choral forces tended to be concentrated on one church or group of churches in an area, the rest managing without. The training of the smaller contingent of choristers required was consequently provided in one particular school, incidentally reducing the functional importance of music as a subject and the attention given to teaching it in other schools. This segregation of choristers had long been the practice in Catholic regions. But Catholic resistance to secularising influence was strong enough to ensure the preservation of musical standards in most churches, with compensatory advantages for their receptive congregations.

The extent to which this restrictive policy damaged conditions in the Protestant north, on the other hand, is forcibly demonstrated in the complaints made by Johann Kuhnau, J. S. Bach, and later Cantors at St Thomas's, Leipzig, about the increasingly meagre forces made available at what was the best musically equipped church in the region.[10] The plight of less eminent musicians serving in smaller churches was far worse; and the constraints placed upon music teaching in their local schools even more damaging.

As a result, local churches ceased to provide the obvious centres of musical activity for a community. In compensation, as it were, there was a marked rise in amateur, secular music-making – something most obviously reflected in the growth of *collegia musica* in university towns. The former concept of schoolroom and choir-loft as the natural scene of universal musical training under the Cantor's direction, now steadily gave place to a general acceptance of home-based private tuition as the norm, for those categorised as musically gifted.

The critical period in which circumstances eventually combined to sever links with ancient tradition can be identified with some confidence as the second decade of the eighteenth century. It was then, in order to induce his countrymen to familiarise themselves with the new styles of French and Italian secular music, that Johann Mattheson published his *Das neu-eröffnete Orchestre* (1713). In that book, besides describing unfamiliar developments in music abroad, Mattheson urged German musicians to re-educate themselves and ensure that the musical education of future generations was rid of exploded theoretical concepts and practices. In particular he attacked the church modes and hexachordal solmisation as outworn survivals preserved rather as hallowed relics than for their utility.

Mattheson's unsparing assault on tradition understandably provoked indignation among those brought up to believe that musical wisdom dwelt in the past. Foremost among such dissentients was Johann Buttstett, the leading organist of Erfurt, who published a vigorous rebuttal of Mattheson's arguments

[10] H. T. David and A. Mendel. *The Bach Reader* (London, 1946), pp. 120–4. A. Schweitzer, *J. S. Bach*, trans. E. Newman (London, 1911; R/1967), vol. 1, pp. 116ff.

in *Ut, mi, sol, re, fa, la, tota musica et harmonica aeterna* (1716). But Mattheson was more than equal to this riposte. Dismissing Buttstett's mystic and symbolic title with a devastating pun: *Todte (nicht tota) Musica*, the sophisticated. cosmopolitan Hamburg musician demolished his provincial opponent in *Das beschützte Orchestre* (1717) with a finality that was to remain unquestioned.[11]

To replace the Guidonian syllables and their cumbersome mutations Mattheson supported the system known as *Abcedieren*. When first daringly introduced in the sixteenth century by Pancratius Crüger this unorthodox method, which used chromatic, alphabetical note-names (*C, Cis, Ces; D, Dis, Des*, etc.) instead of sol-fa, had led to Crüger's dismissal from his post of Rector at Lübeck in 1588. But other teachers dissatisfied with solmisation revived its use during the seventeenth century, and now it was soon to become standard practice.

Another emphatic break with the past came as schools were granted greater independence from the Church, and the State assumed responsibility for educational provision. In the Grand Duchy of Weimar school attendance had been enforced upon both boys and girls as early as 1619.[12] Frederick the Great now extended compulsory education to the whole kingdom of Prussia, making special provision for the teaching of music in a Decree of 18 October 1746:

> Having received many complaints of the decline in the art of singing, and the neglect of it in our gymnasiums and schools, His Majesty commands that the young people in all public schools and gymnasiums shall be exercised more diligently therein, and to that end shall have singing-lessons three times a week.[13]

Thereafter, through the influence of J. B. Basedow and J.-J. Rousseau,[14] schooling underwent notable modification. Greater stress was laid on practical activities, and tentative efforts were made to teach music as an aesthetic experience. After 1800, Rousseau's theories were demonstrated practically in Switzerland by Pestalozzi,[15] whose rationalisation of teaching method was next applied to music by M. T. Pfeiffer and published by Hans Nägeli.[16] As a direct result, through the agency of C. A. Zeller, B. C. L. Natorp, and other

---

[11] B. C. Cannon, *Johann Mattheson, Spectator in Music* (New Haven, 1947), *passim*; W. Blankenburg, 'Der Titel und das Titelbild von J. H. Buttstetts Schrift,' *Die Musikforschung* 3 (1950), p. 64.

[12] W. Boyd and E. J. King, *History of Western Education* (New York, 1973), p. 307.

[13] Translated in Grove, *Dictionary of Music and Musicians* (London, 1948), vol. 2, p. 311.

[14] J. Basedow, *Representations to Philanthropists* (1768); J.-J. Rousseau, *Émile* (1762).

[15] R. De Guimps, *Pestalozzi: His Life and Work*, trans. J. Russell (London, 1890).

[16] H. G. Nägeli, *Die Pestalozzische Gesangbildungslehre* (Zurich, 1809).

influential local teachers, music-reading by means of numeral notation was adopted in several German regions.[17]

That such steps should have been necessary was a clear indictment of *Abcedieren*. Like *solfège*, which it resembled in affording a conveniently singable name for each degree of the scale, this method offered advantages to capable students; but as a teaching aid for beginners it presented more problems than it solved. Its inadequacy was further substantiated by the flood of alternative teaching methods produced by teachers in German teacher-training colleges during the first half of the century. But opportunities to employ those methods fruitfully were minimised as music's traditional place in the curriculum gave way to language and science in Gymnasiums, Realschulen, and Bürgerschulen. With the exception of a few cases where an individual teacher was able to maintain standards in a celebrated school, it was now only in the Volksschulen that music lessons were consistently found.[18]

But in those elementary schools, with their former tradition of teaching in the vernacular, not Latin, a traditional level of 'folkish' simplicity moderated teaching standards generally. Musical aims were commonly limited to teaching hymns and simplistic, so-called folksongs by rote, controlled by the ubiquitous violin that every primary school teacher was trained to rely upon as the standard teaching aid.[19]

The picture that thus emerges of music teaching in German schools later in the nineteenth century largely comprises unsystematic, mechanical activity, often at the hands of indifferent teachers. That this should have been so, just at the time when adulation of the musical powers of the Germans was at its height in England, presents more than a touch or irony. For by curtailing the *universal* musical education of the young – the acknowledged source of those powers – the Germans put at risk a national endowment they had come to take for granted. It was now no longer the school, but the home, that encouraged musical training; the drive often largely supplied by middle-class social ambition. More disturbingly, with the proclamation of the German Empire in 1871, the schools lent themselves to ideological indoctrination through promoting the use of nationalistic songs glorifying militarism.

It was perhaps the thinly veiled antipathy generated between Germany and England after 1871 that prompted John Hullah, the man nominally responsible for music teaching in English schools since 1840, to question whether the Germans in fact possessed greater inherent musical aptitude than other nations.

[17] K. A. Zeller, *Beitrage zur Befoerdurung der Preuss: National Erziehung* (Königsberg, 1810–17); C. L. Natorp, *Anleitung zur Unterweisung im Singen für Lehrer in Volksschulen* (Potsdam, 1813).

[18] H. Kretzschmar, *Musikalische Zeitfragen* (Leipzig, 1903).

[19] J. S. Curwen, *School Music Abroad* (London, 1901), p. 2.

Now government Inspector of Music, as he neared the end of his career Hullah secured the Privy Council's authority in 1879 to investigate music teaching in schools on the continent.

After a tour lasting thirteen weeks and embracing Switzerland, Holland and Belgium, as well as Germany, Hullah compiled a detailed *Report* on his frequently disappointing experiences.[20] Summarising his findings he emphasised a number of points. First, that continental children remained longer at school, and appeared more eager to learn, than was the case in England. Secondly, class numbers were smaller. Thirdly, there was no evidence of any greater aptitude for particular subjects in Swiss, German, Dutch, or Belgian children than in their English counterparts. And fourthly, where music was concerned, repeated opportunities of observing the first attempts of German children to imitate musical sounds had shown the same mixture of aptitude and inaptitude as displayed by English children. There were, in short, as many musically incompetent pupils in Germany and every other continental country as in England.[21]

A mid-nineteenth century German caricature of a music lesson confirms Hullah's findings in that respect (see illus. 1). The presence of a clerical supervisor does nothing to deter the antics of the less able pupils seated at the back of the class. 'In a word,' Hullah maintained, 'I believe that the so-called "natural" musical power of the English people is equal to that of the German or any other people. If the greater musical fecundity of the German nation be adduced as evidence to the contrary, it must be borne in mind that this fecundity is of recent growth, and may in turn prove to be but temporary.'[22]

Finally, Hullah uttered a devastating censure. It was his opinion, he declared, that in spite of their lengthy and thorough training German teachers of music in schools were generally ineffective; the results of their teaching to be described as 'the poorest conceivable.'[23] That finding was borne out in his *Report* by a variety of detailed accounts of visits to schools in Stuttgart, Munich, Vienna, Prague, Dresden, Leipzig, Berlin, and Hanover.

Whatever its effect in his own country, the impact of Hullah's *Report* in Germany can hardly be exaggerated. It was first translated into German by Hermann Kretzschmar, later to become Professor of Music at the University

---

[20] J. Hullah, *Report on Musical Instruction in Elementary Schools on the Continent; Minutes of the Committee of Council on Education* (London, 1880), pp. 529–48; reprinted in J. Hullah and J. S. Curwen, *School Music Abroad*, ed. B. Rainbow, CTME 15 (Kilkenny, 1985).

[21] *Ibid*, pp. 544–5.

[22] *Ibid.*, p. 545.

[23] *Ibid.*, p. 546.

1 J. B. Scholl, *The Singing Lesson* (detail) (1848). The tune on the board is that of 'God save the Queen', sung in Germany to 'Heil Dir im Siegerkranz' and other texts. Following common practice, a robed priest is present to supervise the lesson. The teacher is the clownish figure regularly depicted in such scenes; the pupils, villagers ranging from capable singers to urchins with no interest in the lesson. (From a print in the Kunstmuseum Dusseldorf, Bibliothek, Inv. Nr. 33/152 reproduced with permission.)

of Berlin, and published in the journal *Die Grenzboten* in 1881.[24] Kretzschmar thereupon devoted himself over many years to arresting the decline which it had revealed. His ideals were summarised in the detailed programme of reform published in his *Musikalische Zeitfragen* (1903) and embracing every aspect of musical education. both amateur and professional, from primary school to university, from private teacher to conservatory. In it he acknowledged the impetus given to his efforts by John Hullah's public condemnation of existing conditions.[25]

Among the direct results of Kretzschmar's reforming policy was the re-introduction of the music lesson in Gymnasiums and the adoption of agreed music syllabuses, including sight-singing, in schools generally. Teachers of singing were now required to qualify by examination, their training being widened to include a study of musical history; they were encouraged, moreover, to develop a sense of the emotive and aesthetic potential of music as distinct from the functional and mechanical rote-singing formerly allowed to monopolise music

[24] H. Kretzschmar. 'Ein englische Aktenstück über den deutschen Schulgesang'; in *Die Grenzboten* (Leipzig, 1881), vol. 4, p. 175ff. Also in *Gesammelte Aufsatze über Musik und Anderes* (Leipzig, 1910), p. 45ff.

[25] *Ibid.*

lessons.[26] But perhaps Kretzschmar's greatest achievement was to persuade the Prussian government that reform was needed at all.

Nor was Kretzschmar's a lone voice calling for reform. The *Allgemeine Deutscher Musikverein* had long expressed disapproval of the state of music teaching current in German schools; and among notable innovations on the part of individuals designed to promote more systematic teaching was *Tonika Do*, a German version of Tonic Sol-fa devised by Agnes Hundoegger in 1897.[27] Another was the *Tonwort* system of Carl Eitz, introduced in 1891 and later employed at an elementary level in Bavarian schools, which provided a separate note-name for every chromatic and enharmonic degree of the scale.[28] Both methods were designed to promote sight-singing in schools as an essential basic skill.

The reinstatement of sight-singing at length restored a vital but neglected activity that had held a central place in German school music since Luther's day. The fact that this skill had originally been taught simply to enhance the church service, then been preserved only to build up a store of hymn tunes – both being non-musical ends – in no way reduced its innate capacity to develop greater powers of musical perception in those who acquired it. Generations of ordinary Germans had benefited from that circumstance. Indeed, as we have seen, their reputation as a musical people – as opposed to a nation numbering eminent musicians among its sons – was first engendered in this way. Leo Kestenberg, who followed in Kretzschmar's reforming footsteps after 1918, showed by the policies outlined in his *Musikerziehung und Musikpflege* (1921) that he was aware of this truth. More familiar with the realities of the classroom than Kretzschmar, he was able to concentrate upon attainable ends and to translate his predecessor's idealism into a workable system.[29]

Piecing together this narrative of the slow rise of musical education in Germany, observing its sudden growth and widespread fruits; then discovering how this rich heritage was squandered during the nineteenth century, it is easy to be reminded of a not dissimilar situation at home – where a protracted struggle during that same century saw England at length escape the taunt of being unmusical, then enjoy justified celebrity as a singing nation; only to throw away that new birthright in more recent times, through laxity and would-be populism.

The clearsightedness of such reformers as Kretzschmar and Kestenberg in Germany was enough to bring about a deliberate return to systematic teaching

---

[26] G. Schünemann, *Geschichte der deutschen Schulmusik* (Leipzig, 1928).

[27] A. Hundoegger, *Lehrweise nach Tonika Do*, 10th edn (Köln, 1967), p. 3.

[28] C. A. Eitz, *Das mathematisch-reine Tonsystem* (Leipzig, 1891).

[29] U. Günther. *Die Musikerziehung im Dritten Reich: die Schulmusikerziehung von der Kestenberg-Reform ...* (Berlin, 1967).

in schools there, which halted the Gadarene plunge of self-destruction. So remarkable an instance of the reversal of an apparently fatal tendency toward decay at the eleventh hour perhaps offers hope that, given reformers of similar vision in this country, it is not too late to begin the arduous process of recovery that the impaired state of class music teaching in our schools so evidently demands.

The French Revolution and Music Teaching –
A Bicentennial Review
[1989]

I T PERHAPS SEEMS SCARCELY CREDIBLE that amid the turmoil and bloodshed of the French Revolution the citizen-legislators of Paris spared time to discuss musical training. But after 1789 music was deliberately made a public medium rather than an aristocratic preserve; and musical performances on a massive scale were called for by France's new rulers in a drive to maintain and strengthen revolutionary and patriotic fervour. Most took place in the open air accompanied by pageantry and military spectacle. All demanded vast numbers of performers, and dramatic steps were taken to assemble and train them. The present bicentenary lends new interest to the unlikely sequence of events which resulted, with consequences that have lasted to our own day.

The earliest moves were made after the fall of the Bastille in July 1789, when Bernard Sarrette, a twenty-four-year-old staff-captain in the revolutionary forces took upon himself the task of organising military bands for the National Guard. A typical member of the Girondin intelligentsia within the citizen-militia, Sarrette's first step was to recruit forty-five capable musicians to form a training school. Many of them were distinguished performers formerly in royal service whom he persuaded to earn safety from the Terror by serving the revolutionary cause.

By 1792 Sarrette had been able to secure funds from the municipality to create a Free School of Music in Paris to train further instrumentalists. Pupils were to be admitted between the ages of ten and twenty to receive two lessons in musical rudiments and three instrumental lessons a week. By the following year the newly trained pupils had earned public recognition with a telling contribution to the elaborate musical pageant staged to celebrate the capture of Toulon. As a result the National Convention was called upon to consider granting government support for the Free School.

Thus it was that only a few months after Louis XVI went to the guillotine, members of the Convention met in Paris to hear the poet Marie-Joseph Chénier urge the necessity of promoting training in music – as a powerful agent of political reform. The art of leading men, Chénier argued, depended on directing their sensibilities. That power, he claimed, was signal among music's attributes. And after a ringing speech comparing music's status in Plato's *Republic* with the role it should occupy in their own, Chénier urged his listeners to astonish Europe by showing that even in the present turmoil France could find time for the encouragement of an art that had gained them victories and would soon bring them the delights of peace.[1]

Carried away by Chénier's oratory, his audience adopted the resolution and promptly elevated the Free School of Music to rank as a National Institute. Two years later, in September 1875, after further successful public performances by its pupils, the new institute was made the Conservatoire Nationale de Musique under Sarrette's direction. In line with his policy of admitting as many as sought instruction, the new school had now assumed huge proportions. There were no less than 115 teachers on its staff with 800 pupils covering every branch of instrumental and vocal music, theory and composition.

In a speech at the opening ceremony Sarrette attacked the inadequacy of previous institutions designed to train musicians in France. The former École Royale de Chant earned his particular scorn because it had been limited to supplying the needs of the royal court; earlier institutions for training army bands were denounced for teaching a few marches without attempting to develop musicianship. But Sarrette's greatest condemnation was reserved for the *maîtrises*, the song-schools attached to the cathedrals and greater churches of the land.

> Singing, that essential part of music [Sarrette declared] has always been badly taught in France. The Song Schools were the only institutions for the purpose under the *ancien régime*. Created for the service of religion, their sole aim was to demonstrate how to sing as loudly as possible in order to fill huge spaces with sound. That approach excluded singing with either feeling or expression ... In spite of the existence of more than five hundred of these schools, maintained at an annual cost of some ten million francs and each intended to produce and train musicians, music in France ... had entirely failed to attain the perfection and popularity it enjoyed among both the Germans and Italians.[2]

By then the ancient *maîtrises* had been suppressed in the wave of anti-clerical and atheistic fervour that accompanied the French Revolution, and their endowments confiscated. Part of those funds were now applied to support the new Conservatoire. The five most influential of its teachers, appointed as *inspecteurs de l'enseignement* comprised the country's leading musicians, Méhul, Grétry, Gossec, Lesueur, and Cherubini. But alongside their appointments each was expected to demonstrate loyal support for the Revolution by composing triumphant hymns for the outdoor spectacles that by now formed

---

[1] E. Maruat, 'L'enseignement de la musique en France,' in A. Lavignac and L. de la Laurencie, ed., *Encyclopédie de la musique et Dictionnaire du Conservatoire* (Paris, 1925), 2me partie, vol. 6, pp. 3581–2.

[2] Ibid, p. 3582. [All excerpts translated by BR]

a regular feature of the revolutionary calendar. As a result, several of those eminent musicians had faced the daunting experience of conducting massed open-air rehearsals of their new hymns with the mob of *sans culottes* who made up both audience and chorus on such occasions. To minimise the high risk of disaster – though ostensibly to enhance a fitting atmosphere of neo-classical pageantry – trumpeters of the National Guard were in future stationed about the arena to lead the singing.

The more sumptuous republican festivals organised in Napoleon's day incorporated much more elaborate music. Large-scale choral and orchestral works calling for expert singers and instrumentalists were now composed to honour victorious battles of the French armies. It thus became essential for the Conservatoire to produce thoroughly competent performers rather than a multitude of run-of-the-mill bandsmen. At the same time, as military adventure drew ever more heavily upon the national exchequer, greater economy was forced on the Conservatoire.

Soon, following regular criticism from musicians themselves, Sarrette's original scheme, typical of many grandiose projects conceived during the heady days of the Revolution's early triumphs, had to be modified and made more realistic. By 1802 the staff of the Conservatoire had been drastically cut to thirty-eight and the number of pupils more than halved.[3] Standards of attainment rose correspondingly.

Yet by that time the cult of mammoth musical effects married to pageantry or ceremonial had begun to impose itself upon the national taste. The effect can be recognised unmistakably on one hand in several later works of Berlioz – perhaps particularly the *Grand Messe des Morts* and *Te Deum*. A second, perhaps less familiar aspect of the Revolution's musical monumentalism was to reveal itself in the operatic field.

It was first made apparent in the vogue for 'heroic' operas designed to whip up patriotic feeling, as well as in 'rescue' operas meant to strengthen public morale by celebrating human courage overcoming villainy, misfortune or natural catastrophe. To an unsophisticated popular audience of the new kind cultivated by revolutionary ideals, much of the immediate appeal of those long forgotten works lay with the elaborate staging of the volcanoes, earthquakes, avalanches, or shipwrecks which threatened their heroes; and though much of the dialogue was spoken, the musical scores were designed to balance such spectacular visual effects with large-scale melodramatic devices of their own.

Works of this calibre set new problems for performers. And to equip singers to undertake the dramatic roles concerned – roles so unlike the statuesque operatic heroes and heroines of the *ancien régime* – the Conservatoire was

---

[3] T. Dubois, 'L'enseignement musicale,' in Lavignac and Laurencie, *Encyclopédie*, p. 3446.

obliged to recognise and overcome its weakness in teaching solo singing and discover new methods of developing stage presence. A new department of declamation was now founded and a boarding school for students of singing was opened in 1806. A new concert hall/theatre followed and regular public performances were organised under the title of 'exercises' publics to allow able students to savour audience response while at the same time encouraging their fellows by their example.

Throughout this period of enforced change, in spite of outspoken opposition from several quarters, Sarrette continued to hold the post of Director of the Conservatoire. But with the downfall of Napoleon the post was suspended. François-Louis Perne, a former professor of harmony, was made Inspector-General until Cherubini's epoch-making appointment followed in 1822. After that, under his reforming hand the Conservatoire steadily became recognisable as the forerunner of the institution we know today.

By 1822 the political climate in France had undergone many changes since the Conservatoire was founded. Yet though revolutionary fervour had lapsed and conscious striving to glorify the common man no longer set the tone in the opera house, the challenges to the Conservatoire were unremitting. New operatic styles, the rise of grand opera, the evolution of Romantic orchestration, all increased rather than diminished the demands made upon the institution to produce a worthy elite of singers, instrumentalists and composers. Sarrette's original vision of the Conservatoire as an institution open to every man seeking musical tuition had become a forgotten dream.

Yet elsewhere in post-Revolutionary France the notion persisted of music brought within reach of the common man.

The memorial of popular grievances drawn up in 1789 had stressed the need for educational reform. But below secondary level it produced minimal improvement. Not until a group of philanthropists formed a Society of Elementary Education in 1815 were new schools set up. One of its main supporters was Joseph-Marie, Baron de Gérando, holder of various state posts and a man of unquestionable integrity. He it was who now urged that music lessons should be introduced in the new schools. Presenting realistic arguments to that effect to the Society in July, 1819, de Gérando emphasised the distinction between professional musical training and the type of general initiation through class-singing he was advocating:

> If it is realised that children can be taught to read and write without having to make them into scholars and men of letters, it will be evident that children can be taught music and singing without turning them into finished artists and virtuosos. As to the power which music can exert, without reminding you of circumstances in ancient Greece, I should like to

draw attention to a few hard facts with which everyone is familiar. Music, which in the eyes of some people is just a luxury for the rich, is in fact a most useful helpmeet for a life of laborious toil. Not only does it sustain and refresh, but it governs physical effort, because by making a man's movements more harmonious it renders them less strenuous... You have wisely introduced linear drawing into our schools as a valuable means of improving the precision of hand and eye. Is it not feasible to suppose a little singing would be a natural complement leading to the same goal?[4]

Here was a rationale quite distinct from that of Sarrette. And it was on that basis that music teaching began in French schools in March, 1820. After the decision to introduce it was agreed, various methods of introducing the subject were considered, including those of Alexandre Choron[5] and Pierre Galin,[6] but the choice eventually fell upon that of Guillaume Bocquillon-Wilhem[7] which had been specially devised to allow monitors to assist in teaching it.

By coincidence, Wilhem (to give him his usual name) had been a pupil at the Paris Conservatoire in its early days and had since long felt that curtailment of its activities and the reduction of student numbers had robbed France of the chance to transform itself into a musical national. His ambition, as he put it, was to 'naturalise' music in France. After leaving the Conservatoire in 1803 he had taught music privately. He was now presented with a task that seemed to make his dreams possible.

Both true sons of the Revolution, Sarrette fathered the Conservatoire and Wilhem became the progenitor of school music in France. Their ultimate influence, however, was to be much wider. Most European countries soon imitated the Conservatoire to create Conservatoires of their own. And Wilhem's method was to be formally adopted to teach music in England's schools.

---

[4] H. Radiguer, 'La vie et l'œuvre de B. Wilhem', in Lavignac and Laurencie, *Encyclopédie*, pp. 3720–1.

[5] A. Choron, *Méthode d'instruction primaire pour apprendre à lire et à écrire* (Paris, 1819).

[6] P. Galin, *Exposition d'une nouvelle méthode pour l'enseignement de la musique* (Paris, 1818).

[7] G. L. B. Wilhem, *Manuel musical* (Paris, 1836)

An Excellency in Musick

[1957]

> Musick ... wastes so much of a young Man's Time to gain but a moderate Skill in it; and engages often in such odd Company, that many think it much better spared: and I have amongst Men of Parts and Business so seldom heard anyone commended or esteemed for having an Excellency in Musick, that amongst all those things that ever came into the List of Accomplishments, I think I may give it the last place.
>
> John Locke, *Some Thoughts Concerning Education* (1692)

LOCKE'S unenthusiastic pronouncement on music now appears as readily assailable as his advice on protecting a child from chills: 'Have his Shoes made to leak ... to harden those Parts by a frequent and familiar Use of cold Water.' And indeed, when seen to be the opinion of one of Purcell's contemporaries, his assessment is revealed as rather less than enlightened. Yet Locke is expressing, even explaining, the faintly insolent tolerance with which the English aristocracy tended to regard music during the two centuries which separate the Restoration of Charles II from the middle years of the reign of Victoria. He confirms our impression that Purcell's royal master, whom Pepys saw from his pew at Whitehall Chapel nonchalantly waving his hand in time to the anthem, thought of music only as a minor form of entertainment. He shows us why Lord Chesterfield would allow his son to listen to music, if he must, but emphatically forbade him to learn to play an instrument and so rank as a common fiddler.

The pioneers of popular musical education in England in the nineteenth century achieved their first triumphs because, paradoxically enough, although unaware of Locke's treatise, they successfully contradicted him on both counts. The study and practice of music could no longer be pronounced a time-wasting and useless activity when given an honourable function – that of enabling churchgoers to read and sing their part in the service. Sarah Glover's revolutionary first publication on sight-singing (1828) was significantly entitled *A Scheme for Making Psalmody Congregational*. And as to the propensity of music to lead its devotees into bad company, the early Victorians were to see the tables dramatically turned. John Hullah's mammoth singing classes (1841) earned the weighty approval of the Privy Council not least because they provided such an attractive alternative to the public-house.

This assumption of purposefulness and respectability lent music a new prestige in an age growing increasingly materialistic and conscience-stricken. Evening classes for adults, day schools for the 'Children of the Poor', and new training colleges for their teachers all began to provide facilities for tuition in vocal music. The drive was on to Make England a Musical Nation. As the century proceeded, a phenomenal wave of enthusiasm for sight-singing, nourished by the independent activities of Mainzer and Curwen as well as Hullah, produced those two notable hallmarks of amateur musical life in Victorian England – the local choral society in every town, and the surpliced choir of men and boys in every church.

Both Hullah and Curwen saw that although the immediate success of their movements depended upon the enthusiasm and competence of their adult pupils, lasting achievement would only be secured by teaching young children in the day-and Sunday-schools. Each of these men published manuals and treatises for teachers containing what now appear over-precise instructions:

Now, children, we are going to learn the art of singing a tune.

What are we going to learn? ...

First, then, you must remember that any musical sound is called a note.

What is a musical sound called?

This is a note. ...

I will sing another note. ...

Now I will sing another note.

Could not some of you sing a note?

Hold up hands, those who can sing a note ...[1]

But it was indeed largely through the efforts of these two men, with their pupils and followers, that school music was developed until the establishment of the Board Schools in 1870. They aimed to make *every* teacher competent to teach notation and singing from sight. But since the musical capabilities of many who undertook this task were small, and their teaching conducted largely by rule of thumb, musical activities in most schools were very limited. Most music lessons at this time consisted entirely of unaccompanied singing – very few schools had a piano, though one might occasionally possess a harmonium or seraphine. The teacher would point out notes on the blackboard, on a wall chart, or by hand signals, and the class would attempt to sing them. All too often, depending on the degree of musicianship of the teacher, these notes would bear no relationship to each other, and the exercise would have little connection with music. For the rest, the class learned perhaps a half-dozen simple songs a year.

[1] From one of John Curwen's model lessons in the *Independent Magazine* (1842).

With the introduction of the 'New Code' of 1883, music joined the group of subjects whose efficient teaching decided the amount of the government grant made towards the upkeep of a school. This method of 'payment by results' meant that for every pupil in the school who was able to join in singing songs learned by rote, a grant of sixpence was made. But for every child who could sing *at sight* that amount was doubled. Annual inspections were held to test this competence. Circular No. 219 issued by the Education Department in February, 1883, opens with these canny instructions:

1. If during the examination the Inspector should notice that one or two voices are leading the bulk of the children, such voices must be silenced.

2. Teachers may be allowed to start, but not join in the singing...

Understandably this development produced a flurry of activity, mostly on the part of those teachers with little musical aptitude. And a host of miniature treatises began to appear – crammers for unmusical music teachers – designed, as one issued by the National Society in 1884 admits in its preface, 'to enable scholars to pass the various "tests" at the annual Government examination'.

By the end of the century the singing lesson held an assured place in the timetable of most schools in this country. And if the degree of musicianship to which children were stimulated was very limited, it is generally true that within those narrow limits their training was thorough. That the national standard of musical taste remained low is perhaps partly because the music which these children sang was indifferent, and partly because their singing was performed purely as a task, and in preparation for an examination which their own teachers clearly dreaded.

The standards by which songs for use in school were selected had changed hardly at all since the National Society outlined its method of choice in 1841:

Such tunes will be practised as seem calculated, while they refine the tone of mind, to infuse energy into the will; and such words will be chosen as breathe a devout and loyal spirit – words which will create a correct standard of taste in the learners, so that they may be led to reject, with disgust, songs of a vulgar or degenerating tendency ...

(*33rd Annual Report of the National Society*)

Great attention was given to the 'proper' nature of the words of songs, musical considerations, though loftily expressed, being of a largely undefinable nature. But during the last decade of the century this biased attitude was frequently attacked – notably by John Farmer and C. V. Stanford – and the teaching of traditional 'national' songs recommended instead.

In the twentieth century the importance of singing and of learning to read music has become more and more widely recognised as fundamental. But there has also been increasing a conviction that other forms of musical activity are complementary, and of great value in school. Stewart Macpherson, Walford Davies and Percy Scholes first interested us in ways to stimulate active listening. Then the music masters at our greater boarding schools began to demonstrate that concerted instrumental music-making by school children could be not only edifying and enjoyable to the performers, but tolerable and eventually stimulating to the listeners as well. And so, to the modulator and tuning-fork were added the school piano, the gramophone, and wireless set; the recorder and percussion bands, the violin class and school orchestra.

If the field has grown notably wider, the tools to hand have increased correspondingly – the constant factor being the teacher upon whose integrity, vision, conviction and enthusiasm the whole enterprise still depends. For the task is now seen to be of much greater breadth and complexity than had perhaps been realised; no less than to provide for the continuous development of a means of expression and source of enjoyment throughout life.

The Glass Harmonicon Rediscovered
[1974]

S ARAH GLOVER'S pioneer activity in the field of music education in this country is now widely acknowledged. Every serious student of music in education recognises her as the inventor of a new notation of sol-fa initials which was to form the basis of John Curwen's Tonic Sol-fa. On a recent visit to Norwich, the city where she lived and worked, I made a sentimental pilgrimage to her house in Pottergate, now marked with a commemorative plaque, and to the church of St Lawrence, where her father was vicar and she trained the choir. The church itself, one of the rich heritage of medieval buildings which distinguish the city, is now no longer in use; but among the relics consequently removed to the Church Museum in Hungate I was amazed to come upon Miss Glover's original 'Glass Harmonicon'. Further enquiries revealed that it had lain apparently unrecognised for more than half a century in a room over the church porch at St Lawrence's, miraculously surviving the attentions of generations of the inquisitive of all ages. Still in good working order, it now stands on a table beneath a wall display of 'church gallery' instruments with which – save for its musical nature – it has little in common. The fact that it has survived to be preserved in this way enables some of the misconceptions which have grown up about this unfamiliar instrument to be set right.

In her *History of the Norwich Sol-fa System* which was published in 1844 (and of which only a single copy is known to exist) Sarah Glover spoke of the difficulty of introducing her system of teaching in schools without the supervision of an experienced musician or the aid of a musical instrument. Her remark reminds us that a piano and a pianist were unlikely to be found in most English schools until the last decade of the nineteenth century. To overcome these disadvantages she therefore devised an ingenious but simple keyboard instrument with a compass limited to the range of children's voices and equipped with a device which would enable the less musically accomplished teacher or monitor to fix the keynote and then identify the remaining notes of any major or minor key. The little instrument was manufactured for her by a Norwich cabinet maker and sold for £1 11s 6d. The notes were produced on a row of twenty-five glass bars which, she claimed, would 'unite purity of tone with excellence in tune, and cheapness with durability'. The example which has survived was perhaps a *de luxe* prototype – for it has a sturdy polished mahogany case and could hardly have been produced so cheaply – but it has certainly justified Miss Glover's claim for the durability of her Harmonicon.

The secret of the Harmonicon was a movable roller situated just above the keyboard. This roller could be rotated to expose in turn any one of twelve different placings of the sol-fa scale inscribed along its length. By turning the roller to coincide with a chosen code letter set out on a fixed chart immediately above, the sol-fa names appropriate to any of the twelve major keys could be made to stand above their corresponding notes on the keyboard. This feature can be clearly seen in the photograph below, where the roller has been turned so as to fix the sol-fa scale in the key of C. This is done by making D(oh) on the roller coincide with the code letter 'O' on the fixed chart above, The coding of the various major keys (and thence of their relative minors) which governs the rotation of the roller is as follows:

Key	*Code letter*
A	H
B♭	J
B	K
C	O
D♭	P
D	Q
E♭	U
E	V
F	W
F♯	X
G	Y
A♭	Z

The code letters, it will be seen, run consecutively from the end of the alphabet but excluding those letters which already have a different function in the sol-fa scale (L(ah), M(e), R(ay), S(oh), and T(e)). The relative minor scale according to Sarah Glover's scheme was represented in sol-fa as L(ah), T(e), D(oh), R(ay), M(e), B(a), N(e), L(ah); and the small symbols for Ba and Ne can also be seen in the photograph above the notes F♯ and G♯.

This, then, was the instrument that Sarah Glover used as a cheaper and simpler substitute for a piano to set the pitch for her child singers. It was not, as one writer has suggested, an aural aid placed in the hands of all her pupils – even when sold at a price of £1 11*s* 6*d* so luxurious a refinement would have been beyond the means of schools during the first half of the nineteenth century. The teacher or monitor-in-charge alone employed it.

The school which Miss Glover ran herself, and where the Harmonicon was first introduced, originally stood in a yard behind the Black Boy public house in Colegate – across the River Wensum from her home. The ramshackle buildings which housed the school have since been demolished, leaving no trace of her activities there. The instrument which has survived will have been the one which she used for choir practices – which seem, therefore, to have taken place in the room over the church porch without the aid of the church-organ to give the note. To that fact we owe this remarkable and revealing survival.

Montague, Maddermarket, Norwich

The Miseries of Musick Masters
[1986]

A HUNDED YEARS AGO, when the possession of a piano worth £25 was a new badge of middle-class respectability, armies of boys and girls began to be dragooned through the pages of Ezra Read or William Smallwood, not because they showed musical talent or inclination, but to satisfy the social ambitions of their parents. A century earlier, modest competence at the keyboard stood high on the list of desirable 'accomplishments' of a young woman of gentle birth. Boys were not then expected to acquire this 'lady-like' attribute, but every daughter of a family of means was put to learning to play, however negligible her abilities. At a time when the livelihood of a professional musician largely depended on private teaching, a supply of pupils was thus assured. But the teacher's task provided very little satisfaction. As Hester Chapone drily expressed the matter in 1772, music might afford a young woman with an innocent amusement 'even though it should not enable her to give much pleasure to her friends'.

Together with dancing and deportment, music also formed an essential part of the curriculum in private schools and academies for young ladies. Setting down his recommendations in *A Plan for the Conduct of Female Education* (1797), Erasmus Darwin remarked that music and dancing were generally taught in boarding schools by visiting professional masters. He reminded them to teach with good temper and genteel behaviour, bearing in mind that young ladies should play, dance and sing only so well as to amuse themselves and their friends. To practise those arts so as to 'astonish the public' suggested that more valuable accomplishments had been neglected. Moreover, such activities required 'an exhibition of the person' and were liable to encourage vanity and to extinguish the blush of youthful timidity.

A more outspoken critic of the hours given to music in the education of young women was Hannah More. In her *Strictures on the Modern System of Female Education* (1799) Mrs More vigorously objected to the time 'wasted upon so-called accomplishments'. The hours devoted to music in particular suggested to her a degree of leisure belonging exclusively to affluence. A foreign visitor would be led by prevailing custom to suppose that life in England consisted of a universal holiday.

Confronted with such hostile conditions, few teachers of the untalented, listless daughters of the well-to-do can have regarded their task as more than drudgery necessary to earning a livelihood. Indeed, the traditional pattern of teaching did little to enliven the process or stimulate the pupils' enthusiasm.

The first weeks – even months – of tuition were customarily devoted to rote-learning before allowing the pupil to touch the instrument. And once performance eventually began, for the better part of a century beginners at the piano were always put to learn the same stock piece, known as *Foote's Minuet*. The composer is unknown, the piece has long been lost, and how it came to assume its ritual significance is not obvious. Yet to play *Foote's Minuet* became every beginner's Rubicon. Charles Dibdin, in his memoirs, mentions learning it as a routine part of his musical initiation of 1754, so it was already standard then. It was still used for the same purpose during the Regency sixty years later.

To have stumbled on a copy of *Foote's Minuet*, complete with its contemporary fingering, hardly counts as a musicological triumph. Yet it seems a discovery worth recording – particularly since examination of the piano score explains its long popularity as a beginner' piece. The book in which it came to light represents a wry attempt on the part of a professional musician to introduce a light-hearted note into the field of private music teaching – something that had not previously appeared as a laughing matter to those concerned.

Ambrose Pitman (1763–1817) was a London musician and teacher. His *The Miseries of Musick Masters* was published in 1815. Sub-titled 'A Serio Comick Didactick Poem' it parodies the Augustan manner in almost a thousand lines, adding to the reproaches suggested by its title versified instruction on rudiments and fingering. Something of its style may be conveyed by a few opening couplets:

> What *Miseries* has Heaven designed
> To plague and punish human kind!
> Some more, some less, yet few as much
> As him who well the *Lyre* can touch,
> And, from his merit, oft incurs
> The plaudits of the Theatres.

> But when compelled his *hour* to stay
> And teach Miss Play-ill how to play –
> Unhappy wight! 'tis given to him
> To hear no sweet-ton'd *Seraphim.*
> Yet though discordant is the shock,
> *One* hour his time is – by the clock!

The book is well got up, with a hand-coloured frontispiece by George Cruikshank, and it must have been costly to produce. One is left wondering why Pitman should have gone to the expense of publishing it. For though later sections deal with musical rudiments, the reader being addressed is clearly not a child:

> 'Tis proper first of *Scales* to speak:
> And *Masters*, who can construe *Greek*
> Will tell their *Pupils* there were *three*
> About the time of PTOLEMY.
> But now Philosophers harmonick
> Adopt but *two*, – the *Diatonick*
> And the *Chromatick*: – equal quite
> To form the *Science* of Delight ...

This is designed to amuse – and impress – the adult reader blessed with a classical education, leading us to conclude that Pitman's book was meant to demonstrate not only his musical erudition but his attributes as a well-educated gentleman. Where the daughters of the nobility were concerned, the problem was to come upon teachers sufficiently respectable to be admitted to noble company. The amorous or the comic music master had become a stock figure in both theatre and opera house. Pitman seems to have wanted to establish different credentials.

Moreover, at the time in question, dogging the heels of the old-style professional music master was a growing army of young women anxious to seek in teaching the only 'respectable' means of earning an income – and the independence that went with it. 'The only field at present open for what is considered lady-like employment', wrote an early feminist in 1838, 'is that of educating the young'. And where the mature professional musician found that adjusting his approach to the mental level of a child was difficult, a young woman was often able to do this instinctively.

A notable case in point was the governess to the daughters of the Countess of Leven and Melville, whose *Private Education, or a Practical Plan for the Studies of Young Ladies* (1816) devoted more than thirty of its pages to explaining her views on the reform of music teaching. Elizabeth Appleton maintained that the first duty in teaching was to make progress easy and lessons enjoyable.

The Miseries of
MUSICK MASTERS see v 865

Some teachers, she declared, insisted that no less than six or eight months be spent on musical theory before the pupil was allowed to touch the piano keys. This preliminary study should be drastically curtailed. Technical terms should be avoided. Definitions should not merely be learnt by heart. A child whose early lessons had been conducted sensibly would look forward to her next lesson.

Nor was it only among governesses that rivals to challenge the monopoly of the professional music master were to be found during the first decades of the 19th century. Already Anne Rodwell was offering her services to the public, not just as a governess but as 'Teacher of the Pianoforte'. Her successful career was to be crowned by the publication of a children's instruction book, *The Juvenile Pianist: A Mirror of Music for Infant Minds* (1836).

Ambrose Pitman was clearly aware of the dangers that such rivalry presented. *The Miseries of Musick Masters* represents the personal publicity campaign he mounted to counteract it. For the purposes of this article, however, the main interest in his book lies in its containing the score of that hitherto elusive beginner's piece, *Foote's Minuet*. It will be seen that the great advantage of the piece for a beginner was that the fingers could remain stationary over the keys with no lateral arm movement required. This attribute was obviously responsible for its amazingly lengthy survival. Even the dullest pupil appeared to shine when the fingering alone ensured that the right notes were played.

The Rise of Popular Music Education in Nineteenth-Century England

[1986]

IN THE YEAR OF Victoria's succession to the throne, Thomas Wyse, a vigorous advocate of educational reform in the House of Commons, drew attention to the longstanding neglect of music teaching in the nation's schools:

> Music, even the most elementary, not only does not form an essential of education in this country, but the idea of introducing it is not even dreamt of. It is urged, that it would be fruitless to attempt it, because the people are essentially unmusical; but may not they be anti-musical because it has not been attempted? The people roar and scream, because they have heard nothing but roaring and screaming – no music – from their childhood. Is harmony not to be taught? ... No effort is made in any of our schools; and then we complain that there is no music amongst our scholars. It would be as reasonable to exclude grammar and then complain that we had no grammarians.[1]

The national struggle to reverse that position took place during the queen's reign in conjunction with gradual acceptance by the state of responsibility for popular education as a whole.

Such limited educational progress as in fact occurred in Britain between 1800 and 1837 was largely due to private endeavour. Much of it concerned elementary education, was purely local in effect, and found its inspiration in some particular individual's awareness of continental developments. The rival monitorial systems introduced by Joseph Lancaster and Andrew Bell, each administered by opposing religious bodies, first received a meagre government subsidy to support them in the provision of elementary education in 1833. But the state still failed to accept responsibility for the education of its subjects along lines similar to those of most northern European countries.

The first major effort to readmit music teaching to the elementary curriculum in England since its virtual banishment at the Reformation had occurred in 1790 when Bishop Porteus of London advised the clergy of his diocese that the provision of singing lessons in the nation's many Sunday Schools would go a long way toward correcting the deplorable standard of singing in parochial

---

[1] Thomas Wyse, *Education Reform* (London, 1836), p. 186; quoted in J. Mainzer, *Music and Education* (1848; R/CTME 12, Kilkenny: Boethius, 1985), p. 106. Wyse uses the term 'harmony' here to indicate 'music', not the skill of chord writing.

churches.[2] On the other hand, the first stirrings of an awareness that music deserved a place in its own right in every child's general education can safely be traced to Robert Owen and the model for infant education first presented in his experimental school at New Lanark on the Clyde before its disbanding in 1824. Though evidently unaware of the writings of Rousseau and Johann Heinrich Pestalozzi on education, Owen had formed ideas of his own virtually identical with many of theirs. In his school, memorisation and 'book-learning' were replaced by deliberate exercise of the senses. Practical experiment and observation, play, physical drill, dancing, and singing all became essential features of his little pupils' daily programme; and among the wall charts enlivening their classrooms were found not only pictures of exotic animals and plants, but copies of the tunes they sang written out in musical notation.[3]

Owen's educational experiment was shortlived, and though his ideas were taken up elsewhere in Britain by such disciples as David Stow and Samuel Wilderspin, enlightened teaching received its next important stimulus more directly from Pestalozzi through the activities of enthusiasts who had travelled to Switzerland to work under his direction before setting up private schools of their own in Britain. Charles Mayo at Epsom and J. P. Greaves at Ham, are best known among those who brought Pestalozzian methods – including recreational song – into currency. And in his *Letters on Early Education Addressed to J. P. Greaves* Pestalozzi expressed his regret that in spite of its beneficial influence music did not form a more prominent feature in general education in England.[4]

But before music could earn a place in subsidised schools run by the supporters of Bell and Lancaster middle class scepticism had to be persuaded, Hardheaded school governors who failed to respond to Pestalozzi's declaration that music was 'beneficial' were more readily convinced when it could be shown that music teaching was 'useful'. And the first school music textbook to appear in England in modem times was careful to underline this functional aspect on its title page. John Turner's *Manual of Instruction in Vocal Music* (1833) was subtitled *chiefly with a view to Psalmody*.[5] Its immediate successor Sarah Glover's Scheme *for Rendering Psalmody Congregational* (1835),[6] was even more

---

[2] Beilby Porteus, *Works,* 6 vols. (London: Cadell & Davies, 1811), vol. 6, p. 243.

[3] H. Silver, ed., *Robert Owen on Education* (London: Cambridge University Press, 1969), pp. 161–3.

[4] Johann Heinrich Pestalozzi, *Letters on Early Education Addressed to J. P. Greaves* (London: Sherwood, Gilbert & Piper, 1827), Letter 23, 18 February 1827, pp. 93–9.

[5] John Turner, *Manual of Instruction in Vocal Music* (1833; R/CTME 6, Kilkenny: Boethius, 1983).

[6] Sarah Glover, *Scheme for Rendering Psalmody Congregational* (1835; R/CTME 5, Kilkenny: Boethius, 1982).

specifically titled. And only when W. E. Hickson's The *Singing Master* (1836) followed, was the connection between singing in school and singing in church less heavily emphasised, to be replaced by the argument that something more was required 'to improve the mind, and hearts, and promote the happiness of the rising generation than has hitherto been attempted'.[7] All three books were soon enjoying local use in a few areas.

Each of the pioneers concerned in these prime ventures, from Bishop Porteus onward, sought (often unwittingly) to restore music teaching to the place it had held in popular education before the Reformation swept away the song schools, chantry, and monastic schools providing it. As Thomas Wyse's statement suggests, early efforts in this direction remained little known nationally. But in the warmer educational climate that followed the passing of the first Reform Bill, it is no coincidence to find three school music textbooks making their unprecedented appearance within as many years. For when the first state grant for education was belatedly approved by Parliament in 1833, a turning point had been reached. Subsequently, governmental apathy in such matters steadily gave place to reluctant awareness that educational provision in Britain was shamefully inadequate. The situation was slowly corrected during Victoria's reign.

I

One striking feature of the century's educational advance was its initial polarity. At the outset, reforming energy was centred upon schools catering to extreme elements in the population: the children of the labouring poor and of the aristocratic rich were its principal beneficiaries, leaving the sons and daughters of a rapidly growing middle class largely unprovided for. Religious differences complicated the situation. According to whether their parents subscribed to Prayer Book or Dissent, the children of the poor went to 'National' or 'British' elementary schools; the sons of the wealthy folk either to ancient public schools or those nonconformist academies established during the previous century. The curriculum content, religious instruction, and methods of teaching in these schools varied greatly, and no music was taught in any of them.

An increase in the government grant subsidising voluntary elementary schools heralded the appointment in 1839 of school inspectors whose reports were soon exposing conditions of scandalous neglect and incompetence in existing schools and their teachers. Six years previously a special committee of the Privy Council had been appointed to consider educational provision; and in 1835 £10,000 was voted for the building or a state training college for teachers.

---

[7] W. E. Hickson, *The Singing Master* (1836; R/CTME 10, Kilkenny: Boethius, 1984), p. 3.

But it was not until the true scale of educational shortcomings was revealed during 1839 that urgent remedies were sought and the new Committee of Council on Education braced itself to undertake substantial reform of elementary education. An indirect consequence was the reinstatement of the music lesson in schools for the children of the poor. Meanwhile, following the example of Thomas Arnold at Rugby, reform began from within the almost equally ill-conducted schools of the wealthier classes. But it required the courageous unorthodoxy of another famous headmaster, Edward Thring of Uppingham, before music was admitted to the curriculum of a public school a generation later.

Although much of the substance of the Education Bill of 1839 may be traced to earlier proposals made by Wyse, the principal architect of the policy implemented by the Committee of Council on Education was its secretary, James Kay. A medical man rather than a teacher and later to become Sir James Kay-Shuttleworth, he owed his influential appointment to his known devotion to progressive educational ideals and the success with which he had applied them in his capacity as assistant poor law commissioner to improve the lot of pauper children immured in the workhouses of rural England.

The members of the committee itself – Henry Petty-Fitzmaurice, John William Ponsonby, John Russell, and Thomas Spring Rice – relied heavily upon their secretary for the formulation of educational strategy. To prepare himself for the responsible task of advising them, Kay undertook in 1839 a three-months' tour of Holland, France, Prussia, and Switzerland, to examine for himself the methods and conditions prevailing in the schools of the four countries which had already introduced state systems of education. On his return, armed with a substantial collection of the primers and manuals employed in those schools, Kay's belief in the automatic superiority of continental reaching methods was reinforced, and his faith in Pestalozzi as the inspired fount of educational wisdom confirmed.

During Kay's absence abroad, however, Parliament again deferred the establishment of a national training college for teachers. No compromise could be reached between Church and Dissent upon their differences over religious instruction in the proposed institution, and the issue was shelved. Faced with this obstacle, Kay promptly and boldly decided to found a private institution himself, to demonstrate how such an establishment could be conducted without sacrificing religious principles. With the financial backing of his friends he set up a small-scale training college to accommodate a dozen youths in what was then the Thames-side village of Battersea. There he put into practice the lessons learnt during his recent educational tour and laid the framework of a model curriculum for the elementary schools of the future. No longer restricted to religious instruction and the three 'Rs', Kay's enlarged syllabus included both music and drawing, taught according to methods which he attributed to Pestalozzi. At that time Kay's conception of the nature of Pestalozzian teaching was summarised by him as 'leading children from the known to the unknown by gradual steps'.[8] Valid so far as it went, that definition failed to recognise the method's sensory and synthetic characteristics. As a result Kay often tended to attribute to Pestalozzi teaching methods which owed little or nothing to his tenets.

An example of this misconception can be seen by comparing the methods adopted at Battersea for teaching reading, writing, drawing, and music. The reading primer was an English adaptation of the German method devised by a pupil of Pestalozzi named Lautier. The writing primer was by another of his pupils named Muhlhauser. Both were authentic applications of the Swiss educationist's principles.[9] But drawing was taught using Alexandre Dupuis's geometrical objects, and this had no connection with Pestalozzian theories, though Kay justified their use as allowing the student 'to proceed by gradual steps through a series of combinations until he was able to draw faithfully any object, however complex'.[10] And music was also taught by a French system, devised for use in the monitorial schools of Paris by Guillaume Wilhem and owing nothing at all to Pestalozzi's principles, in spite of Kay's confident declaration that 'the method of Wilhem is simply an application of the Pestalozzian method of ascending from the simple to the general through a clearly analysed series' (*Minutes*, 1842–3, p. 226).

To start his training institution, Kay relied for the most part upon volunteers among his friends; but the choice of a musician able to teach by means of an unfamiliar continental method presented a very real problem. Eventually, however, Kay met John Hullah, a young composer who had for some time been attracted to the idea of setting up in London a series of public singing classes similar to those which were then enjoying remarkable popularity in Paris.[11] Begun in 1836, two rival courses for adults were attracting hundreds of aspiring singers from the Parisian labouring classes. One course was directed by Joseph Mainzer, a German ex-priest who had formerly taught music in the seminary in Trier. The other was run by Wilhem, employing the monitorial

[8] James Kay-Shuttleworth, *The Training of Pauper Children* (London: Clowes, 1839), p. 5.

[9] James Kay-Shuttleworth, *Minutes of the Committee of Council on Education* (London: Clowes, 1841), pp. 33–51.

[10] James Kay-Shuttleworth, *Four Periods of Public Education* (London: Longmans, 1862), p. 345.

[11] Frances Hullah, *Life of John Hullah* (London: Longmans, 1886), p. 25.

system which he had already introduced for teaching music in the *commune* schools of Paris.[12]

Hullah had first become aware of the singing classes in Paris from an article in the *Athenaeum,* London's leading journal treating the arts, late in 1837. Written by H. F. Chorley, the paper's music critic, it spoke of Mainzer's classes with sufficient enthusiasm to make Hullah decide to visit Paris to witness so unusual an educational venture for himself. Chorley had written: 'I was present at one of the meetings of M. Mainzer's singing class of workmen and artisans, at a room in the Place de l'Estrapade. This gentlemen's success should encourage all those who wish to diffuse a musical taste among the humbler orders.'[13] Making Chorley's acquaintance, Hullah sought further details; and in 1839 the two men journeyed to Paris to enable Hullah to see Mainzer at work. They were disappointed because Mainzer's classes had just been discontinued; but they were able to visit those of Wilhem instead (F. Hullah, p. 25).

It was thus through accident rather than design that Hullah became acquainted with the Wilhem system which was to occupy his labours for the next forty years. Soon after his return home he was introduced to Kay, presented with the challenge of adapting Wilhem's system to English use, and invited to instruct the apprentice teachers at the new institution in Battersea. Hullah's own description of these events is revealing:

> Shortly before this the Normal School for schoolmasters had been opened at Battersea – the only school for schoolmasters then existing in England. It consisted at first of some ten or twelve youths, two or three of whom only had any knowledge of music, and as many any voice or apparent knowledge of the subject. Any beginning less encouraging could hardy be conceived. I remember, after walking some time before the gates of the establishment, at length summoning up courage to make my appearance ... and I found myself, for the first time in my life – called upon to give a lesson in music. In this I believe, I was considered to have been fairly successful.   (F. Hullah, pp. 25–6)

Completely inexperienced as a teacher, at the age of twenty-seven Hullah was able to rely on a combination of charm, enthusiasm, and a natural talent for exposition for his early success. His pupils, hand-picked boys just rescued from the workhouses where their future had seemed without hope, reacted eagerly to his kindly instruction. Visitors to Battersea, many of them eminent,

---

[12] F. J. Fétis, *Biographie universelle des musiciens,* 8 vols. (Paris: Fournier, 1835–1860), 'Mainzer', vol. 6, p. 231; 'G. B. Wilhem' (Brussels: Meline, Cans et Cie, 1844), vol. 8, pp. 563–6.

[13] Henry Fothergill Chorley, 'Foreign Correspondence', *Athenaeum* no. 527 (2 December 1837), p. 881.

expressed their surprise at the efficiency with which these youngsters were soon performing the exercises from Wilhem's course. The boys were soon called upon to demonstrate their powers to the public at large. On witnessing these unsophisticated lads displaying musical skill beyond that of most adults, delighted audiences in London and the provinces responded with incredulous applause. The Battersea Boys, clad in their green uniforms, were soon known nationally as 'Hullah's Greenbirds'.[14]

Encouraged by this early success, Kay urged the Committee of Council to approve the foundation of a singing school for schoolmasters where the teachers of London might be taught the secrets of Hullah's triumph. Sanction was given, and on 1 February 1841 the first class was enrolled at London's largest public arena, Exeter Hall. Two further classes were formed in the following March, when the first course for schoolmistresses also began. Each class met twice weekly for sixty nights under Hullah's personal tuition; the course cost fifteen shillings, thus making the venture self-supporting.[15]

The *Minute* of the Committee of Council on Education that announced the formation of the Exeter Hall Singing School was a substantial document designed not only to publicise Hullah's classes, but to justify the inclusion of the music lesson in schools generally. In it Kay summarised the arguments employed to sway influential opinion in government circles and public debate. He reiterated them in a single sentence when he declared that vocal music was an 'important means of forming an industrious, brave, loyal, and religious working class' (quoted in J. Hullah, *Method*, p. iv). He also emphasised the merit of song as a promoter of patriotism, civilising agent, innocent pastime, counter-attraction to the beerhouse, and the means of making attendance at public worship more attractive to the uneducated. 'A relish for such pursuits', Kay's Minute went on, 'would in itself be an advance in civilisation, as it would doubtless prove in time the means of weaning the population from debasing pleasures, and would associate their amusements with their duties' (quoted in J. Hullah, *Method*, p. v). It was with this moralistic preamble – in itself a seasoned foretaste of the high Victorian manner – that Hullah's adaptation of a French method of teaching music was first presented to the public at large.

Just how warmly it was received may be discovered from the way in which the initial success of the classes for teachers at Exeter Hall promptly led to the formation, at vigorous public demand, of additional classes 'wherein the working classes, and the apprentices and foremen of shops and handicraft trades' might acquire this innocent and useful recreation (*Minutes*, 1841–2, p. 75). By

[14] T. Adkins, *History of St. Johns College, Battersea* (London: National Society's Repository, 1906), p. 8off.

[15] John Hullah, *Wilhem's Method of Teaching Singing adapted to English Use* (2nd edn 1842; R/CTME 7, Kilkenny: Boethius, 1983), p. xiv.

the end of 1841, according to a contemporary estimate, at least 50,000 children of the working classes in London had also begun to receive instruction at school in singing from notes (*Minutes*, 1841–2, p. 75). Just as their teachers had so recently been, those children were led through the pages of Hullah's *Method*, slowly learning to find their way up and down the scale and to sing such edifying ditties as:

> How pleasant it is, at the close of the day,
>   No follies to have to repent;
> But reflect on the past and be able to say,
>   My time has been properly spent!
> When I've finished my business with patience and care,
>   And been good, and obliging, and kind,
> I lie on my pillow, and sleep away there,
>   With a happy and peaceable mind.
>   (J. Hullah, *Method*, p. 65)

II

Some witnesses of this apparent triumph for Kay's idiosyncratic musical policy were less than enthusiastic. Few professional musicians were persuaded that Hullah's singing school would achieve worthwhile results. Ultra-conservatives among the upper classes clung to their conviction that any attempt to educate the humbler members of society must lead to an increase in discontent and subversion. Even staunch advocates of the development of popular education, and of music education in particular, voiced their disapprobation of the Committee of Council's haste in putting Kay's recommendations into practice without first consulting informed opinion as to the suitability of the French method he had chosen. Soon after the publication of Hullah's adaptation of Wilhem's manual, a stern but well-informed criticism of it appeared in the *Westminster Review*:

> In our visits to continental schools we have accumulated among other school books, a great number upon singing, but we have not one in our collection so overlaid with the technical pedantries of the science, so abounding in difficulties insuperable to children, so little of the character of a work adapted for the self-instruction of an adult, as this English adaptation of Wilhem's method. Indeed without a master to explain it, the book is perfectly useless.[16]

[16] W. E. Hickson, 'Music, and the Committee of Council on Education', *Westminster Review*, vol. 37 no. 1 (January 1842), p. 29.

The writer was W. E. Hickson, the vigorous promoter of the cause of national education whose *Singing Master* has already been mentioned. Since its publication, however, Hickson's wider philanthropic and educational activities had included service on a government commission to examine the circumstances of unemployed handloom operators (1837) and an educational tour of North Germany and the Low Countries (1839).[17] These pursuits had increased his stature as a public figure, lending added authority to the pronouncements on educational matters which he published in the *Westminster Review,* a journal he had purchased in 1840 as a vehicle for his utterances.

Hickson's detailed criticism of Hullah's singing manual took exception to several of its essential features and was restated in subsequent articles in the *Spectator* in 1841 and the *Illustrated London* News two years later.[18] For Hullah's natural talent as a teacher Hickson spoke with unqualified approval; his objections were wholly against the government for overlooking indigenous methods within their reach while prepared to occupy themselves in 'rambling researches' in Switzerland, Holland, the German States, Prussia, Austria, and France. And contrary to the Committee of Council's declaration that no method had previously existed to simplify the teaching of vocal music in elementary schools, Hickson pointed out the existence of many such works, 'fully as clear and quite as useful as the one now adopted', not a few of them native products. There were, moreover, other treatises of a more authentically Pestalozzian cast in use both in Germany and America.

Perhaps the most radical of Hickson's objections was directed against Hullah's adoption of French nomenclature for the degrees of the scale. Instead of employing the customary alphabetical note-names, in his manual Hullah justified the continental usage in these terms:

> In England the eight sounds of this scale are called C, D, E, F, G, A, B, C, and it may be useful, at some future time, to become familiar with these names. The syllables ... (commonly used in France and Italy) have, however, many advantages over the letters, and will therefore be used throughout this method. ... Thus, by using the syllables Do, Re, Mi, Fa, Sol, La, and Si over and over again, we find names for as many sounds as we need. (J. Hullah, *Method*, p. 6).

Hickson justifiably questioned this policy, pointing out that a pupil taught in this way would 'begin and finish his course of lessons without being acquainted

[17] *Dictionary of National Biography*, compact edition, 2 vols. (London: Oxford University Press, 1975), vol. 1, p. 969.

[18] W. E. Hickson, 'Wilhem's Method of Teaching Singing', *Spectator* vol. 14 (10 July 1841), pp. 667–8; 'The Singing Classes of Exeter Hall', *Illustrated London* News, vol. 1 (11 June 1842), pp. 76–7.

with the names of the notes as they are universally used in England' ('Singing Classes', p. 77). He would be unable to sing or understand anything but the contents of his own singing manual.

Later experience was to expose an even more damaging disadvantage of the use of this continental system. The whole or the first course of lessons in Hullah's manual was limited to the key of C, where the sol-fa names established a sense of note-relationships. And the marked success of his early teaching occurred while pupils were at this initial stage. But when keys other than C were introduced in the second course of lessons, the sol-fa names no longer identified familiar note patterns, and pupils grew increasingly confused as a result. Thereafter, only the naturally talented were able to progress.

In undertaking his search on the continent for the means to redeems England from her educational sloth, Kay more than once exposed his own limited understanding of technical considerations. Nowhere was the discrepancy more obviously revealed than in his choice of Wilhem's system of teaching music. Because he had selected in Hullah a man with no previous teaching experience to introduce the new method, its most obvious shortcomings were left unexplained to him before he sought for it the government's approval. The chosen method was to prove deficient; and Hickson's castigation of it was more than justified by the consistent failure of the Hullah–Wilhem system to develop real competence in either the average child or his teachers. After its first dramatic success, the survival of Hullah's manual was assured only by the official backing of the Committee of Council on Education who insisted on its being taught to teachers in training. Twenty years after its first introduction, most practising teachers had abandoned using it in their classrooms. Yet the importation of Wilhem's method to the schools of early Victorian England should not be hastily dismissed as heralding a false dawn. However misguided the policy formulated by Kay and followed by his lieutenant, Hullah, their joint efforts were to prove far from fruitless. Ten years after the first lessons at Battersea and Exeter Hall had begun to arouse unprecedented public interest in learning to sing at sight, Dickens's *Household Words* recorded the appearance of a new attitude toward music in the school curriculum: 'Music is becoming a regular branch of popular education. ... Already its effects are striking and encouraging. Music – well, badly, or indifferently taught – forms a part of the business of the great majority of schools, national, public, and private, throughout the country.'[19]

By 1850 – when those words were written – a considerable number of alternative methods of teaching music were employed. The annual reports issued by government inspectors of schools during the 1840s reveal that in spite of

---

[19] [George Hogarth?], 'Music in Humble Life', *Household Words*, vol. 1 (1850), p. 164.

the official recognition accorded to Hullah's manual, outside the metropolis itself individual teachers were still using one of the earlier primers published by the three native pioneers in the field: Turner, Glover, or Hickson (see *Minutes*, 1841–2, p. 179). The accepted aim of the music lesson in all these primers was to teach children to sing melodies at sight while acquiring a growing repertory of moral texts. But examination of their books shows that Turner and Hickson both assumed that by explaining the meaning of the symbols of notation to children they were automatically enabling them to read music. Only Sarah Glover made use of movable sol-fa, anglicising the syllables as Doh, Ra, Me, Fah, Sole, Lah, and Te, and using those initial letters as an ancillary form of notation from which her pupils gradually learned to sing with confidence.

Elsewhere, individual teachers who chanced to be members of church choirs made what use they could of the methods by which they themselves had been trained. The most common of these was the traditional 'fasola' system which named the notes of the scale fa, sol, la, fa, sol, la, mi, and consequently presented the beginner with ambiguities likely to baffle all but the brightest child.[20] Another more straightforward method then being taught nationwide to nonconformists by one of their ministers, the Reverend J. J. Waite, used numerals as a form of notation, representing the degrees of the major scale by the figures 1–7, as Rousseau had recommended.[21] A third system, the 'interval method', introduced no ancillary notation but attempted to reduce the element of chance in reading from standard notes by drilling the pupil in striking different intervals from a given keynote. This was the method favoured by most professional singing teachers and the one also adopted by John Turner in his *Manual*.

The range of possible approaches to teaching sight-singing in schools was yet further increased in May 1841, when Joseph Mainzer – whose singing classes in Paris appear to have been regarded as potentially treasonable assemblies and were thus closed by the police – crossed to London and started classes in rivalry to those which Hullah had then been holding for four months at Exeter Hall. Mainzer's classes were held in assembly halls in various London districts under the catch phrase 'Singing for the Million'.[22] They each attracted hundreds of devotees and contributed decisively to producing the 'singing mania' which was to become one of the most remarkable social phenomena of early Victorian England.

Mainzer used the same catch phrase as the title of his teaching manual, *Singing for the Million* (1841), a much less pedantic treatise than Hullah's and

[20] B. Rainbow, *English Psalmody Prefaces*, CTME 2 (Kilkenny: Boethius, 1982), pp. 4–6.

[21] J. J. Waite, *The Hallelujah* (London: Snow, 1852), preface.

[22] J. Mainzer, *Singing for the Million* (1841; R/CTME 9, Kilkenny: Boethius, 1984), introduction, pp. 4–5.

one clearly based upon many years' practical teaching experience, Mainzer summarised his policy as follows:

> To impart a general knowledge of the principles of music, a different method of teaching is indispensable to distinguish it from a purely musical education; and it is a great error to apply to elementary schools, or public classes, methods which are not founded on this rigorous distinction. ... In the latter it is only necessary to communicate a general knowledge of the art, to incite a taste for it, to prepare the physical organs – the ear and the throat – to awaken the intelligence and the heart, and to afford to infancy and youth a participation in the attractions and noble sentiment inspired by its mysterious power. To attain this object, it suffices to study the few rules applied to the reading of music, explained in this little work. ... These are the simple and only means I have employed in gratuitous classes opened in Paris in favour of workmen.
>
> (Mainzer, *Singing*, pp. i–ii)

The straightforwardness of Mainzer's early lessons and the simple vocal exercises they employed made encouraging progress possible for the beginner. But as the course continued and the singer began to meet sharps, flats, and key signatures, the French background to Mainzer's method and its consequent use of fixed sol-fa no longer provided a reliable method of pitching intervals correctly. It was at this stage that enthusiasm began to wane and attendance at Mainzer's classes began to fall off. As with Hullah's method (and for precisely the same reason) Mainzer's *Singing for the Million* encouraged many thousands of ordinary folk to become aware of the pleasure that choral music could afford, without enabling them to take more than the first steps into mastering its demands. Hullah and Mainzer both depended more upon their own enthusiasm, natural aptitude for teaching, and personal charm for their success than upon the merits of their systems of instruction. Yet it was natural for schoolteachers attending their classes to attempt to pass on to their own pupils what little skill they had managed to acquire themselves.

By 1846 the number of alternative methods of teaching sight-singing had grown so profuse that James Turle, the organist of Westminster Abbey, and Edward Taylor, Gresham Professor of Music, joined forces to produce *The Singing Book* (1846) which emphasised that there were no short cuts to proficiency, that once the essentials of musical rudiments had been acquired by a pupil, practice must do the rest, and that the existence of so many different systems led to nothing but confusion.[23] There were few subjects, their preface declared, which the wit and ingenuity of man had encumbered with more

---

[23] James Turle and Edward Taylor, *The Singing Book* (London: Bogue, 1846), pp. i–vii.

needless words and presented to a young mind in a less attractive form than the art of singing from notes. Instead of removing gratuitous obstacles to progress, individual teachers seemed determined to multiply them – not least by the addition to the regular musical alphabet of a host of arbitrary and unmeaning syllables. Usually called, and often supposed to be, 'the Sol-fa system', no description of it could be more incorrect. For scarcely any two writers in modern times had used the system in the same way. The Italians and the French had their own ways of handling it; the English were not only at variance with both but with each other.

Examination of various elementary works on singing showed that far from being founded upon any well-established and universally accepted principle, the details and application of sol-fa varied in different countries and were 'altered according to the fancy of individual instructors' (p. iv). Recent attempts (such as Hullah's) to substitute sol-fa names for the alphabetical names of the notes simply exasperated Turle and Taylor: 'The alphabetic notation must be known by every musician, because it is of universal employment. No other is used in any choir or orchestra in the kingdom. The student may add to it some other, but he must learn this' (p. v). For all these reasons *The Singing Book* dispensed with sol-fa altogether, adopting instead, for its preliminary exercises numerals together with alphabetical note names printed beneath the staff. In this way, it was claimed, 'a correct idea of distance' was developed in the mind of the beginner (p. v). Thus the multiplicity of methods was further increased.

III

In the hands of a talented and musical teacher each of the methods that have so far taken our attention offered a possible approach to teaching sight-singing. But it seems evident today that something more specific was required to enable the teacher to overcome personal musical limitations and then satisfactorily guide pupils. What was needed was not so much a textbook prepared by an expert musician as one prepared by an expert teacher. Only then would the accomplished musician's innate tendency to underestimate the learner's problems be avoided and recent advances in the techniques of teaching other subjects be applied to music also.

Even so earnest a music teacher as John Turner, the pioneer who produced the first school music text in English in 1833, had underestimated the task he was undertaking, as this summary of his aims makes clear: 'It is proposed that the children should be taught the names of the notes, and other marks of music, their nature and their use; that they should be practised in singing the scale, and in the proper use of the voice: that they should learn to pronounce words so as to preserve the organs of the throat in free exercise,

and be by these means instructed in the rudiments of melody and harmony'
(Turner, p. 26). Faith in rote-learning of facts had long dominated all teaching in schools. Understandably, it dominated most early attempts to teach
music there. Indeed, Sarah Glover alone among those whose work has been
considered revealed an awareness of the need to organise her teaching along
other than factual lines: 'In teaching children music, I think it best to instruct
them on the same principle as they are taught speech: viz., by deducing theory
from practice, rather than practice from theory.'[24] She also deliberately chose
to employ movable sol-fa (which emphasises the regular pattern of tones and
semitones in the major scale whatever the key) instead of fixed sol-fa, the continental counterpart adopted by both Mainzer and Hullah. As the name implies,
the latter system attached the sol-fa names permanently to the key of C, thus
robbing them of their value in other keys. It fell to John Curwen, a young man
in his early twenties already known in Congregationalist circles for his remarkable skill in teaching young children and his insight into educational theory, to
contrive a method of teaching music which made it available to musically inexperienced teachers and their pupils. The fact that when he undertook the task
he was equally inexperienced himself was to prove an advantage rather than a
handicap in the long run.

Even as an undergraduate at London's new University College in 1833,
Curwen's intense interest in teaching children impressed his fellow students.
Every Sunday he taught in a school held in the Barbican for children obliged
to work on weekdays, developing there his 'Look and Say' method of teaching them to read words as a whole instead of spelling them out letter by letter.
This ability to analyse the processes of instruction and then plan teaching procedures to accommodate them was partly instinctive and partly the result of
conscious study of the writings of the progressive teachers of his day. Perhaps
above all he was indebted to Pestalozzi for his radical views on teaching; but
that influence came to him at first indirectly through the books of Elizabeth
Mayo, David Stow, Horace Grant, and Jacob Abbott.[25]

In 1838 Curwen was appointed assistant minister at the Independent Chapel
at Basingstoke, Hampshire, where once again it was his remarkable powers
with children that impressed local people. The amazing success of a deliberately simple storybook for children which he now published soon made his
name widely known among parents and teachers. As a result he found himself
invited to address meetings and conferences of teachers in many parts of the
country. On one such occasion in 1841, when the rival classes of Hullah and

---

[24] Sarah Glover, *A Manual of the Norwich Sol-fa System* (London: Hamilton, Adams,
1845), p. 66.

[25] B. Rainbow, *John Curwen: A Short Critical Biography* (London, Novello, 1980),
pp. 10–13; see pp. 94–138 above.

Mainzer were first attracting general public interest, a conference chairman, impressed by Curwen's evident grasp of educational values, commissioned him to review existing methods of teaching singing and to 'recommend some simple method to the churches which should enable all to sing with ease and propriety'.[26] Aware of his own musical limitations, Curwen accepted the task with misgiving. But he regarded it as a solemn undertaking and, though he could not anticipate the consequences, it was to become his life work.

A year later Curwen published the first results of his investigation in a series of 'Lessons on Singing' in a Congregationalist journal, the *Independent Magazine*.[27] Utterly unlike the standard music primer which traditionally began by defining the difference between 'noise' and 'music' and then introduced the symbols of notation, Curwen's approach was essentially practical, dispensed with rote-learning, and was couched in the simplest language.

He presented his lessons in the form of 'letter to a friend who had undertaken to train a class of children':

> I must suppose you, with your blackboard and chalk at your side. ... I shall enclose your words in inverted commas, and where I suppose a pause while anything is done, I will mark it by an asterisk.
>
> 'Now, children, we are going to learn the art of singing in tune. What are we going to learn? First, then, you must remember that any musical sound is called a *note*. What is a musical sound called? This is a note.' (I hear you singing to the sound a*h* any note you please.) 'I will sing another note. * Now I will sing another note. * Could not some of you sing a note? Hold up hands – those who can sing a note. *Do* you – * and you; * I want you now to distinguish the *same* note from a *different* one. Sing the *same* note as this. * Sing the *same* note as this. * Hold up hands – those who will sing me a note, and I will sing the same. Do you – * and you.
>
> (J. Curwen, 'Lessons', pp. 23–4)

Curwen had found so many shortcomings in existing methods – particularly in Hullah's – that he decided to develop one of his own. For its basis he chose Sarah Glover's 'Norwich Sol-fa' with its simple notation of sol-fa initial letters and movable do. But he amended many of its details before incorporating further material from other methods which his own experience – first as learner, then as teacher – showed to be valuable. Curwen acknowledged indebtedness for 'borrowed' teaching devices and other intrinsic matter to his fellow countrymen, J. J. Waite, and W. E. Hickson; to the Irish teacher, R. J. Bryce; to the

---

[26] John Curwen, *The Teacher's Manual* (1882; R/CTME 19, Kilkenny: Boethius, 1986), p. 153.

[27] John Curwen, 'Lessons on Singing', *Independent Magazine*, vol. 1 (January 1842), pp. 23–4.

Frenchmen, Jue de Berneval and Aimé Paris; the American, Lowell Mason; the Swiss, H. G. Nägeli; and the Bavarian, M. T. Pfeiffer. Thus began the process of synthesis by which, over a period of thirty years or more, Curwen's Tonic Sol-fa system was engendered.[28]

Following its first tentative introduction to the limited readership of the *Independent Magazine* early in 1842, the Tonic Sol-fa method slowly became more widely known through meetings and classes for Sunday school teachers and temperance workers. Evening classes for adults were also started and, as a result, Curwen was invited to contribute a series of articles on music to John Cassell's new magazine, the *Popular Educator*, in 1851. The magazine's enormous circulation among readers anxious for 'self-improvement' brought Curwen's first article, published in April 1852, into thousands of homes, marking a welcome upward trend in his affairs. Further classes were soon begun in London's Crosby Hall attended by many teachers and educationists; and though Curwen's solitary crusade had neither the government support accorded to Hullah nor the resources of Exeter Hall at its disposal, during the following three years he had attracted some twenty thousand pupils.[29] By 1860 Tonic Sol-fa had eclipsed both the Hullah and Mainzer methods to stand alone in public estimation as the humble person's method of learning to sing from notes. Following the passing of the Forster Education Act of 1870 and the introduction of compulsory elementary schooling, Tonic Sol-fa became the accepted method of teaching singing in the nation's new Board Schools,

The testing ground where the viability of music as a subject in the modem school curriculum was first demonstrated and the merits and disadvantages of alternative methods of teaching it were gradually assessed was thus found in the elementary schools established and developed during the first half of Victoria's reign. And although the apparent success of Hullah's early teaching encouraged the headmaster of Eton College to invite him to teach there experimentally in 1842, the venture was shortlived and not repeated in other independent schools. No doubt partly because the boys at Eton lacked the docility of their humbler counterparts, once the novelty of learning to sing faded, the pedestrian progress of Hullah's lessons quickly lost their interest. Nor was the opportunity taken to link the singing lessons with the music of the college chapel. The services there were sung by the choir of St George's Chapel, Windsor, the youthful congregation – like their highborn parents – convinced that it was 'not genteel to sing in church'.[30]

---

[28] B. Rainbow, *The Land without Music* (London: Novello, 1967; R/Aberystwyth, Boethius Press; R/Woodbridge: Boydell Press, 2001), pp. 139–55.

[29] J. S. Curwen, *Memorials of John Curwen* (London: J. Curwen & Sons, 1882), p. 153.

[30] John Hullah, *The Psalter* (London: Parker, 1843), preface.

IV

The first successful attempts to introduce music teaching in secondary education came with the development of a new type of boarding school for the sons of middle-class parents during the 1840s. The new energy in educational matters which had first given rise to the establishment of schools for the children of the poor was now turned to the provision of others where less expensive secondary education was made available, particularly to the sons of the clergy. Founded as boarding schools, both Marlborough (1843) and Rossall (1844) were sufficiently influenced by the model of Arnold's Rugby to attach great importance to the influence of well-chosen prefects and the sobering impulse of daily worship. But at Radley (1847) the daily chapel service was made a central feature of the school's life. The chapel building was furnished with elaborate care and contained 'one of the finest organs in the country'.[31] One of the first four members appointed to its staff was E. G. Monk, the chapel organist and school music master, under whose direction a musical tradition was steadily built up in which the whole school shared in choral worship whether from choirstall or pew.

This new ideal, further stimulated by the liturgical reforms associated with the Oxford Movement, was taken up in other new boarding schools at Lancing (1848), Hurstpierpoint (1849), Bradfield (1850), and elsewhere, to establish a generally accepted view of music in the curriculum of a Victorian boarding school as the natural adjunct to well-ordered communal worship.[32]

Because music was taught in such schools by specialists rather than novices, the lengthy struggle to select and test teaching methods which had complicated the introduction of music lessons in elementary schools was avoided. Much of the chapel repertoire, however, was learned by rote, natural ability rather than systematic coaching having to provide the sight readers necessary to maintain the choir. Far less attention was given to formal teaching of music in class than was the case in elementary schools.

In the older public schools there was no similar call to entrust the choral element in worship to the boys and masters. At Eton, as we have seen, visiting choristers from Windsor Castle sang the chapel services; at Winchester the cathedral choir sang in the college chapel; at Westminster the boys of the school attended services in the Abbey; at Harrow they went to the adjacent parish church; at Rugby the simple congregational service familiar to Thomas Arnold was jealously preserved. There was thus no immediate demand

---

[31] E. Bryans and T. D. Raike, *History of St Peters College, Radley* (London: Blackwell, 1925), chap. 1.

[32] B. Rainbow, The *Choral Revival in the Anglican Church, 1839–1872* (London: Barrie & Jenkins, 1970), pp. 220–42.

to introduce music lessons in these schools as a means of enhancing choral worship. Moreover, social snobbery played its part. The popular enthusiasm aroused by the massed singing classes at Exeter Hall and elsewhere in London seemed to make simultaneous instruction in singing a pursuit appropriate only to the labouring classes. When music eventually came to be taught in the public schools, both the motivation for it and the form were quite different from music instruction in the elementary schools. The first move in that new direction was made at Uppingham in 1856.

When Edward Thring was appointed headmaster in 1853, Uppingham was an unremarkable rural grammar school of twenty-five boys. He left it thirty-five years later among the foremost of English public schools, transformed by a new attitude toward the curriculum which widened it beyond the Classics to embrace a range of pursuits designed to meet the needs and aptitudes of every pupil. Part of every day was devoted to French, German, chemistry, lathework, drawing, carpentry, or music; each boy was required to choose one or more of these besides the traditional range of classical studies.

One of Thring's biographers has emphasised the fact that though he was the first to introduce music teaching into a public school; he was himself quite unmusical:

> The importance of musical teaching was probably brought under his notice by his wife, who had brought from her German home a warm love of music and interest in it. The refining and elevating influence of *serious* music on those who were able and trained to appreciate it could not escape Thring's rare powers of observation. An art which appealed at least as much to feeling and imagination as to the intellect, that bugbear of his, could not fail to attract him greatly. And furthermore, the power of vocal music to enhance and emphasise the meaning of words appeared to him of great value, it was with a view to their being set to music and sung, and thus brought forcibly home to a large number of performers and listeners, that he wrote his school songs.[33]

Yet the school songs which Thring introduced were not, as one might expect today, designed to be performed by the whole school. From an entry in his diary describing a school concert in 1873 we learn that a performance of the school song was encored 'again and again, and all rose and stood while it was being sung'.[34] It was performed by a trained group of singers whose attendance at rehearsals was made compulsory once they had joined the singing class,

---

[33] G. R. Parkin, *Life and Letters of Edward Thring*, 2 vols. (London: Macmilian, 1898), vol. 2, pp. 306–9.

[34] Quoted in P. A. Scholes, *The Mirror of Music* (London: Oxford University Press, 1947), p. 627.

while Thring would often be present to demonstrate his support for the activity. The rest of the school did not join in.

Instead of basing music teaching in the classroom, as a discipline common to all and centring on vocal activity, Thring chose to foster an instrumental approach dependent on individual coaching and made available only to those who chose it. The school as a whole, however, was invited to share the experience as listeners by attending concerts given by the school choir and orchestra (stiffened by the instrumental coaches themselves) as well as by visiting soloists. To effect this policy Thring appointed Paul David, son of the eminent German violinist, Ferdinand David, to direct music teaching throughout the school.

The model presented at Uppingham was not immediately imitated elsewhere. But as former bias against musical performance as a time-wasting activity and sign of degeneracy gave way to a more balanced opinion among public school headmasters, Thring's policy was slowly adopted in other schools of similar calibre. The school song and the school concert both became generally accepted features of the life of a superior boarding school as the century progressed. Some part of the influence prompting their acceptance came also from Harrow, where the introduction of music teaching was not first instigated by the headmaster.

The circumstances of John Farmer's appointment to teach music at Harrow are not fully documented. Tradition has it that he was invited teach the piano there by individual boys themselves in 1862; and that he was not made a formal member of staff for some years after that. However that may be, his influence upon the school during the next twenty years was indelible, involving a lasting tradition of house-singing and a collection of school songs which eventually came to enjoy immense circulation. At Harrow under Farmer's direction the whole school sang. Gradually his 'wonderful power of making nearly everyone with whom he came into contact enthusiastic for music' turned many of the boys formerly brought up to scorn music into music-lovers (Scholes, p. 626).

That the admission of music to the curriculum of these two leading schools for boys took place at this particular time was a reflection of the changed attitude toward it in society generally. From an 1863 article in the *Cornhill Magazine* we find clear evidence of the broader acceptance of music at all social levels:

The cultivation of music as a recreation is not now confined in England to one class. While striking its roots down lower in the social scale, its topmost branches have also widened and strengthened. The study is not alone more general, it is also better understood and more seriously undertaken. ... A reaction set in some years ago; yet not so long since but Lady Blessington could venture in one of her books to pronounce openly against a man's occupying himself with music. ... It is a great gain that all the barriers of prejudice against music have been broken down; that boys are permitted to be taught the art; and that it is now generally held to be a rational and humanising occupation for men of all conditions.[35]

The steady growth of music teaching in independent schools for boys fostered by this new tolerance owed its character to a combination of the methods adopted in the types of boarding schools already examined. In general the pattern adopted, and largely retained today, included the provision of music in the school chapel by both choir and congregation, the performance of works by a voluntary choral society, individual instrumental coaching for those who sought it, and the consequent establishment of a school orchestra. House-singing was allowed to develop into music competitions between houses where the spirit of rivalry found on the sports field might be brought into play. In general, music was not treated as a classroom discipline, no doubt partly because most boys lost their singing voices early in their secondary school career.

Hitherto the daughters of the well-to-do had received their education at home before going on to a 'finishing school'. But after mid-century a new pattern for their education was established with the foundation of Cheltenham Ladies' College and the North London School for Girls under the pioneer headmistresses, Dorothea Beale and Frances Buss. Modest musical proficiency had long been regarded as a desirable accomplishment in a young woman. In addition to the lessons in history, geography, grammar, writing, arithmetic, and needlework specified in the entrance rules for the girls' school attended by Charlotte Brontë in 1823, an additional charge of £3 a year was made for music or drawing.[36] What was provided under the heading of music was private tuition in playing the piano or harp, and singing. This was the usual pattern in similar schools at the time.

That this tradition was largely preserved in the new schools for girls as they came into being is evident from Dorothea Beale's account of music teaching at Cheltenham Ladies' College in 1865:

Music is taught in the usual way, by private lessons; but there are also classes for the practice of concerted music, to which only advanced pupils are admitted. There may be from 4 to 12 performers, two to each piano; thus the pupils are enabled to obtain an intimate acquaintance with those works of the great masters (as Cherubini, Bach, Haydn, &c.) which are usually performed by an orchestra, and this promotes, also, decision, accuracy, and facility in reading. Twice a year we have a musical

---

[35] 'Amateur Music', *Cornhill Magazine*, vol. 8 no. 43 (1863), pp. 93–8.

[36] Elizabeth Gaskell, *The Life of Charlotte Brontë* (1857); quoted in A. F. Scott, *An Age of Elegance* (Woking: Gresham Books, 1979), p. 97.

examination, i.e., each pupil is required to play some piece in the presence of her companions and as many parents as wish to attend; no strangers are admitted.[37]

Just how far instrumental teaching in the new schools fell short of thorough competence was emphasised at a meeting of the National Association for the Promotion of Social Sciences which took place in Cheltenham in 1878. During the discussion which followed a paper on music in schools, one speaker claimed that 'the musical instruction in ladies' schools was in a most deficient state. He had often found ladies who could play a piece well, but when asked what key it was in were unable to give any answer' (*Transactions*, 1878, p. 675). The tendency in such schools, he claimed, was to concentrate on empty display. And it seems obvious today that the accepted image of the drawing-room pianist who dazzled suitors with empty technique or earned their affectionate indulgence with faltering execution obliged every young lady to learn to play the piano whether she had aptitude or not. The failure of many girls to benefit fully from their lessons must cause little surprise.

Yet this was a time of remarkable advance in the provision of educational resources for young women and girls. The foundation of Girton College, Cambridge in 1869, of Anne Clough's residential house for women students there in 1871, and of the first high school for girls in 1880 marked a decade of unprecedented progress. It was in the new high schools that class singing was first consistently developed. Maintained by the body later known as the Girls' Public Day School Trust (GPDST) and noted for its enlightened attitude toward music teaching, several of the schools appointed John Farmer to supervise this side of their activities, with results which earned the attention of the *Musical Times* in 1890:

> Perhaps the Girls' High School Company does more to encourage the study of singing than other schools of this class. This Company has now nearly 4,000 pupils attending its numerous schools. To place themselves well in evidence before die public, they have arranged to hold a great demonstration at the Crystal Palace. ... Mr John Farmer, who is to conduct, has decided to include only unison songs.
>
> (quoted in Scholes, pp. 627–8)

A subsequent report of the occasion, published in the same paper, found the programme 'decidedly monotonous' though the 'sweetness and purity of tone of the voices' afforded a redeeming feature. Yet the editor doubted whether

---

[37] Dorothea Beale in *Transactions of the National Association for the Promotion of Science* (London: n.p., 1866), p. 285.

these high school girls would have been as successful as their board school counterparts in singing at sight.

The editor of the *Musical Times* was W. A. Barrett who also held a post as inspector of music in schools and training colleges between 1871 and 1891. As such he was unusually well placed to comment on existing standards. His comparison of the differing potential of high school and board school pupils in the field of sight-singing pinpoints what was perhaps the most remarkable and ambivalent aspect of popular musical education throughout Queen Victoria's long reign.

Among tokens of the class distinction which led Disraeli to speak of the Queen's subjects as comprising Two Nations, none seems more bizarre than the opposing interpretations placed upon the content of the music lesson in schools catering for different classes. We have already noticed the 'improving' benefits that music teaching was designed to bring to both old and young among the 'lower orders' of Victorian society. Their social superiors, it seems, were not in need of singing lessons on this account. But as Sarah Glover pointed out in 1835, the reform of congregational singing – that other purpose of the singing class movement – required the participation of all branches of society:

> Amongst the superior orders of the community. singing is at present very rarely cultivated at all by gentlemen: and few ladies have such an acquaintance with intervals, as to venture to sing the simplest psalm tune, unprompted or unsupported by an instrument. Psalmody is therefore usually abandoned to the care of the illiterate ... most of whom are accustomed, in their youth, to strengthen their vocal organs in various ways which would be deemed unseemly in nurseries and academies for the children of gentlefolk. ... [But] let singing become a branch of national education, not only in schools for the children of labourers and mechanics, but in academies for young ladies and gentlemen, and the main point will be attained towards rendering psalmody truly congregational.
>
> (Glover, *Scheme,* pp. 5–6)

Her injunction, however, met with small response, though a few new boarding schools for boys began to encourage singing in their chapels a decade or so later. When a more general drive to introduce music teaching in similar schools took place toward the end of the century, it favoured instrumental activity,

That this choice was influenced by the occurrence of the boy's changing voice early in his secondary school career draws attention to another reason for the differences in music teaching in different types of schools: the widely differing ages of their pupils. The school-leaving age for elementary school pupils was fixed at ten years in 1880, rising to eleven in 1893 and twelve in 1899. Only in 1918 – as a new wave of reform began – was school attendance made compulsory between the ages of five and fourteen. The leaving age for a boy in an independent secondary boarding school, on the other hand, was normally eighteen.

An influence quite as great was the kind of musical training which the teachers in each of the two types of school had received. Music was taught in elementary schools by general class teachers whose musical knowledge and skill were commonly limited to basic matters included in a general teacher-training course. On the other hand, specialist teachers of music appointed in independent secondary schools (never in grammar schools for boys at this time) had generally received their training at a college of music or a university. Invariably instrumentalists – usually organists – they carried with them into their schools the unconscious bias of the instrumental performer.

The comparative weakness of secondary school pupils in the field of sight-singing, to which W. A. Barrett referred, was one consequence of their teachers' instrumental outlook. That this was a longstanding circumstance and not a by-product of the times is apparent from a discussion of music teaching published in France in 1818:

> One thing that constantly puzzles observers is that among the vast number of those who have learned music, so few can sing at sight. Most of them have to consult their violin, their pianoforte, or their flute, in order to learn a new tune; and it is actually the instrument which does the reading for them. It is as if, in order to read books, one learned to operate a machine designed for the purpose instead of adopting the more direct medium of the words themselves.[38]

In that passage from his *Exposition d'une nouvelle méthode pour l'enseignement de la musique* Pierre Galin laid bare, perhaps for the first time, a fundamental shortcoming In the average instrumental performer's musical equipment: an inability to 'hear' a written melody before playing it. It was his contention that this skill had come to be regarded as rare only because teachers failed to concentrate on training the beginner's ear before training the eye to identify the symbols of music. Other, later teachers were to share his belief that by encouraging singing from sol-fa their pupils developed a more accurate sense of relative pitch than instrumental experience alone could afford.

Most of those who came to share Galin's belief also shared his amateur status. Few of the attempts to reform musical instruction which occurred during the nineteenth century were made by professional musicians; almost all were the work of amateurs with sufficient understanding of children to question traditional methods which presented obstacles to all but the talented. Foremost

---

[38] P. Galin, *Rationale for a New Way of Teaching Music* (1818), ed. and trans., B. Rainbow, CTME 8 (Kilkenny: Boethius, 1983), pp. 41–2.

among such pioneers in England was John Curwen whose Tonic Sol-fa was designed specifically to ease the beginner's path.

But Curwen's amateur status, and his temerity in presuming to 'interfere' in the jealously guarded field of music teaching, incensed professional musicians. The situation was not eased by his being a nonconformist minister of known radical sympathies whose massive popular following embraced the unfashionable, the teetotallers, and the poor. Above all, the ancillary notation of sol-fa initials used in Curwen's vocal scores was anathema to the orthodox; and the resulting combination of outrage and musical snobbery was enough to outlaw Tonic Sol-fa – even after the professors of music at Oxford and Cambridge both commended its usefulness (Scholes, p. 16). It is thus unsurprising that specialist teachers of music in independent schools were not anxious to introduce Tonic Sol-fa, or that general standards of sight-singing there were as relatively disappointing as Barrett had suggested.

In spite of such differences, the state of music teaching in schools at the close of Victoria's reign presented a very different picture from the desolation prevailing when the Queen came to the throne. Then, it had proved necessary to justify music teaching to the nation and Parliament on other than purely musical grounds. Now, the choice of school songs no longer depended principally upon the message of their words, and a wide array of national and folk songs were being brought back into currency through children's participation. Then it had seemed politic to summon patriotic support by comparing native sloth with Prussian achievement. Just how far that situation had changed by the end of the century is shown by an article published in *Child Life* in 1899:

> It is the belief that only in Germany is there any musical education worth the name. This was true once upon a time, but nobody who knows anything about it could say that it is so today. 'England,' writes my German friend, 'needs another twenty years of musical education before the teaching will be efficient.' Most true! And when she has had it, Germany will need another twenty in which to catch her up. For during the past half-century England has been making strides, while Germany has been living on her reputation.[39]

Nor was this outspoken reproach just a reflection of the growing animosity between the two nations which marked those times. The 'myth' of German supremacy in popular musical education had been under attack since the publication of Hullah's formal *Report on Musical Instruction in Elementary Schools on the Continent* in 1880. After visiting schools in Württemberg,

---

[39] A. J. Curwen, 'Should All Children Be Taught Music, or only the Gifted?', *Child* Life (October 1899); reprinted in A. J. Curwen, *Music and Psychology* (London: J. Curwen & Sons, 1901), pp. 291–6.

Bavaria, Austria, Bohemia, Saxony, and Prussia, Hullah dismissed the generality of the teachers' achievements as 'the poorest conceivable'.[40] Indeed, the decline of musical instruction in German schools was shamefacedly acknowledged by Hermann Kretzschmar in his *Musikalische Zeitfragen* (1903) and a policy of reform proposed.[41] At the same time, the two types of English school whose different interpretations of musical education had hitherto been so distinct now began to experience a process akin to cross-fertilisation. The first example of the trend appeared when classes in violin-playing were introduced in a number of elementary schools in 1905. The venture was made possible by an astute London music firm which supplied instruments by hire-purchase at a low rate, boosting the enterprise by organising the attendance of private teachers in urban schools throughout the country. By 1910 a massed 'orchestra' of several thousand elementary school violinists trained in this way performed impressively at the Crystal Palace (Scholes, p. 623), and the beginnings of a new tradition of instrumental playing appeared in state schools which was to continue and develop to our own day.

A movement also began in the same decade to improve aural training and sight-singing in secondary schools. The prime mover was Mary Agnes Langdale, whose challenging articles on 'A Plea for Broader Treatment of Music in our Schools' appeared in a little-known Roman Catholic educational journal, *The Crucible*, in 1908.[42] Recommending that the teaching of music should more closely resemble the teaching of literature, Langdale urged the teaching of intelligent listening in addition to class singing. Piano and violin teaching would continue to rank with other optional studies, but obligatory lessons should be provided to 'ensure to all pupils the benefits of a sound musical training'. No amount of individual instrumental reaching or practice should be allowed to interfere with this regular class work so as to afford those who took up an instrument the general musical knowledge which was essential to intelligent performance. Lessons in musical rudiments and aural training for juniors would lead to the teaching of 'Musical Appreciation' for seniors.

That policy was first formally implemented by Stewart Macpherson, a teacher at the Royal Academy of Music, who obtained permission to try out the scheme at Streatham Hill High School (GPDST) with gratifying success, The school soon became virtually a normal school where would-be teachers studying at the Royal Academy could practice teaching under Macpherson's supervision, while other girls' high schools were not slow to imitate the Streatham

---

[40] J. S. Curwen and J. Hullah, *School Music Abroad* (1880; R/CTME 15, Kilkenny: Boethius, 1985), p. 18.

[41] Hermann Kretszchmar, *Musikalische Zeitfragen* (Leipzig: Peters, 1903), throughout.

[42] M. A. Langdale and S. Macpherson, *Early Essays in Musical Appreciation*, CTME 11 (Kilkenny: Boethius, 1984), contains both articles in facsimile.

pattern. The creation of the Music Teachers' Association under Macpherson's leadership in 1908 'to promote progressive ideas upon the teaching of music, especially with a view to the more educational treatment of the subject in schools', accelerated the process.

As a result of these developments, by the first decade of the twentieth century music had found a place in the curriculum of a wide variety of schools whether independent or maintained by the state. Only the academically slanted, examination-haunted grammar schools for boys generally failed to admit music teaching. They continued to do so until the implementation of the Butler Education Act of 1944. Elsewhere syllabuses attempting broader treatment of the subject were consistently introduced to encourage greater musical understanding and wider familiarity with she masterpieces of the art than singing lessons alone could afford. Efforts of this kind were at first necessarily limited to the playing of pieces on the secondary school piano; the pianola, the gramophone, and the radio would enlarge the scope of this work in the future. But within the resources available at the time, well before Victorian self-confidence and earnestness had evaporated, a pattern of music teaching had been developed in schools nationally which was recognisably the forerunner of the scheme existing today.

Plato and Music Today
[1981]

D EFENDING MUSIC'S PLACE in the curriculum has once again become
a valid preoccupation. Once again we must now expect to meet quotations from Plato trotted out to justify music as an essential feature in education 'because it helps to develop character'. Automatic respect for that great
philosopher perhaps prompts us to accept such claims without question. But
are they true? Beethoven, we suddenly recall, swindled his publisher; Mozart
wrote childishly scatological letters; Gesualdo murdered his wife ... Yet all
those thorough-going musicians should (if these claims were true) have displayed impeccable integrity. The matter seems to invite further investigation.

Quotations wrenched from their context are invariably unreliable. When
citing Plato on Music we must remember that he uses the term *mousikē* in its
original sense to embrace the territory of all the Muses – those divine daughters of Zeus who preside over poetry, tragedy, comedy, history, dance and
astronomy, as well as song. Nor must we forget Plato's uncompromising opinion that melody unaccompanied by verse is meaningless. For him, melody was
simply the inspired and inspiring medium that carried words and fused them
into the memory. These facts change the meaning of the often glib quotations
from his *Republic* where, before treating the topic of music in our sense of the
word, he pays detailed attention to children's literary upbringing and discusses
the kind of verses they should encounter. Only then does he consider the types
of melody suitable (Apollonian) or unsuitable (Dionysian) when reciting those
verses.

However, this does not mean that we can now afford to shrug off Plato's
opinions as irrelevant today. On the contrary, seen in that new light his observations on the choice of suitable texts and appropriate music convey a message
which has recently obtained all too little attention in curriculum planning. He
is not telling us that music has some magic power to develop character, but that
both words and music used in schools must be carefully chosen if the effect
upon character is not to be harmful. And that is a very different matter.

Dr Burney found it possible in 1789 to define music as 'an innocent luxury'.
Innocence is perhaps the last thing that strikes one about much of the stuff
hammered out to the accompaniment of flashing lights and tom-toms in dis-
cos today. There the Dionysian as opposed to Apollonian aspect of music is
regularly demonstrated with a vengeance. It is this barbarous music that Plato
warns against when discussing a child's musical upbringing. Not so many years
ago it may have been possible to introduce 'pop' in the classroom at minimal

risk by selecting songs from the Beatles (surrogates for Apollo) rather than those of the Rolling Stones (standing in for Dionysus). It was certainly at that time that the trend began. But those days have gone, taking with them the immediacy of pop songs then current.

The present vogue, including the insidious 'punk rock' with its malicious overtones, makes a selective approach less practicable and certainly less advisable. In any case, the time has surely now come to admit that pop music is more a social phenomenon than a musical manifestation. Attempts to apply the standards of orthodox musical criticism to 'hit' records in the classroom seem as unprofitable as trying to debate the literary style of a mob-orator at an extremist rally. To expect a class of young addicts to assess the quality of a favoured pop number objectively, when their judgement has already been formed subjectively – and under the formidable influence of 'peer group' mentality – is indeed an ungrateful task. For that matter, its devotees know that you don't *listen* to a pop song – you *react*.

This article began by questioning the tired claim that music helps to build character. We now find that its indiscriminate use can do exactly the opposite – can indeed reinforce the cult of violence, a phenomenon horrifyingly apparent today.

When seeking to defend music's place in the curriculum we must first make sure that the position we have chosen to adopt is defensible. If we wish to cite Plato in support of our policies, those policies must not contradict his tenets. But whether we rely on Plato to lend authority to our arguments or not, we ignore his warnings about the harmful potential of the Dionysian element in music at our peril. Merely to make our goal the performance of music of whatever kind in the classroom is heading for trouble.

It is pitifully easy to base activities upon familiar precepts from great educators only to find that they can lead to disaster. Sometimes (as with Plato) failure may be due to misunderstanding of the precept itself; sometimes excess of zeal or lack of common sense is responsible. Pestalozzi's dictum, 'Proceed from the known to the unknown', is a case in point. Applied indiscriminately it could lead to courses in accurate brick-throwing for juvenile delinquents. Some trendy music teaching seems to fall into this category. Often it is due to the earnest teacher's wish to get nearer his class by showing that he can share their tastes. But the invisible barrier that initially exists between pupil and teacher (no matter how young!) is not demolished so easily.

Need we feel ashamed at omitting from the music lesson those aspects of the 'known' that seem unlikely to encourage the development of what is at present the 'unknown'? Will further doses of the over-familiar make the unfamiliar more acceptable? Or, to return to Plato, should we not ensure that all music introduced in schools is carefully chosen if the effect upon character is not to be harmful?

For some of those young teachers who have been given a smattering of Sociology in their colleges the problem that now arises is how to reconcile Plato with Max Weber. According to Weber, value-judgements should be avoided when discussing human or social affairs scientifically. This tenet is too often taken to mean that any attempt to distinguish between 'right' and 'wrong' in everyday affairs is somehow socially reprehensible. What was intended as a methodological ideal for scientific evaluation (*Wertfreiheit*) has been treated as a ban on assessment of any kind.

Consequently, a vague desire to be 'democratic' can lead a young teacher (or an older one) to adopt a policy of musical *laissez-faire* – anything goes, as they say. Cases where children are invited to bring to school favourite records to play during lesson time are by no means unknown. The choice is nearly always predictable – another pop song. The result: not only a waste of scarce lesson time, but the apparent addition of a stamp of authority to the inferior. Such lapses are regrettable; for although it is now thought politically unsound to dare to speak of 'good taste', musical values still exist. And it remains the teacher's duty to preserve and encourage them. Alas, all too often where this is not done, policy has been dictated by despair rather than trendiness.

Onward From Butler: School Music, 1945–1985
[1984]

THE PRESENT TRIPARTITE SYSTEM of education in this country with its stages of Primary, Secondary and Further Education was brought about by the Butler Act of 1944 which implemented the findings of the McNair Report and thus incidentally strengthened the place of Music in general education. Music teaching in schools was quickly expanded as a result and has since undergone a further series of revolutions often influenced by social and political circumstances rather than purely musical considerations. The concurrent and similarly prompted shift of values which took place in young people's ideals, sense of independence and behaviour generally during the 1960s further sharpened the atmosphere of change. This year's anniversary of the passing of the Butler Act presents a symbolic occasion for reviewing some of the events which have so radically altered the pattern of school music teaching during the past forty years.

THE EDUCATION AND TRAINING OF TEACHERS

Anticipating the need for additional teachers due to the introduction of tripartite education the McNair Report made careful recommendations with different disciplines in mind. The shortage of music teachers would at first be most pronounced in the secondary schools for boys, where the subject had traditionally been neglected. As a first step headmasters were advised to recruit new staff from among local private teachers and organists; thereafter, in addition to the universities and music colleges, new or expanded music departments in teacher training colleges would eventually supply a generation of specialist teachers. At the same time the whole question of 'educating' rather than 'training' nongraduate teachers was placed under review. Earlier attitudes toward teacher training were criticised as doing little more than offering 'tips for teachers' without continuing the student's education appreciably beyond the elementary stage.

To remedy that deficiency students in training colleges were required in future to select a 'main study', followed for their own personal advancement, and not necessarily as a subject which they chose to teach. On the pedagogical side the general policy was to encourage teaching skill by the systematic study of 'Principles of Education' and supervised teaching practice, rather than by a demonstration of teaching methods in the lecture room.

Where the majority of subjects in the school curriculum are concerned, grasp of subject matter coupled with reasonable competence in planned verbal exposition enables the young teacher to survive in the classroom. But however adequate that equipment may prove for teaching English, History, Mathematics, Geography or the like, additional resources are essential to teachers of Music – where practical experience and understanding of how to develop such basic techniques as singing and aural perception must precede success in teaching them to children.

Yet in the struggle to attain academic respectability prompted by the new concept of 'teacher education' music syllabuses during the postwar era commonly imitated the theoretical content characteristic of earlier university courses. As a result, would-be teachers who lacked the levels of musicianship to earn a university place received a watered-down version of a university course rather than one designed to develop practical skills essential to successful work in schools. Instead of being taught choral techniques students learned to analyse fugues; before learning to hear a melody from the page they were asked to harmonise it; though largely unfamiliar with classroom repertoire their attention was first drawn to Haydn's string quartets. Ideally of course, both aspects of musical experience should have been made theirs. But limitations of lecture time and the reaction against 'tips for teachers' saw to it that priority was given to 'academic' music, consideration of classroom needs coming a very poor second and being seen as an inferior appendix rather than an integral part of the course. This attitude was further hardened with the eventual introduction of graduate courses for the BEd.

Entrants to teaching from the universities and colleges of music were not at first required to undergo training for teaching. The possession of a degree or a 'recognised' diploma was accepted as an adequate initial qualification. An attempt on the part of the colleges of music to introduce a graduate diploma incorporating methodology was found not to produce satisfactory teachers and soon abandoned. It was replaced by a voluntary scheme which took diploma-holders to one of the few training colleges selected by the Ministry of Education's inspectors to run a special one-year course in Education, teaching preparation and practice, leading to the award of a teaching certificate. This procedure was later made compulsory for entrants from the music colleges.

University graduates in music were not obliged to undergo professional training for teaching until very recently. Those who chose to might enrol for training at one of the selected training colleges – though some opted to attend a general postgraduate course in a university department. Only when the patent disadvantage of allowing music teachers to be trained in general courses which made no provision for their special needs was later realised were postgraduate courses exclusively designed for music teachers established at the Universities of Reading and London. Even so, many music graduates continued to enrol for general postgraduate training which left them ill-equipped for the realities of the classroom.

Fortunately, the naturally talented among those entering the teaching profession soon overcame such limitations. And whether from training college, music college, or university, most elected to teach in secondary schools. In the wider range of schools for boys and girls over the age of eleven, opportunities now opened to pursue higher levels of musical achievement. Existing Grammar Schools for boys or High Schools for girls fortunate enough to have a capable musician on their staff were soon undertaking ambitious performances with choirs and orchestras backed by soundly organised sixth-form Music courses. And although academic standards were necessarily lower in the new Secondary Modern Schools, experience soon showed that under inspiring teaching very satisfactory (and rewarding) levels of musical performance were attainable by children not otherwise much given to shine. Yet in both types of secondary school it was in the classroom that the limitations of the existing system of music in general education were frequently revealed.

It proved virtually impossible in secondary schools generally for teachers to avoid starting music lessons from scratch if they meant to tackle the subject seriously. With each new intake of children the disparity between those who came from Primary Schools where Music was taught competently and those from others where it was neglected or taught badly was regularly emphasised. It seemed difficult to avoid the conclusion that since there was no commonly accepted standard as to what could or should be achieved in the Primary School continuity of teaching throughout the child's school career was simply unattainable. Discussion always revealed general conviction that it was during the formative years in the Primary School that basic musical skills and perceptions were best cultivated. But circumstances in Primary Schools, staffed as they were by general class teachers rather than specialists, presented problems of organisation and teacher training to which answers had not been found – and which remain unresolved to this day.

In the early days of teacher training in this country midway through the nineteenth century it was taken for granted that every elementary school teacher should teach singing, and initial training consequently included instruction in approved methods of learning to read music and sing from notes. In spite of changes in the choice of methods approved for the purpose this remained the state of affairs until the 1920s – by which time our elementary schools had gained an international reputation for the ability of their pupils to sing at sight.

Disregarding for the time being the question as to whether learning to sing at sight is a desirable pursuit or no, but acknowledging that standards of teaching it varied considerably among elementary teachers depending upon ability and enthusiasm, it seems evident that the state of music in the elementary schools of the 1920s demonstrated adequately enough what can be achieved in spite of individual limitations when modest aims are set and those aims are made clear to the teachers concerned. The same might be said, after all, about most of the subjects in the Junior School curriculum.

But this argument was not allowed to influence policy when the pattern of postwar training for general class teachers was decided. It was argued instead that the potential content of the Junior School curriculum had grown to such an extent that teachers should not be called upon to teach in all areas; and that since Music was a subject best taught by those with a liking for it, it should be made an optional choice in the training college syllabus. One unforeseen result of this decision was that most of the students choosing to engage in an optional music course were those who had already learned to play an instrument from childhood and who consequently entertained certain misconceptions about the learning process in music. Almost more unfortunate was the impression created in the child's mind that since Music was not taught (like other Junior School subjects) by every class teacher there was something 'peculiar' about it; and that if a favourite teacher didn't seem to care for music there was no reason for her pupils to do so either.

A further complication, which particularly affected secondary teaching but also impinged on the Primary School, was the amazing growth of the music curriculum during the postwar decades. What had been an exclusively song-based activity in the nineteenth century now offered a multiplicity of possible opportunities involving instrumental music making, guided listening, interpretational movement, and creative work. This development, which demands closer examination, made the choice of classroom musical activities much more dependent upon the teachers' own individual enthusiasms, and the adoption of an authorised core curriculum for the Primary School less than congenial in the liberalised atmosphere of the postwar era.

THE BROADENING MUSIC CURRICULUM

Innovations widening the scope of music teaching in our schools began to appear quite early in the twentieth century, but since they were confined to independent schools and spread only slowly even there, the Musical Appreciation movement, Dalcroze Eurhythmics, the use of the gramophone in the classroom, and infants' percussion bands made little impact in state schools before the 1930s. By then, however, listening to music had become a domestic pastime through the advent of gramophone and radio. And though in many households the music broadcast received little conscious attention, the 'Foundations of Music' talks given by Walford Davies became a surprisingly popular feature among middle-class listeners. The climate of public response to music was gradually changing, and with it attitudes to music in schools began to change, too.

Emphasis began to shift from vocally based activity to instrumental work with the introduction of the bamboo pipe followed by the recorder during the 1930s. The move was hailed, and with some justification, as adding purpose to music lessons by providing an end product for theory. Elsewhere attention turned from singing to listening to recorded music. This innovation in turn was applauded as a realistic preparation for future enjoyment. In both cases older children whose early music lessons had been adequate and whose grasp of basic musical essentials was sound were able to benefit from the new element of variety in their later lessons. But without that foundation, at the hands of less competent teachers both types of activity invited misuse of limited lesson time. The Board of Education found it advisable to warn teachers not to regard the new activities as alternatives but as adjuncts to former methods. That warning was in a sense prophetic – for the immense variety of alternative musical activities introduced in schools since the Butler Act has led to a situation in which hardly any two secondary schools have a concordant policy, while such basic skills as singing and aural training are quite neglected in a very high proportion of our primary schools.

Although the outbreak of war in 1939 seriously affected the day-to-day running of schools, planning for postwar development continued. And contrary to what might be supposed, the war years were to see further growth in popular response to music – a circumstance aided by the creation of a national Council for the Encouragement of Music and the Arts, later to become the present Arts Council. The first postwar decade was dominated by austerity, but special resources were made available for building houses and schools. To begin with only the bare essentials of the Butler Act were implemented, but during the 1950s the number of pupils remaining at school until the age of seventeen rose to double that of the prewar total. Most of the schools which they attended were now better equipped to teach music and had begun to introduce wider activities with resources hitherto found only in independent schools.

At the same time social and technological advances were boosting average weekly incomes which rose by 34 per cent between 1955 and 1960. Ten years later they had risen by 130 per cent. The Affluent Society symbolised by a car, a washing machine and a television set to every household had arrived. With it came the creation of a new consumer society from among the formerly underprivileged (and their children) whose unprecedented purchasing power now made them a tempting target for predatory commercialism. This development helps to explain the rise of the 'pop' music phenomenon supported as it was by the prodigious growth of recording sales among young people in the 1960s. Calculated populism encouraged triviality, and following the pattern of teenagers in the United States their counterparts on this side of the Atlantic soon adopted the deliberately non-intellectual repertoire provided for them, as a badge of identity.

To begin with, the attitude of the bulk of teachers toward their pupils' odd musical preferences was no different from that of their predecessors. Although not dignified as was now the case by such pretentious labels as 'youth culture' or 'popular culture' a type of popular song formerly regarded as merely vulgar had always existed. Under the influence of Arthur Somervell, H.M. Inspector of Music at the beginning of the century, and Cecil Sharp, the folk-song revivalist, teachers had accepted that an important part of their task was to wean adherents away from 'the raucous notes of coarse music-hall songs'. The same attitude had been adopted following the advent of the 'crooner'. The pop-singer seemed to present an identical problem and to merit the same treatment. But then experience with growing numbers of secondary pupils revealed that young people were able to compartmentalise their musical response – finding satisfaction from both 'pop' and 'serious' music. Only with the birth of the 'generation gap' and the adoption of leaders of the pop scene as cult figures, did the true scale of the problem confronting music teachers in schools reveal itself.

Meanwhile attention turned to new opportunities of extending classroom musical activity. Rumour had it that the German composer Carl Orff had revolutionised music lessons in his homeland simply by introducing new pitched percussion instruments with detachable tone-bars to suit different levels of ability. Cheaper versions of his glockenspiels and xylophones were promptly marketed in this country together with simple performing scores imitating his originals. Classrooms everywhere began to echo with the clink and bong of metal and wood. Many teachers felt they had found a simpler and more enjoyable way of developing musical literacy. But when authentic English versions of Orff's *Schulwerk* were later published, they revealed that instrumental work provided only a part of his programme, to complement carefully developed basic aural and vocal skills. Yet for every teacher who examined Orff's instructions books there were hundreds with only second-hand acquaintance with his methods. And by this time the vogue for pseudo-Orff was too well established, backed by wide commercial support, to halt the decline which had taken place in the development of aural skills and class singing.

The teachers who joined the rush to adopt classroom instruments were not simpletons; an instrumental stance appealed to them particularly because most were themselves instrumentalists – mainly pianists – and their own mental approach to the interpretation of musical notation was instrumentally based. During their early lessons they had learnt to 'find' a note on a keyboard rather than to 'hear' it in their heads after identifying the symbol concerned on the page. Even those of them who could play at sight confidently, commonly lacked the ability to sing quite a simple tune from the page. More to the point, as we have seen during their training as teachers the deficiency had not been corrected and the paradox which explained it had not been thoroughly exposed.

This was a time, too, when instrumental activity had begun to dominate school music exclusively. As developing secondary schools flexed their muscles the creation of a school orchestra became a common goal and the employment of peripatetic instrumental teachers the essential means to that end. The unusual appointment now of a former leading orchestral player to the post of H.M. Inspector of music in schools served to strengthen what was a growing trend. With the creation of the first three Comprehensive Schools by the Labour-controlled London County Council in 1955, the large number of pupils enrolled increased both the range of choice for membership of an orchestra and the *per capita* financial grant to provide the instruments and tuition to equip and service it. As more Comprehensive Schools were created during the 1960s, often catering for more than a thousand pupils of mixed ability, music blossomed in them as an extra-curricular activity just as evidently as it declined in effectiveness and popularity as a classroom discipline.

The truth of this situation failed to secure public attention. Scarce references to school music in the press largely consisted of self-congratulatory accounts of performances by school orchestras or the often admittedly excellent youth orchestras which they fed. But the children concerned had been selected for their talent and given special coaching to reach such standards; far from typifying the well-being of Music in schools these exceptional pupils served rather to emphasise the poverty of the rest – whose unenthusiastic response to their music lessons in the secondary school can readily be traced to awareness of their own musical incompetence. Lacking basic skills best taught at an early age but all too often neglected in our Primary Schools, the musically untalented pupil quickly lost interest in a teacher's efforts to build upon foundations that were simply not there. And given the special place that music of a particular sort occupied in the adolescent's life-style, active rebellion of a vigour spared to teachers of other subjects was regularly aroused during and after the 1960s.

As a result of this stalemate music's renown as an all-embracing educational force seemed subject to direct challenge in Secondary Schools. Some thought it should survive there only as an optional subject. Others suggested that radical revision of the music curriculum itself was necessary to meet changed circumstances. There were, needless to say, many rival theories as to the desirable content of future music lessons ranging from egalitarian pressures in support of populism to equally extreme *avant-garde* calls to outlaw the diatonic scale. Each school of thought had its followers and the current assumption was that salvation lay only in novelty; but partisan interest and support centred particularly around three policies.

The first was based on the argument that it was a mistake to try to educate children to respond to music which it was claimed had been written for the edification of an upper-class audience – a 'cultural elite'. Instead, teachers should aim at strengthening the sub-culture presently enjoyed by their pupils, first entering and coming to terms with it themselves. Efforts to bring the cultural heritage of the past to the children of the present were unlikely to succeed and were, it was said, of doubtful educational value. The 'broad mass of people' did not respond to the heritage of the past, according to radical opinion.

Where this policy was implemented (notably in inner-city areas) musical appreciation lessons were dropped, and the song repertoire shifted away from former tradition by introducing songs of the very type that Somervell and Sharp had condemned. To identify the stratum of sub-culture common to all pupils in the wide range of a comprehensive school meant selecting the lowest. And so the process of 'levelling-down' already familiar in other schemes of social engineering began its debasing progress in the unlikely field of music teaching.

The second proposal was an off-shoot of the first. The requisite sub-culture selected here for investigation and development was the 'pop' music so favoured among young people of school age. The declared aim was to heighten discrimination within the sub-culture itself, as well as to develop a wider response to music generally. Supporters of this policy included many young teachers whose limited knowledge of the background of pop found them poorly placed to teach its devotees – who resented this incompetent invasion of their preserve. Hence the aims of this revisionist policy were seldom realised. Then, otherwise capable and enthusiastic teachers became disenchanted as pop's obvious associations with drug abuse and youthful revolt became inescapable, making serious attempts at criticism and assessment less than realistic. Few teachers were equipped to deal with problems of this magnitude and complexity.

A third alternative syllabus sought to apply the currently favoured technique of 'creativity' to the music lesson. Even if confident that a child was as able to experiment with sound in the music lesson as with design and colour in the art lesson, teachers had hitherto been brought to a halt by their pupil's inability to record in standard notation the sound patterns he could easily invent. With the adoption of graphic musical notation by *avant-garde* composers a way of overcoming this handicap presented itself; and through their spontaneous use of sound without trying to ape the formal structures of earlier music, children's efforts even acquired a 'contemporary' quality. After George Self's pioneering work in this vein at a London school, other influential teachers adopted what came to be known as 'Experimental Music in Schools'.

The new technique, so adventurous in concept compared with traditional methods, attracted many young teachers who started creative work with their classes. But an element essential to success in this activity was an ability on the teacher's part to guide and sustain positive criticism of children's efforts in performance. And this attribute, owing to a combination of immaturity and limited acquaintance with contemporary music, proved to be sadly beyond the reach of many of the teachers concerned. Moreover, since the new activity made a virtue of musical illiteracy, an already strong movement to abandon teaching the use of standard notation received further impetus.

In pursuit of spontaneity a generation of schoolchildren had already grown up without skills previously regarded as essential in elementary education. Theories that children should not be pestered to learn to spell, write grammatically, or learn multiplication tables later found a musical counterpart in arguments against teaching the use of notation. Its opponents reinforced their position by remarking that sight-singing had first been added to the school curriculum largely in order to improve congregational singing in churches. That policy was clearly no longer justifiable and the time given to the exercise should now be devoted to other 'more enjoyable' musical activity. In spite of the weakness of their case, advocates of child-centred education were aware that fashion supported them; and encouraged by this apparently erudite and historically sound argument unsuccessful teachers of sight-singing were glad to abandon the pursuit. Tonic Sol-fa, the standby of elementary teachers at the beginning of the century, had never gained wholehearted support from the instrumentally biased teachers who succeeded them. Sol-fa syllables did not help a pianist to find his notes, and the letter-notation designed to help beginners was seen as an old-fashioned expedient which had outlived its usefulness. The first English announcement, early in the 1960s, of Kodály's Method and its successful application in the schools of Hungary aroused a stir of interest – but without revealing to teachers generally that the inspiration of Kodály's achievement lay in their own neglected Tonic Sol-fa. And while a limited number introduced the Kodály Method in their schools, news of Carl Orff's *Schulwerk* with its instrumental bias – also first circulating at this time – attracted much greater interest and support from the new generation of teachers. It was widely felt that instrumental activity in the classroom satisfactorily replaced sight-singing, making the use of sol-fa unnecessary, it was generally abandoned.

Another casualty to current iconoclasm was class singing itself. Former high standards of school singing now earned scornful rejection as being artifically reminiscent of the cathedral chorister – that outmoded elitist. Already sadly undermined by the introduction of rowdy songs into the repertoire and perhaps even more seriously assailed by the deliberately unformed voices modelled by pop-idols, voice training finally disappeared from most schools. Gruff low-pitched voices producing either an ugly uproar or a husky mutter now regularly went unchecked in junior classrooms, while older pupils sulkily refused to sing at all.

During the 1970s the wheel turned full circle as former children who had received this impaired musical education themselves became teachers. To existing problems of the Junior School was now added the class teacher who had never learned to sing and who believed that children's voices should not use the upper register. This opinion was echoed in research documents which claimed that (judging by existing standards in schools) all previous theories and experience touching children's singing voices were mistaken, and that the true compass was in the contralto range. At a stroke the entire repertoire of treble songs drawn from the past four centuries was consigned to the dustbin. All told, the future looked far from bright.

THE AFTERMATH

It is not unusual to find the phenomenal growth of new teaching methods which has taken place since the 1950s described as an Explosion. Like other explosions this one has emphatically produced its roll of casualties. But however serious that consequence may have been it is not just what was destroyed that gives rise to misgiving in this case. There seems as much cause for concern in the very prodigality of what has been created. For though methods and resources have expanded to an unprecedented extent, the allotment for music on the school timetable remains much what it was a century ago; and this means that instead of producing a general broadening of the music curriculum, the range of alternative procedures presented to teachers has left them to decide what to include and what to omit in the time available.

While there is much to be said for enabling individual teachers to bring to their pupils the benefits of their own preferences and enthusiasms, this can only become a satisfactory general policy where a basic core syllabus exists – at least at Primary School level. But this, as we have seen, is something entirely lacking as things stand. As a result, indiscriminate growth in the upper reaches of the syllabus has meant fragmentation of effort and a situation where no two secondary schools teach the same range of musical activities. The position of a pupil transferred from one school to another is thus an unenviable one. At the same time the absence of continuity in musical education between Primary and Secondary levels results in failure to realise music's intellectual and educational potential. And the child's own musical experience and sensibility are left to depend less on what is taught at school than on the choice of television channel at home.

The process of disintegration begun in the 1960s was accelerated by an absence of leadership. The withdrawal of H.M. Inspectorate from its former role as classroom adviser and critic perhaps reflected awareness of the unfortunate effect of excessive zeal on earlier generations of teachers. Whatever the reason may have been, the resulting vacuum remained unfilled in spite of the existence of such bodies as the Incorporated Society of Musicians and the more recent United Kingdom Council for Music Education and Training. For though subcommittees were appointed to make recommendations on school music in either case, their findings were constrained by compromise, and lacked weight. No assembly of 'experts' today, it seems, should be expected to agree a forthright statement which might tread on partisan corns. One vexed issue raised at these discussion meetings concerned the development of musical literacy. And while earlier opposition to teaching the use of notation had given way by the seventies to more general realisation of the value of this skill in developing aural sensitivity, agreed statements on the subject were yet discreetly worded to recommend only 'the use of an appropriate form of notation' in order to accommodate the Experimental Music lobby.

The situation which this impasse reveals is a particularly interesting one showing that the fragmentation which has taken place in the pattern of school music is no more than a reflection of the over-specialisation which now divides would-be authorities on music education – each of them concentrating his energies upon the establishment and maintenance of an exclusive facet while defending it from encroachment by other factions. Only rarely, it seems, is an 'expert' to be found with a universal attitude toward the whole range of aspects now available – one ready, moreover, to agree the detail of a core curriculum around which other optional activity might take place to complement it. Without such a policy the present spiral of thriftlessness and dissipation seems bound to continue.

Meanwhile there is plenty of evidence to show that between them the new teaching methods introduced during the 1960s still command support from large numbers of teachers. What is not so readily apparent is how often this support is forthcoming only because such activities keep pupils 'busy', and not because of the educational expectations they arouse. For that matter, when faced with problems of the kind regularly confronting secondary teachers in urban areas today, the teacher whose prime aim in planning a music lesson is to find undemanding ways of filling up the time must earn at least some sympathy. Yet the consequence of this all too common policy has been to treat the music lesson as an occasion for entertainment rather than for learning. When policy is dictated by despair in place of resolve, educational aims necessarily carry little weight. Music has been seriously undervalued as a result.

Yet there are signs that the long flirtation with unorthodoxy in music teaching is waning. Teachers are rediscovering methods and attitudes rejected by their predecessors during the years when excellence was equated with novelty.

In-service training has revealed to many Junior School teachers that properly directed effort enables them first to overcome their own shortcomings, then to develop children's skills usefully. Subsequent experience with their classes has shown that contrary to hearsay children enjoy learning to use their musical sense, while short regular sessions of aural training soon develop new skills contributing toward that adventure of discovery which plays so important a part in a child's gratification. Quite as much as any other subject in the curriculum Music offers opportunities for enjoyment through achievement. The conviction is now widespread that much of the secondary pupil's lack of enthusiasm for his music lessons is due to the absence of early training in aural-skills. Misguided attempts to make good the starvation years of the Primary School with a prodigal menu in the Secondary School now merely call to mind Marie Antoinette's hare-brained proposal to feed the breadless poor: Let them eat cake!

NOVEMBER 1984

SOME PERSONAL AFTERTHOUGHTS (1990)
Walter Heise

WHEN I WENT to London in the middle of the 1980s to one of the yearly conferences of the Curwen Institute, this happened at that time out of a purely historical interest. Agnes Hundoegger[1] and her circle had received their fundamental ideas regarding the Tonika-Do-Lehre at the London Tonic Sol-fa College before the turn of the century and had tried to transpose them to Germany. For various reasons however, this stood contrary to the music-educational *Zeitgeist* of the turn of the century.

The cosmopolitan attitude of German educators at the beginning of the nineteenth century became increasingly engrossed in the second half of the century with its own self-sufficiency. Moreover, at the end of the century nationalistic biases made influences from abroad ('foreignness') so suspect, that special justifications were required, if one had been attempting to undertake in this country what had long been tried and tested abroad. This is substantiated by the following sentences from Agnes Hundoegger's preface to *Lehrweise nach Tonika-Do* (1897): 'We Germans like to bask in the knowledge of being more advanced in things musical than every other nation, and it is especially towards

---

[1] Agnes Hundoegger, who grew up in a home of very musical parents, met Joseph Joachim, Johannes Brahms, Clara Schumann and Julius Stockhausen very early on. She studied music in Berlin, gave concerts for several years as a singer and pianist and later taught in Hannover. As a teacher of instrumental and vocal music she found ear-training methods lacking until she finally found satisfaction from the Tonic Sol-fa College.

England that we would least like to acknowledge any superiority. Contrary to belief rather, here it is not just about the revolutionary efforts of music as such, but only a carefully thought-out teaching method, proven over more than a generation, in which ... the educational direction of the practical English are ahead of us.'

But there were other obstacles that stood in the way of integrating Tonika-Do in the schools.

1. The method developed by the teacher Carl Eitz[2] around the same period, was trusted as a method by school teachers more than the method which grew out of the field of private instrumental and vocal tuition.

2. There were reservations by the – mostly male – teachers regarding a method, which was being propagated by women.

3. Until 1918, methods for instruction by the schools were set by the state. Only after the implementation of freedom of instructional methodology could Tonika-Do integrate itself into many schools; it became embroiled at the same time, however, in a long-drawn-out fight over methods between the 'Eitzianer' and the 'Tedisten'. Out of this fight over methods a compromise was born, Richard Münnich's Jale.

4. After the national-socialist state had hardly done anything to encourage solmisation methods, Jale was made the official state method after the end of the Second World War in East Germany (DDR) (until 1989). In West Germany, the methods of Carl Eitz and Tonika-Do were reintroduced, of which only the Tonika-Do survived until the end of the 1950s.

Even though I had still been taught Tonika-Do during my university studies in the 1950s, in practice I could only observe its disappearance. My last dealings with Tonika-Do were triggered by conversations with my predecessor. Prof. Kurt Sydow. He had been asked by the remaining members of the Tonika-Do Federation to take over its direction. His hesitation had something to do with the actual possibilities, that he thought such a method could still succeed in today's educational climate. The ideal of a 'singing school' had become less certain for many reasons:

1. After song had been constantly misused for ideological ends during National Socialism (which was continued in East Germany with a different emphasis), many teachers regarded singing as an elemental part of the teaching curriculum with increasing scepticism.

---

[2] Carl Eitz (1848–1924). He developed a very elaborate method of teaching elementary singing. He gave different pitch names to the diatonic, chromatic and enharmonic degrees of the seven notes in the rising scale from C. The result was a scale of thirty-one names – too complicated for general acceptance. Eventually it was banned from school use!

2. At the same time, however, other alternatives began to appear, there were new, easily played instruments (Orff instruments) for school children, who hadn't learned a 'classical' instrument. It rapidly became clear that a meaningful use of the Orff instruments demanded the systematic direction of school children by musically well-trained teachers. These prerequisites, although, were not on hand in many of the schools, and so, with frustration, the instruments were set aside little by little.

3. With the development of cheaper electronic playback units a broad repertoire of high-quality music recordings of every kind became available in the space of just a few years. Many teachers began to totally replace singing and instrumental playing with 'listening to music'. They soon began to realise however, that even hearing has to be learned, and that skills are necessary for that, which could best be learned by actively singing and playing music. Naturally, teachers were also reminded of the fact that pupils can't concentrate as long as they like in always the same way, and so the educational principle of 'changing methods' finally led to music being sung and played in the classroom again. The question, although, of how the ear can systematically be trained in this way, still remains unanswered.

Back to the yearly conference of the Curwen Institute! In contrast to my expectations of meeting a group of honourable notables, the yearly conference of the Curwen Institute gave the impression of being a very lively and contemporary event for teacher in-service training. Very persuasive examples of teaching were varied with lectures, among others from the internationally recognised choir director John Alldis, who specialises in avant-garde music. The most important dividend of this meeting however, was the encounter with Bernarr Rainbow, whose work *The Land without Music* (London 1967, R/1990/1) I had known and valued since its publication. In the meantime, an extensive exchange of letters about questions over the history of the profession grew out of this short encounter, mostly based on the existing or planned volumes of the series 'Classic Texts in Music Education' (CTME), which he had published himself. With about fifty planned titles, of which over twenty have already appeared, the CTME series, begun in 1982, is by far the most comprehensive documentation on the history of this subject that has ever appeared. A more intensive reading of some of his 'Classic Texts' led me almost inevitably to translate them. That several of these translated texts from Sarah Glover, John Hullah, John Spencer Curwen, Mary Langdale and Stewart Macpherson are in the meantime available to us here, is thanks to my working together with Reinhold Schmitt-Thomas, whose source works for the MPZ series could no longer be continued after twenty volumes. The different situation between England and Germany became loud and evident; while Bernarr Rainbow first began his work with CTME and other projects at the end of his active service, Reinhold Schmitt-Thomas had to put a stop to the MPZ source writings, as neither his Institute nor an appropriate publisher were interested in such a series. In reality, this situation mirrored the extensive lack of history in German school music's own view of itself. Again and again, Bernarr Rainbow has attempted to show the historical connections of the European history of the profession. Among these include the small cross-section of German developments on aspects of the question of the gifted ('The Land with Music', in the Arnold Bentley Festschrift, translation in *Zeitschrift für Musikpädagogik*), the extensive collection of sources in *Music in Educational Thought and Practice: A Survey from 800 BC* (1989/2006) and *Four Centuries of Music Teaching Manuals, 1518–1932* (2009).

In London, Bernarr had given me the small publication 'Onward from Butler' as a present, and on first reading I thought it to be the argument of a notorious traditionalist. Only later did the numerous parallels to the German position occur to me.

Today 'Onward from Butler' seems to me to be the concerned plea of one of the best-informed authorities on the European history of the profession, to whom the radical changes in society are equally current, like the realistic conditions today of teacher education and working in the schools. From this point of view, the reader may compare the developments in England with those in Germany. Alone the names Carl Orff and George Self (who are named in this text) prove not only the lively transfer of ideas but the mentioning of similar problems as well, of which the most serious appears to me to be the absence of obligatory and realisable fundamentals for elementary/primary school.

In a single issue of a daily newspaper I recently read several direct or indirect allusions to the situation of music education in Germany: in two actual cases, it referred to the streamlining of the whole course of instruction in the schools and the possible reduction in the number of instruction hours which would then result. A State Minister for Education and Culture expressly ruled out any reductions to teaching music in the schools, but in a letter to the editor, a music teacher in Frankfurt delivered the missing rationale: music classes in the schools would be discontinued anyway because there were not enough music teachers.

But why should such a lack of qualified teachers be surprising, when even after remedying the situation, one could not succeed in precisely showing which fundamentals are truly being learned by primary school children and being reliably introduced in teaching at secondary schools?

Translated by Dr Scott Swope

Freedom and its Price
[1989]

THAT CELEBRATED MUSICAL *The King and I* told the story of an English governess who was engaged to bring up the numerous children of the King of Siam – now Thailand. While many details of her own account of what happened have since been revealed as apocryphal, the main events she described there actually took place.[1] King Mongkut of Siam did in fact engage Anna Leonowens in 1862 – as part of his plan to transform the country into a modern state. She held the post until 1867; and her considerable influence on the early upbringing of the princes of the blood is a matter of record.

What happened after that is not so widely known. The eldest of Anna Leonowens' twenty-two royal pupils had been Crown Prince Chulalongkorn. In 1873 he succeeded Mongkut as King of Siam, whereupon he in turn set up a school in the palace for his children under an English teacher. And when his eldest son, the new Crown Prince, came of age in 1886 a tutor was brought from England to undertake his further education.

The responsible post of tutor to the King's heir was awarded to Robert Morant, a twenty-three-year-old Oxford graduate educated at Winchester and New College, who had taught briefly in an English preparatory school before going out to Siam.[2] Through his influential new appointment he soon became recognised as the ultimate authority on educational matters in Siam and went on to lay the foundations of a national scheme of public education there. But perhaps inevitably, so much influence made him the subject of jealousy, and eight years later, with the growth of anti-European feeling, he resigned from the Siamese service, returning to England in 1894 to engage in social and educational work at Toynbee Hall.

In the following year Morant successfully applied for a post in the Education Department in London – the predecessor of the present Department of Education and Science – where he worked on compiling a series of reports on the organisation of education in other lands. His ability, energy, and administrative skill were early recognised in this branch of the Civil Service; and a rapid sequence of departmental promotions saw him pass from comparatively junior rank to that of Permanent Secretary of the newly formed Board of

[1] A. Leonowens, *The English Governess at the Siamese Court* (London: Chatto & Windus, 1870), *passim*, and W. Bristowe, *Louis and the King of Siam* (London: Trubner, 1976), chap. 2.

[2] *Dictionary of National Biography*, compact edn (1975), vol. 2, p. 2081.

Education in less than ten years. The passing of the Education Act of 1902 is acknowledged to have been 'largely due to his vision, courage, and ingenuity'.

You have been introduced to this remarkable man and his romantically improbable background because his weighty influence on the educational scene in this country – based as it was on actual experience of laying the foundations of a system of national education elsewhere – saw Victorian cheese-paring, improvisation, compromise, and muddle replaced by measures recognisable as the fore-runners of conditions as we know them, for better or worse, today. And I want to draw attention in particular to one edict of his which crystallised that difference. Indeed, the central focus of my remarks will be upon the consequences of one of Morant's decrees.

The Victorians, faced with the immense task of recruiting and training teachers to staff the new elementary schools of their era, adopted a policy of standardisation. Every teacher was a class teacher trained to teach religious knowledge, reading and recitation, music, arithmetic, English grammar, geography and history. The coverage given to these subjects in teacher-training could seldom be more than shallow, and lessons in schools were consequently long dominated by teaching manuals, known as *Methods*, each designed to show the inexperienced what to teach and how to teach it. The narrowness of 'monitorial' teaching, in which selected pupils were formerly made to challenge their fellows' ability to recover facts committed to memory, was perhaps by now outgrown, yet notions of teaching continued to favour the assembling of facts. As a result the design of most *Methods* was to arrange factual material in an appropriate order for presentation. Not that the educational reforms introduced by Pestalozzi and his followers were unknown in this country, but attempts to present them for general use too often led to their dilution and distortion.

It was Morant's thesis that good teachers could not be mass-produced. And in 1905 he published a substantial pamphlet from the Board of Education redefining the teacher's role and the scope and purpose of the accepted subjects in the school curriculum. The very title of this publication was revolutionary. Instead of presenting instructions to teachers upon their duties it was entitled *Suggestions for the Consideration of Teachers and others concerned in the work of Public Elementary Schools.*[3] In his Prefatory Memorandum Morant stated categorically that the new policy was not to impose regulations upon teachers. Instead, the uniformity of practice hitherto required was now considered to be as undesirable as it had proved unattainable:

The only uniformity of practice that the Board of Education desire to see

---

[3] Board of Education, *Suggestions for the Consideration of Teachers* (London: HMSO, 1905).

in the teaching of Public Elementary Schools [Morant wrote] is that each teacher shall think for himself, and work out for himself such methods of teaching as may use his powers to the best advantage and be best suited to the particular needs and conditions of the school.[4]

That stipulation, regularly repeated in government statements on education for the next thirty years and never since rescinded, was designed to heighten teachers' intellectual involvement with their task, not just to give them greater freedom or self-respect. It was introduced when the pattern of compulsory education for every child set the school-leaving age at eleven and levels of instruction were correspondingly limited. But ever since that time the implications of Morant's policy statement have continued to confer upon teachers the freedom to select methods and contrive syllabuses to suit their needs. Even today, the Department of Education and Science overtly refuses to specify, recommend, or support the use of particular teaching methods or systems.

Yet, though the freedom conferred by Morant's edict has been meticulously maintained and the terms in which he pronounced it have often been restated, less has been said about one essential condition he was careful to add to his original statement. 'Freedom,' he declared, 'implies a corresponding responsibility in its use.'

Music, more than any other subject in the school curriculum, plunged the Victorian student-teacher into the unfamiliar. The Manual introduced to guide him through the hazards of a music lesson was consequently made more than usually specific. In the opening paragraph of John Hullah's government-sanctioned *Method of Teaching Singing* (1841) teachers had put into their mouths the precise words to be used in distinguishing between musical and unmusical sounds. Then followed the instruction, '*The Teacher will strike the wall with his wand or stamp on the floor*, exclaiming, "That is Noise." He must next sing a short passage, written out for him in notes, and say, "That is Music."'[5]

The lessons that followed were all spelt out in detail with the same masterful inflexibility. Conducting the specified 'Recapitulatory Exercises' at the end of the first year's work the teacher was still to follow precise instructions stated in the same dictatorial manner as when the course began:

The exercise on *Intervals* is to be studied thus: the Teacher will point to various bars, at random: demanding first of one pupil, then of another, what intervals they contain, and whether they are major or minor, perfect

---

[4] *Ibid.*, p. 6.

[5] J. Hullah, *Wilhem's Method of Teaching Singing* (London: J. W. Parker, 2/1842), p. 3; reprinted as CTME 7.

or imperfect, &c. exercises will then be sol-fa-ed by the whole class, in strict time; any errors being corrected ...[6]

It is, of course, possible to point to other manuals in use at this time – in Music as in other disciplines – where teachers were allowed greater freedom in exposition. But Hullah's *Method* had been sanctioned for use by the government, as such it was taught to every teacher in training and, more to the point, was eventually examined at the end of the student's course by John Hullah himself as Inspector of Music in training colleges. It is ironical in this situation to discover that by 1860 most teachers chose to abandon the use of Hullah's *Method* as soon as they obtained school posts, preferring to use the indigenous Tonic Sol-fa system rather than the continental sol-fa favoured by Hullah. A strong though unacknowledged reaction against imposed teaching methods was already making itself felt even at that early date.

By Morant's day a school music lesson was still limited to singing and learning to read simple tunes at sight. The main changes to take place during the nineteenth century concerned the choice of songs for use in schools. After the 'Moral Songs' and psalm-tunes favoured since the 1830s came a preference for traditional 'National Songs' introduced during John Stainer's tenure of the inspectorate from 1882. In the early 1900s selected examples of true English folksong were added to the repertoire – though in bowdlerised and harmonised form that disappointed later purists. Apart from this widening of the repertory there were fewer opportunities to exercise new-found freedom when teaching singing than was the case with other areas of the curriculum. But this situation was to change dramatically as the new century unfolded. The raising of the school-leaving age and the development of secondary education both encouraged an increase in the scope of music teaching; and new resources designed to stimulate wider interest in the subject began to appear.

By the 1920s the subject previously labelled as 'Singing' on school timetables was renamed as 'Music'. Children were now taught to write simple tunes as well as read them, to listen to music as well as sing. These additional, more technically demanding activities among older pupils brought with them a realisation that beyond the earliest stages not all teachers were capable of effective music teaching; that a teacher who had little taste for music would produce no results of value if forced to teach it. In larger schools head teachers learned to share out music lessons among the musically disposed members of staff, in very small rural schools the activity had sometimes to be dropped.

---

[6] *Ibid.*, p. 75. Incidentally, even this short extract from Hullah's *Manual* makes it easy to see why one critic found the book unequalled among comparable instruction books for 'technical pedantries of the science ... and abounding in difficulties insuperable to children'; W. E. Hickson, *Westminster Review*, vol. 37 no. 1, p. 29.

The problem has never left us, its cause regularly lies in teachers' own early upbringing.

During the 1930s still further musical activities were introduced in schools. Simple instruments calling for limited technique were now brought into the classroom: toy percussion instruments such as triangles, drums, and cymbals enabled children to read rhythm-notation and then perform from it. Elsewhere classes were taught to make pipes from bamboo, then learn how to play them. New activities of this kind were first introduced by individual teachers, then copied in neighbouring schools, to be spotted by visiting school inspectors and, where thought successful, made widely known through the Board of Education's circulars. One such circular, entitled *Recent Developments in School Music*, published in 1933, brought both percussion bands and bamboo-pipe bands to wider notice.[7] And the *Handbook of Suggestions* first issued by Morant in 1905 and regularly revised and republished until 1937, also helped to spread awareness of new teaching devices.[8] Morant's original statement allowing freedom of choice in teaching methods was still deliberately included in it, but teachers adopting new forms of musical activity in their lesson schemes were now warned that such things should follow, not replace, singing and aural training.

Just how far the scope of music in schools had increased by 1937 is demonstrated in the last edition of the *Handbook of Suggestions*. Activities listed there include Singing, Ear Training and Sight Reading, Rhythmic Movement, Folk Dancing, Percussion Bands, Appreciation of Music, School Broadcasts, Festivals, Concerts for Schools, and the School Orchestra. The hazards of presenting so wide a choice to teachers had already become apparent to those responsible for superintending music in schools. Ten years earlier Dr John Borland, London County Council inspector of music, had uttered a warning:

> A chief hindrance to laying the foundations of a musical education may be termed 'departmentalism'. We have the folk-song enthusiast who can see no good in sight-singing or part-music, the voice-producing enthusiast who looks at everything from the point of view of the tone-producer, the pianoforte-trained person who will try to put the clock back a long way on some matter of mere notation, the enthusiast for the 'appreciation' of music who thinks that all definite ear-training should go by the board, and that children should be given instead some washy sort of general impression of masterpieces ... and lastly, we still have that Methuselah amongst us who thinks that music in schools should consist only of song-singing,

[7] Board of Education, *Recent Developments in School Music* (London: HMSO, 1933).

[8] Ministry of Education, *Handbook of Suggestions for the Consideration of Teachers* (London: HMSO, 1937).

and that the number of songs was limited either by Magna Charta or by the Education Act of 1870 ...[9]

Firmer admonition was contained in the Board of Education's pamphlet, *Recent Developments* in 1933:

> The class teacher of music is today suffering from an *embarras de richesses*. Very different was the position of his predecessor of fifty years ago. A few songs to satisfy an Inspector furnished all he needed to ask. In these days a problem has to be solved by a teacher who wishes to keep abreast of the times, both in the sense of adopting modern methods, and of getting in all he wishes to teach in the few hours per term at his disposal. He will certainly not find it possible to pursue all the recent developments ... A wise teacher does not allow the complement, or supplement, to take the place of the subject itself, and his sense of values enables him to plan a course of lessons, carefully apportioning the time at his disposal, with due regard to the practical and the cultural. The singing of songs must ever have pride of place in the music syllabus ... Voice-training, the training of ear in pitch and rhythm, and sight-singing are also essentials, together with a minimum of theory taught incidentally. So long as there is no interference with these essentials, there can be no valid objection to the introduction in the syllabus of one or more of the newer forms of activity.[10]

Half a century ago, that is to say, the freedom that Morant had granted to teachers was already proving a mixed blessing.

An outstanding feature of the Education Act of 1944 was the provision of secondary education for all. Previously, secondary schools had offered a traditional form of 'liberal education' to fee-paying pupils plus a minority of scholarship-holders admitted after passing a qualifying examination. Boys and girls were educated separately: the boys in Grammar Schools, often ancient foundations, the girls in much more recently founded High Schools. The curriculum in each type of school differed sharply. The boys' schools aimed overtly at university entrance and clung to the traditional core of the Classics with the addition of a range of academic studies. Aesthetic activities, music among them, seldom if ever featured in the curriculum. Girls' schools, on the other hand, were notably fewer in number and less obviously directed toward matriculation. But music regularly found a place in them together with other pursuits regarded as

[9] J. Borland, *Musical Foundations* (London: Oxford University Press, 1927), pp. 7–8.
[10] *Ibid.*, pp. 8–10.

suitably 'ladylike'. A similar situation was found in private schools including the exclusively fee-paying Public Schools.

After 1944 new Secondary Modern schools were created in order to supply a less academic form of secondary education for those requiring it. But increasing criticism of testing pupils' attainment and abilities at the age of eleven led to the introduction of comprehensive schools designed to embrace all types of secondary education. Given these resources, children enjoying state education now moved at the age of eleven from a primary to a secondary school. The term 'elementary school', felt to be somewhat patronising, was now dropped.

The physical move from one institution to another necessarily involved a complete break with familiar teachers and their methods and syllabuses. Yet it is reasonable to maintain that with most subjects in the primary school curriculum such a break was not difficult to negotiate. A child who had followed a progressive course of study in arithmetic, history, or geography, for instance, could soon be expected to pick up the traces and link what he had already learnt with the fresh (but closely related) information now to be provided. Even if the intake of a secondary school was drawn, as was usually the case, from a variety of primary schools, the same applied. The nature of the subjects themselves discouraged the creation of peculiarly orientated syllabuses. With music it was a different story.

Children coming to their new secondary school from half-a-dozen primary schools might previously have spent their music lessons in totally different activities decided by their teachers' preferences. Assembled in their new school, their teacher would be hard pressed to find a common starting point. According to Borland, such a group would include some who had spent their time exclusively singing folksongs or listening to recordings with no experience at all of aural training or sight-singing. Others from rural areas, as we have seen, might never have had any musical tuition at all.

Faced with this recurrent situation teachers of music in secondary schools invariably felt obliged to 'start from scratch' ‑ to the understandable exasperation of those children who had covered the ground before. Meanwhile, the less experienced found themselves having to start learning, at the age of eleven, skills that properly belonged to early childhood, and would have been mastered far more easily then. Once again, Morant's gift of freedom was found to impose unforeseen penalties for later generations of teachers.

❋ ❋ ❋

But it is time to turn to the present day. What has been said so far can hardly have struck you as the view of an inveterate admirer of the past setting out to belittle the present. In what remains to be said I shall continue to view past and present with the same perhaps slightly jaundiced but impersonal eye.

These days, on the rare occasions that music in schools is mentioned at all in the newspapers, what appears is invariably a self-congratulatory notice of one of our Youth Orchestras. There can be no doubt at all, I hasten to add, that the standards of performance reached by these young people under their meticulous coaches and skilful conductors is very high indeed. It is said that students entering our colleges of music today have already reached the levels of those leaving them a generation ago. But to cite the achievements of these hand-picked and talented youngsters as an indication of the healthy state of music in schools generally – as sometimes happens and is often implied – calls for firm contradiction.

We owe the astonishing growth of instrumental standards among young people still at school largely to the rise of the Comprehensive school. With its very large roll – often between one and two thousand pupils – a high capitation budget made possible the purchase of expensive orchestral instruments and provision of skilled individual tuition on them. The fruits have indeed been remarkable. But we cannot blind ourselves to the fact that what goes on in the classroom during a music lesson, even in a school with a high reputation for its concert activities, is often of an extremely disappointing standard.

Class music teaching today finds itself the victim of the Morant phenomenon at its peak. So many new facets and aspects of musical activity are now available – I shall not attempt to detail them – that it is only rarely that two schools are found to follow the same music programme. What *can* be said, however, is that in most schools music teaching has acquired an instrumental basis. A trend that began with percussion bands and bamboo pipes in the twenties and thirties led later to the use of more sophisticated Carl Orff instruments and the treble recorder. What has made this trend so attractive to perplexed teachers is its capacity to produce quick, tangible results. Instead of seeming to fumble about with crotchets and quavers on paper, children could now convert notes into sound mechanically – a much more gratifying experience and one that did not fail to cheer their teachers, too.

But pleasurable and entertaining as this might be, more thoughtful teachers have found themselves questioning whether this essentially mechanical way of 'learning to read music' is quite as educational an activity as it seems. It is not easy to get out of one's head the objection raised by a French teacher early in the nineteenth century:

> One thing that constantly puzzles observers is that among the vast number of those who have learned music, so few can sing at sight. Most of them have to consult their violin, their pianoforte, or their flute, in

order to learn a new tune, and it is actually the instrument which does the reading for them.[11]

Faced with that challenge we are left wondering how far instrumental work in schools simply trains children's eyes and fingers – instead of their ears. On the other hand, wherever a systematic course of sol-fa singing in their junior schools has taught young children to associate sound and symbol accurately, later instrumental work will heighten their responses. But how many children entering secondary schools have had that training? Far too few. Of course it is not too late to undertake the task at eleven, but it is a matter of great regret that such basic skills have not been taught in the junior school where they could be acquired so much more quickly and easily.

When we ask why this is not happening we shall be told that many junior school teachers lack the skill to teach music at any level. If that is so, the main reason is the inadequate musical tuition those teachers received in their own early schooldays. It is encouraging to find recent experience showing that this vicious circle can be broken by in-service training. Cases regularly come to light on in-service courses of experienced teachers who discover, to their surprise, that with skilled guidance they can first acquire and then pass on to their classes basic musical skills that they thought were beyond them. The discovery is regularly greeted with as much pleasure as amazement, making these teachers ask themselves why they had not made the attempt before.

That unspoken question invites some attempt at an answer. It seems justifiable to claim that the freedom which Morant first bestowed on teachers to select their own methods of teaching has been tacitly extended to cover a much wider range of options. At the same time, his declaration that 'freedom implies a corresponding responsibility in its use' has been conveniently forgotten. Very many more junior school teachers are capable of teaching elementary musical skills than do so. They have often chosen not to do so through self-doubt: but they have seldom been encouraged to change their minds either during their training or afterwards.

The whole question of 'freedom' in teaching seems a matter deserving further thought. Since Morant persuaded the Board of Education in 1905 to publish *Suggestions* rather than *Instructions*, social change has vastly increased the individual's sense of independence. In line with that shift the modern equivalent of *Suggestions* has become a series of 'discussion documents' inviting comments and suggestions *from* teachers. Where music is concerned, the document on *Music from 5 to 16* cautiously offers 'a framework within which each school

---

[11] P. Galin, *Exposition d'une nouvelle méthode* ... (Paris, 1818), translated B. Rainbow as *Rationale for a New Way of Teaching Music*, CTME 8 (Kilkenny: Boethius Press, 1983), pp. 41–2.

might develop a music programme appropriate to its needs'. The use of the subjunctive in that statement is significant, and many parts of the document display masterly avoidance of decision.

One questions whether injunctions offered to teachers in such cautious terms are even minimally effective – whether, indeed, they are so much as thoughtfully read by many teachers. To take a case in point rather than speculate: there is an opportunity in the recent pamphlet to follow up a matter we have just been considering. In one of its more decisive paragraphs it has this to say:

> Pupils entering a new school bring with them varied experiences and perspectives of music. [*How true; but how cleverly put!*] The music teachers of the receiving school should be in close touch with the schools from which the pupils have come.[12]

At face value that seems to offer sound advice and to be a novel proposal designed (at last) to overcome the lack of continuity regularly caused by the switch from junior to secondary school. A novel proposal, that is, until one turns to the *Handbook of Suggestions* published exactly fifty years ago, in 1937. There we find:

> It is important that a unified scheme of Music teaching should be followed by the same children at different stages of their school life in a particular group of schools. Those responsible for the teaching of music at the Infant, Junior, and Senior School stages respectively, should keep in touch with one another, in order to ensure that a pupil is not subject to a disconcerting variety of method, or an irksome repetition of subjects to be studied.[13]

No evidence exists to suggest that this injunction was ever generally acted upon. And there seems little reason to suppose the present-day version is being more widely observed. Meanwhile many teachers would welcome firm guidance on the task that confronts them in schools. There are some encouraging signs that the Department of Education and Science is at length abandoning the role of Voiceless Oracle it has assumed in recent decades. Though disappointingly indecisive, the Discussion Document on *Music from 5 to 16* specifically invites comments and suggestions. This surely suggests that before long the Department means to publish a further document reporting its findings. The welcome inclusion of music among the subjects recently announced as

---

[12] Department of Education and Science, *Music 5–16* (London: HMSO, 1985), pp. 10–11.
[13] *Ibid.*, pp. 177–8.

forming part of a national curriculum should add urgency to the inspectors' deliberations.

Of the options before them one seems to claim precedence. Teachers of music today are swamped by alternatives, as they first were in 1933. Now as then the prime need is for a clear ruling on what is essential in music education and what is optional. Teachers would hardly feel their freedom threatened by such a rationalisation. After all, the charm of liberty wears thin when one is stranded in the wilderness.

Some New Music Teaching Devices from France
[1961]

JUST OVER A CENTURY AGO when English education first began to receive state support, it was apparent that continental schools – already in a flourishing infancy – had much to offer in the way of tried teaching devices. And English educationists, both philanthropists and teachers, made their way across the Channel to inspect the schools of western Europe. The *Reports*, *Accounts*, and *Itineraries* which they published on their return are full of details of school organisation which had impressed the writers, and which, in a number of cases, provided the basis of methods adopted in the new schools and training colleges of this country.

Music was no exception in this respect. The first authorised method employed in teaching music in our National schools was imported lock, stock and barrel: John Hullah's translation and adaptation of *Wilhem's Method*. A later immigrant was the *Galin–Paris–Chevé Method* – with the 'French Time-Names' which John Curwen fostered. These still enjoy a flourishing existence in many enlightened schools.

It was with these thoughts in mind that on a recent visit to France I sought an opportunity to watch music being taught in a junior school by a French training college lecturer. Not that the foreign article is bound to be better than the native product – but that fresh experience is usually salutary. One of the impressions which remain indelibly with me after seeing this teacher at work is that although in this country we have widened our music syllabus so as to include a variety of new aspects and activities, we have done so on the whole at the expense of developing basic ability in reading from notes. Some teachers would defend this policy, saying that the number of children who will want to sing at sight in adult life is so small, that to attempt to develop the skill in all children is uneconomic. But the same argument would apply equally to the teaching of algebra, foreign languages, and a considerable part of the curriculum.

And surely the point is this: that a skill such as reading notation is best developed when the mind is tractable, and when *in-learning* of the kind involved is comparatively easy. One has only to look around the members of an average choral society to confirm how difficult it is for an adult who cannot already read music to learn to do so. Further, it is my own experience as a teacher that very many children, who would not otherwise have done so, have taken up a musical instrument and come to find a deep satisfaction in music, through first learning to read notation at school. And, in any case, it is arguable that the mental exercise involved in learning to use notation is every bit as valuable as that provided by other school subjects. But a purely functional attitude to the content of the curriculum will quickly argue music out of its place in schools altogether.

One assumes, in defending the teaching of sight-singing, that the teaching will be done adequately; that the child will not be asked merely to memorise the symbols of notation – juggling with them in a kind of musical algebra. Nor is the answer to be found merely by teaching music-reading in terms of some simple instrument such as a recorder or harmonica. These are very desirable additions, but they must supplement sight-singing. My reason for saying this it that when one plays at sight, the symbols are interpreted not in terms of the sounds which they represent, but in terms of the keys which have to be pressed, the holes which have to be stopped, or the positions which the fingers have to assume. Any piano teacher knows how confidently beginners play wrong notes, quite unaware that they are wrong – since the symbol has conveyed to them no precise idea of the sound involved. Certainly in the music teaching which I saw in France, training in sight-singing played a very considerable part – as it does in Holland, Germany and Switzerland as well. Some of the methods used were new to me and, I thought, of considerable interest.

The children were boys of nine to ten years of age – mixed classes are rare in France. The lessons began with sol-fa exercises on the common chord. In spite of the protests of Rousseau in the eighteenth century, and many others since, the fixed *doh* is still generally used, I found. There was no piano in the class-room – the teacher gave the pitch on a tiny table-top reed organ, or patterned the notes vocally. And in this early part of the lesson I began to feel a sense of disappointment – or rather I did not find my hopes raised. But in no time at all the class had been divided into two sections which began to sing at sight *from the staff notation* in two-part counterpoint *alla Palestrina*! This miracle was achieved quite simply, but it was no less impressive for all that.

What happened was this. The teacher set up on the board the common chord and the remaining notes of the scale in this form:

Then using two pointers, one white, the other red, and pointing to the notes on the board, he led the two halves of the class simultaneously through a two-part exercise of this nature:

The musical effect was greatly enhanced by the presence of the counterpoint, and indeed it seemed clear that the children were helped by the existence of the other part to find their own notes, as well as to gain musical satisfaction from the exercise. Later I saw another device which was new to me. This was something like the Curwen Hand Signs, but I thought it simpler to use from the child's point of view, and on the whole much easier for the teacher to supervise effectively. It is known as *phonomimie*, and has been developed by Maurice Chevais.

With this, each degree of the scale is represented by a gesture of the hand in relation to a definite part of the body – so as to record quite accurately the rise and fall of melody. *Doh* is at the waist, *me* at the neck, *soh* on the forehead, upper *doh* a few inches above the head. *Ray* on the shoulder, *fah* at the ear, *lah* resting on top of the head, *te* (or *si* as they prefer it) with the hand at an angle of 45 degrees just above the head.

All these gestures involve the same flattened palm. Consequently the teacher is easily able to watch the whole class as they 'translate' a sung melody directly into this visual notation. As I saw it done, the class worked sitting down and with their eyes closed, so that each child was obliged to think for himself – there was no copying the gestures from a neighbour. And while the teacher first sounded *doh*, then proceeded slowly through a simple melody, the whole class responded by translating each note into an appropriate gesture. It was virtually an exercise in musical dictation; but one which could be supervised and corrected at each stage, so that mistakes were dealt with at once, and the less capable were quickly identified and helped.

Since there is no royal road to success, and one of the surest ways of getting a point home to a class is to be able to present the same fact in a variety of different ways, both these devices seem to me to be useful additions to music teaching technique. I certainly mean to try them out myself!

Curwen, Kodály and the Future

[1979]

IT IS NOT ALWAYS REALISED that the basis of Kodály's methods was his discovery of John Curwen's Tonic Sol-fa teaching during visits to this country at an earlier stage of his career in the 1920s. Anxious to develop the teaching of music in Hungarian schools, and deeply impressed by the standards of singing then found in English elementary schools, Kodály made Curwen's principles the basis of his own teaching: the Hand Signs for the degrees of the scale, the movable role of *doh*, the concept of inner hearing, and a vocal rather than instrumental approach to note-reading, all these sprang from Curwen's teaching. They have remained the foundation of all Kodály's work.

The remarkable development of music in Hungarian schools in the last thirty years has understandably attracted worldwide interest followed by attempts to introduce Kodály's methods in other countries. Where Britain is concerned, the liberal system which gives almost complete autonomy to every music teacher does not provide congenial ground for the introduction of a system so highly regimented as that adopted in the state-controlled schools of Hungary; and such attempts to introduce Kodály's methods as have taken place here remain purely local and tentative.

Yet there is no doubt that the worth of Kodály's system has been effectively demonstrated in his own country, with nationwide musical literacy and a network of special music schools for those who show pronounced talent. In neglecting to preserve and develop Curwen's teaching we have allowed a part of our national musical heritage to fall into decay. Should we now attempt to reconvert to English use what Kodály has already adapted to suit Hungarian needs? A more reasonable course would be to start from Curwen and frame methods to suit present needs in our own schools.

At this point it would be well to consider why Curwen's teaching was allowed to fall into disuse in his own country. The answer is complex and includes reference to the introduction of new aspects of school music in the early decades of this century: a new instrumental trend displayed in bamboo-pipe playing, followed by recorder and percussion playing; the musical appreciation movement and the advent of the classroom gramophone. This broadening of the music curriculum inevitably reduced the vocal element in the music lesson and inadvertently discouraged the notion of aural training associated with the voice. But there was another, more damaging influence for which Curwen's own most zealous followers must be held responsible. Tonic Sol-fa was increasingly taught, not as a method of aural training but as a rival form of notation. Just how seriously this development damaged the method may be seen by the fact that, even today, the term *Tonic Sol-fa* conjures up a picture of an outmoded form of letter-notation to many observers. Its true role as a way of developing aural sensitivity has been forgotten.

The letter-notation of Tonic Sol-fa was first introduced only as an ancillary device and an approach to staff notation. Its exclusive use at a later stage of the movement's history was an unfortunate consequence (from our own point of view) of a desire to print music cheaply, thus bringing song books, hymnals and oratorio scores within reach of the poor. But the fact that armies of amateur singers were brought up to read only from this 'peculiar' notation brought the movement into disrepute among more orthodox musicians. Disgusted by the notation, the professional musician refused to treat Tonic Sol-fa seriously and seldom appreciated the remarkable standards of sight-singing achieved by its devotees. That this skill was due to Curwen's method of training the ear, and had nothing to do with the form of notation employed, was seldom realised.

With the advent of a new generation of music teachers in schools, most of them instrumentally trained, distaste for Tonic Sol-fa notation hardened. By mid-century the method had acquired an effete, old-fashioned image discouraging its use in teacher training institutions. With the coming of the new Colleges of Education, the struggle to attain intellectual respectability for music courses led to emphasis on purely academic content at the expense of the study of teaching technique. In such an atmosphere the problems of training the ear – the true basis of all fruitful music teaching – were too easily eclipsed.

It is this essential feature that the broadening of the music curriculum in past decades has driven into decline. To restore it would both provide the common core at present absent from music programmes in different schools, and also enhance standards of achievement. To be most effective, it is suggested, courses of in-service training could be organised on a local basis with the teachers from the primary schools which feed a central secondary school meeting there for a co-ordinated programme of work. Experiment in Colchester has already shown the advantage of such a procedure.

CURWEN PROJECT

Indeed, what is being discussed here is not just a matter of speculation. Over the past few years action has been taken to translate theory into practice. Beginning with the lesson learned from Kodály, the first need was to revive Curwen's teaching; but to redeem Tonic Sol-fa from the outdated image caused by its letter-notation. A Working Party of experienced teachers meeting during 1970–1 at the Institute of Education at London University undertook that task, linking sol-fa with staff notation throughout. Next, the Curwen

Institute was established in 1974 to promote the revised system. More recently, a prototype scheme was launched in 1978 at a large comprehensive school at Colchester. Teachers from surrounding primary schools were brought together for an introduction to Curwen's teaching illustrated by a class of young children recently introduced to the use of Hand Signs. This was followed last July by a short residential course. Meanwhile, an introductory text book was prepared by Dr W. H. Swinburne, containing 'lessonettes', each lasting from five to ten minutes in which Curwen's principles are thoroughly taught. The aim of the book is to establish those mental concepts without which any attempt to 'read music' is likely to be disappointing.

As a trial ground for the text book, last year a school in which Tonic Sol-fa had not previously been taught was asked to help; and three music teachers, none of whom was a 'solfaist', agreed to co-operate. The 'lessonettes' were given to half classes, the remaining half going on with instrumental work for the short period involved in each lesson. It thus became possible to make a rough comparison and assess the effect of the Tonic Sol-fa teaching. The teachers' report was encouraging. Children who had received the special teaching 'had acquired a more critical ear for intonation and could learn a song by rote more quickly. They were able to sing a tune before playing it on their recorders and their performance was notably more musical and alert. They were able to improvise short phrases and point these out on a stave. Because part-singing, by rote and by sight, was an integral part of the teaching, the children's musical awareness was increased, and because of this there was certainly no falling off of interest in the subject.'

Encouraged by this response to a few terms' work in a single school, the Curwen Institute now plans to undertake a more extensive trial of the principles adumbrated first by Curwen (1816–80) and then by Kodály (1882–1967) in some twenty schools or groups of schools in different parts of the country. The 'lessonettes' will be employed as a guideline over a three-year course; and the children's attainment will be assessed under an agreed plan at the end of each year. Teachers involved will meet each term to discuss progress and problems, and will finally present a report.[1]

It is perhaps particularly appropriate that this 'Curwen Project' should be launched at the present time. The year 1980 marks the centenary of Curwen's death. In his own day John Curwen launched a method which revolutionised

---

[1] See W. H. Swinburne, *The New Curwen Method*, book 1: *Tonic Sol-fa in Class* (London: Curwen Institute, 1980); book 2: *Notation: The First Steps in Sight-Reading* (London: Stainer & Bell, 1981); book 3: *Notation: Reading the Stave* (London: Stainer & Bell, 1984). W. H. Swinburne OBE (1907–94) spent most of his life in Colchester, and it was due to his vision that an influential Music Department grew up in what became the Colchester Institute. Initially he taught Music and Physics at the Royal

popular musical education throughout the world. In our own time Kodály's revival of his principles has demonstrated their lasting worth. The restoration of Curwen's neglected principles to their merited place in more of the schools of his own land would fittingly mark the centenary year.

Grammar School; later became Music Advisor to the county of Essex; was President of the National Association of Teachers of Singing; and was awarded an honorary doctorate from Essex University. He was organist and choirmaster of Lion Walk Church, Colchester, and founded the Colchester Chamber Orchestra. Throughout his life he was involved with many musical organisations in the region and was widely respected as a teacher. Ed.

An Ear for Music[1]

[1980]

T HE WIND OF CHANGE has increasingly been blowing over music
teaching in schools during this century. Today, as it approaches gale force,
it is only necessary to turn the pages of a music publisher's catalogue to see the
astonishing variety of alternative musical activities available in the classroom.
I know that many teachers find this wealth of opportunity bewildering – they
have said as much. The children's position, although less easily assessed, can
hardly be more satisfactory.

As things stand, the most obvious disadvantage is a lack of continuity. A
child, moved from one school to another, or from primary to secondary level,
will be very lucky to find what he has done in one school continued and developed in another. Is there a secondary music teacher anywhere who doesn't take
for granted that he must start again from scratch? But what *is* 'scratch'? And
is it reasonable to have to assume that a fresh start must always be made in the
secondary school?

I can see some junior teachers stirring crossly at this. In *their* school, they
are anxious to point out, the children enjoy their music lessons; they play on
recorders and chime-bars; they can read a simple tune; they sing, and enjoy it.
That's splendid! We trust there are such schools, such teachers, and such fortunate children. But what happens to those children when they arrive in their
secondary schools? They find themselves in a class with children from other
schools who have not had this experience. As a result, they have to mark time
while the rest catch up – and that is a very discouraging experience for keen,
able youngsters, you will agree. Or, what's worse, they find that the recorder-
playing and instrumental work at which they have become so proficient is not
going on in the secondary school at all. Instead, they are now invited to shake a
detergent pack filled with dry peas – but only at the moment when the teacher
points a finger at them.

You may think that I just want to poke fun at advocates of the so-called
'experimental' style of school music or that I don't know enough of their aims
when I lampoon them in this way. In fact, both George Self and Brian Dennis
have been colleagues of mine. I *do* understand and respect their aims; but I
repeat now what I have often said to each of them: that 'experimental' music
in schools should augment, not replace, the development of basic skills – skills
which are neither too difficult nor too boring for children to acquire if they

[1] A shortened version of the Curwen Centenary Lecture delivered at the London
University Institute of Education on 21 March 1980.

are tackled early enough; skills which children quickly show that they enjoy acquiring, if tackled in the right way; and skills which should then continue to be employed and consistently developed once they have been acquired. The problem, of course, is to find time for all the things we should like to do in schools today!

I think we need to remind ourselves how little time is in fact available for music teaching in a school, before we decide what use to make of it. The muddle we have got ourselves into often seems to spring from excess of zeal rather than the reverse. Two forty-minute periods is about all the most generous head teacher can be expected to allot for class music. We try to crowd into it too many diverse things. It is almost as if we imagine that a child's musical life is over once he leaves school. And when we plump for some new and apparently attractive aspect of music in an attempt to arouse his interest, the lesson plan often becomes uncoordinated; and there is not time to get anything done thoroughly.

This is an example of what I call the 'spin-drier syndrome' at work. Load half a dozen articles into a spin-drier and switch on. When you open it again you find the contents packed tight around the edges, with an empty space in the middle. A lot of music teaching today seems rather like that. There's plenty going on the edges and next to nothing in the centre. Although we often hear about *parameters* in music teaching, we seem less concerned with parameters than perimeters! Let me describe what I think that empty space in the middle should contain.

The briefest examination of the phenomenon we know as Music will show that, fundamentally, it depends for its influence, effect, even its existence, upon one thing alone – the ear. Since this is so, the basis of all successful music teaching must surely be the training of the ear. Yet much of the instrumental work going on in classrooms today concentrates on training the hand and eye while neglecting the ear's essential role. 'Look at the note, find the chime-bar, and hit it,' has become a widely accepted method of working. With no expectation of the required sound, the child hits the wrong note as cheerfully as the right one. The process is mechanical rather than musical – in a parallel situation, it is like giving a child a pocket calculator to do sums with, before he understands the value of numbers.

Agreed, that after a few bosh shots a class armed with chime-bars and copies of the music will eventually produce a satisfying recognisable tune. But are they then really 'reading music'? For that matter, is 'reading music' the prime aim in schools today?

I suggest that well before attempting to teach reading, the skill of listening must be consciously developed. Not just 'hearing', for that is a passive condition; but the active and deliberate process of listening to ordered sounds.

You may say that is just what the 'experimental' school of thought is try-ing to develop. Isn't it their aim to encourage children to respond to musical sounds, events, textures and colours? To invent sound patterns for themselves and respond to them as they emerge?

Yes, indeed it is. But the 'experimental' people, it seems to me, don't go far enough with the process – or at least they devote their energy too exclusively to particular areas of the sound spectrum at the expense of the melodic compo-nent. Today, despite technology, the computer, the synthesiser and all the rest, the most natural medium for music-making is still, as it always has been, the human voice. Melody should therefore provide the prime element in a planned course of aural exploration.

The fact that straightforwardly singable melody has lost its appeal for many composers is a fact to be acknowledged. It is no doubt this fact that has made the 'experimental' music enthusiasts fasten attention so largely upon texture and dramatic dissonance. But in their anxiety to familiarise children with a contemporary musical idiom they seem too willing to abandon the language of the great mass of our musical heritage. And you will not need me to remind you that (whatever you may hear to the contrary) one of the accepted aims of education in a civilised community is the preservation of a cultural heritage. Do art teachers forbid their pupils to enter the National Gallery lest the experi-ence should deaden their eyes to contemporary painting?

Alas, however stimulating and enjoyable 'experimental' music-making may be (and I agree that it can be both those things) a course *dominated* by it does not satisfy our needs. In any case, work of this kind can only be carried out successfully by a teacher really familiar with contemporary musical styles. In the hands of a musically inexperienced teacher, no matter how willing, 'experi-mental' music can easily degenerate into so much clinking and bonging. What I am looking for is an approach which can be adopted – and started in the junior school – by an enthusiastic teacher prepared to undertake realistic first steps in developing aural awareness. Steps that can lead on to further stages in a consistently developing programme of aural perception. Such a programme is within reach if a few minutes – no more than that – in *every* lesson are devoted to ear training with sol-fa. Far from handicapping other musical activities, this work will quickly be found to enhance them. Nor would teachers be deprived of that freedom to introduce aspects of music which particularly attract them. On the contrary, they would find them far more rewarding once the children had been shown how to use their ears ...

I have already mentioned the problems caused by a lack of consistency and continuity in our apparently random choice of musical activities in schools. The acceptance of aural training as an essential basic element would provide the common core at present lacking.

But how is this miracle to be achieved?

The first step is to encourage greater communication between junior and secondary schools. Co-ordination and continuity cannot be obtained if neither school knows – except by hearsay – or cares, what the other is doing. May I urge you very seriously to consider establishing some suitable means of communication between your own school and its neighbours? What is wanted is not the imposition of a programme (such as an illiberal government might insist upon) but preliminary discussion of the disadvantages at present brought about by a lack of awareness of each other's programmes and policies. A next step might then lead to the discovery that it would not be too difficult to introduce a common element by way of unification.

As to the feasibility of introducing and training with sol-fa in schools generally, we have only to look at the schools of Hungary. This does not mean that you have to go to Hungary to study the Kodály Method, although if you did so, you would find his programme superbly organised. Each type of school follows a closely organised syllabus, from kindergarten to conservatoire. Every child and every teacher is told what to do at each stage. The course begins in the kindergarten and its first steps are designed for children of that age.

For better or worse, teachers in this country have grown used to greater freedom; and under prevailing conditions here the starting point for music teaching varies considerably. A uniform start with material designed for kindergarten use is therefore hardly feasible. Nor has every class teacher the musical background required to teach the Kodály Method.

This does not mean, however, that we have nothing to learn from Kodály. And an examination of his Method is not only worth while, but highly revealing. We find that he adopts as the basis of his Method, a number of standpoints and devices:

(i) that a partnership of ear and voice provides the most profitable approach

(ii) that sol-fa names enable the character of notes and note relationships to be identified easily

(iii) that Hand Signs for individual notes reinforce that awareness

(iv) that the name *doh* should always represent the keynote of a major scale, the other names retaining their position relative to it

(v) that note-reading should be developed on a vocal rather than instrumental basis.

The whole of Kodály's Method is based upon that foundation. In our search for a method of training the ear of children in the schools of this country it is therefore distinctly encouraging to discover that these devices which Kodály has adopted are English in origin. He has acknowledged so much himself. They were first propounded by John Curwen.

While still in his twenties John Curwen was celebrated for his skill as a teacher of young children. Innate ability coupled with wide study of the teaching methods of others had given him a remarkable instinct for analysing the processes of the learner's mind. An early disciple of Pestalozzi in this country, he was often invited to lecture on general teaching methods in various parts of the country. And it was on an occasion of that kind that he was first called upon to investigate and recommend the most suitable way of teaching schoolchildren to sing. With next to no experience in that field, Curwen found the task a daunting one. But he accepted the commission and began the systematic examination of existing methods, both native and foreign, in the light of his own experience and insight as a teacher.

He found, in fact, that while no single method completely satisfied him, many of them contained features which appealed to his critical sense as a teacher. These he assembled and incorporated into an ideal system of his own. The result was soon to be known as Tonic Sol-fa. He was to spend the rest of his days perfecting it ... When Curwen first began teaching Tonic Sol-fa in 1841, the schools of this country were as yet in an embryonic state. Many children were, in any case, obliged to work throughout the week to augment the family income, receiving such education as they might by attending a school organised by the churches on Sundays. It was at a Sunday School of this kind that Curwen gave his first Tonic Sol-fa lessons. He was at that time himself a Congregationalist minister; and his first aim, as he put it, was to get children to enjoy their Sunday School.

The philanthropic and religious aims apparent in Curwen's early teaching were always to colour his attitude. Once the effectiveness of Tonic Sol-fa had been demonstrated with classes of children, he began to teach adults. A second of his aims was to improve singing in churches, particularly among the poor, who could not afford music lessons. As his adult classes grew, Curwen soon realised that his pupils could not afford to buy hymn books either. Musical scores were laboriously engraved by hand in those days; and the cost of a hymn book with tunes, or a collection of songs, was considerable in 1841.

To overcome that problem Curwen made a decision which was to have an unforeseeable sequel in what must then have seemed the remote future – the twentieth century. To help the beginner, he was already using in his lessons a simplified form of musical notation: instead of crotchets and quavers on a five-line stave, he employed the initials of the sol-fa syllables. *Doh* was *d*, *ray* was *r*, *me* was *m*, and so on. He now decided to adopt this letter-notation, not just as an approach device in early lessons, but as a standard form of notation in all Tonic Sol-fa publications. Printed in this way, his music copies could be produced for a penny or two and come within the reach of the poor.

An unfortunate consequence was that many of Curwen's followers came to regard Tonic Sol-fa notation as a rival to staff notation – instead of an approach device. Professional musicians were not slow to demonstrate their disapproval of this development. Almost without exception they looked on Tonic Sol-fa with scorn, refusing to treat Curwen's aims seriously and quite failing, as a result, to discover the remarkable merit of Curwen's method of training the ear – the true source of his success. In spite of this professional opposition, the Tonic Sol-fa movement continued to flourish.

At Curwen's death, in 1880, Tonic Sol-fa was employed in schools and amateur choral circles throughout the world. It was still enjoying that wide popularity and success when Kodály visited this country late in the 1920s. At that time the Hungarian composer was eager to develop the teaching of singing in the schools of his own country. And deeply impressed by the high standards of singing *then* found in English elementary schools, he discovered that Tonic Sol-fa formed the basis of the children's teaching. On his return to Hungary, Kodály began the long process of adapting Curwen's principles to suit the needs of the schools of his own land. His adaptation, once complete, was only finally adopted there on a national basis in 1945.

Looking back on all this today, it seems obvious that because he came upon Tonic Sol-fa with none of the prejudices of English professional musicians, Kodály was able to see past the peculiarities of its letter-notation to the heart of the method itself. The notation, he quickly realised, was not an essential feature. It could be abandoned at an early stage of teaching without destroying the method itself. And so, without realising what he was doing, Kodály in fact restored Curwen's original way of teaching – as it had been before the needs of the poor led to the permanent use of letter-notation.

By the 1920s it was too late, of course, for Tonic Solfaists as a whole to change their ways. The movement was too widely and firmly established, with an immense published literature of its own. Indeed, in the public mind, the letter-notation *was* Tonic Sol-fa! It was that misconception and the impossibility of changing the movement's course, as it were in midstream, that eventually led to its decline. During the thirties, Tonic Sol-fa was increasingly regarded as outmoded; by midcentury it had largely disappeared from our schools, strangled by the notation.

The central feature of school music lessons had by that time rightly ceased to be learning to sing at sight. Other aspects now took an increasing share of the time for music. Even class singing itself began to lose its importance for some schools. And it was at this time, too, that aural training began to disappear from the list of aims that most music teachers set themselves.

Experience teaches that progress is not always made in a forward direction, and attractive short-cuts often turn out to lead into blind alleys. I believe we are now in one of those enticing cul-de-sacs. When that happens, we have the choice of banging our heads against impenetrable walls, or retracing our steps.

I shall be accused of trying to 'put the clock back'. This is a favourite phrase among progressives in many fields today. But it was Mozart's determination to put the clock back to counterpoint that gave us the 'Jupiter' Symphony.

To change the metaphor: we have sown our wild oats in profusion; let us try growing a few roses! You may think the 'soil' in your school is not very suitable. But more than one gardening book will tell you that with good cultivation *and the proper fertiliser* almost any garden in the British Isles can produce roses; the same books will tell you to prepare the soil as long as possible with fertiliser before you try growing the rose. The fertiliser for a musical rose is Ear Training. If it is only provided early enough, with good cultivation almost any classroom in the British Isles can flower. The 'make' I recommend is John Curwen. Today's 'band wagons' attract because they are new, not because they are necessarily better. We can hardly fail to notice that a generation of children who cannot spell is the product of one widely patronised band wagon of recent times; and I'm sure you can think of others without my prompting.

But to be reasonable in Curwen's centenary year, it would be folly to think of simply reissuing his original books for use in schools. However sound his analysis of the teacher's problems, circumstances today call for different teaching attitudes, different methods of presentation, and different repertoire, from those current in Victorian England. During his lifetime, Curwen was constantly adding to his method refinements and improvements in the light of current teaching. After his death, that process was not continued; the Tonic Sol-fa method was allowed to petrify.

Those of us who are so convinced of the value of Curwen's principles as to work for their revival today, are very much aware of the need to present them in a form to suit modern needs, It was one thing to abandon the use of the old letter notation. The modification necessary was undertaken readily enough at the London University Institute of Education early in the seventies.

But the compilation of an up-to-date treatise on Tonic Sol-fa was quite another matter. To find combined in one man the qualities of distinguished teacher, scholarly musician and convinced sol-faist seemed impossible. In the end, good fortune – or could it have been the personal intervention of St Cecilia? – found for us in the person of Dr William Swinburne a man who not only combines those qualities, but is also an internationally respected music educationist.

That I have chosen to speak less about Curwen as an historical figure, than as the originator of a living force to revitalise music teaching today, is no accident.

That is how I have come to regard him. He is not a remote, forgotten pioneer from the past. Instead, current happenings enable me to link the past with the future; to acknowledge the debt which we all owe to John Curwen for his long and virtually unaided struggle to bring music within the reach of the public at large; to remark the determination which enabled him to continue that struggle in the face of professional indifference; and to forecast the vindication of those efforts in the revival of his principles in our schools today. For what Curwen offers to us is an attribute which the accepted phrase describes with such penetrating terseness and clarity – an Ear for Music!

The New Curwen Method:
A Partnership of Ear, Eye and Voice
[1988]

'OH, I've tried sol-fa,' said the young teacher. 'I taught them the song from *The Sound of Music* that introduces all the names of the notes. Then I wrote the names up on the board and we practised singing them from my pointing.' 'How did it go?' asked her friend. 'Oh, it got very boring. They could climb up and down, one note at a time; but most of the jumps were beyond them. To tell the truth I couldn't do some of them myself.' 'I'd thought of trying it,' said her friend haplessly, 'but people say that sort of thing is old fashioned and just a waste of time anyway.'

This glum conversation, overheard on the top of my Hammersmith bus, describes what happens when sol-fa is used haphazardly – as if just knowing the sol-fa names magically enables the child to pitch notes correctly. As to wasting time, any unsystematic process in the classroom runs that risk. On the other hand, the enjoyment that any primary child finds in growing mastery of a new skill applies as much to music as to other activities. Those who have never seen a class of youngsters during a music lesson may need reassurance on this point. Recent experience in many parts of the country since the New Curwen method was launched has shown that, once encouraged to overcome their own self-doubts, ordinary class teachers can play a contributory but essential part in this work. Not only have they proved that a desirable element in the primary school curriculum is generally attainable; many have also been gratified to find themselves developing skills they had previously thought beyond their reach.

As to sol-fa being old fashioned, former opponents of the English version known as Tonic Sol-fa made a point of emphasising that it was first introduced into our schools by John Curwen to improve current standards of hymn-singing, a justification no longer applicable. Yet the fact remains that generations of ungifted schoolchildren who learned to sing from Tonic Sol-fa – for whatever reason –found their musical sense sharpened to an extent their modern counterparts simply cannot rival. And today, since it proves possible to strip the old-fashioned trappings of the Victorian classroom from Curwen's Tonic Sol-fa without sacrificing its essential qualities, what we have chosen to call the 'New Curwen Method' has been devised to bring back to currency resources otherwise lost which we cannot afford to abandon. The aim is no longer to teach sight-singing as an end in itself but to train the musical ear and sharpen sensitivity.

At the same time as scrapping outmoded features Dr W. H. Swinburne, the Method's distinguished author, has introduced a number of important innovations drawn from his own teaching experience and carefully tested in schools. The nature and value of these new features will become apparent from a brief account of the Method as a whole. The first stages of teaching concentrate on developing the 'inner ear' (that is, the ability to hear a note mentally before singing it), on exercising the musical memory, on pleasant, controlled singing and on active listening. As a general rule throughout this early work no symbol is introduced until the sound it represents has been experienced.

It is important to note that the programme is designed to occupy only *a few minutes in each music lesson* – a deliberate policy which takes into account the high level of concentration expected of the children concerned. The rest of the lesson remains available for other forms of musical activity already being practised. These in turn are soon found to benefit from the children's growing aural awareness.

Class songs of a traditional cast, most of them in general use, are made the starting point. A large number of easily learnt tunes should be known and regularly sung with enjoyment before aural training begins. The importance of soft, musical singing is emphasised. A notion has got about that children be allowed to sing down in their boots. Our own experience contradicts this, and a compass centring around treble G is encouraged. The singing voice plays an essential role in the New Curwen Method – not least because it is only by singing a note that it can be shown to have been heard mentally in the first place.

To encourage early acquaintance with staff notation standard notes are always used to depict rhythms. Quite young children can use crotchets, quavers and minims for simple instrumental work. Avoid introducing a wide range of note values at the outset and equating them with coinage. The concept of duration is best revealed by hearing a pattern of crotchet followed by two quavers in a repeated formula, rather than by arithmetical description. For young children the French Time Names

taa ta-tai
(taa ta-te)   ♩ ♫

provide a readily understood nomenclature. In the early stages of the course short repeated rhythmic formulas are employed as pulse structures on which to build melodic variations. A class which can read and perform a formula of

is ready to begin work on the complementary study of pitch.

Teachers whose own musical background is instrumental are commonly tempted to tackle pitch discrimination in terms of the five-line stave. Instead, with the New Curwen Method, the children meet *sounds* rather than *diagrams*. The aim is to familiarise them with the aural effect or 'character' of individual intervals which can be recognised when met again. The scale is slowly built up, not introduced as a series of sounds called 'Doh, ray, me' etc. Each interval is presented, in a carefully designed order, through tunes which are already familiar.

The first interval encountered is the falling minor third, arguably the basic musical utterance; familiar in the cry 'coo-ee' and regularly heard in the chants of football supporters and children at play. Selecting from a list of suggested tunes the teacher indicates the interval when it occurs in the song which the children are actually singing. This is done by using the Hand Signs (first devised by John Curwen in 1870) for the notes *soh* and *me*. For example:

The aim, at this important initial stage, is to establish the memory of this interval, in permanent association with these Hand Signs, firmly in the mind. Children are found to respond quickly to this device. They are soon singing the notes concerned as soon as the appropriate Hand Signs are made. And if the Signs are given in reverse order they will sing the rising interval. At this early stage the names soh and me are not mentioned. The notes can be hummed or vocalised for the time being. The names are introduced only when the sounds have become instinctive.

In a subsequent lesson, when every child is able to recall and sing these notes on seeing the Hand Signs, the note *doh* is added, together with its Hand Sign. Once again this is done in the context of a known tune. The final phrase of 'This old man' suits the purpose very well:

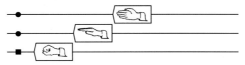

The fact that the word 'home' is associated with *doh* in this song makes it a happy choice for the purpose. Yorke Trotter's term for the tonic – the 'Home Note' springs to mind. Other songs introducing the three notes learnt should now be used to familiarise the pattern *soh–me–doh*. 'Oranges and Lemons', 'The Mulberry Bush' and 'Ten in the Bed' are some useful examples. Make the Hand Signs whenever the notes are sung. Those who have met the Kodály Method (itself based on Curwen's principles, as Kodály himself stated) may be surprised to find the note *doh* introduced at this stage rather than *lah*. But examination of our national children's songs shows that the melodic pattern *soh–me–lah* is uncharacteristic. The regular appearance of that phrase in Hungarian folk tunes lies behind Kodály's introduction of *lah* at an early stage in his Method. But that is another matter.

Once familiarity with the notes *soh–me–doh* in conjunction with their Hand Signs has been established and consolidated, several organisational steps follow. The sol-fa names can now be introduced, and the concept of the stave approached by employing a three-line blackboard stave to record the relative position of the three notes in visual terms. The place of *doh* is now marked with a square note-head (Curwen's original device).

The square note-head provides an embryonic clef which can be moved into a space at a later stage as the range of notes in use increases. But the stave is not used as yet to accommodate *written* notes. Instead, its purpose is to give precision to the levels at which the Hand Signs are made. Thus, when the clenched fist of *doh* is made against the bottom line, the horizontal palm for *me* stands on the second line, and the vertical palm for *soh* against the top line. The Hand Signs themselves are in fact being used as *a preliminary form of staff notation*.

Even with the limited material now available children can be invited to recognise and then sing short phrases from Hand Signs. The crotchet–crotchet–minim or crotchet–quaver–quaver formulas mentioned earlier will provide suitable rhythmic structures on which to build. To assist in this work a standard blackboard lay-out is now adopted. First, the chosen rhythmic formula is written in conventional notation at the head of the board. Below stand the lines of the stave employed so far, with *doh*'s position shown by its square note-head. These three features form a consistent lay-out for all blackboard work during the early stages of the Method.

There is a further point, the importance of which can hardly be over-stressed as it forms an essential feature of the Method's individual character. From this stage onward, whenever a melodic phrase is being introduced to the class by means of Hand Signs, instead of following the usual practice of singing each note as its Hand Sign is given, the children should first *hear the whole phrase in their heads*. Notes should not be sung until this has been done. This device is one of Dr Swinburne's innovations which proves highly effective in developing the musical memory. When, later in the course, the phrases 'dictated' by Hand Signs extend to a range of seven or eight notes, the usefulness of this device becomes even more apparent. Experience has shown that children taught in this way soon rival experienced adults in memorising melodic material. The ease with which they can learn a new song by rote is an obvious advantage.

Another point to be stressed is that children should *make the Hand Signs themselves* while singing dictated phrases. This helps in the processes of identifying and retaining the sense of relative pitch as additional notes are learnt. The physical action of making the signs prompts the mind to recall the intervals involved – something that becomes extremely valuable as the range of notes in use increases. The practice has been found highly effective in first steps in true sight-singing later in the course. One group of secondary children was able to sing at sight in three parts using Hand Signs to prompt their recall – and this after only a few terms' preliminary work.

Once Hand Signs can be used instinctively, they can also be used in a form of musical dictation. It will be obvious to teachers that when a whole class sings a phrase together in unison, the less able child's deficiencies are easily concealed. The more able lead the rest. But when children have learnt (as they should) to accept individual singing as an unremarkable challenge, this difficulty can be overcome readily enough. Meanwhile, however, teachers can obtain a clear idea of individual ability in a class by singing a phrase which the children then translate into Hand Signs *with their eyes closed*. In this way the weaker brethren can be identified and the teacher is not falsely encouraged to press on to further steps prematurely.

Before going on to describe later stages of the course, there are a few more procedural matters to mention. Although aural training is carried out in a separate, concentrated part of each lesson, it should be related wherever possible to other activities. For instance, once a class can sing a phrase before playing it on the recorder intonation will automatically improve. As aural skills grow they will be fertilised by relating them to other musical activities within the lesson.

The class is best arranged in a horseshoe grouping, to allow for antiphonal singing. As one half sings while the other listens, active attention is further encouraged; and when a known song is shared in this way, phrase by phrase, much is unconsciously learnt about musical structure. In addition, the way is prepared for part-singing – something which is made to follow on naturally later in the first year's work.

A creative element is introduced quite early. Using Hand Signs, the teacher dictates a short phrase whose rhythm is already written at the top of the board. The class sings it. Then one child is invited to signal a balancing phrase using the same rhythm and notes already in use. This phrase, too, is sung by the class. Soon, this device can be shared between two pupils, one starting the process, the other completing it. It can start as soon as *soh–me–doh* is known and familiar, the limited number of notes making success more likely and consequently building confidence.

So much for basic procedures. The essence of the New Curwen Method is contained in these early steps. Everyone seems to agree that the Primary School is the place to provide a firm basis for musical education. The New Curwen Method provides class teachers with a realistic way to guide young children through the complexities of learning to listen. Aware of their own limitations many class teachers fight shy of teaching music. Some may be disposed to argue that learning to listen is a dull business compared with the joy of banging a drum. The New Curwen Method both contradicts the claim of dullness and leaves plenty of lesson time for other musical activities. It aims to simplify instruction for both teacher and pupil, thus enabling the general class teacher to co-operate with the music specialist in providing systematic musical training during the child's formative years.

The bold, four-square relationship between the notes of the common chord, *doh, me, soh,* makes learning to distinguish between them encouragingly straightforward. Progress in the earliest stages of the New Curwen Method is not difficult to attain provided the teacher adjusts the pace to include slower learners. Such a relatively trouble-free start might possibly mislead teachers into supposing that additional notes of the scale can all be made familiar as easily. The next step in the course involves the note *ray*; and here the aural challenge of recognition is far greater for some children than might be supposed. It is as well to be ready to meet this challenge before it reveals itself.

As before, the new note is identified in a known tune. 'Frère Jacques' and 'Three Blind Mice' are suitable, while 'Au clair de la lune' has a long opening phrase using only *doh ray*, and *me*. Once again a new Hand Sign is used to identify the position of the new note in these songs:

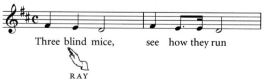

Three blind mice,   see how they run

RAY

Patience will be called for before a whole class can find the note securely. Working with children in schools Dr Swinburne finds that, given the signs for *soh–me–ray*, half the class will at first sing *soh–me–doh* because the memory-trail is so strong. To overcome this he recommends concentrating on 'inner-hearing' of *ray* before trying to sing it. Give the signs for *soh–me–ray* but stop the class before they try to sing *ray*, and ask them to 'sing it in their heads.' Repeat this treatment twice, then allow the whole phrase to be sung. Not only will *ray* be sung without difficulty, but it will give no trouble in future. Just to press on at this stage, before the identity of *ray* is clear in children's minds, is likely to cause a loss of confidence difficult to remedy later on. It is a mistake to assume that, once a new note-name has been learnt, the sound it represents has become equally familiar. This misconception, far more common than might be supposed, has bedevilled many past attempts to employ *sol-fa* productively in the classroom. It is for this reason, too, that the temptation to introduce the whole scale at once, together with all the Hand Signs, must be resisted. In the blackboard exercises *ray* now finds its place in the first space of the three-line stave:

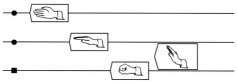

The additional note considerably extends the possibilities of balanced phrase-making, already a regular feature of the lesson; and using the three-line stave the teacher can begin to develop the class's ability to 'hear' a melody as it is pointed out in silence. Two examples using only the notes learned so far suggest themselves for this work: 'Jingle bells, jingle bells, jingle all the way' employs *me, me, me –; me, me, me –; me, soh, doh, ray, me –*. 'I know a girl that you don't know' (Li'l Liza Jane) uses *me, me, me, ray, doh; me, soh, soh –*. The teacher should make these Hand Signs in turn against the stave, carefully preserving the rhythm of the piece and inviting the class to recognise the tune as they hear it in their heads. Two or three repetitions, with the children's hands going up as they spot the tunes are followed by the whole class singing it together. This marks another breakthrough: the children have taken the first step in reading music. It is something that can be achieved after a few weeks' work with the New Curwen Method.

In most classes a few children will be learning to play an instrument and growing familiar with standard notation. It is obviously desirable to avoid an impression that work with *sol-fa* bears no relationship to 'real music'. As a first step toward reconciliation crotchets, quavers and minims have been used con-sistently from the outset in creating balanced phrases. It is now time to carry the association further by introducing alphabetical note-names. By adding the marking 'Doh is G' to the usual blackboard lay-out, and then ensuring that a G chime-bar regularly fixes the pitch, the way is prepared for children to discover, as further lines are added, that this is the familiar set of lines and spaces after all. The next stage of the course brings that situation closer.

With *ray* established the next note to be introduced is lower *soh*. The last phrase of 'Frère Jacques' and the first of 'Hot Cross Buns' both employ this note memorably. In both cases it resolves characteristically upon *doh:*

This note is deliberately introduced at this point because it forms a regular feature of English melody – particularly as an opening. To accommodate it on the blackboard a new line is now added, bring the stave a step nearer completion:

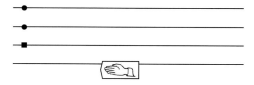

Next follows *lah*, demonstrated in 'One more river' and now given its new Hand Sign following the usual pattern in introducing a new note:

While this pattern has already been established and can be described here in a few words, the introduction of *lah* calls for the same deliberate, careful procedure as its predecessors.

The fifth line is now added to the blackboard stave to contain the new note. With the stave complete, the treble clef, alphabetical note-names, and the key signature of one sharp can now be introduced. Theoretical justifications for clef and key signature are not needed at this stage; the symbols win be familiar to children from their song books and recorder pieces. Explanations can follow later.

Lower *lah*, like lower *soh* previously, is a note calling for special treatment. It is less easily pitched by beginners than upper *lah*; but is conveniently demonstrated in 'I've been to Harlem':

Arrival at this stage opens the way to the use of a wide repertoire of well-known tunes which can be sung with Hand Signs for all their notes; which can be recognised from the teacher's Hand Signs given in silence; or which can be employed in a novel form of dictation – the teacher singing a phrase which the class then repeats while making the appropriate Hand Signs *with their eyes closed*. 'Shut-eye' tests of this sort are immensely valuable in spotting pupils who need help with aural skills; with their eyes shut, the less able cannot mask their shortcomings by copying their neighbours.

The remaining two notes of the scale and other necessary details are now carefully introduced in the following order:

1. The next new note is *fah*, discovered in 'Good King Wenceslas':

'Oranges and lemons' and 'Cockles and mussels' are two more tunes that prove useful in familiarising *fah*.

2. The last note in the major scale to be learnt is *te*. 'Good King Wenceslas' can again be used:

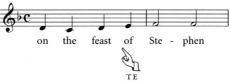

The last phrase of 'Bobby Shaftoe' will also serve.

3. So far, *doh* has stood on G. The fact that any note can become *doh* – because the same tune can be sung higher or lower – is now explained; and practical work follows with *doh* on F. This means moving the square note-head on the board to a new position in the first space, and then building confidence in using Hand Signs at the new pitch. The children now learn that when *doh* is F a flat sign stands on the third line. They also find that lower *soh* now needs a line below the stave to accommodate it.

With the major scale completed, a very wide range of tunes can now be sung and recognised from Hand Signs. Individual improvisation can also be much more adventurous. Practical activities of this sort form an essential part of the New Curwen Method, being introduced deliberately to underline what is being learnt. This will be a convenient point at which to summarise the main classroom procedures which should form a regular feature of every lesson.

Singing

Almost every aspect of work in the New Curwen Method depends on the use of the singing voice as the infallible way of confirming that what has been 'heard in the head' is accurate. Moreover, since the notes of the scale are introduced in terms of well-known songs, a repertoire of such songs needs to be built up in preparation. Teachers find that the standard of singing automatically improves as aural sensitivity is developed: ear and voice are mutually supportive.

Rhythmic work

Alongside the work in pitch discrimination which has taken most of our attention because of its more demanding nature regular work in clapping and tapping rhythmic phrases should find a place. Associated with this practical work (and not as an arithmetical exercise) children soon learn the use of rhythmic notation. By the time they have learnt to use the notes of the major scale, they can become familiar with crotchets, quavers, minims, and semibreves. Even the apparent complexities of compound time lose their dread if first encountered through clapping 'One more river' – instead of being treated as an intellectual exercise.

Recognition of known tunes

From time to time, phrases of well-known tunes that have been used to introduce new notes should be signalled in Hand Signs for the children to recognise. 'This old man', 'Oranges and lemons', 'I've been to Harlem', and the rest will stimulate memory for intervals while helping to make the Hand Signs instinctive in use. By the time the pentatonic scale has been covered a much wider choice of tunes, some of which have not been used for teaching intervals but are otherwise well known, can be suitably employed. The class should follow the Hand Signs in silence – not sing with them – making this an exercise for the 'inner ear'. When the tune has been recognised it should be sung by all, making the Hand Signs as they go along.

Dictation

Starting with short phrases of three or four notes whose Hand Signs are known, this exercise can be built up until quite long phrases are employed. In every case, however, the whole phrase must be completed before an attempt is made to record it. To tackle this work a note at a time is to minimise its benefit. Instead of writing the notes down, the class should interpret each phrase in Hand Signs with their eyes closed. The teacher will find this provides an immediate indication of individual abilities and shortcomings in the class every bit as revealing, and far less tedious than the collecting and marking of written work. As further notes are learnt the dictated passages can become longer. This not only develops the sense of pitch discrimination but also strengthens the ability to memorise whole musical phrases – an important, but often neglected feature of musical response.

Regular use of Hand Signs

The true value of the Hand Signs is not gained until they have become instinctive. For this reason they should be used as often as possible during the lesson. It must be stressed that they should be used to emphasise the convention of 'Rise and Fall' in pitch by being made at appropriate levels from waist to head as need be. Gestures should be smooth, not jerky; and the hand position should be accurate. At a later stage in the course variants of the seven original Signs will be used for accidentals. At this stage the Sign for *soh*, if made carelessly with the thumb in the air, will be found to have a different meaning.

Creative work

From the very earliest lessons children should learn to make answering phrases to balance those dictated by the teacher. This can only be done individually, and a simple blackboard drill enables it to be done effectively. Teacher and pupil (and at a later stage, pairs of pupils) stand on either side of the board which bears a standard framework to accommodate the exercise. Details of key, rhythmic formula and time signature are first chosen by the class and written up:

> Teacher makes Hand Signs on the stave: *doh, me, doh, soh*
> Class sings, making the Hand Signs: *doh, me, doh, soh*
> Pupil makes Hand Signs on the stave: *soh, me, soh, doh*
> Class sings, making Hand Signals: *soh, me, soh, doh*

The Hand Signs are made at the board in silence, but according to the given rhythm, and with a tambour or foot-tap to maintain an accurate pulse. As competence grows the phrases become longer and involve more notes. It helps to instil confidence in this exercise if the pupil's answer starts on the last note of the given phrase.

Part singing

To encourage attentive listening as well as prepare for part-singing the class should become used to singing in two alternate groups, exchanging short phrases signalled by the teacher or a selected pupil. At a later stage two-part singing can start with the teacher dictating a separate simultaneous part with each hand, one for either half of the class. This calls for skilful control by the teacher; but once begun, the remarkable effect immediately obtained will encourage the teacher to practise until two-handed dictation at a simple level loses its apparent trickiness. To prepare for this it is a good idea to use the left hand as often as the right hand when giving Hand Signs in the general way. Here are some simple phrases in two parts which can be used to start this work:

Others will be found in Book I of the New Curwen Method, the teacher's manual published by Stainer & Bell, which summarises the first year's work along me lines briefly described in these articles so far.

At the beginning it was claimed that 'ordinary class teachers can play a contributory but essential part in this work'. Now that the content of the first year's programme has been outlined that claim perhaps seems too optimistic. But where the teacher in charge of a primary school's music is ready to persuade, recruit, and guide class teachers to tackle Hand Sign practice with their own pupils this aim is far from unattainable. Experience has repeatedly shown that, once persuaded to try, non-specialists surprise themselves with what they can achieve. By keeping one step ahead of the children and tackling just a little each day, their own skill increases alongside their confidence. The specialist, meanwhile, finds that two or three minutes' daily 'brush-up' taken by the class teacher reinforces children's aural ability to an amazing extent.

Ideally, of course, the most favourable starting point from which to launch the New Curwen Method is an in-service course of the kind regularly organised by the Curwen Institute – either on its own initiative or at the invitation of an LEA. But once the teacher-in-charge at a particular school has successfully introduced the Method there, the class teachers can readily pick up what is required of them by sitting-in at a few of the regular lessons. This approach has the great advantage of letting any doubters witness for themselves the children's growing satisfaction at what they can achieve. As one class teacher among many in primary schools has reported, 'It is delightful to watch the concentration on their faces and the pleasure they get from their own achievements ... Apart from the children's obvious enjoyment, I am myself enjoying using this method, so it is a two-way thing.'

Those thinking of launching the New Curwen Method in their schools will no doubt be glad to know of two devices now made available to assist in the early stages. The first is a video suitable for viewing by staff and pupils of the 7–10 age-group outlining the basis of the Method in simple terms. Made by children and teachers from junior schools in Coventry, its running time is one hour; but it can be shown to advantage in two separate parts. Entitled 'It's All in the Mind', this video provides a suitable introduction to an in-service course or when staff propose to introduce the New Curwen Method as a curriculum subject.

The second is a computer software self-testing programme available on forty-track disc for the BBC microcomputer, specifically written to supplement the New Curwen Method of aural training. Easy to use, it provides pupil (and teacher!) with a range of graded tunes, from simple, three-note phrases to four-bar sentences using all the notes of the scale. The pupil listens to the phrase, then, subject to the computer's correction, writes in pitch and time symbols using Hand Signs, standard notes, and the stave. The keys of G and F are used and the programme can be extended by the teacher to provide an unlimited number of melodies. Entitled 'Hand in Hand', and requiring no previous computer experience, this visual and aural aid combines the attraction of a fashionable diversion with the advantages of disciplined instruction.

Book I of the New Curwen Method, which covers the first year's programme, is a teacher's book. There are no supplementary books for children's use, so the decision to introduce the Method does not involve a lot of expense. Well over 3000 copies of Book I have been sold since it was published eight years ago – an encouraging indication of the way in which its use has spread nationally. Book II applies what has already been learnt and tackles sight-reading from the stave. Once again it is a teacher's book; but it has been deliberately designed of a size to suit overhead projection so as to enable classes to see plenty of notation.

The lesson material in Book II is very carefully graded to help combine progress with retention. The plan remains to devote only a small part of each lesson to aural training and reading; and the content of this book is sufficient for two years' work. Although the eventual aim is to enable pupils to work from staff notation alone, in the early stages the familiar devices used during the first year are deliberately retained. Conversely, many of the first examples wholly written in staff notation consist of tunes, or phrases from tunes, already learnt from Book I. Rhythmic and melodic problems and challenges are tackled independently before the pupil meets them in combination.

The range of keys is now extended to three flats and four sharps; both simple and compound time-signatures are successively introduced. Some very simple two-part songs were used in Book I in addition to the exercises in singing from double Hand Signs. Building on to that early experience, more extended two-part songs now appear. The first of these comprise known tunes arranged on two staves – at first antiphonally, then in a simple harmonisation. Often the tune passes from one voice to the other, the harmonised part reversing the process for the sake of interest. Part-singing is regarded as an essential element in sight-singing – to be tackled as soon as basic reading skills are established. The exercises provided are intended for sight-singing purposes only, and should not be allowed to occupy too much of the limited lesson time. But the experience gained from their use will lead to much more proficient handling of part-singing when more ambitious works are being rehearsed.

Opportunity is found in Book II to touch on matters that will assume much greater importance later in the pupils' musical development – or which may already have been encountered by children who are gaining proficiency on a musical instrument. The first is the question of scales and modes other than the major which has monopolised attention in the elementary stages so far. It is sometimes maintained that the term 'Tonic Sol-fa' implies that a keynote is always to be called *doh*. John Curwen did not think so himself. As the inventor of the term he intended it to mean that, unlike 'continental' sol-fa, *doh* is not always the note C.

We can be certain of this because by the time Tonic Sol-fa was being introduced by missionaries in remoter parts of the globe, John Curwen urged his followers to realise that the music of eastern nations was not confined to the same bounds as that more familiar at home. Missionaries, he warned, must 'expect to find tunes based on ray or me, or soh as the keynote'. This enlightened attitude – not then shared by most practical musicians among his countrymen – leaves no possibility of argument as to his intentions. For Curwen, as for Rousseau and a host of other adherents to sol-fa, the keynote of a minor scale was to be called *lah*, not *doh*. As to the viability of making *ray* the 'keynote' of a Dorian melody, doubters are recommended to try sol-fa-ing 'What shall we do with a drunken sailor' first based on *doh*, then on *ray*. The result will be conclusive for most.

None of this concerns the child, of course. It is a matter for teachers. But it seems appropriate to discuss this vexed question here before going on to say that in Book II the existence of tunes based on notes other than *doh* is mentioned and an opportunity provided to practise singing scales based on *lah*, *ray* and *me*. In this way the path is prepared to teach the minor scale based on *fah* at a later stage.

Another technical point introduced at this stage is the concept of *chords*. As well as describing the make-up of chords, opportunities are found to sing them from Hand Signs, with the class divided into groups. The primary triads on *doh*, *soh* and *fah* are examined and performed separately, then traced as elements in various harmonic melodies. The *sequence* as a structural device in a melody is also explained. Examples are then sung in groups – at first from notation, while making the appropriate Hand Signs, then by improvising at indicated points in an incomplete score. Elsewhere verbal aspects of vocal music are explored. Verbal rhythms are examined on a monotone and short verses provided for the children to notate in suitable rhythmic form as a preparation for melody-writing. This is not just a dull rule-of-thumb exercise, as the following example will reveal:

One, two, three, four, five,
Once I caught a fish alive.
Six, seven, eight, nine, ten,
Then I let it go again.

Considerable variety and subtlety are possible here. The teacher who is surprised at the children's unexpected ability in this work will enjoy finding and setting further verses to stimulate their efforts.

Teachers who have already made the New Curwen Method a regular part of their music work in primary schools report finding marked improvement in general musical activities: songs are learnt by rote more quickly and accurately, recorder playing has better intonation, children learn to *listen*, and enjoy having something definite to learn. It is often claimed, too, that by learning to concentrate, the children's general level of attention is raised with benefit to the rest of their classroom work. It seems highly regrettable that at least some of those who have had so beneficial a music course in their primary schools should later find themselves in secondary schools where next to nothing is done systematically to follow up their previous experience with sol-fa.

A lack of continuity between primary and secondary schooling is a short-coming not easily overcome in an educational system which favours teachers' independence. In a recent Discussion Paper (*Music from 5 to 16*) the Department of Education and Science referred to this problem, urging music teachers in secondary schools to 'be in close touch with' the schools from which their new intakes come. At face value this seems an encouraging development designed to overcome a long-standing weakness. Alas, there is nothing new about the advice. In 1937, some fifty years ago, the *Handbook of Suggestions for Teachers* published by the Ministry of Education had this to say:

> Those responsible for the teaching of music at the Infant, Junior, and Senior School stages respectively, should keep in touch with one another, in order to ensure that a pupil is not subject to a disconcerting variety of method.

What makes the disruption of continuity even more acute is the flood of attractive alternatives that swamp music teachers in secondary schools nowadays. With so much to choose from it is tempting to ignore basic skills. At the same time, the structured courses available for developing those skills are commonly so exclusively designed and so time-consuming that room for other forms of musical activity cannot be found alongside them. Only the fanatic among teachers is attracted by this sort of thing.

As we have already seen, this last objection cannot be levelled against the New Curwen Method which has been consistently planned to occupy only a small part of available lesson time, thus freeing the remainder for other activities. The same policy has been adopted in planning the secondary component, outlined in Book III. Here the aim is to broaden the pupil's experience and knowledge, while retaining the attitudes and teaching devices whose value has been successfully demonstrated earlier. We urge the secondary teacher not to regard these as 'childish'. More than one secondary teacher to our knowledge, dismayed at the inability of potential examination candidates to tackle necessary ear tests, has introduced New Curwen Method techniques to fourth-formers with gratifying results. The pupils concerned were too pleased by their new-found aural awareness to look down on Hand Signs as beneath their dignity.

Among the new skills developed at the secondary stage are modulation, and the use of minor keys. Both require the use of accidentals and involve the introduction of a few new Hand Signs. It is at this point that the importance of making the Hand Signs accurately in earlier stages of the course becomes more obvious. The new signs prove to be quite slight modifications of those already in use, representing as they do the raising or lowering of a note by no more than a semitone:

Sharpened *fah* becomes *fe*

Sharpened *soh* becomes *se*

Flattened *te* becomes *ta*

Following the policy adopted earlier in the Method, in Book III all these innovations are incorporated into melodies designed to be sung – thus ensuring that each new detail is experienced in *sound*, not just committed to memory as a fact to be remembered. In a similar way frequent opportunities are presented for part-singing, not just for its own sake but to encourage better intonation and develop the pupil's harmonic sense. Modulation is both explained grammatically and experienced aurally through singing what is written down. Disciplined exercises in improvisation lead the way to written composition of melodies where the writer can 'hear' what has been written – something by no means certain otherwise.

In all these activities the early ideals of the Method are carefully preserved: intervals, especially those including 'difficult' notes, are always heard 'in the head' before trying to sing them; the musical memory is constantly stimulated by storing up whole phrases before singing them, whole rhythms before tapping them out. It is through the consistent application of such devices, and the author's refusal to try to press ahead too fast, that the New Curwen Method achieves its status as a 'structured' course. As such it has come to attract growing favour with teachers who realise that at a time of immense diversity in school music it has become all too easy for results to appear haphazard and uncoordinated.

Although it requires only a moment's thought to decide that all successful music teaching must depend on training the ear to fulfil its function adequately, much of what goes on in music lessons nowadays concentrates on training the hand and the eye rather than the ear. By introducing the New Curwen Method to fertilise what already takes place in an adventurous music programme, the missing element can readily be supplied, restoring to music lessons their lost backbone.

Sol-fa as an Ethnic Link
[1982]

ANYTHING that helps teachers to meet the needs or multi-racial classes is to be welcomed. Where a learning process common to different cultures can be found it should certainly be developed. Once identified, similar thought patterns adopted by different races in teaching must help in this respect.

An example of such parallelism in the early stages of learning music comes to light in the widespread, wellnigh universal use of syllables sung in a particular order to represent and identify the rising notes of the scale. Systems of this kind are common to the principal musical cultures of the world and have existed in many cases for more than a thousand years. Nor was Europe the first place to develop them. Both India and China were employing the equivalent of sol-fa systems in the 3rd century BC. A few examples of the syllables sung for this purpose in various parts of the world will serve to illustrate the similarity of attitude that exists:

China	*kung, shang, cheuh, chih, yu*	Pentatonic scale
India	*sa, ri, ga, ma, pa, dha, ni*	Major scale
Japan	*ni, ho, te, to, i, ro, ha*	Major scale
Korea	*toong, tung, tang, tong, ting*	Pentatonic scale
Bali	*ding, dong, deng, dung, dang*	Pentatonic scale
Java	*be, ja, da, po, gang, ne, ba*	Pelog scale
Arabia	*sad, lam, sim, dal, ra, mim, fa*	Major scale
Ancient Greece	*té, ta, tee, toh*	Tetrachordal scale
Medieval Christendom	*ut, re, mi, fa, sol, la*	Hexachordal scale
Tonic Sol-fa	*doh, ray, me, fah, soh, lah, te*	Major scale

The wide range of different syllables employed is very apparent; but it is the similarity of purpose which is important – the fact that children from widely separated cultures have grown up in a musical situation where it is customary to identify the character of the different notes of the scale by singing them to syllabic names. We can hardly afford to ignore a similarity so advantageous when teaching music to groups of children of diverse ethnic origin. And recent visits to schools have shown that sol-fa-based teaching is highly successful with children of non-European origin whose enthusiasm and aptitude for it act as a spur both to themselves and to the rest of the class.

Indeed it is not only the non-Europeans who respond well to a sol-fa approach. Nor should it cause surprise that a universally adopted teaching device continues to find ready response when it is used in schools today. In those cases where sol-fa-based teaching has proved disappointing in the past it was invariably because it had been allowed to degenerate into boring drills kept up for too long and taught unmusically. To counteract such shortcomings, in-service courses are now being held in many parts of the country to help teachers to introduce sol-fa more realistically using modern methods. The Curwen Institute has been founded to promote this activity and enquiries from teachers and advisers interested in attending or organising such courses are welcomed.

The sol-fa approach to music teaching is best developed through short spells in every lesson and associated with the singing voice. A few minutes is enough when the work is well planned, leaving the rest of the lesson time for other musical activities. Recent experiments have shown that young children taught in this way soon learn to listen with attention, to recognise and discriminate in matters of pitch, rhythm and phrasing, and to use their Singing voices naturally. They consequently develop an ability to use the 'inner ear' and to memorise more efficiently. These skills in turn enhance their work in other parts of the music lesson. Out-of-tune recorder playing ceases to be the norm: instrumental work is undertaken more musically.

It seems reasonable to claim that the worldwide existence of a sol-fa approach in music teaching is not just a chance phenomenon. That so many races have developed similar ways to conjure precise notes 'out of the air', to give them singable names which identify their individual character, and to enable tunes to be indexed and stored in the memory in large numbers, suggests instinctive wisdom rather than chance. It is perhaps our own more recent fascination with instrumental music in schools and elsewhere that has been responsible for a present lack of enthusiasm for the sol-fa approach. Grown accustomed to think of musical notation as a device which tells what to do with our hands to make an instrument produce the requisite sounds for us, most of us have failed to develop the ability to 'hear' from the page. Many adult amateur instrumentalists who can play quite difficult music at sight cannot sing simple tunes from the notes. To prevent that shortcoming the 'inner ear' should be trained in childhood – the task is much more formidable for an adult.

What is at stake here, then, is the musical education of future generations assembled from many quarters of the globe and now settled in the schools of this country. In sol-fa-based teaching we have resources at our disposal which are themselves universal in origin and of immemorial effectiveness.

The Kodály Concept and its Pedigree
[1990]

ECLECTICISM PROVIDES THE BASIS of many successful teaching methods. Kodály's method of teaching music, originally designed for use in Hungarian schools, was no exception. And in an authorised account of its origins published in English translation in 1966 Erszébet Szőnyi described the influences brought to bear upon it by sundry teachers from different parts of Europe, and claimed to define their specific contributions.[1] Yet since certain of the sources she quoted now appear open to serious question, in the interest of historical accuracy a closer look at the situation seems called for.

In Erszébet Szőnyi's account we find six references to borrowed devices, components, and influences, enumerated in this order.

1. The letters and hand-signs of John Curwen's Tonic Sol-fa system.[2]

2. Jean Weber's principle of the shifting place of *doh*.[3]

3. Émile Chevé's use of Arabic numerals for the degrees of the scale.[4]

4. 'A few practical passages from Fritz Jöde and Agnes Hundoegger's *Tonika-Do-Lehre*.'[5]

5. Guido d'Arezzo's solfeggio syllables.[6]

6. Jöde's hand-signs.[7]

This list of six separate sources does not stand up to close analysis. Moreover, where a particular attribution proves questionable – especially in the cases of Weber and Jöde – an unfortunate impression is created, however unintentionally, of an attempt to understate Kodály's indebtedness elsewhere. Let us look at these various claims in turn.

Zoltán Kodály's open acknowledgement of the influence of Curwen's Tonic Sol-fa upon his own efforts to reform music teaching in Hungarian schools

---

[1] F. Sándor, ed., *Musical Education in Hungary* (London: Barrie & Jenkins, 1966), pp. 26ff.

[2] *Ibid.*, p. 26.

[3] *Ibid.*, p. 27.

[4] *Ibid.*

[5] *Ibid.*

[6] *Ibid.*

[7] *Ibid.*, p. 39.

makes Szőnyi's first attribution almost unnecessary. But before leaving it, in view of some of her later claims we should note the precise reference she makes in it to 'the letters *and hand-signs* of John Curwen's Tonic Sol-fa system'.

In her second attribution Szőnyi claims for Jean (actually Johann Rudolf) Weber the 'principle of the shifting place of *doh*'. J. R. Weber (1819–75), a leading Swiss music educationist, did indeed produce one of the most influential Swiss music primers to follow the Pestalozzian manual published by Nägeli and Pfeiffer in 1810. But that primer, Weber's *Theoretische-praktische Gesanglehre*, was not published until 1849,[8] by which time the *Do-re-mi* system outlined in it had long been anticipated by Tonic Sol-fa – whose very name had, of course, been coined to emphasise 'the shifting place of *doh*'. So much, then, for Weber as a prime influence.

For her third ascription Szőnyi justifiably attributes to Émile Chevé Kodály's use of Arabic numerals to represent the degrees of the scale. Yet she fails to observe that Chevé had inherited the device in turn from Galin, Rousseau and other earlier teachers. This omission is one of several examples of apparent unawareness of developments in musical education outside Hungary that regularly characterise the post-war statements of some of Kodály's young, very self-confident, but politically sequestered and thence insular disciples.

The same criticism applies to Szőnyi's subsequent reference to Fritz Jöde as a collaborator with Agnes Hundoegger in producing the *Tonika Do* manual. *Tonika Do*, it should perhaps be explained, was the name given to a German adaptation of Tonic Sol-fa devised in 1897 by Agnes Hundoegger (1856–1927) after studying Curwen's system in England. Apart from using specifically German tunes as examples, her adaptation was largely a matter of translation, most features of the original system being retained – including the hand signs. But in one admitted improvement Hundoegger replaced Curwen's use of punctuation marks to designate rhythmic values by printing the stems and tails of crotchet, quaver, etc., above the pitch symbols – rather as Galin had done.

Since Hundoegger was herself a private teacher of singing and piano, not a class teacher in school, acceptance of her *Tonika Do* system was at first limited. But by 1909 a Tonika-Do Association had been formed, a manual was in circulation, and courses and examinations were made available. Among her later supporters in getting *Tonika Do* widely known in German primary and kindergarten schools were Maria Leo, Dora Gotzmann and Elisabeth Noack. Unlike Hundoegger herself, each was involved with schoolteaching, Noack in particular being a lecturer at the Kiel Teacher Training College. Another influential supporter was Frieda Loebenstein, a piano teacher at the Stern'sches

[8] J. R. Weber, [*Relative*] *Theoretische-praktische Gesanglehre* (n.p., 1849).

Konservatorium in Berlin, who used *Tonika Do* with her pupils there. With the help of these allies *Tonika Do* began to flourish.[9]

Fritz Jöde (1887–1970), whom Szőnyi mistakenly links so closely with Agnes Hundoegger, came of a much later generation, was quite unknown to her, and was only ten years of age when *Tonika Do* first made its appearance. He became, however, a well-known music educator whose books enjoyed a large circulation in Germany. In a final section of his manual, *Elementarlehre der Musik* (1927), Jöde referred to Curwen's influence upon his own work.[10] That influence had been gained indirectly through acquaintance with *Tonika Do* –whose originator in fact died in the year Jöde's book was published. But despite his tribute to Curwen, and Jöde's claim elsewhere in that book to have 'applied Tonic Sol-fa to the needs of our time', neither Maria Leo nor Elisabeth Noack thought highly of Jöde. A letter from Leo to Noack dated March 1926, and preserved in the Hessische Landesbibliothek, Darmstadt, leaves no room for doubt on that score.[11]

> As you say, [wrote Maria Leo] Jöde seems very musical; but why does he write such unmusical stuff? ... As for his knowledge of *Tonika Do*, he may use it properly himself but his pupils make nonsense of it. In any case he never learnt it thoroughly!! How could that be done in a single lecture? – after which he began using it here [in Berlin] ... Yet his pupils were all convinced that Jöde had invented the whole system himself. That was the final absurdity.[12]

There is certainly no suggestion of a partnership between Jöde and any of the proponents of the *Tonika Do* movement there.

We shall not split hairs over Szőnyi's mistakenly ascribing the sol-fa syllables *do* and *si* to Guido. But her use of the term *solfeggio* in this context is disconcerting to an English reader. While this might be considered just a question of semantics we note that László Eősze in his book, *Zoltán Kodály: his Life and*

---

[9] A. Hundoegger, *Lehrweise nach Tonika Do* (Köln: Kistner & Siegel, 1897; rev. E. Noack, 1967), pp. 3 f.

[10] F. Jöde, *Elementarlehre der Musik* (Wolfenbüttel: Kallmeyer, 1927), vol. 1, pt 1, pp. 138ff.

[11] A photocopy of this letter has kindly been provided by Professor Walter Heise of the University of Osnabrück, whose help in clarifying details of the German background to this whole controversy is gratefully acknowledged.

[12] The original runs: 'Du sagst, Jöde selbst [sei] eine eminent musikalische Natur. Gut, warum hat er dann aber so viel unmisikalisches Zeug geschrieben ... Das, was ich gesagt habe ... ist, dass Jöde selbst wahrscheinlich die Sache tadellos macht, dass aber unter seinen Schülern ... Unfug daraus erwachst ... Jöde hat doch TD nie richtig kennen gelernt!! Kann man denn das in *einem* Vortrag (nachdem er namlich 1924 angefangen hat, es hier zu benutzen) ... aber bei dem Kreis hat das alles erst Herr Jöde erfunden. Das ist die Unsinnigkeit.'

Work (1962), astonishingly defines *solmisation* as 'the Hungarian version of the Curwen Tonic Sol-fa pedagogical system'.[13] There is evidently both confusion and room for more careful use of terminology here.

After attributing them to Guido, Szőnyi goes on to describe how Kodály used the sol-fa syllables. '*Tee* is used instead of *see*,' she writes, 'to avoid confusion between *soh* and *see*'.[14] Even when deciphered, this remark altogether fails to acknowledge either the borrowing of the English name of the seventh sol-fa degree or its true source, Sarah Glover – again demonstrating what seems a nonchalant lack of concern with details of music education outside Hungary's borders.

Szőnyi's final claim – that Fritz Jöde was the originator of the hand signs – is quite the most preposterous of her gaffes. Not only have we already noted her earlier and correct attribution of the device to Curwen, but Jöde's own *Elementarlehre* (mentioned above) itself includes diagrams of all seven of Curwen's diatonic hand signs in its pages.

A partial explanation is perhaps to be found in Maria Leo's letter, already cited, where she maintains that Jöde's pupils declared *he had invented the hand signs himself.* Moreover, she went on, he never so much as mentioned *Tonika Do* to them, but allowed them to use the hand signs mechanically, *ohne funktionelles Hören* – without mentally hearing their implications.[15] Szőnyi's groundless claim therefore seems based on hearsay first spread by Jöde's misinformed pupils.

As to her faulty statement on another page that John Spencer Curwen (1847–1916) 'introduced Tonic Sol-fa in the 1840s',[16] the confusion of John Curwen with his son no doubt springs from the *Lehrweise nach Tonika Do,* where J. S. Curwen (a mere child at her death) is mistakenly named as Sarah Glover's fellow-worker. The reference survives in all later editions of that book to mislead Erszébet Szőnyi and any other reader content to rely on secondary sources.

It seems evident, then, that while no doubt compiled in good faith, Erszébet Szőnyi's somewhat casually assembled account needs extensive revision. The central, unquestioned fact it exposed is one now commonly recognised – that the so-called Kodály Concept was the result of composite efforts by the master's disciples and pupils, rather than a strict summary of his own practice. But

---

[13] L. Eősze, *Zoltán Kodály: His Life and Work*, trans. I. Farkas and G. Gulyás (London: Collet, 1962), p. 170.

[14] Sándor, *Musical Education in Hungary*, p. 27.

[15] The original runs: 'Dass tatsächlich nicht nur bei einer Generation im Institut die Ansicht bestand, das sind "die Handzeichen von Herrn Jöde" und von TD nie die Rede war, ist mir jedenfalls berichtet worden.'

[16] Sándor, *Musical Education in Hungary*, p. 30.

to serve its purpose such an account should be both reliable and comprehensive. Nor is it unreasonable to expect to find even its subsidiary detail free from mis-statements and omissions, to find in it a reliable account of what actually took place, and not to be left with doubts or misgivings about significant features.

To take a case in point: although hand signs form an important element in the Kodály Concept as evolved, there is no evidence that Kodály himself ever used hand signs in teaching. A vital question that consequently remains unanswered in Szőnyi's summary concerns not only the manner in which this feature of the Concept was introduced, but more importantly who was responsible for changes made to certain of the hand signs.

At some stage the original gestures for *fah*, sharpened *fah* = *fe*, sharpened *soh* = *se*, and flattened *te* = *ta*, were each altered. All these alterations, incidentally, are now recognised as advantageous compared with Curwen's originals.[17] But if Kodály himself did not employ hand signs, who then made these changes? At one time, before Szőnyi's claims were seen to be questionable, we had all been led to believe that Fritz Jöde was responsible. Szőnyi presumably thought so herself. But now that possibility has been scouted one wonders if it is already too late to discover who really did alter them.

On another question, it would be useful to have the term *Relative Sol-fa*, regularly used to describe Kodály usage, explained. It frequently appears in contexts where an English reader is at a loss to understand the precise meaning. In a somewhat similar way the terms 'sol-fa', 'solfeggio', 'solfège' and 'solmisation' are employed indiscriminately, without the clear shades of distinction they properly hold for English musicians. Perhaps such problems are to some extent due to translation difficulties. But the term Relative Sol-fa is often made to seem to relate to some exotic feature of musical practice that has no obvious parallel in English use.

It cannot, surely, be intended only to emphasise the fact that Kodály not only employed a movable *doh* but allowed other degrees than *doh* to stand as finals: *ray* with the Dorian, *me* with the Phrygian mode, and so on. That would be to assume that the same liberal policy had not always been followed in the use of Tonic Sol-fa – which is not the case.[18] These are all questions that deserve answering with something more positive than a peremptory rap on the knuckles.

What is sought, then, is a valid account which identifies the true sources of the Kodály Concept. In the early paragraphs of this article details are given of some sadly misleading statements. Something over twenty years has passed

---

[17] See the diagram of Hand Signs in 'John Curwen: A Short Critical Biography', p. 131 above.

[18] J. Curwen, *The Teacher's Manual* (London: Curwen & Sons, 1875; R/CTME 19, Kilkenny: Boethius Press 1986), p. 314.

since F. Sándor's *Musical Education in Hungary* gave them wide circulation. It is not perhaps too sanguine to suppose that, during the interim, aware- ness of historical circumstances in the development of musical education in other countries has become more accessible in Hungary – so as to reveal the true source of every 'borrowed' feature of the Kodály Concept. Particularly if undertaken by one of Kodály's surviving disciples, a new and more accurate account of this hitherto somewhat arcane aspect of its evolution would both serve to remove present misgivings and contradict any suggestion that existing errors and omissions had been anything other than accidental.

Cheironomy
[1979]

A RANGE OF STYLISED GESTURES with the hand forms a medium of human communication possibly older than speech. The priestly blessing and the military salute represent formal instances; but in everyday situations the handshake, the outstretched palm of the beggar, the heavenward-pointing finger of one seeking a taxi, and the vertical palm of the replete diner all convey an unambiguous message requiring no spoken clarification. An entire conversation may be conducted in silence with the sign language of the deaf and dumb, while the plot of most early ballets was conveyed to the audience through an elaborate mimetic code. Less familiar is the age-old use of hand gestures as a form of musical notation under the name of *Cheironomy*.

Case 233 at the Egyptian Museum, Cairo, contains a painted limestone relief taken from the tomb of Nekheft-Ka at Sakkara in the Valley of the Nobles on the bank of the Nile opposite Luxor. Dating from about 2700 BC, it represents the scene at a feast. There are five linen-skirted girls dancing to the music of a group of instrumentalists playing transverse flute, double aulos and harp. Facing each of the players sits another man who indicates the melody by means of gestures. Each has his right hand extended with finger and thumb joined to form a rough circle. The left hand of one is held up with the palm flat against the side of his head; the others have their left palms cupped on their raised left knees.

Some observers have attempted to claim that the fingers and thumbs of these cheironomists are not being used in a musical sign language but are merely producing finger snaps to emphasise the rhythmic beat of the music. But we notice that two girls who stand beside the dancers are fulfilling that task by clapping their hands. More to the point, in the Egyptian Rooms of the Louvre in Paris there is another limestone relief from a similar tomb in which the same arrangement of players and cheironomists is depicted. But here the gestures are different ones. By locating further examples it would be theoretically possible to reconstruct the system employed and the form of notation itself.

Nor was the use of cheironomy limited to ancient Egypt. Late in the twelfth century Nicholas Mesarites wrote an account in Greek of the schools attached to the church of the Apostles at Constantinople. On the west side of the cloisters was found an elementary school whose young pupils were taught singing – not by learning to read written notation, but by following hand signs. Their teachers, he wrote, made 'movements of their hands in order to guide the beginner in following the mode with his voice, that he may not slip away from

the melodic line, drop out of rhythm, nor fall away from the other voices, nor sing tunelessly.'

Nothing further is known of the hand signs then employed. Indeed, only chance has given us that brief account of a practice that may well have been so general in the song schools of the Eastern Church as not to call for comment. In the Latin-speaking Western Church, however, various medieval texts and later sources show that although the hand was used as a teaching aid in music lessons it was employed in a different manner. Teachers of Grammar, Arithmetic and Music all used the hand as an aid to the memory, laying out upon the joints and tips of the fingers an array of data to be committed to memory and then recited at the teacher's bidding. Where music was concerned, the twenty syllables of the Gamut were distributed in an anti-clockwise spiral beginning at the tip of the thumb and ending above the middle finger. There is no evidence, however, that pupils were required to *sing* notes from the Guidonian Hand; rather was it a mnemonic device and a conveniently accessible substitute for a textbook in days before the invention of printing. A woodcut from the Psalter of 1563 shows a father teaching his children their notes from the Guidonian Hand in Elizabethan times. The device was to survive well into the next century.

In the eighteenth century a new form of cheironomy made its appearance in the training of French cathedral choristers. With this method, the extended fingers of the hand were used to represent the lines and spaces of the staff, the learner singing notes as they were pointed out one at a time with the other hand. The device was first mentioned by Rameau in his *Code de musique pratique*:

It will be seen readily enough that the five fingers of the hand are very capable of representing the five lines upon which music is written: for if one contemplates or imagines a hand held well open, the little finger nearest the ground, one may see the five lines with their spaces – which are the gaps separating the lines formed by the fingers.

Rameau's book was not written until 1760 – four years before his death. But it contained the result of a lifetime's experience as a church musician involving the training of choristers at Avignon, Paris, Lyons and Clermont. Moreover, his father had been organist at Dijon before him; and it would be unwise to assume that Rameau's mention of the use of the hand to guide singers in this way marked its first introduction at so late a date.

Singing from the hand held as a staff was later to be a basic element in the popular singing classes organised by G. L. B. Wilhem in Paris following his appointment as Director-Inspector of Singing in 1835. Indeed, Wilhem added several refinements to the simple system outlined by Rameau. First, he moved his ring from one finger to another to denote the position of the clef; next, he used his right hand to represent the treble staff, and the left hand, the bass. Thirdly, he allowed for the indication of chromatic degrees by reserving the central joint of each finger to denote a *natural*, while the tip and root, respectively, were to indicate *flat* and *sharp*. From 1840 onward, 'singing from the hand' became a feature of the singing classes introduced in London by John Hullah, in acknowledged imitation of Wilhem's model and employing an English 'adaptation' of his system. Nor has the device lost its usefulness in the early stages of learning to read music to this day.

Another system of cheironomy, devised by Maurice Chevais in the 1930s and still popular in France, is known as *phonomimie*. With this, the notes of the major scale are identified with parts of the pupil's own frame: the waist, shoulders, neck, crown of the head, etc. Individual notes are signalled by holding the hand, palm down, horizontally against the part of the body concerned. Apart from singing to the teacher's signals, pupils taught *phonomimie* use it in a form of musical dictation. A capable class, with eyes firmly closed as the rubric requires, seen identifying the notes of a melody sung by their teacher makes a memorable picture of youthful concentration in a French elementary school.

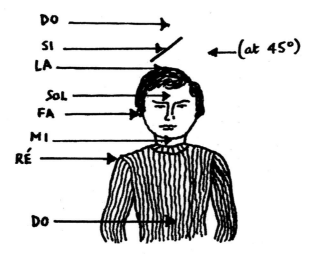

Most widely known and employed of all recent systems of cheironomy, however, are the Hand Signs representing the degrees of the scale first introduced
by John Curwen in 1870. The occasion was a gathering of Welsh singers at
Ruthin, Denbighshire. Many of those present could neither speak nor understand much English; and Curwen chose to demonstrate and employ the new
Hand Signs as a means of communication where ordinary speech failed. Each
sign had been skilfully designed to portray the 'character' of the degree of the
scale concerned: the firmness of *doh*, the calm of *me*, the melancholy of *lah* and
rising trend of *te*, for example.

Later teachers were not slow to realise the advantages offered by Hand Signs
for class teaching – among them Zoltán Kodály, who adopted them together
with Curwen's other principles for use in Hungarian schools. In a similar
way Agnes Hundoegger introduced the Tonic Sol-fa system to Germany as
Tonika Do.

Kodály's championship of Curwen's principles has had the effect of giving them new and wider currency in our own day. Indeed, there are many
who suppose that Kodály was the sole originator of the method of teaching
music which is now publicised under his name. That impression was notably
reinforced in the recent space epic *Close Encounters of the Third Kind*,[1] where
music was made an extra-terrestrial common language with the Hand Signs its
means of personal communication.

Seldom have teachers of music in junior schools received so unexpected
and powerful a boost to their efforts as this film provided. In it, we follow
the adventures of a team of scientists who pick up a mysterious code signal
from outer space: *ray–me–doh–doh₁–soh*. Following an increase in the number

[1] 1977 American science-fiction film written and directed by Steven Spielberg. Ed.

of UFOs, they decide to return the signal. In secret conclave they are briefed about the sol-fa names and the Hand Signals used to represent them. These, they are unreliably told, were Kodály's invention. Eventually, a spaceship on something of the scale of the Albert Hall descends to bring an emissary to treat with Earth. And at the film's climax this awesome personage emerges mistily from his spacecraft to greet them by solemnly translating the notes of the code signal into Hand Signs. (If, as we are left to suppose, his knowledge of those signs sprang from infinite wisdom, he alone among those present will have known that they originated in Curwen, not Kodály.)

Cinemas have been thronged for months past with youngsters eagerly watching the visitor from outer space signalling his friendship to humanity with musical Hand Signs. Few alert teachers aware of this film's content will have failed to respond by seizing the opportunity to teach their younger pupils how to employ for themselves the Cheironomy of the Space Age.

Victorian Street Music

[1998]

S EEKING A THEME to illustrate the month of November in his *Comic Almanack* for 1837, George Cruikshank has fastened on 22 November, the day chosen to celebrate the patron saint of music, St Cecilia. But where another artist will have treated the subject with veneration, Cruikshank's alert sense of the droll has led him to satirise rather than extol. Though less ribald than Rowlandson, more genial then Gillray, Cruikshank was their legitimate heir, seldom losing an opportunity to ridicule the absurd, taunt pomposity, or laugh down social folly. In this case he has chosen to depict music in the streets rather than in celestial regions, exposing with jocular realism the continuing survival of a public indiscretion Hogarth had treated with far less good nature in his *Enraged Musician* a hundred years earlier.

Cruikshank's mastery of crowd scenes enables him to assemble in one spot a collection of the street performers to be encountered all over London in his day. Varying from the preposterous to the pathetic, all the characters included are recognisable in contemporary literature and repay closer examination. Some, like the strolling bagpiper, are still to be seen in London today; others have been replaced by later versions of themselves; but most demonstrate music in her less dignified role as a means of extracting charitable contributions from the parsimonious. In that respect part of the humour of Cruikshank's portrayal lies in the complete absence of any passers-by from whom this army of impoverished but determined musicians might secure a contribution.

Just joining the throng on the left is a typical cockney butcher-boy and
his mate. Both carry a marrow-bone and cleaver. The traditional 'music' of
butchers in Britain was the ringing rhythmic clatter produced by striking a
meatchopper with a large bone. Apart from its everyday use in attracting the
attention of customers, over the ages this butchers' music acquired the esoteric
function of saluting a newly-married couple as they left the church after their
wedding.

Describing a scene in London early in the nineteenth century a contributor
to the *City Press* wrote:

> There has been a wedding in Milk Street, and Cheapside is alive with the
> marrow-bones and cleavers, as they pass in procession to serenade the
> bride and bridegroom ...[1]

Such an event was common enough then not to require further explanation.
In the previous century Hogarth had included the marrow-bone and cleaver
among the street-band celebrating the wedding of his *Industrious Apprentice*.
Long after the custom was commonly abandoned it was continued in the twentieth century at the weddings of butchers themselves. Even today this rough
music may occasionally be revived at a traditionalist's wedding.

Flanking Cruikshank's leading butcher-boy in his oversleeves and apron we
find the very different figure of a boy treble accompanying himself on what
seems to be a mandolin. In a survey of the London poor, published in the daily
press during the 1840s, Henry Mayhew reported several conversations with
street musicians. According to one of them 'the great majority' of the fraternity
had been brought up from childhood to be street-performers. Taught early, few
of them afterwards left 'the profession' for any other business. The better sort,
Mayhew was told, were prudent and struggled hard for a decent living.[2] The
sensitive looking child Cruikshank has set alongside his tough butcher-boy
clearly belongs to this more respectable class of performer.

Walking towards him, with his back to us, is an organ grinder who deftly
turns the handle of his barrel-organ while it is still slung across his back. By
mid-century with the coming of larger, louder, instruments trundled around
on carts, the organ grinder was to become the noisiest and most exasperating of
street-performers; but this modest instrument seems inoffensive enough – so
long as its pipes are kept regularly tuned. How seldom this was the case is made
clear by the comment of another writer on London street-musicians:

---

[1] Reprinted in Aleph [W. Harvey], *London Scenes and London People* (London: W. H.
Collingridge, City Press, 1863), p 351.

[2] P. Quennel, *Mayhew's London* (selections from H. Mayhew's *London Labour and the
London* Poor [1851]) (London: Spring Books, 1961), p. 521.

In some of the German cities, the police have summary jurisdiction in offences musical, and are empowered to demand a certificate, with which every grinder is bound to be furnished, showing the date of the last tuning of his instrument ... Such a bye-law would be a real bonus in London.[3]

Almost without exception organ grinders were foreigners – usually Savoyards or Italians. Mayhew interviewed one who had come to London from Parma as a child of nine or ten, but now spoke English well enough to tell his own story.[4] The small organ he carried around played a cosmopolitan repertoire ranging from Italian opera – *Il trovatore* and *I Lombardi* – to such English favourites as the *Liverpool Hornpipe* and *The Rat-catcher's Daughter*. He had found, though – like most of his trade – that while the poor enjoyed simple native tunes 'the gentlemen's they like more the opera'. But he could also provide a Scottish country-dance and a polka. Finally, there was a Viennese waltz which had been added especially at his request:

I don't know which one, [he explained engagingly to Mayhew] but I say to the organ-man, 'I want a valtz of Vienna'; and he say, 'Which one? because there is plenty of valtz of Vienna.' Of course, there is nine of them. After the opera music, the valtz and the polka is the best ...[5]

Cruikshank's organ-grinder will doubtless have had a similar story to tell.

Over the grinder's head in the engraving can be seen a forest of bayonets as a regiment of soldiers marches past headed by their band. But these were the days when the vogue for 'Turkish' music still flourished in military bands; and so we see two turbanned Negroes ceremoniously wielding tambourine and cymbals above their heads, while behind them the ornate 'Turkish Crescent' nicknamed the 'Jingling Johnny' and covered with small bells is being vigorously shaken in time with the music. Not long since, Haydn, Mozart and Beethoven had all introduced features reminiscent of these exotic percussion instruments into their compositions. At a more mundane level domestic pianos at this time were often equipped with extra pedals to operate drum, tambourine and other percussion effects in imitation of the fad for 'Turkish' music. 'Jingling Johnny' and tambourine were to be included in British army bands only until 1856, though the cymbals and triangle still survive.

Rising up alongside the soldiers' line of march is the tall frame of a Punch and Judy show. In front of it the drum and panpipes traditionally associated with this entertainment are sounding vigorously. As we can see, while being played, the pandean pipes – a title always insisted on by practitioners – were

---

[3] C. M. Smith, *Curiosities of London Life* (London: W. & F. G. Cash, 1853), p. 5 note.

[4] Quennel, *Mayhew's London*, pp. 527ff.

[5] *Ibid.*, p. 536.

held in place at chin level by a scarf or stock around the neck and then blown by turning the head from side to side. This left the hands free to play the drum – or, in the case of players accompanying *fantoccini* shows, tambourine, cymbals, triangle, and other 'Turkish' instruments.

Besides the important preliminary duty of attracting an audience for the show, the pipe-and-drum man once took an active part in the performance itself. On his first entrance Mr Punch would address him from the stage, 'How do you do, Master? – play up; play up a hornpipe; I'm a most excellent dancer'; and then Punch danced to the pipes and drum. Later he would say, 'Master, I shall call my wife up, and have a dance.'[6] At the end of the first act the drum and pipes would strike up again to mark a break in the performance. Then at various points Punch and other characters would sing well-known songs or topical doggerel such as:

> I'm a roarer on the fiddle
> Down in the ole Virginny;
> And I plays it scientific,
> Like Master Paganini.[7]

Cruikshank, then, is not mistaken – as might be supposed – in showing Mr Punch on the stage at the same time as the pipes and drum are sounding.

But, however accurate in detail, the purpose of this picture is satirical; and so, less than a foot from the pipes-and-drum player we find a town crier in his tricorne, hand to mouth, bawling out his message and ringing his bell. Then, well within arm's reach of this stentorian performer stands the central group of figures in our picture; an impoverished family of six, yet all singing their hearts out.

From the slim bunches several of them hold in their hands they seem to be lavender-sellers; but they have been cynically depicted as members of a highly trained ensemble – enthusiasts to a man, well-drilled in voice production and proficient in placement. Even the babe-in-arms has the look of an experienced vocalist, while his elder sister, hands clasped modestly in the classical attitude, fixes us with the arch but challenging eye of an established diva. With such performers, one feels, even that simple street cry, 'Who'll buy my sweet lavender?' is ready to rival the 'Hailstone' Chorus.

Advancing from behind these accomplished choralists comes a less assured pair playing a triangle and a tambourine. Mere children, they seem to form part of a team with the string-bass and fiddle players following close behind. Their headgear gives all four the look of foreigners, no doubt Germans; but

---

[6] *Ibid.*, p. 455.

[7] *Ibid.*, p. 458.

these are quieter forerunners of the noisy German brass bands that came to haunt London's streets after mid-century. Unpopular with other street musicians – Germans were invariably more capable – they lived their lives apart, mixing only with their own countrymen working in London, as sugar-bakers for instance, and patronising one of the few public-houses then kept by Germans.[8]

Standing alone in front of this group is an even more obvious foreigner, this time playing a hurdy-gurdy. Short in stature, his sun-hat suggesting a Mediterranean origin, despite his unimposing presence this is no mere organ-grinder. Unlike the barrel-organist, whose tunes were produced mechanically, the hurdy-gurdy player must pick out his own melodies on a keyboard; the handle he turned only set the strings vibrating.

In London at that time, we are told, there were two classes of hurdy-gurdy player. Young boys, who danced and sang as they turned their handles, but played no recognisable tune; and more mature performers who produced melodies and even harmonies with something like precision. There were likewise two types of instrument: those of the boys having but few keys, often not even a complete octave. The instrument of true performers, on the other hand, had a scale of an octave and a half, sometimes two octaves.[9]

In the case in point Cruikshank's drawing sufficiently reveals an instrument with a keyboard of quite an octave and a half, partly covered though it is by the diminutive youth's surprisingly broad left hand. But at the moment his playing is not perhaps at its best – for his attention is fixed on a nearby dog (seldom a friend to itinerant strangers) that distractedly howls its protest at a tartaned bagpiper. The dog in turn is joined by a braying donkey whose costermonger driver struggles vainly to get it back to work.

Amid the undulation the Scot plays away on his pipes unmoved. Perhaps, like another street bagpiper interviewed later by Henry Mayhew, he is a former member of a Highland regiment and hence accustomed to more formidable opposition.[10]

Tucked away behind the bagpiper and his critics is an insignificant figure who in fact represents the doyen of all street musicians. This is the ballad singer, then still continuing the seventeenth-century trade of selling broadside prints of the words of his songs. His two-fold repertoire comprised traditional songs, moral tales, and hymns on one hand, and doggerel accounts of sensational happenings – explosions, fires, murders, seductions, courtroom and gaol scenes – on the other. Both types of ballad were printed on narrow 'slips' of

[8] *Ibid.*, p. 59.

[9] Smith, *Curiosities of London Life*, p. 16.

[10] Quennel, *Mayhew's London*, pp. 523–5.

extremely cheap paper and illustrated with wood-blocks drawn from the specialist printer's stock-in-trade.

> These peripatetic vocalists [we are told by a contemporary], having retentive memories and abundance of assurance, never encumbered themselves with sheet music; they carried a bundle of ballads, printed separately, on slips of dirt-coloured paper, and the type very indistinct – all the letters seeming afflicted with *delirium tremens*. Each slip was about twelve inches long by four wide, embellished at the top with a smudgy ornament, libellously called the 'royal arms'. This people's edition of popular songs was sold by the publisher, who dwelt somewhere in Seven Dials, at threepence a dozen, but the street price was a halfpenny each.[11]

When Charles Dickens referred mysteriously in *Sketches by Boz* to Seven Dials as a region of song 'hallowed by the names of Catnach and Pitts,'[12] the reference was to James Catnach and John Pitts, the rival broadside printers who published these ballads and provided singing salesmen with their livelihood.[13] During the 1840s, shortly after Cruikshank's caricature appeared, longer song sheetswere being offered for sale with the cry, 'Popular songs! Three yards for a penny!'[14] This gave rise to the easily misinterpreted term 'long songs.'

On a raised platform behind our ballad singer a booth has been set up and a showman wearing the traditional dress of a Tower of London beefeaters[15] loudly summons an audience. At fairs and other popular outdoor entertainments unfortunate freaks of all kinds – dwarfs, fat ladies, Siamese twins, and all manner of performing animals – were commonly made central features of rare shows of this sort. What readily came to be regarded as their musical equivalent, the infant prodigy, we now see being put on show in much the same way under the title of the *Infant Orpheus*.

Fascination with the exploits of precocious children is not uncommon among adults. But when that precocity extends to musical skill it acquires an irresistible fascination for the unmusical. The nineteenth century was an age of extreme susceptibility in this respect, the serious interest shown earlier in the cases of Mozart and Crotch steadily giving way to open-mounted wonderment at far less deserving attempts to repeat their feats. Very occasionally one of the resulting army of infant marvels would attain mature celebrity; but none

---

[11] Aleph, *London Scenes and London People*, p. 347.

[12] C. Dickens, *Sketches by Boz* (1836), chap. 5, 'Seven Dials'.

[13] T. Gretton, *Murders and Moralities: English Catchpenny Prints, 1800–1860* (London: Colonnade Books, British Museum, 1980), p. 11.

[14] J. W. Dodds, *The Age of Paradox* (London: Gollancz, 1953), p. 411.

[15] Similarly dressed showmen appear in other nineteenth-century prints, e.g. Cruikshank's own *The Shows* in the *Comic Almanack* for 1835.

had been recruited from a street booth. By the turn of the century popular interest in the fad diminished. As *The Musical Times* put it: 'No doubt there have been sea-serpents, and it is equally certain that Mozart and Liszt were youthful prodigies. But these phenomena are so very rare that scepticism is fully justified.'[16]

Sharing the platform with the showman is a wind consort of trumpet, oboe, and bass trombone. No doubt there to give a foretaste of the musical treat awaiting those who paid to hear the Infant Orpheus, these bandsmen seem obviously English. Even discounting their Pickwickian toppers, the masterly drawing and characterisation of the cocky trumpeter and the sketchier but no less revealing portrayal of the old hacks with him leave us in no doubt as to that. If these men had learned to read music they could have earned extra money by playing at concerts, balls, parties, processions, and water excursions, as well as in the streets. But native street performers were invariably brought up from childhood to play by ear. This was to become a major source of friction between them and the more thoroughly trained German players – who consequently secured such engagements. Yet, as one English bandsman objected to Henry Mayhew, 'numbers of street musicians (playing by ear) are better instrumentalists than many educated musicians.'[17]

A large Concert Room – forbidden territory to the buskers playing so vigorously outside – is seen rising elegantly behind the showman's booth, its Corinthian columns and proportions reminiscent of those seen in engravings of the Hanover Square Rooms, then London's foremost concert hall. Although there are no signs of a concert in progress here, we are doubtless being reminded that Cecilia is honoured indoors as well as out.

The same point is made, yet more subtly, on the opposite side of our picture where the view is closed, first by a tall warehouse, then by a larger building alongside. Careful examination shows on it the faint inscriptions, APOLLONI-CON. This, of course, was the name given to the largest and most elaborate barrel-organ ever built in England. It had been constructed 1817 by Flight and Robson, the leading English manufacturers of mechanical organs, and gave regular performances in the capital for more than thirty years. Intended to reproduce the effect of a full orchestra, it was equipped with powerful reeds and percussion instruments as well as standard organ pipes. Three pinned barrels were required to operate it mechanically, but it could also be played manually at separate consoles by as many as six performers. Soon established among middle-class audiences as one of London's main musical attractions the Apollonicon was long to be heard at Flight and Robson's showrooms in

---

[16] P. A. Scholes, *The Mirror of Music*, 2 vols. (London: Novello, 1947), vol. 2, p. 847.

[17] Quennel, *Mayhew's London*, pp. 520–1.

St Martin's Lane. It was still attracting large attendances in Cruikshank's day, but by then had been removed to premises near Regent's Park.

The inclusion of Apollonicon and Concert Room in the background of this panorama completes for us a summary of the musical resources separately available to different levels of society in 1837. The effect is to heighten the impression of uncouthness and cacophony in the street scene itself – though without destroying its humour. Such is the artist's magic.

In the middle distance stands the parish church. Its clock, we can see, has just struck the hour. The chimes, then, are now making their own contribution to the clamour below. Meanwhile, dead on time, with a final touch of drama a hackney-coach driver whips up his horses. His passengers peer from the windows bemusedly as the coach moves off and they make their escape from the uproar surrounding them.

George Cruikshank's *St Cecilia's Day* provides a comic but authentic picture of street music in London in the year Victoria came to the throne. During her reign its consistent degeneration into street noise aroused growing outrage among householders and others whose professional activities were disturbed daily by the ceaseless clamour outside their windows. In 1864 and again in 1882 Acts were passed designed to subdue this nuisance. The success of those enactments and sundry later by-laws introduced with similar intention was never more than partial. Indeed, the phenomenon is still with us – though with certain new twists. In London many performers, some of them highly competent, have literally 'gone Underground' – more for the increased resonance of the tile-lined passageways than to escape the weather. There is a *volte-face,* too, among those still favouring the pavements for their recitals. Foreigners no longer do much of the performing. Today, at least in those shopping streets of the metropolis favoured by tourists, it is foreigners who have become the involuntary audience.

The English Promenade Concert
[1995–6]

I N 1833 Phillipe Musard began holding informal concerts of light music in a hall on the Rue St Honoré in Paris. Advertised as *promenade concerts* – because the audience stood or strolled about during the performance – they ranged from short symphonic movements to quadrilles which the audience might choose to dance, and enjoyed great popularity. Four years later they were being continued with a ninety-piece orchestra in a large marquee on the Champs-Élysées. News of their success soon prompted an attempt to imitate their innovation in London; and in 1838 a series of *Promenade Concerts à la Musard* was announced at the Lyceum Theatre where they attracted large attendances.

It was these Musard Promenade Concerts that introduced the term still used to describe an informal concert with a perambulating audience; but an abiding impression that all such concerts had their origin in France is groundless. They form part of a much older English tradition, possess a distinguished history of their own, and are closely linked with the once fashionable custom known as 'parading'.

During the eighteenth century the social promenade was a convention as evident in Britain as any *passeggiata*, *paseo* or *promenoir* of continental Europe. For 150 years from its construction in Charles II's day the Mall in St James' Park was London's most fashionable parade. Society came to walk here on fine days from 7.00 to 10.00 in the evening, and in the winter from 1.00 to 3.00. Gainsborough's painting of 1783 showing elegantly attired beauties and their escorts parading in the Mall compares revealingly with the picture of fashionable Parisians at the Palais Royal in Debucourt's *La Promenade Publique* of 1792. There is no mistaking English lambency and reserve in the one for French sparkle and dash in the other; but these two contrasting portrayals of polite society assembled to see and be seen depict precisely the same custom in vogue on either side of the Channel.

Early in the eighteenth century formal public walks were being constructed all over England. Brighton, Scarborough and Weymouth were soon building esplanades to keep pace with the promenades of Bath, Tunbridge Wells, Epsom and Cheltenham. Adjoining many of them were tea rooms, shops, gardens, perhaps even a bandstand. But London led the way in providing suburban 'pleasure gardens' as commercial concerns where such amenities were combined; and it was there, over a century before Musard, that the English promenade concert had its formal inception.

The most celebrated of these establishments was Vauxhall; but Marylebone Gardens at the northern end of Marylebone High Street was a shade earlier, beginning unsalubriously in 1650 as a centre for bear-baiting, cockfights, boxing matches and the like. When Gay placed his *Beggar's Opera* here in 1728 Macheath's gang mirrored the mingled card-sharpers, pick-pockets, highwaymen and trollops still favouring the place. Dick Turpin was at Marylebone Gardens as late as 1730. But by then the building of new streets and squares north of Oxford Street was encouraging the disreputable to seek a remoter playground.

The transformation of Marylebone Gardens into a formal promenade was achieved in 1738. The lessee, John Trusler, had introduced an entrance fee and hired soldiers to protect patrons making their way along lanes still separating the hamlet of St Mary le Bone from the houses going up in Wigmore Street. A reward of ten guineas cannily offered for the arrest of any highwayman found in the vicinity remained unclaimed.

Meanwhile a grand tree-lined circular walk, hedged and latticed alcoves, various assembly rooms and a concert stage with an organ were added. Excellent refreshments were served, and during the summer months, when the gardens were now alone open, an orchestra played to the perambulating audience each evening from six to ten o'clock directed by an expatriate Neapolitan, the elder Stephen Storace. The resident organist was Stephen Philpot, and a typical programme comprised overtures, symphonies and concertos for a variety of solo instruments including the organ, interspersed with vocal solos, duets and choruses.

Small-scale operas were soon added and in 1758 Storace presented a concert version of Pergolesi's *La serva padrona* which he had translated into English for the occasion with an additional scene of his own in the middle. This proved highly popular, was often revived, and led Storace to translate and mount other Italian *intermezzi* at Marylebone. Then in 1769 Trusler sold the lease of the gardens to Samuel Arnold, formerly harpsichordist and répétiteur at Covent Garden. A future organist of the Chapel Royal and Westminster Abbey, Arnold was then only twenty-nine and had recently married an heiress. He could thus afford to give up his post at the opera-house and devote himself to composing and presenting concerts and operatic performances on his own premises.

James Hook, the former musical prodigy from Norwich, now in his early twenties and currently organist at a Clerkenwell tea-garden, was now appointed organist and composer at Marylebone. He was a prolific composer capable of writing such engaging songs as *The Lass of Richmond Hill* as well as pantomimes, comic operas, serenatas and a host of overtures, concertos and symphonies. His light-hearted compositions were to delight audiences at Marylebone for as long as the gardens survived.

To replace the ageing Storace as leader of the orchestra Arnold engaged François-Hippolyte Barthélémon, a French musician of exactly his own age recognised as one of the best violinists of the day and an instrumental composer of merit. His new young English wife was a fine singer who often appeared with him at the ambitious concerts now regularly given at Marylebone. Besides Hook's compositions there were others by Barthélémon and Arnold himself, as well as those by international composers; and Storace's version of Pergolesi's *La serva padrona* still held a popular place in the programmes.

In 1773, Hook left to accept a similar post at Vauxhall. But by this time the heyday of Marylebone Gardens was over. A trusted employee had for some time been embezzling the takings; and in 1776 Arnold was obliged to sell the gardens and return to earning a living in church and theatre. Two years later a tide of new streets and houses had submerged the site.

The rival gardens at Vauxhall were first known as New Spring Gardens. When the earlier and notorious Spring Gardens at Charing Cross had been closed down late in the Commonwealth a new site was found for them away from Whitehall across the river at Vauxhall. Admission here was at first free of charge and after a visit in 1667 Samuel Pepys remarked approvingly,

> I by water to Fox-hall, and there walked in Spring Gardens. A great deal of company, and the weather and garden pleasant: and it is very cheap going thither, for a man may go and spend what he will, or nothing, all is one – but to hear the nightingale and other birds, and here fiddles and there a harp, and here a Jews trump, and here laughing, and there fine people walking, is mighty diverting.

With the main walks lit at night a little modest music-making was already among the attractions of this popular resort.

From 1728 Jonathan Tyers leased the gardens, greatly increased their amenities and determined to make them respectable. Chinese pavilions and supper boxes, artificial ruins with a resident 'hermit', ornamental arches, statues, and a cascade were in turn erected while in the central promenading area a roofed 'Gothick Orchestra' was built to accommodate the band. With these additional features the gardens were formally reopened in June, 1732, for a *ridotto al fresco* attended by the Prince of Wales. Annual season tickets now became *de rigueur* and while still attracting Londoners of all classes Vauxhall Gardens became a highly fashionable resort.

An astute and adventurous organiser, Jonathan Tyers was ever at pains to attract popular audiences with sideshows, elaborate illuminations and fireworks. But aware that for many of his patrons – and not merely the *beau monde* – the concerts given at the gardens provided an important attraction he was careful to provide varied programmes ranging from orchestral items to glees, choruses and comic songs. Tyers engaged only competent performers or established singers and a new organ was installed in 1737 with James Worgan to play it. He held the post of organist for fourteen years until succeeded by his brother, John, a most distinguished performer who remained at Vauxhall as organist and composer until 1774.

But Tyers set his sights high. In 1745 he appointed Thomas Arne, the most eminent native musician of the day, as Composer to the Gardens. In a series of new songs, ballads, glees, pastoral settings and cantatas with orchestral accompaniment Arne was to set a model for his successors at Vauxhall. James Hook (1774), Thomas Cooke (1823) and Henry Rowley Bishop (*c.* 1826) – besides providing a repertory pirated in the dozens of minor pleasure gardens now established around London.

In April 1749 a public rehearsal of Handel's *Music for the Royal Fireworks* was held at Vauxhall. No less than 12,000 persons monopolised the Thames ferries and blocked London Bridge with coaches for several hours in their determination to reach the gardens. But this was a unique occasion and it is less easy to discover the programmes of more typical concerts given at Vauxhall then. Only later, when full details are advertised in the newspapers, can a clear idea be formed of just what was performed – and especially of the orchestral items known to have been regularly included. These prove to have comprised overtures, symphonies and concertos by composers ranging from Corelli and Handel to Haydn and J. C. Bach besides similar works by leading English composers of the day.

Just as the eighteenth-century fashion for promenading produced the London 'pleasure garden', so the desire to continue the practice out of season encouraged the building of Assembly Rooms. By the 1770s all but the smallest towns in England had assembly rooms ranging from the palatial saloons of Bath or York to less splendid accommodation attached to provincial inns.

London's first indoor alternative to Vauxhall Gardens was Ranelagh – a vast circular assembly room opened at Chelsea in 1742 and soon claimed by Horace Walpole to have 'totally beat Vauxhall'. Ranelagh Gardens had been established by Lacy, the patentee of Drury Lane Theatre, in the grounds of a riverside house adjoining Chelsea Hospital and formerly owned by Lord Ranelagh. Like Vauxhall these gardens boasted sideshows, tree-lined walks, illuminations, fireworks, refreshment booths, and a Chinese Pavilion. But the centre-piece here was the huge new and luxurious-seeming rotunda said to have been inspired by the Pantheon in Rome. Canaletto's painting of 1754 has made Ranelagh's interior familiar. Yet the account of a German visitor who discovered the rotunda only after losing himself at night in the ill-lit and largely deserted gardens surrounding it merits quotation:

> But what a sight I saw as I came from the darkness of that garden into the glare of a round building lit with hundreds of lamps, surpassing in splendour and beauty any I had ever seen before! Everything here was circular. Above stood a gallery with private boxes; in one part of the gallery stood an organ and a well-built choir apse, from which poured forth music both vocal and instrumental. Round the building, all of fashionable London revolved like a gaily coloured distaff, sauntering in a compact throng.

Musical programmes given at Ranelagh resembled those at Marylebone and Vauxhall, though the marked gentility of this audience favoured the inclusion of Mannheim symphonies and concerti grossi at the expense of comic songs. Significantly, too, it was only at Ranelagh the castrato, Tenducci, sang during the 1760s; only there that the boy Mozart played his own compositions on both organ and harpsichord in 1764. Although masquerades were sometimes held, promenading while a concert was given remained Ranelagh's principal attraction.

London's second indoor centre for assemblies, sometimes described as the 'winter Ranelagh' was a beautiful building named the Pantheon erected for the purpose at the junction of Oxford Street and Poland Street in 1772. More conveniently situated for residents of London's rapidly expanding West End than either Ranelagh or Vauxhall, in wintry weather aristocratic patrons were able to descend from their carriages at its very doors sheltered by a stone portico. Within were to be found vestibules, tea rooms, card rooms, supper rooms and a great rotunda with coffered dome and pillars in simulated *giallo antico* all closely modelled on the Pantheon in Rome.

Horace Walpole names it 'the most beautiful edifice in England'. Here were held not only masquerades, ridottos and fetes, but well attended fortnightly concerts at which famous opera singers such as Mara and Pachierotti sang. It was only later when a concert forming part of the 1784 Handel Commemoration took place at the Pantheon in the presence of the royal family that the tradition of a promenading audience was finally abandoned.

The Pantheon was converted to an opera house in 1791 and burnt down in a suspicious fire shortly afterwards; Ranelagh next lost its appeal and was demolished in 1805; but Vauxhall survived. Of all the centres where concerts were given before a standing or strolling audience Vauxhall still enjoyed popularity with all classes of society – and perhaps for that reason proved the most enduring. Acclaimed retrospectively in Thackeray's *Vanity Fair* as late as

1848, the appeal of Vauxhall was nowhere more charmingly recorded than in Rowlandson's famous aquatint of 1784.

There, beneath the lamp-lit trees many celebrities can be recognised. James Boswell, Dr Johnson and Mrs Thrale are seen in their supper-box; Captain Topham, 'the macaroni of the day', stands isolated in the foreground boldly quizzing the Duchess of Devonshire and her sister; the Prince of Wales flirts with Perdita Robinson under the resentful gaze of her diminutive husband; a lackey struggles to uncork a bottle for a party of cockney wine-bibbers. Meanwhile within the 'Gothick Orchestra' that outstandingly popular English soprano, Frederica Weichsell, serenades the assembly to the accompaniment of a sizeable uniformed band. All these details provide a faithful record of the Promenade Concert as a longstanding English institution; they also help refute any suggestion of a French origin for it.

If Rowlandson's *Vauxhall* (1784) is carefully compared with Debucourt's *La Promenade Publique* (1792) several points of resemblance immediately stand out. Captain Topham's stance, the group with Perdita Robinson and her tiny spouse, the waiter serving at table – all are either mirrored or parodied much too closely by Debucourt for this to be coincidental. Nor is it difficult to prove that this French artist admired, studied and often imitated English colour-prints; and the present masterly paraphrase that transmutes an easy-going Vauxhall audience into a gathering of frivolous Parisian pleasure-seekers on the very eve of the Reign of Terror is known to have been inspired by Rowlandson's original. For present purposes the closeness with which *La Promenade Publique* deliberately echoes Rowlandson's *Vauxhall* makes the absence of a musical element in it all the more striking. We are able to feel confident that had Parisian promenades ever taken place accompanied by noteworthy music Debucourt would have shown this happening here – if only to complete the parallel with Rowlandson's Vauxhall. The omission of such a feature from La Promenade Publique points to the absence at that time of a French counterpart to London's outdoor promenade concerts – a valid conjecture, as it proves.

Foreign visitors to England in those days often mentioned the London pleasure garden as unique in Europe. Many successful attempts were made to imitate it abroad; but a solitary venture to do so in Paris is known to have gone astray. In 1772 two French officials responsible for the royal fireworks came to London to study pyrotechnic displays there.

Impressed by Vauxhall and Ranelagh they determined to establish a similar pleasure garden in Paris. Obtaining an official concession on land adjoining the Bois de Boulogne they built there a combined playhouse, cafe, and assembly room surrounded by extensive lawns and named it Petit Ranelagh. The place quickly became *à la mode* once Marie Antoinette took to coming there with members of the court to dance; but as a result any resemblance to an English pleasure garden promptly and permanently evaporated. Today the Jardins du Ranelagh, a municipal park, alone remains to record the site.

The failure of that attempt left Paris without a counterpart to either Vauxhall or Ranelagh. The incident serves to emphasise that it was not until after 1789 that music on anything approaching an elaborate scale became a public medium rather than a royal or aristocratic preserve in France.

The shift from chateau to concert hall was to take place only gradually in times dominated by more drastic change. The revolutionary turmoil of 1792 saw the royal family swept into prison and the Republic proclaimed. In the same year the newly composed *Marseillaise* was transformed from a zestful marching song to a feverish revolutionary hymn. In that heady atmosphere the citizen-legislators of Paris next declared their intention to confer on music a 'political existence' by incorporating it in public ceremonies designed to boost popular morale.

The leaders of the Paris commune had already replaced the École Royal de Chant with a Free School of Music formed to train bandsmen for all fourteen armies of the Republic. This training ground was now enlarged into a National Institute (direct parent of the Conservatoire Nationale founded in 1795) to provide singers and instrumentalists for republican pageants.

Elaborate open-air spectacles designed by the artist, Jacques-Louis David, and involving national and municipal dignitaries, costumed crowds, vast choirs and wind-ensembles, were now mounted on the Champ-de-Mars and elsewhere to mark such annual festivals as the storming of the Bastille (14 July), the death of Louis XVI (21 January), the fall of the Girondins (31 May), and the Festival of the Supreme Being (8 June).

Events of this order brought open-air music to the people at large with a vengeance. The mammoth patriotic cantatas commissioned for such celebrations from Méhul, Gossec, Catel, and their contemporaries helped stimulate a later penchant for showy grand opera and the polychoral œuvres that culminated in the Berlioz Requiem. Similar large-scale works were mounted to celebrate Napoleon's victories and his coronation in 1804. But there was nothing of the promenade concert about all these heavy-handed attempts to make music glorify either the nobility of the revolutionary cause or the splendour of the Empire that succeeded it.

Not until after the Paris uprising of 1830 brought Louis-Phillipe, the citizen-king, to the throne and 'tilted the political balance towards the middle classes' was relaxed concert-going to play a significant part in the wider social life of Paris. Programmes of light classical works and dance music now became extremely popular, with a promenading audience often dancing to the quadrilles that fashion demanded. As we have already remarked, Phillipe Musard initiated this trend, soon attracting several imitators by his success.

From the little that is known of him one point is particularly relevant here. A large number of the quadrilles Musard himself wrote were first published, not in Paris but in London as early as 1817, when he was only twenty-four and as yet unrecognised in France. The supposition must be that their publication took place here because he was at this time himself working in London as a rank-and-file musician. By then the great days of Vauxhall were past. The Gardens were opened on only three nights a week. Concert programmes now included fewer concertos – to make way for quadrilles and waltzes interspersed with items by the military band of the Coldstream Guards. Musical taste was fast changing: lavish firework displays and the tightrope walking of Madame Saqui were now thought necessary to attract audiences.

As a result, what Musard will have witnessed when he visited Vauxhall – it is absurd not to suppose he did so – was a type of entertainment and a repertory far more unbuttoned than in Arne's day. It was one that will have struck him as likely to appeal to pleasure-seeking Parisians. That the new Promenade Concerts he introduced in Paris on his eventual return had about them an unmistakable stamp of Vauxhall should cause little surprise.

Whether or not they still owed anything to their originator's youthful experience in London the Promenade Concerts *à la* Musard introduced at the Lyceum in 1838 started a notable vogue. Several competing series were soon being held under various conductors; and in 1840 Musard was invited to London to direct two seasons himself at Drury Lane and the Lyceum.

By that time his most successful imitator in Paris, Louis Jullien, conductor at the Jardin Turc and twenty years his junior, had been tempted to settle in London. Prompted by Musard's visits Jullien now mounted ever more sensational concerts of his own where the number of performers was often decided only by the size of the stage available. His mastery of the new cult of the show-man-conductor aroused sufficient acclaim for him to remain in England for the next eighteen years.

In the event, Jullien's concerts offered a travesty rather than a rejuvenation of Vauxhall. An orchestra of three hundred players joined by three or four uniformed military bands; a programme of galops, waltzes, quadrilles, overtures and marches that yet found a place for a complete Beethoven symphony (provided with additional wind parts); his own dandified presence clad in tailcoat and white waistcoat, wielding a jewel-encrusted baton; the ceremonious donning of white kid gloves to conduct Beethoven, and reclining on the platform in a velvet and gilt chair between items – all these made Jullien at once a figure of fantasy for the multitude and the target of such satirical caricaturists and George Cruikshank.

Yet despite his musical megalomania Jullien's influence in bringing a wide variety of music to a new public in many parts of the country must not be underestimated. One of his near contemporaries has left this level view of him:

> It is true he frequently resorted to clap-trap (often very needlessly, as his singers and players were excellent), but the fact remains that he was the first to familiarise the masses of Great Britain with the works of Mozart, Beethoven, Mendelssohn, and others, and so proved himself to be a great practical reformer.

Following a series of financial misadventures Jullien at length returned to Paris in 1859 and died prematurely in the following year. Other conductors now continued the promenade tradition he had established. Not until the end of the century were the excesses that had become his hallmarks effaced from London's Promenade Concerts. Then, between 1895 and 1941 under Robert Newton's management and Henry Wood's conducting, greater respectability was gradually restored – though without destroying an underlying light-heartedness that has made what are now affectionately known as 'The Proms' unique.

Nowadays it is only on that unpredictable occasion, The Last Night of the Proms, that anything approaching spectacular excess occurs – and then it takes place off, rather than on, the concert platform. It is not only on such occasions, however, that the spirit of Vauxhall is still clearly perceptible.

BIBLIOGRAPHY/SOURCES

Baptie, D., *A Handbook of Musical Biography* (London, 1883; R/Clarabricken: Boethius Press, 1986) [CTME 17]

Cudworth, C., 'The Vauxhall Lists', *Galpin Society Journal* 20 (1967)

Fétis, F.-J., *Biographie universelle des musiciens* (Paris, Brussels, 1835–44) [CTME 13]

Girouard, M., *The English Town* (New Haven, 1990)

Hillairet, J., *Connaissance du vieux Paris* (Paris, 1969)

Hobsbawm, E. J., *The Age of Revolution: Europe, 1789–1848* (London, 1977)

Lavignac, A., and L. de la Laurencie, ed., *Encyclopédie de la musique* (Paris, 1925–30)

Moritz, P., *Journeys of a German in England* (London, 1795)

Norwich, J. J., *A Taste for Travel* (London, 1985)

Piper, D., *Artists' London* (London, 1982)

Ribeiro, A., *Fashion in the French Revolution* (1988)

Sadie, S., ed., *The New Grove Dictionary of Music and Musicians*, 6th edn (London, 1980)

Salmon, M. C., ed., *P. L. Debucourt*, Masters of the Colour Print, vol. 5 (London, 1929)

Scholes, P. A., *The Mirror of Music* (London, 1947)

Snowden, W. C., *London 200 Years Ago* (London, 1946)

Temperley, N., ed., *The Athlone History of Music in Britain*, vol. 5: *The Romantic Age* (London, 1981)

Weinreb, B., and C. Hibbert, ed., *The London Encyclopaedia* (London, 1983)

Thomas Helmore and
the Anglican Plainsong Revival
[1959]

T HE FIRST STIRRINGS of a new interest in plainsong in England, after its virtual abolition by the Puritans, followed the publication of Vincent Novello's *Evening Service* (1822), with its music for Compline, Vespers and Tenebrae, and the Gregorian hymns. The subsequent appearance of William Dyce's *Order of Daily Service with Plain Tune* (1843) awakened the Anglican Church to its own peculiar heritage in this direction. And Richard Redhead's *Laudes Diurnae* (1843) marked the first attempt to provide an English psalter pointed to the Psalm Tones. But the costliness of Dyce's sumptuous work, and the artificial awkwardness of Redhead's pointing, prevented either book from achieving wide acceptance.

The first practical plainsong psalter in English – the one which under successive editors has retained its influence to this day – was Thomas Helmore's *Psalter Noted* (1849), the direct ancestor of Briggs and Frere's *Manual of Plainsong*.

The circumstances which permitted Helmore to produce a workable Psalter at a time when next to nothing was known of the idiom are not unlike those which enabled Haydn at Esterháza to evolve his classical orchestral manner by experiment.

Upon coming down from Oxford where he graduated in 1840 – an Oxford ringing with the *Tracts for the Times* – Helmore spent two years as Priest-Vicar at Lichfield Cathedral. He was then appointed vice-principal of the training college for teachers which the National Society had newly established at Chelsea, subsequently known as St Mark's College. Under the principalship of the Rev. Derwent Coleridge, this institution developed along near-monastic lines, the young students rising at 5.30 a.m. to undertake domestic duties before attending their classes, with the daily service in the college chapel integral in their training.

An important part of Helmore's duties lay in the ordering of these chapel services, and in the preparation of the students to take a full vocal part in them. There was no organ, the services were sung by the whole assembly, the prayers were intoned, and a select surpliced choir sang anthems and settings from Moxley and Ingram's *Sacred Music* (1842), the publications of the Motett Society, and Boyce's *Collection*. A service of this musically elaborate nature was unique in London at that time, and the college chapel quickly became a place of pilgrimage for the musical and the curious, while minor anti-popery riots occasionally occurred outside in the Fulham Road.

Under the tuition of John Hullah all the students at St Mark's were taught sight-singing, and Helmore would declare, 'Hullah hones them; I strop them.' But in spite of this tuition, the task of transforming these youths into an assembly capable of singing an elaborate, unaccompanied musical service remained formidable.

For the first year the chants for the psalms were taken from Burns's *Gregorian and other Chants* (1841). But many of these proved to be spurious, and in the following year Helmore began experiments in adapting the true Psalm Tones to the words of the English psalter, basing his work largely upon the principles set out by Dyce in the appendix to his *Order of Daily Service*. The opportunity for patient experiment which his appointment at St Mark's provided alone enabled Helmore later to publish his *Psalter Noted*, which he himself described as being 'originally prepared (some six years before its publication) for the special use of St Mark's College'.[1]

The success of the *Psalter Noted* led to the publication of its companion volumes in which the Canticles and remaining sections of the Prayer Book services were set – the whole being issued in 1850 as the *Manual of Plainsong*. A result of greater consequence was the introduction of Helmore to J. M. Neale, then industriously issuing his learned tracts, first hymns and translations from the seclusion of Sackville College. Together they undertook the task of producing the *Hymnal Noted* with the support of the Ecclesiological Society. This book provided for the first time English translations of the ancient Latin hymns, principally from the Sarum books, associated with their original melodies. It was the source of most of the familiar plainsong hymns in use today. The first part appeared in 1851, followed by a concluding part in which Neale, as textual editor, was joined by Benjamin Webb, while Helmore shared the musical editorship with S. S. Greatheed and H. L. Jenner. It was in this second part – with its widened editorial responsibility that *Veni, Emmanuel* appeared – about which so many inaccurate postulations have been made (including its outright attribution to Helmore in *Songs of Praise*), and whose source still remains a mystery.

THE MYSTERY OF *VENI EMMANUEL*

The 'plainsong' tune to 'O come, O come, Emmanuel' has long enjoyed such popularity in England as to carry the hymn itself beyond the High Anglican circles for which it was first intended, across many boundaries of

---

[1] T. Helmore, *St. Mark's Chant Book* (London, 1863), Preface.

churchmanship, to find an established place in the hymnals both of the Roman Catholic and Free Churches. Yet very little is known of the origin of the melody, and accepted accounts of it – even those quoted with the weighty authority of Dearmer and Jacob's *Songs of Praise Discussed* (1933), or Routley's *Music of Christian Hymnody* (1957) – prove upon examination to be readily contestible and must now be refuted.

The former says of it: '*Veni Emmanuel* is found in the *Hymnal Noted* (Pt. II, 1856) where the melody is said to be 'From a French Missal in the National Library, Lisbon'. These Missals have all been examined by the Rev. W. Hilton of the English College, Lisbon, but this melody is not to be found in them.' This, as far as it goes, is indisputable. Almost the whole passage has indeed been taken verbatim from Cowan and Love's earlier treatise, *The Music of the Church Hymnary* (1901), which goes on: 'In all probability it is not a genuine medieval melody, but has been made up of a number of plainsong phrases, most of them being found in settings of the *Kyrie*. The tune in its present form cannot be traced to an earlier source than *The Hymnal Noted*, and the likelihood is therefore that the adaptation was made for that book to suit Dr. Neale's translation.'

This, it will be seen, admits to being conjectural, and clear evidence will be produced to contradict the claim of adaptation. But the music editor of *Songs of Praise Discussed* continues his duplication of Cowan and Love's text, rounding it off with an even less circumscribed hypothesis: '... and the likelihood is therefore that the adaptation *was made by Thomas Helmore* [my italics] for that book to suit Dr. Neale's translation'. The claim is pressed with still less reserve in *Songs of Praise* itself which, alone of all the hymn-books, gives the source as 'Adapted by Thomas Helmore "from a French Missal"'. Dr Erik Routley too, in his *Music of Christian Hymnody* repeats and emphasises this supposition: 'When he deals with genuine plainsong tunes, Helmore is not unreliable. ... And, in one case, it seems that he actually composed a quasi-plainsong tune, *Veni Immanuel*.'

All these commentators appear to have overlooked that the musical editorship of Part II of the *Hymnal Noted* was widened by the appointment of the Revs. H. L. Jenner and S. S. Greatheed – Helmore was no longer alone responsible. Further, that *Veni Emmanuel* was harmonised not by Helmore, but by Greatheed. This weakens the case. But it is sent tumbling down by Helmore's own account – also overlooked it seems. This is contained in the article 'Plainsong' which he subscribed to Stainer and Barrett's *Dictionary of Musical Terms* (1881). Here he states explicitly that *Veni Emmanuel* was 'copied by the late J. M. Neale from a French Missal'. This amounts to a categorical denial of adaptation which cannot be ignored.

It was indeed Neale's custom to take down himself, or secure copies of, texts and music which interested him on his Continental travels.[2] And in 1853, as the result of a commission to write a guide book, he is known to have visited Spain and Portugal. In the resulting *Handbook of Portugal* (1856) he had this to say of the Bibliotheca Publica at Lisbon: 'It is difficult to estimate the number of volumes, since so many duplicates, from the libraries of suppressed convents, *are now in course of distribution and exchange* [my italics]. ... The library is not well arranged, is very dark, and does not possess a general catalogue. Some of the most valuable books lie in heaps without any attempt at order.' If what Helmore has set down is correct – and there seems no reason to doubt him – it was amidst this confusion that Neale took down the melody. And the Rev. W. Hilton's subsequent search may well have failed to locate a particular volume because it was only temporarily housed at Lisbon.

There remains another possibility. While it is not to be questioned, in view of Helmore's statement, that it was Neale himself who made the copy, the source given may be inaccurate. At least one other case is known in which a source cited in the *Hymnal Noted* is questionable. This is *Corde Natus*, there described as 'from a MS. at Wolfenbüttel'. This manuscript, too, has never been traced. But the tune in question appears in *Piae Cantiones* (1582) – a book which Neale and Helmore drew upon for other hymns and carols at this time. And certain errors in the verbal underlaying of *Corde Natus* as it appeared in the *Hymnal Noted* are only to be explained by reference to *Piae Cantiones*.[3]

Neale's memory can have been at fault as to the occasion on which he copied the melody of *Veni Emmanuel*. He visited many libraries, taking copies, while in Spain and Portugal. From Valladolid he writes: 'Then to the Library of the Museum ... I found a Palencia Breviary of 1545, and a Compostella one of 1569, and got some hymns from them ...' All of which leads one to suppose that *Veni Emmanuel* may still be lying, in the book from which Neale copied it, in some Iberian library, awaiting rediscovery.

HELMORE AND THE REVIVAL OF CAROL SINGING

When in 1823 William Hone produced his short treatise on Christmas Carols[4] he expressed a fear that they might 'at no distant period become obsolete'. His list of eighty-nine surviving examples was largely compiled from the crudely printed broadside texts, illustrated with primitive woodcuts, then still published for street-pedlars by Batchelor of Moorfields. To these were added a few personally gathered from country singers. Only the words were recorded.

---

[2] J. M. Neale, *Letters* (n.p., 1910), p. 194.

[3] See *Hymns Ancient and Modern, Historical Edition* (London, 1909), p. 77.

[4] W. Hone, *Ancient Mysteries Described* (London, 1823), pp. 90–106

Tunes were sung from memory, and Hone had not the musical skill to note them: '... in the country I have heard old women sing an old Carol, and brought back the Carol in my pocket with less chance of its escape, than the tune in my head'.

The same romantic delight in the 'Antient', which prompted Hone's research, simultaneously led Davies Gilbert to produce his set of eight *Ancient Christmas Carols, with the tunes to which they were formerly sung in the West of England.* Independently Hone and Gilbert seem to have sensed that the era of the neglect of carols as old-fashioned relics for the entertainment of the poor, was about to give place to their revival as antique pleasantries worthy of the attention of the well-to-do. Ten years later William Sandys published his further collection, *A Selection of Christmas Carols* (1833). And by their publications all these men helped to initiate a revival – which may be said to have reached its zenith after the publication in 1867 of Bramley and Stainer's *Christmas Carols New and Old.*

No doubt partly because both were priests, Thomas Helmore and John Mason Neale lent added authority, and gave great impetus to this revival when they brought out in a popular form a further range of attractive carols taken from a previously untapped source. While examining early documents for material for the *Hymnal Noted*, they were given by the British Minister in Stockholm a rare copy of Nyland's *Piae Cantiones* of 1582. Besides hymns, this contained a number of carols, and some of these Helmore and Neale decided to prepare for English use, thus deliberately extending the repertory beyond the purely indigenous.

Upon the completion of Part 1 of the *Hymnal*, they turned to these carols and produced a set of twelve *Carols for Christmastide*, in 1853, and a further twelve *Carols for Eastertide* in 1854. Helmore's task was to decipher, transcribe and harmonise the melodies, and so enable Neale to provide rhythmic texts, which he elected to make 'for the most part, in imitation of the general tone of ancient Carols'.

Of these, his version of *In Dulci Jubilo* made that early German carol widely known in this country as *Good Christian Men, Rejoice* – in which form it is still often heard, although Pearsall's superb choral arrangement gave us something much closer to the original macaronic text. A comparison of these two versions of *In Dulci Jubilo* reveals how considerably Neale departed from the original in some of these carols. And many later authorities have expressed regret at this. But it seems clear that he did so in order to provide words for simple folk, like those who first sang them.

Hence it is not perhaps surprising that the quality which seems a shortcoming in *Good Christian Men* should have obtained for another carol in the same collection overwhelming and lasting popularity. This is *Good King Wenceslas* which, as everyone now realises, was originally a spring carol – *Tempus Adest Floridum* – but which every carol party yet insists on sinking to Neale's words.

Helmore's active part in the revival of the carol was not limited to his work as editor. Already established as a leading authority on church music – the very name Helmore was synonymous with plainsong for two generations at least – he addressed audiences all over the country on the various aspects of choral worship. In the course of these talks the carol was not forgotten. And it was as the admitted authority upon the subject that, towards the end of his life, he subscribed the article on Carols to Julian's *Dictionary of Hymnology*.

His intense purposefulness, tremendous energy, and the curiously contradictory blend of sternness and emotionalism which marked his relationship with his pupils – Arthur Sullivan among them remarked it – make Thomas Helmore appear a prototype Victorian. His energy never left him. When at the age of nearly eighty he was still striding about London, habitually walking from Chelsea to the Strand to visit his barber, his doctor suggested curtailing these activities. Helmore responded by giving up playing the flute.

Today, a century after the appearance of his major contributions to the literature of church music – in psalm, hymn and carol – and remote from the battles of churchmanship that surrounded them, we are able to appreciate the value of Helmore's pioneer labours, to note his understandable errors as well as his achievements, and to pay him homage.

Notes from Two French Organ Lofts

[1961]

To an English organist there is something fascinatingly exotic about the liturgical music at the Cathedral of Notre Dame in Paris. And it provides an experience which I seldom fail to renew when the opportunity arises. The bold antiphonal outbursts of the great west-end organ which interrupt the accompanied chanting in the chancel make dramatic use of the vastness of the building in a manner reminiscent of the Venetian *concerti ecclesiastici* of Gabrieli. From the crowded nave the impact of these improvised organ interludes is remarkable; I found myself professionally curious as to how such skilful synchronisation – performers at either end of the cathedral taking over instantly from each other – was achieved.

On a recent visit I had the privilege of attending a service in the loft of the great west-end organ. It was a memorable experience. Reached by way of a stone spiral stair set in the south-west tower, the loft itself is vaster and very much higher than its counterpart in English cathedrals. Unlike them, too, it is invariably the meeting-place at Mass of a sizable assembly of pupils and professional and social acquaintances of the *maître*; there is something strongly reminiscent of the *levée* about the occasion.

The *maître* (on this occasion not M. Cochereau himself, who was in America) – the *maître* presides – that is the only apposite term – at a detached Cavaillé-Coll console, raised on a substantial tiered *tribune*, so as to face the high altar and command full view of the vista towards the east. In the remote chancel the mass proceeds – the plainsong sung by men's voices accompanied by the altar-organ, the polyphonic settings sung by an unaccompanied choir of boys and men. The first organ interludes occur during the Credo. This is sung to plainsong, but divided at the paragraphs by pungent modal outbursts of extemporised, deliberately 'primitive' homophonic organ music from the west end. These were played during my visit largely on manual reeds at 16′, 8′ and 4′ – a registration which seemed thick to English ears, but which filled the cathedral with a pageantry of sound – and as each ended the choir instantly took up the plainsong at their conductor's signal. At other times during the mass the great organ played further interludes – while the celebrant was officiating at the altar, and during the communion of the people. Some of these were extemporised, some consisted of chorale-preludes of Bach, a toccata by Muffat, and a prelude of César Franck.

At the conclusion of the mass, as the priest's procession left the high altar, the organ burst into a final extemporisation. This seemed at first a typical toccata in the French manner, with a busy repetitive figure on the manuals to which the pedal reeds were added *ostinato* fashion. But it quickly developed into something quite extravagantly unorthodox, with daring discordant embellishments and several *glissandi* from top to bottom of the pedal-board. In another, smaller building it might have sounded merely cacophonous, but here it seemed no more than daring. One was reminded curiously of the bold primitive brilliance of the illuminations of Froissart's *Chronicle*.

On another Sunday morning the organ loft at Saint-Sulpice provided the same atmosphere of the *levée*, its smaller size making it appear congested with those privileged to be there. But everything else about the occasion was quite different. M. Marcel Dupré matched the Italianate elegance of the architecture with corresponding musical suavity. A noble, near-motionless figure at the console, he surveys the drama at the altar dispassionately, and reflects this in his extemporisations. All the organ music at this service was, as far as I could tell, improvised. There is no robed choir at Saint-Sulpice, and the mass was sung in unison by the congregation at large to the conducting of a priest near the altar. The final extemporisation to High Mass was a splendid formal fugue *à la Franck*.

The organs themselves differed in these two churches. At Notre Dame, the reeds sounded almost rough to English ears. At St Sulpice, while they lacked this quality, they were notably fiercer than one would find in this country. Even orchestral reeds were extremely telling, and as used by M. Dupré during my visit as solo stops, but played at 16', 8' and 4', the effect was most unexpected and striking. Each organ, and the style in which it was played, matched the architectural style and atmosphere of its building in a manner as remarkable as it was appropriate.

William Dyce

[1964]

T HE CENTENARY EXHIBITION of William Dyce's paintings held at
Agnew's earlier this year served to nudge church musicians into recalling
the contribution which that prodigally talented but elusive early Victorian worthy made in their own field. Whenever the Responses to the Commandments
are sung in Merbecke's *Communion Service*, it is music composed by William
Dyce the painter which is being performed.

The Dyce Papers among the archives at the Aberdeen Art Gallery reveal
something of the background to that paradox. An MA at the age of sixteen,
Dyce had gone on to read theology with the intention of entering the priesthood, but the very range of his natural talents soon led him to abandon his academic studies in favour of the career of a professional painter. Thenceforward
the three main interests of his youth – 'painting, music, and the Church' –
were to exert their combined influence upon his activities. The religious subjects which he found so congenial in his meticulously executed canvases display
one aspect of that merging of influences. Another is to be found in his scholarly
endeavours for the reform of church music.

Early in 1841, a year after his appointment as Professor of the Theory of
Fine Art at King's College, London, Dyce turned his attention to the subject
of church music. At the age of twelve he had taught himself to play the organ
and 'could extemporise with great facility'. And in 1841 circumstances had
made serious endeavour towards musical reform in the Church particularly
apposite. By that time the seeds sown by the early Tractarians were springing to vigorous life; and the mammoth singing classes of Hullah and Mainzer
had made the citizens of London more musically conscious than they had ever
been.

With the support of Gladstone, a fellow High Churchman, Dyce founded
the Motett Society for the study and practice of church music of the 16th
and 17th centuries, and for republishing selections of standard cathedral
music. From November 1841 the Society issued an imposing series of Services,
Anthems, and Motets, including works by Tallis, Gibbons, Palestrina, and
Vittoria, many of the Latin works having English texts provided by Dyce
himself. The influence of the Society's publications, at a time when the price
of printed music was high, and the current church repertory thin, was very
considerable.

It was not only with the field covered by the publications of the Motett
Society that Dyce was concerned; his aim was not limited to providing music

suitable for choirs. He sought also to make available authentic versions of
ancient music for congregational participation. With that intention he set
about the study of medieval plainsong, seeking in particular the means of
adapting the Latin psalm tones to English words. His model there was to be
the practice of Merbecke as revealed in the *Book of Common Prayer Noted* of
1550. In July 1841 Dyce thus sought the aid of J. H. Newman at Oriel College,
Oxford, to obtain permission to consult the rare copy of Merbecke's Prayer
Book treasured in the library of Brasenose College. Two years later James
Burns published Dyce's beautiful new version of that book with red initials
and staves, engraved margins, and the whole text set in black-letter, together
with copious notes, and an extended preface and appendix.

Subsequent revisions of the Prayer Book had made much of Merbecke's
original music inappropriate to the existing liturgy; and Dyce had bravely
undertaken to remedy that situation by adaptation or more drastic means
where he found such a course necessary. Every instance where alteration
had taken place was recorded in his appendix, where he argued the merits
of each case. Defending his general course of action, Dyce maintained that
since the labour of Merbecke himself had not been that of invention, but of
adapting, correcting, or simplifying music already in use, similar action upon
his own part was equally justifiable. 'If anyone nowadays,' he argued, 'understands the conditions of Gregorian music sufficiently to become an inventor of new compositions in that kind, there is no reason either against the
exercise of his skill, or against the employment of his productions in divine
service.'

To illustrate an example of Merbecke's own adaptation in the Kyrie, Dyce
quoted from a Requiem in the *Sarum Manual* of 1543:

This passage may be clearly recognsed as the source of Merbecke's English Kyrie.
Its influence remains as clear in the subsequent adaptation which Dyce undertook to accommodate the revised text, 'Lord have mercy upon us, and incline
our hearts to keep this law':

People. Lord, have mercy upon us, and write all these thy laws in our hearts, we beseech thee.

People. Lord, have mercy upon us, and incline our hearts to keep this law.

At a meeting of the Motett Society after Dyce's death in 1864, the chairman reminded members that William Dyce was not only an accomplished musician but a learned scholar, an eminent theologian, a skilful disputant, and a painter of the highest repute. The recent Centenary Exhibition of his works has seen him acknowledged as one of the most universally accomplished men of his generation, and the creator of a number of works which are among the masterpieces of British nineteenth-century painting. A tribute today to Dyce's part in reviving the unique Anglican choral tradition seems no less to be required.

Walmisley's Psychedelic Magnificat
[1980]

T HE *Evening Service* in D minor, which Thomas Attwood Walmisley wrote in 1855, holds an established place among the classics of English church music. Noted for its dignity, spaciousness and that indefinable quality of style which prevents a work 'dating', at once conservative yet highly original, the D minor *Service* is unmatched by any of Walmisley's other pieces and has always appeared on that account something of an enigma. In his book *The Singing Church*, C. H. Phillips exclaims, 'How this work of genius came to be written by the author of most of the anthems of Walmisley is a mystery perhaps solvable by the devotees of reincarnation.'[1] The present article offers a solution less supernatural but quite as strange: *Walmisley in D minor* was composed under the influence of opium.

The effect of drugs on human utterance and artistic expression has been widely observed, from the Delphic oracle to Aldous Huxley; from the *Carceri* of Piranesi to the portraits of Francis Bacon. Perhaps the most familiar and closely documented instance is provided by Samuel Taylor Coleridge's *Kubla Khan*. In his preface to that remarkable poem, Coleridge described its genesis. Then in ill-health, he had retired to a lonely farmhouse on Exmoor. Laudanum had been prescribed, from the effects of which he fell asleep in his chair while reading a passage in 'Purchases Pilgrimage' which ran, 'Here the Khan Kubla commanded a palace to be built ...'

> The author [he wrote] continued for about three hours in a profound sleep, at least of the external senses, during which time he has the most vivid confidence that he could not have composed less than from two to three hundred lines ... without any sensation or consciousness of effort. On awakening, he appeared to himself to have a distinct recollection of the whole, and taking his pen, ink and paper, instantly and eagerly wrote down the lines that are here preserved ...

After an exhaustive examination of Coleridge's note books, J. L. Lowes has shown[2] that his poetry was commonly based upon jottings made during his omnivorous reading. Thus, he claims, to follow Coleridge through his reading is to 'retrace the obliterated vestiges of creation'.[3] But while the width of his

---

[1] C. H. Phillips, *The Singing Church* (London, 1945), p. 166.
[2] J. L. Lowes, *The Road to Xanadu* (London, 1927), *passim*.
[3] *Ibid*. p. 37.

reading enabled a poet who had never been to sea to produce from his imagination the convincing and fantastic scenery of *The Ancient Mariner*, with *Kubla Khan* the case was a different one. There, the results of Coleridge's reading were transmuted into a phantasmagoria without the intervention of a waking intelligence, intent upon a plan, to obliterate or blur them. Coleridge himself declared that he published the resulting poem with some misgiving as 'a psychological curiosity' rather than on the grounds of any supposed poetic merits.[4]

Walmisley, too, was perplexed by his D minor *Service* and the story goes that 'he at first intended to put it into the fire'.[5] Nor does the resemblance between the two situations cease there. Those further affinities, however, will not be pursued profitably until evidence is produced that Walmisley – the respected Professor of Music at Cambridge – was addicted to opium. Expressed in such brusque terms, the suggestion perhaps appears simply outrageous. But we must remember that, until comparatively recent times and the introduction of aspirin and other analgesics, tincture of opium – commonly called laudanum – was the commonplace remedy employed by sufferers from rheumatism, toothache and kindred ailments. As such it was readily and regularly purchased – notably, in this connection, by the fen-dwellers who came into Cambridge from the surrounding damp-infested countryside on market days. Among those who passed from an occasional use of the drug to allay pain or insomnia, to its habitual use as an amnesiac, was Walmisley himself. So much is clear from the cautiously expressed but unmistakeably reproving words of one of his biographers:

> To a highly-strung organization such as Walmisley possessed, the desire to be free from the burning current of his thoughts which led he knew not whither, suggested, alas! an unwise indulgence in lethal remedies. His pleasures may have been thus augmented, but his life was shortened, and he died comparatively a young man, having completed his forty-second year all but four days. His death took place on 17 January, 1856.[6]

Walmisley died prematurely, then, less than a year after writing the D minor Service; and that work thus unquestionably belong to the period of his 'unwise indulgence'.

That being so, other evidence to support the theory that this particular piece was the product of an opium dream becomes admissable. Besides Coleridge, another nineteenth-century writer who recorded his own experience of opium was Thomas de Quincey. And from de Quincey's detailed accounts of his

---

[4] Prefatory Note to 'Kubla Khan', *Poems*, vol. 1, p. 295.

[5] Phillips, *Singing Church*, p. 166.

[6] J. S. Bumpus, *History of English Cathedral Music*, 2 vols. (London, 1900), p. 477.

opium dreams more can be learned of the nature of the narcotic dream-state and the 'visions' which accompanied it. 'Such dreams', he declared, 'repeat with marvellous accuracy the longest succession of phenomena derived either from reading or from actual experience ... The symbol restored the theme, but under new combinations of form or colouring; gives back, but changes; restores, but idealises.'[7]

With these observations in mind, it now becomes appropriate to consider Walmisley's setting of *Magnificat*. As 'the strange beauty' of its opening verses unfolds, the analytical ear becomes aware that it is the boldly antiphonal structure of the music that largely accounts for its individual flavour. The unison verses for men's voices relentlessly alternating with lighter-textured three-part verses for trebles and altos strike one as quite uncharacteristic of the period. Structurally, this is not at all the style of the mid-nineteenth century; instead, it echoes the pattern of the plainchant and *fauxbourdon* settings of three hundred years before:

[7] T. de Quincey, *Autobiographic Sketches* (London, 1853), p. 28.

Now Walmisley, we know, was a musical scholar more deeply versed than most of his contemporaries in the music of the past. Moreover, he was familiar from his childhood in Westminster with the cathedral repertoire, and was also accustomed to entertain his friends at Cambridge with 'clever imitations of the fantasies of Bull and Gibbons'.[8] Had he wished to do so, then, he certainly possessed the technique to produce a deliberate *pastiche* setting.

We are able to feel confident that no such enterprise would seriously have entered his head. The modal style of the sixteenth century held small appeal for the mid-nineteenth century churchgoer; and Mendelssohn spoke for his musical contemporaries when he described his disappointment with the traditional *fauxbourdon*-type service music of Holy Week at the Sistine Chapel in 1831. The Allegri *Miserere*, he declared, lacked for him the unearthly quality earlier listeners had claimed for it; and the Victoria *Passion* he found 'trivial and monotonous'.[9]

Consequently, what the men sing in the unison verses of Walmisley's D minor *Service* is emphatically not plainchant; nor do the responsive voices answer in modal harmonies. Instead, a change, a transmutation of the kind referred to by de Quincey, has occurred. What results is an 'idealised' *fauxbourdon* setting in contemporary attire. It must appear at least remarkable that this enigmatic work, known to have been composed at a time when Walmisley was influenced by 'an unwise indulgence in lethal remedies', should have about it so much of that atmosphere of transmutation described by de Quincey and demonstrated in *Kubla Khan*. But that is not the end of the matter.

Although the present article is thought to comprise the first public statement of the opium theory to explain the strange qualities of the D minor *Service*, it is possible to suppose that C. H. Phillips was also reaching toward precisely the same opinion when he wrote *The Singing Church* a generation ago. There, after referring to Walmisley's D minor *Service* as 'one of those extraordinary and unaccountable products which sometimes appear in art', he went on 'Here was something rich and strangely beautiful such as had seldom been achieved; even Walmisley himself could hardly understand it. It might be called his "Kubla Khan" ...'[10]

The direct reference to Coleridge's opium-induced poem is startling in that context. But this should not make us fail to observe the highly significant but surely subliminal reference to Shakespeare's 'Full fathom five' which occurs in the previous sentence:

---

[8] Bumpus, *History of English Cathedral Music*, p. 477.

[9] F. Mendelssohn-Bartholdy, *Letters from Italy and Switzerland* (London, 1862), pp. 132, 183.

[10] Phillips, *Singing Church*, p. 166.

> Nothing ... doth fade,
> But doth suffer a sea-change
> Into *something rich and strange* ...

Once Walmisley's *Magnificat* has been accepted as a musical equivalent of Coleridge's *Kubla Khan* – the abnormal product of an abnormal nature under abnormal conditions[11] – hitherto inexplicable features of its style and provenance are readily explained. At the same time, indeed, another longstanding puzzle presented by this work can then be solved.

Towards the end of the *Gloria* the composer has added a footnote identifying the bass in the organ part as an extract from an *Agnus Dei* by Dumont. Few thoughtful musicians confronted by this unusual feature in the published score can have failed to wonder why a composer, so inspired as Walmisley shows himself to have been in this piece, should have found it necessary at the climax of the work to insert a few bars lifted from an obscure Belgian organist – and to acknowledge the fact in the score.

But if we accept the opium theory to explain the unusual nature of this work as a whole, the incorporation of that extract is also explained – and thus reinforces the theory – for the substance of an opium 'vision' is an assemblage of material recovered from the unconscious memory. As de Quincey put it, such dreams repeat with marvellous accuracy memories 'waiting to be revealed when the obscuring daylight shall have withdrawn'.[12] Walmisley, then, has not consciously *inserted* this extract from Dumont. On waking and writing down the content of his dream, he has *recognised* part of its material, and wonderingly identified its source upon the manuscript. Small wonder that the piece, unpublished before his death, perplexed him; or that Walmisley considered throwing the manuscript into the fire!

The theories presented in this article first began to form themselves in the writer's mind many years back at a time when, as a parish church organist, he sometimes accompanied *Walmisley in D minor* at Evensong. After reading J. L. Lowes' study in the ways of the imagination, *The Road to Xanadu*, some ten years ago. he became more convinced that Walmisley's masterpiece paralleled Coleridge's. Since that time he has found numerous excuses for not publishing his opinion to a wider audience than a few of his former undergraduate students at Chelsea. But now that the effort has at last been made to organise

---

[11] J. M. Robertson, *New Essays towards a Critical Method* (London, 1897), p. 187

[12] T. de Quincey, *Confessions of an English Opium Eater*, Camelot Classics (London, 1888), p. 90.

these ideas on paper, it will perhaps not be amiss to add two further brief points – both matters of speculation.

As the perhaps somewhat catchpenny title of this article suggests, it is only the *Magnificat* in this Service which Walmisley is believed to have 'dreamed'. The companion *Nunc Dimittis* is thought to have been consciously composed afterwards as a matching piece, complete with a symmetrical, though shorter and almost apologetic extract from Dumont in its *Gloria*. It will be seen that the *fauxbourdon* pattern is followed less consistently in the *Nunc Dimittis*, where the music also appears rather less intensely felt.

As to the identity of the 'model' *fauxbourdon*, retrieved from Walmisley's memory, upon which the *Magnificat* itself was founded, short of identifying and combing Walmisley's original library, it is not possible to do more than conjecture. Let us do so – and wildly! Walmisley was a pupil of his godfather, Thomas Attwood. Attwood had been Mozart's 'favourite' pupil. As a child, Mozart had taken down from memory Allegri's *Miserere* after hearing the work rehearsed in the Sistine Chapel. The story was an attractive one which inevitably passed on from teacher to pupil over the generations and gave to the work a special aura. Can Walmisley's *Magnificat* be a nineteenth-century English reincarnation of the Allegri *Miserere*?

The Hymn-Singing American
[1982]

T HE FIRST PUBLISHED COLLECTION of wholly American music was a
book of psalm tunes, *The New-England Psalm-Singer*, written by William
Billings and published in Boston in 1770. It represents the first milestone in the
musical progress of a new country and reveals the important place that simple
music for worship occupied during the formative years since settlement began.

The Puritans who landed at Plymouth Rock 150 years earlier brought with
them their Protestant psalm tunes, and many of those who sailed from Delft
in 1620 were accounted 'very expert in music'. But the religious conviction that
had prompted their voyage to the New World dominated their lives when they
arrived. For them, sacred and secular represented opposite poles, and little in
the way of folk music, still less in instrumental music, was at first produced. The
metrical psalm, sole musical feature of the Calvinist order of service, became
the central musical feature of their lives. As settlement grew and amenities
increased to include the printing press, it is significant that almost the first
book to be published in America was the *Bay Psalm Book* (1640).

Yet many of the tunes sung by the Pilgrim Fathers were soon forgotten by
their sons, and a century later fewer than ten tunes were commonly sung at
public worship in New England. Indeed, a superstition grew that it was sinful
for a congregation to sing anything more than these. And in spite of the efforts
of more enlightened ministers to combat it, dogmatic resistance to learning
new tunes, either by rote or through learning to 'sing from notes', persisted.
Thomas Symmes published a sermon on *The Reasonableness of Regular Singing
or Singing by Note* in 1720, which was followed by John Eliot's *Brief Discourse
Concerning Regular Singing* in 1725. John Tufts, the more venturesome pastor
of Newbury, was so bold as to publish his own practical instruction book on
sight-singing, *A Very Plain & Easy Instruction to the Art of Singing Psalm Tunes*,
in 1721. In such ways opposition was slowly overcome, allowing New England to
lead the way in forming singing-schools of the type William Billings founded
and for which his pioneer collection of 123 original tunes was designed.

Meanwhile other settlers were arriving from different parts of persecuted
Europe to make their homes in the New World. Musically prominent among
them, and again bound together by shared religious conviction, were Moravian
Brethren who settled in Pennsylvania in 1741 and North Carolina in 1753. Not
only was hymn singing an integral traditional feature of their worship, but
their views on the use of the organ and other instruments in the service was
less narrow than the Puritans' and Calvinists'. Their hymn settings were thus

elaborately harmonised and stood in bold contrast to the plain psalm tunes of New England.

The religious tolerance shown to settlers in Pennsylvania encouraged others among Europe's persecuted sects to settle there. Pietists, Baptists, Lutherans, Mennonites and many others soon founded communities, bringing their chorales and hymns. Huguenot refugees had already made Charleston and New Orleans their home after expulsion from France in 1685; with them came the subtly rhythmic Genevan tunes now forbidden in their homeland. The scattered settlements along the Atlantic coast after the mid-18th century were thus as distinguishable by the religious songs of their inhabitants as by language.

The long chain of events that eventually enabled the descendants of those early settlers to think of themselves as Americans rather than foreign refugees only added to the quantity and diversity of the music designed for use in public worship. To an increasing variety of denominational hymns were now added folk hymns and spirituals as well as the idiosyncratic revival and gospel songs of the camp meeting. But, like the people who now sang them, these new tunes had become essentially American.

The task of making from this mass of material a selection to typify the American hymn is an unenviable one. Obviously it calls for familiarity with a large number of musical miniatures of widely varying standards. That not only purely musical judgment is required is less obvious. The compilation of historical notes on the hymns chosen and the addition of biographical notes on authors and composers also call for highly specialised skills only found among the diminishing number of those who recognise the integrity of church music. These are the qualities that the three editors have brought to their anthology *American Hymns, Old and New.*[1]

It is perhaps tempting, but certainly misleading, for a reader on this side of the Atlantic to interpret the title of the anthology as a paraphrase of that given to its familiar Anglican near-namesake, *Hymns, Ancient & Modern*. Until he has turned some of its pages, such a reader risks being misled in other respects as well. For what is assembled and discussed here as American necessarily has its roots widely spread throughout the Old World, and what is categorised here as a hymn often stretches the meaning of that hitherto precise term to desperate lengths. Rather than beat about for a definition to suit the word in its new context, it is as well to accept that what is under consideration here is American religious song. Some such umbrella term becomes essential to embrace the 625 examples included in this panoramic survey covering four centuries and ranging from the austere to the rumty-tum.

The idea of producing what is described as a 'historical singing book' evolved

---

[1] 2 vols., edited by Albert Christ-Janer, Charles W. Hughes and Carleton Sprague Smith (New York: Columbia University Press, 1980), 1459pp.

only gradually. The original aim, long treasured by the first of the three compilers, had been to assemble and publish a collection of new hymns commissioned from contemporary poets and composers. With the co-operation of Roy Harris the venture was begun in 1952, resulting in the substantial group of pieces that now form the book's last section. Varying from the four-square to the tonally and rhythmically complex, many of them are more suited to choir than congregation. And whether modern American churchgoers are as obstinate about accepting novelty as were their New England forebears remains to be seen.

As assembly of these commissioned hymns proceeded, it was decided (wisely, one feels) to publish them not in isolation but 'displayed against the rich background of hymns which the colonies and the United States could supply'. To achieve this, two further compilers lent their musicological skills, selecting and fully annotating texts and tunes sung at different times and in different parts of the land to create a chronological tapestry.

The resulting publication consequently becomes somewhat reminiscent of the Historical Edition of *Hymns, Ancient & Modern*, but the form it takes is closer to that of *Songs of Praise Discussed*, where hymnal and glossary are bound separately. Those who have found enlightenment and pleasure in such pages will be equally rewarded here. The standard of scholarship is generally high, but at least one observation must not pass without comment. 'In the seventeenth and eighteenth centuries', says the Introduction, 'the tenor frequently sang the tune rather than the soprano.' It is also true that many hymns printed in open score during the 18th and early 19th centuries had the tune on the third staff down. But that was done to bring soprano and bass lines close together for the organist's convenience, not to require the tenor to sing the melody. Mid-nineteenth-century manuals specifically warned singers against misinterpreting this earlier functional layout, pointing out that tenor and soprano parts had been interchanged.

Also somewhat misleading is the inclusion of a number of tunes from other lands to provide settings for devotional verses not hitherto sung as hymns. Orlando Gibbons's *Song 1* is thus married to verses from Thomas Tillam's poem *Upon the First Sight of New England*. The tune fits well and is roughly contemporary, but the musical reader must be alert for such interpolations.

The compilers have not allowed serious scholarship to exclude from their notes the welcome sense of humour that necessarily illuminates the organ loft: we learn that the members of a sect who had announced the Second Coming as due in 1843, only to be disappointed, promptly produced a new couplet running, 'O praise the Lord, we do not fear/To tell the world He'll come next year'.

Although it is impossible (and certainly was not in the minds of the compilers) to imagine *American Hymns, Old and New* settling comfortably in English choir-stalls, these two handsome volumes will make welcome and worthy neighbours for Julian, Frere, Frost, Dearmer and Lightwood on the shelves of a thoroughgoing music library.

Charity Children: Singing for their Supper
[1984]

'NOT for a long time', wrote Haydn in his diary, 'has music moved me so much.' Few would guess that the composer's pleasure sprang from the singing of hundreds of London schoolchildren in June 1791.

During the eighteenth century many so-called charity schools had been founded in English towns through bequests and donations. The children attending them were marched to church every Sunday wearing their school uniforms. Seated in the organ gallery under the supervision of a beadle, they then led the singing of the metrical psalms which formed the main musical feature of the service in most parish churches. To equip them for this role charity children, as they were commonly called, were taught a few common tunes at school. This rote-learning formed their only musical instruction, and the result was seldom edifying. Yet it was a massed choir of charity children which had so moved Haydn in 1791. The custom of bringing them together annually to sing originated almost at the beginning of the century.

In 1704 it was resolved that the children from all the charity schools of London should assemble to sing a festival service together at St Andrew's Church, Holborn. This event was to provide them with both an outing and the encouragement of singing *en masse* under the direction of a more capable musician and to the accompaniment of a finer organ than most of their own parishes could provide. The success of that first festival led to its repetition the following year at the larger neighbouring church of St Sepulchre, where it was held annually until 1738. After that it took place at Christ Church, Newgate Street, until 1801, when the growing numbers of the children and the popularity of the event itself led to its transfer to St Paul's Cathedral. There it was to remain an annual event throughout most of the nineteenth century.

The idea of holding the annual meeting of the charity children at the metropolitan cathedral seems to have arisen almost by chance. When plans were being made to celebrate George III's return to health in 1789, a thanksgiving service was arranged at the cathedral which the monarch would attend in state. To lend grandeur to the occasion, it was decided to add to the cathedral choir the forces of the charity children, now grown in number from a few hundred to several thousand, who should join in singing the psalms and hymns. A huge circular scaffold was erected to seat them in tiers beneath the dome, while the cathedral choir occupied seats in front of the organ, still situated in those days on a screen across the chancel arch.

Much of the success on that occasion, which led to the permanent transfer of the annual meeting to St Paul's, was undoubtedly due to the power of so unusual a number of young voices, to which the astonishing acoustic properties of the vast dome lent a new quality. The love for grandiose musical effects which we often attribute to the Victorians was, in fact, engendered well before their day at the mammoth Handel Commemoration performances in Westminster Abbey in 1784. No fewer than 525 performers took part. And at similar concerts given in the abbey during the next few years that number was increased to over a thousand. Sheer volume of sound had become a new musical luxury; it is no accident that the odd term 'grand crash' appears so often in the contemporary accounts of orchestral performances during the years Haydn was in London.

Given the weight of thousands of admittedly untrained young voices setting the echoes rolling under the dome of St Paul's, we need add only the influence of sentimentality to see how the annual meetings of the charity children earned their regular place in the London calendar – as well as the elderly Haydn's emotional tribute. Some such explanation is called for, since the children's usual weekly performances in their own churches earned nothing but protest and abuse from contemporary writers. Bishop Gibson of London charged his diocesan clergy to undertake the urgent reform of parochial psalmody in 1724. His successor, Bishop Porteus, repeated that challenge more weightily in 1790, appending a particular reference to the limitations of charity children in the enforced role of choristers:

> In London and a part of Westminster this business is in great measure confined to the charity children, who though they exert their little abilities to sing their Maker's praises in the best manner they can, yet for want of right instruction to modulate their voices properly, almost constantly strain them to so high a pitch as to disgust and offend the ear, and repel instead of raising the devout affections of the hearers. And it is generally a contest between them and the organ which shall be the loudest, and give most pain to the ear.

That emphatic condemnation leaves little room for doubt. Not every church, however, was served by a choir of charity children. Where congregations were sufficiently affluent to subscribe to their fees, it was common to find a professional choir of adult singers tucked away behind a curtain in the organ loft. Poorer parishes often had no choral assistance beyond the parish clerk and his pitchpipe.

Yet there was one choir of children in London which regularly drew large attendances to the services which they sang in the chapel of the Foundling Hospital. First established by Thomas Coram in 1739, the Foundling Hospital was created for the education and shelter of young children, accepted as babies abandoned by their parents. As the first inmates grew up, larger premises were built and a chapel was added in 1747, which all the older children attended. Handel presented the organ, and the Foundling Chapel was soon made a centre for professional musical performances, including *Messiah* with the composer himself at the organ. The younger J. C. Smith, Handel's pupil and amanuensis, became the first regular organist at the chapel in 1750. In that musical atmosphere it was not surprising to find that more than usual attention was given to the singing of the children in preparation for the chapel service.

One of the first signs of that special care appears in the minutes of the general committee where, on 20 March 1758, we find recorded 'that Tom Greville, a boy of this Hospital, born blind, be taught music by the assistant to the organist of the chapel ... at the price of two guineas per quarter'. Two or three other blind children were similarly treated, and attention was thus drawn to the question of teaching the children generally. Soon, to the 'admirable choir' which the children formed, were added some half-dozen professional voices, the donations of the public attending the musical services which resulted 'contributed greatly to the prosperity of the institution'. An account of the Foundling Chapel accompanying the illustration reproduced here, which appeared in 1851, speaks of the mingled crowd of the pious, the wealthy and the fashionable which occupied the gallery facing that filled with the children themselves. The boys in their dark costume on the right, the girls in white on the left, sit on either side of the organ, in front of which are the professional soloists. 'In that gallery', the account goes on, 'centre the attractions which make the Foundling Hospital Chapel one of the most popular of London places of worship.'

While the singing of individual parish choirs of charity children could offer little to compare with the choral splendours of the Foundling Hospital Chapel, the massive effect achieved at their annual festival service at St Paul's continued to fill the cathedral for many years. But by the 1830s a few critics had begun to voice objections to that event, based on other than musical grounds. The exhibition before their neighbours of street processions of boys and girls known to be educated 'on the parish' was thought to cause unwarranted embarrassment to their unfortunate parents. And while the ancient dress of cassock and yellow stockings worn by the boys of Christ's Hospital seemed an archaism befitting English respect for tradition, the 18th-century dress of the charity child now appeared merely old-fashioned. Not least among other objections was the fact that, obliged to leave school early in the morning for rehearsal in the cathedral, the children remained without a meal until they reached their schools again after the long day's proceedings were over. All these matters were brought before the public in some sardonic lines published under a bitter title in the *Comic Almanack* for 1838:

The Martyrdom of St Paul's

Oh, Charity! celestial dame! – I cannot call thee maid,
While ev'ry year thy children dear make such a grand parade.
The girls all clad in worsted gowns, mob caps, and aprons white,
Like Lilliputian grandmothers, – a venerable sight:
The boys in pretty blanket coats of green or brickdust red,
With tawny leather breeches, and a thrum cap on their head;
And then that splendid pewter badge, worth all the rest beside;
No medal worn by hero could inspire more honest pride.
While to the neighbours they're a mark of pleasant observation,
How must their happy mothers bless a parish education!
Oh! merry day of jubilee to every little sinner,
When ev'ry one receives a bun and goes without a dinner.

On the other hand, one of George Cruikshank's most charming illustrations, dating from this period, records in a light-hearted and affectionate manner seldom found in his caricatures the departure of a group of charity children for St Paul's. The whole scene is skilfully handled: first come the self-important beadles, parish clerk, usher and churchwardens; then the boys, one of them receiving from an anxious mother something to eat during the day, another getting only a reprimanding prod from an officious marshal in the doorway; finally, the girls in their mob caps making their way down the stairs to bring up the rear. Nothing here suggests disapproval – unless it be the portrayal of the smug Dickensian figures who lead the way.

The charity children's meetings were to continue for many more years with

Charity children on their way to St Paul's, a caricature by George Cruikshank

renewed support. By mid-century between five and six thousand children were assembling annually at St Paul's on their curious wooden amphitheatre. The area which it surrounded was 'filled with persons of rank, fashion and intellectual distinction', while as many of the public as could obtain tickets thronged the nave. In 1851 Berlioz took the opportunity, while in London, to judge the musical exhibits at the Great Exhibition, to attend that year's meeting of the charity children, finding it as moving as Haydn had done. Yet the old paradox remained: though the splendid effect of the children's massed singing regularly earned the praise of observers, their raucous performance, Sunday by Sunday in their own churches, was described by another contemporary as 'the compulsory scream of the charity children'.

But the era of the charity choir was nearing its end. Churches everywhere were now introducing surpliced choristers. And, in the end, the annual festival at St Paul's was to be discontinued for the most prosaic of reasons. The erection of the cumbersome scaffold tiers in the cathedral each year always led to the closing of the building for a week beforehand. In 1870 the Chapter decided that this was no longer acceptable. The promoters were told that the scaffolding could not be erected in future: the children must occupy seats on the floor with the rest of the assembly. After that the event was abruptly discontinued.

PRINCIPAL SOURCES

Anon., *The Excellent Use of Psalmody* (London, 1801)

Brownlow, J., *History and Design of the Foundling Hospital* (London, 1858)

Burney, C., *An Account of the Handel Commemoration* (London, 1785)

The Comic Almanack (1838)

Knight, C., ed., *London Pictorially Illustrated*, vol. 4 (London, 1851)

Milman, H. H., *Annals of St Paul's Cathedral* (London, 1868)

Porteous, B., *Complete Works* (London, 1811)

Simpson, W. S., *Gleanings from Old St Paul's* (London, 1889)

Sinclair, W., *Memorials of St Paul's Cathedral* (London, 1901)

John Jebb (1805–1886) and the Choral Service
[1986]

N OT SO MANY YEARS AGO most members of a parish church congregation took for granted the presence of a surpliced choir of men and boys in
the chancel. Comparatively few were aware that robed choirs of this kind had
first been introduced in parish churches only during the nineteenth century in
an attempt to increase decorum in public worship. Prominent among those who
encouraged this change was the Revd John Jebb, an Anglo-Irish clergyman the
centenary of whose death occurs this year. Details of his career – Prebendary
of Limerick (1832), Rector of Peterstow (1843), Prebendary of Hereford (1858)
and Canon Residentiary there (1870) – are found in the *Dictionary of National
Biography*. But reliance has too often been placed on unsubstantiated anecdote
for the part Jebb played in the reform of choral music. The present anniversary
prompts a fuller, less misleading picture.

Throughout the eighteenth century and for much of the nineteenth the
neglected state of the singing in English churches was regularly condemned.
Bishops reprimanded their diocesan clergy on a number of occasions, and the
literature of the time contains many reports of scandalously irreverent behaviour on the part of rustic 'cock and hen' choirs. The open warfare between
singers and minister mentioned in Parson Woodforde's *Diary* readily springs
to mind. Although town churches often had more disciplined choirs of boys
and girls who were marched there in uniform from the local Charity School,
their raucous performance was summed up by a contemporary writer as 'the
compulsory scream of a school of children'; and Dr Burney's tart claim that
the greatest blessing for lovers of music attending a parish church was to find
there an organ sufficiently powerful to drown the singing disdainfully states
the general situation. In more opulent urban parishes a professional quartet
would regularly be engaged to sing in the organ loft; but though this arrangement produced a more musical effect it encouraged the people to be content to
have the service sung for them.

It was to be a prime aim of those who first sought improvement in this
state of affairs to encourage congregations generally to take a more active and
devout part in the church service. Instead of lolling in their pews while the
metrical psalms were sung they should stand and join in. The part already
played by massed singing in the Methodist movement provided an example
not to be ignored; and the Evangelical clergy in particular began to introduce
hymns already familiar in Methodist circles but hitherto excluded from use in
churches. In a few instances, notably in the north of England, attempts were

even made to chant the prose psalms congregationally. But according to J. A. Latrobe's *The Music of the Church* (1831) the custom of chanting the psalms was still 'generally confined to Cathedrals'.

Three early instances are known where an individual clergyman's sense of propriety led him to introduce a small choir of men and boys wearing surplices into a local church. All took place between 1818 and 1838 and seem to have been prompted by the example of university chapels rather than the cathedrals. In no case was the development imitated in neighbouring churches; and these spontaneous events, taking place in Yorkshire, Limerick, and the Isle of Wight, cannot be seen as the start of a deliberate movement to encourage the adoption of robed choirs in parochial churches generally. That development sprang instead from the example of an obscure London chapel where the unusual atmosphere of devotion established was soon attracting fervent congregations. Many prominent citizens as well as the younger clergy from neighbouring parishes attended the daily services introduced by the Revd Frederick Oakeley when he was made incumbent of Margaret Chapel, Marylebone, in 1839.[1]

By that time the joint impact of the Oxford Movement and its minor counterpart, the Cambridge Camden Society, had already stimulated efforts to improve the conduct of services and the restoration of buildings in a number of other parishes. But at Margaret Chapel Frederick Oakeley extended the range of reforms to embrace 'aesthetic' aspects generally ignored by Anglicans though never underestimated by the Roman Church. In particular, attention was diverted from the pulpit and reading desk to the altar, hitherto a neglected and unadorned feature of most churches; and a repertoire of appropriate music was carefully selected and published which regular churchgoers should learn to sing in accordance with the rubrics.

Oakeley was not unaware that the task of creating a singing congregation was a considerable one. But he was convinced that the provision of a well trained choir to lead the people made this possible. Such a choir should be recruited afresh from boys and not comprise the tyrannical performers who customarily monopolised singing galleries. The essential step was to persuade churchgoers generally to turn from doing nothing to doing something:

> If the assembled worshippers [he wrote] one and all positively decline to chant, a mere choir of boys is almost or quite worse than nothing; for in that case it will operate only in relieving the congregation from a part of its duty. This, however, we look upon as an imaginary difficulty; we never yet heard of the instance, nor do we believe it possible without mismanagement, in which the disposition to promote chanting on the part of a

---

[1] The Church of All Saints, Margaret Street, now stands on its site.

clergyman has been otherwise than cordially met by the better disposed of his flock. An experienced choirmaster is absolutely necessary ...[2]

Besides chanting the responses, Oakeley's congregation also learned to sing the psalms for the day – at first to Anglican chants, then to plainchant, using *Laudes Diurnae* (1843) the Gregorian psalter he hid prepared for them.

As the passage quoted above from his own observations makes clear, Oakeley meant the choir established at Margaret Chapel to be the prototype for others. And a Society for Promoting Church Music was soon formed by sympathetic Tractarians with this end in view. The society published its own monthly journal, appositely named *The Parish Choir*, offering guidance on how to introduce musical improvements according to 'sound religious principles'. Each issue of the paper included a music supplement providing simple settings of the Responses and Litany, Anglican chants and metrical psalm tunes, together with anthems suited to newly formed choirs; but it was emphasised that the provision of anthems must not prevent the people from taking full vocal part in those portions of the service allotted to them by the rubrics.

Another influential Tractarian paper to support the musical policy adopted at Margaret Chapel was *The Ecclesiologist*, the journal of the Cambridge Camden Society. Although principally concerned with the fabric and furnishing of churches the society made the ordering of services another of its interests; and when the experiment of chanting the psalms to Gregorian tones using Oakeley's *Laudes Diurnae* began in 1843 the paper voiced its approval of a step so prone, it felt, to encourage congregational participation. *The Ecclesiologist* never doubted that the role of a newly introduced surpliced choir was to lead the people. 'No music for the *common* parts of our offices is admissible,' it declared, 'which cannot be sung by all.'[3] And it expressed admiration for the stimulus provided to the nationwide creation of surpliced choirs by another institution, St Mark's College, Chelsea. At this training institution for teachers in church schools, founded in 1841, all the students were taught to take part in daily choral services in the college chapel so that when they became teachers they might be able to conduct with greater skill the sacred music of public worship.'[4] *The Parish Choir*, too, voiced its approval of the efforts of the Revd Thomas Helmore to produce a new race of musical schoolmasters at this church training college: 'There is perhaps no institution of modern times which has done so much for the choral music of the Church of England as St Mark's Training College.'[5] And when Helmore produced his definitive plainsong *Psalter Noted*

[2] *The British Critic*, October 1843, p. 313.
[3] *Ecclesiologist*, vol. 5 (1846) p. 173.
[4] *The Parish Choir*, vol. 11 (1846) p. 105.
[5] *Ibid.*

following extended trial at St Mark's, *The Ecclesiologist* complimented him on a task 'accomplished with exquisite skill and perspicuity'.[6]

As a result of all these endeavours surpliced choirs of the type first demonstrated by Frederick Oakeley at Margaret Chapel in 1839 were soon established in other churches with similar liturgical aspirations. Their congregations, suitably furnished with simple tunes and chants, accordingly began to take a fuller, more devout, and increasingly competent vocal part in the services. But now, at another level of churchmanship a different, diametrically opposed model for the parochial choir was presented – one not designed to lead the people's song but to sing while the congregation remained silent. This new prototype first appeared at Leeds parish church in 1841 while Dr W. F. Hook was vicar. The man responsible for the musical policy which it implemented was John Jebb.

To the parish church at Leeds belongs the distinction of being the first to introduce a surpliced choir since the Reformation. But this innovation did not occur, as has been repeatedly claimed, under Dr Hook with John Jebb as his lieutenant in 1841. A body of professional singers was recruited there by the Revd Richard Fawcett when he became vicar in 1815; and a robed choir of boys and men was introduced by him in 1818.[7] Their duties were limited to singing metrical psalms and anthems. But well before Dr Hook became vicar of the parish in 1837 objections by Dissenters to the payment of church rates had led to various retrenchments and the former choir had been discontinued.

After steadily gaining the confidence and support of the townsfolk Hook made it one of his first tasks at Leeds to replace the overcrowded and dilapidated parish church with an entirely new building. And early in 1841, while building went on, a deputation of parishioners requested that a robed choir be re-established when the new church was complete, Hook agreed that provided adequate funds were made available to maintain an efficient choir, its presence would accord with his wish to provide a worthy and noble centre for worship. But the introduction of such a choir was clearly not due to personal preference on his own part – for Hook was unmusical to the extent of being unable to recognise one tune from another.[8]

The request to re-establish a choir agreed, Hook sought expert opinion upon the musical policy to be adopted. No Tractarian, he had always carefully avoided extreme positions in churchmanship; and the model supplied by Margaret Chapel will have had little attraction for him. Yet he was able to

---

[6] *Ecclesiologist*, vol. 2 (1849) p. 208.

[7] *Leeds Mercury*, 26 Nov. 1826, reporting the Vestry Meeting.

[8] W. R. W. Stephens, *Life & Letters of W. F. Hook* (London, 1878), vol. 2, p. 334.

rationalise the arguments for and against the introduction of choral services as presented by High and Low churchmen, outlining them in a letter to one of his parishioners with impressive penetration:

> A Protestant goes to church to get good to his soul, a Catholic to glorify God; a Protestant to have his own mind impressed, a Catholic to do God service ... According, then, as your feelings are more Catholic or more Protestant, you will like or dislike cathedral service ... During the last century the mind of England became thoroughly Protestantised, therefore choral service fell into disuse: it is now becoming again Catholicised, and Choral service is coming in.[9]

He was aware, moreover, that many of his congregation would regard as most appropriate, the way of conducting the service to which long use had accustomed them. He therefore sought advice, not only for himself but for local churchgoers as a whole, calling three public meetings at which expert opinion should be presented to the townsfolk on the subject of the choral service.

A nephew of Bishop Jebb of Limerick, himself Hook's longstanding spiritual mentor, John Jebb seemed a natural choice to provide that advice. He had made a deep study of the Anglican liturgy, and as Prebendary of Limerick Cathedral since 1832 had gained considerable practical experience of church music. But his background as a cathedral dignitary made his interpretation of the term 'choral service' synonymous with 'cathedral service'; and his recommendations to Dr Hook and the churchgoers of Leeds were precisely opposed to those currently voiced in Tractarian circles.

A very clear picture of John Jebb's views on the desirable roles of choir and congregation may be found in his exhaustive survey of the *The Choral Service of the United Church of England and Ireland* (1843). Following radical clamour questioning the function of the cathedral and the need to continue its existence, parliamentary debate had led to the passing of the Dean and Chapter Act of 1840 which limited the number of cathedral posts. Jebb's treatise was the most substantial by far of several publications which set out to reassess an ancient institution which had fallen into disesteem.

In the course of some seventy-nine chapters Jebb scrupulously detailed every aspect of the liturgical system of the Anglican communion, relating each particular to an appropriate authority and source. Forthright in his condemnation of neglect, he had determined that ignorance of the proper manner of administering the liturgy should no longer excuse church dignitaries. Examples of unjustifiable disregard of statutes at particular cathedrals were specifically cited; and whether it was the wilfulness of minor canons in refusing to chant

---

[9] *Ibid.* p. 133.

the office, or the incompetence and carelessness that prevailed among the ill-paid, inexpert and commonly irreverent lay-clerks, Jebb did not hesitate to identify the offending cathedral concerned, often in outspokenly abrasive terms:

> Till I heard the choir at Gloucester, I imagined that the acme of irreverent and careless chanting was to be found at Lincoln. At Gloucester half the words of the psalms were inaudible: I doubt whether they were uttered at all.[10]

The passage exemplifies the ruthless candour with which Jebb uttered his exasperated criticisms. But the main purpose of his treatise was to describe and justify what should take place, rather than to rate the misguided for their shortcomings.

John Jebb's scholarly investigation of authenticity in the celebration of the Anglican offices produced a monumental handbook for the future guidance of cathedral dignitaries upon which his fame deservedly depends. Yet his name has tended to be more closely associated in the folk-memory of church musicians with inaccurately reported events surrounding the introduction of the surpliced choir at Leeds parish church. For though, as we have seen, the choir formed at Leeds in 1841 was neither the first to be established at that or any other parish church in the land, its role in 'performing' the choral service to a listening congregation soon attracted emulation among non-Tractarians, allowing it to become a factional rival to the model demonstrated at Margaret Chapel three years previously.

As one might expect, John Jebb's views on singing the service of the Common Prayer were formed long before his major treatise appeared in 1843. And though expressed there in terms of cathedral practice, earlier observations of his clearly indicate his conviction that wherever a recognised choir was introduced, the musical effect aimed at should not be marred by the congregation's inexpert participation. Moreover, his disapproval of what he classed as 'the roar of the congregation' was not left unspoken. When *The Ecclesiologist* published its first substantial article on church music in September, 1843, maintaining that the key to the development of congregational singing lay in the revival of plainchant rather than in Anglican chants and metrical psalmody, John Jebb wrote to protest his disagreement. His letter was subsequently acknowledged in the paper without formal reply.[11]

But following the introduction of choral services at Leeds the pattern of service adopted there was increasingly imitated elsewhere; and a phrase whose

[10] J. Jebb, *The Choral Service of the United Church of England and Ireland* (London, 1843), p. 439.

[11] *Ecclesiologist*, February 1844, p. 83.

period flavour is inescapable was adopted to distinguish between less ambitious musical endeavours and the type of service referred to as 'fully choral'. The guide lines which John Jebb had laid down in contradistinction to those of Oakeley, and which now hardened to become the hallmarks of a rival school of thought on the subject of choral worship, are firmly stated in his writings and may be summarised as follows.

Where a parish church chose to establish a choir to perform the choral service it should consist of men and boys, be surpliced, and occupy facing stalls situated in the chancel. Placing a choir in a gallery Jebb considered 'popish' and a late innovation. The organ should be sited as near to the choir as possible, preferably on the north side. These were the arrangements discovered at Leeds when the new parish church was consecrated in September, 1841. The *Parish Choir* reported that public response to the 'full choral service' was generally favourable though opposition was evident in some quarters. Clearly the public meetings which Hook had called to prepare the townsfolk for the changes had been largely effective.

On the congregation's role in the choral service Jebb was forthright. If, in line with currently expressed views on the subject, everyone no matter how unskilled ought as a matter of duty to sing in church, he felt that it would be better to drop all pretence of choral music. Where chanting of the psalms was concerned, it was essential for the choir itself to undergo regular daily practice in order to fulfill this part of its duty adequately. That being so, congregational chanting could not be seriously considered. Moreover, the suggestion that reviving the use of Gregorian tones would help the people to chant the psalms, only aroused Jebb's indignation further. To him the ancient tones seemed musically impoverished, revealing the defects, not the advantages, of antiquity. What would be said, he demanded, if new churches were restricted in their architecture to 'the debasements of the age of Constantine'?

But Jebb's objections to the use of plainchant were not limited to purely musical considerations. The rehabilitation of music drawn from ancient breviaries and missals offended his staunch Protestantism. Why, he demanded, should so much be made of the musical example of Rome? In his view the Anglican chant sufficiently expressed gravity, strength, and religious awe to reflect 'true Church of England devotion'. And where anthems were concerned, whatever might be said for the music of Palestrina, John Jebb felt that his English contemporaries – Byrd, Farrant and Gibbons – were at least his equals in every essential quality. For that matter, the selection of anthems should be made a matter of deliberate study on both musical and liturgical grounds. And once selected, they should be meticulously rehearsed, announced in a *Weekly Table of Services and Anthems* and never subsequently changed 'by the solicitation of amateurs and others who desire some favourite Anthem, however inappropriate'.

All these circumstances, first introduced at Leeds under John Jebb's leadership, were further emphasised in the following year when S. S. Wesley was appointed organist at the parish church. After ten frustrated years in the organ lofts of Hereford and Exeter cathedrals Wesley looked forward to working in what must have seemed ideal conditions – where the concept of the choral service was already established along lines closely parallel to his own aims, and where Hook evidently agreed with his own contention that 'whatever is offered to God should be as faultless as man can make it'.[12]

Under Wesley's influence the 'cathedral' nature of the service at Leeds was further developed. For him the beauty of the choral service, far from encouraging singing by the people generally, must compel silent awe from those who heard it. The use of Gregorian tones and the formation of amateur choirs simply aroused his scorn. Those who promoted such ideas were doing great harm to the cause of church music – for plainchant seemed to Wesley the musical counterpart of Stonehenge. He responded by writing elaborate music and pointing a new *Psalter* for the choir; by extemporising voluntaries of 'the grandest, most beautiful, and elaborate character'[13] which edified (and greatly enlarged) the listening congregations. Understandably, then, churches elsewhere, not already committed to Tractarianism, eagerly imitated the musical policy so beguilingly demonstrated at Leeds. That they sought to do so without the professionalism and genius that Leeds could muster led to inadequacies without, however, halting the trend.

In 1711, at a time when church music in England remained sadly deficient, Alexander Pope could yet write

> ... as some to Church repair
> Not for the Doctrine but the Musick there.[14]

How much more appositely might those lines have been uttered during the nineteenth century following the adoption of 'fully choral' services in many churches. Indeed, an account of church attendance in 1872, while expressed in prose rather than Augustan couplets and carefully avoiding censure, leaves a very similar impression:

> Churches in which plain, simple, but assuredly cold parochial services prevail, are comparatively deserted, in spite of the efficiency of the preach-

---

[12] S. S. Wesley, *A Few Words on Cathedral Music* (London, 1849), p. 75.
[13] W. Spark, *Musical Reminiscences* (London, 1892), p. 166.
[14] A. Pope, *Essay on Criticism* (London, 1711), p. 342.

ers, whilst those where a choral or cathedral service has been introduced overflow with congregations.[15]

Contemporary accounts show that in churches where surpliced choirs were introduced at this time interpretations of the term 'choral service' varied extravagantly according to standards of churchmanship, the musical disposition of incumbents and church wardens, the competence of organists and choirs, and the funds made available for music. Cases where new choirs precisely resembled the model of either Oakeley or Jebb were far outnumbered by hybrid choirs with no settled musical policy. Most were robed – even where women were included, most sang occasional anthems, all chanted the psalms mid-responses; but a vague spirit of hopeful compromise was left to decide what vocal part the congregation should play apart from singing the hymns.

This state of affairs was not unwelcome to the well-to-do and those who imitated them in believing that it was 'not genteel to sing in church'.[16] And in spite of the objections of some parishioners, in many churches the congregation were content to take a passive musical role. In urban areas at least, something of a solution was provided as further churches were built to meet the current rise in population. Each new church adopted its own musical policy; and with the improvement of public transport churchgoers generally were free to choose which church best suited their ideal levels of churchmanship and musical practice.

In a populous urban area there might consequently be found a 'fashionable' church whose congregation scarcely uttered a note during the whole service; another where, however tentatively, the people sang their Gregorian psalm tones and plainsong hymns with genuine devotion; in others, choir and congregation made whatever contribution to the singing local resources could muster. In extreme cases a church might build a tradition of unison singing by both choir and people; or present services of a musical elaboration that earned for St Anne's, Soho, for instance, the popular nickname of 'The Sunday Opera'.

Neither Jebb nor Oakeley can have approved the way in which their separate models of a parochial choir became distorted. Oakeley's chagrin over the matter was to be comparatively short-lived but compounded by constant attacks from Low Churchmen upon his 'ritualistic practices'. After six uncomfortable years at Margaret Chapel he eventually seceded to Rome in 1845. John Jebb's disappointment was to be more lengthy. Although his personal vision of a parochial choir was effectively realised to wide acclaim at Leeds, his ultimate aim – the reform of cathedral music – seemed for long unattainable.

The shortcomings which Jebb had pointed out in his *The Choral Service* in

---

[15] J. E. Cox, *Musical Recollections of the Last Half-Century* (London, 1872), p. 7.

[16] J. Hullah, *The Psalter* (London, 1843), Preface.

1843 were taken up again by *The Parish Choir* in an article on 'Defects in the Cathedral Service' in July, 1846. The irreverence, incompetence and negligence of choirs and cathedral dignitaries alike were castigated. Subsequent articles appeared in the same paper during the six years of its existence, reporting continued failings in the musical arrangements at a dozen English cathedrals. In 1849 S. S. Wesley added his voice to the accusations with his *A Few Words on Cathedral Music*. There was not a cathedral choir in the land, he declared, 'competent to give effect to the evident intentions of the Church with regard to music'.[17] Moreover, he felt that cathedral dignitaries would be unlikely to remedy matters without parliamentary intervention.

By that time the contrast between the reforming energy being displayed by the younger parochial clergy and the elderly indolence characterising most cathedral dignitaries had become inescapable. And in 1853 the *Edinburgh Review* was drawing attention to the discrepancy: 'The deadness of a former age has passed away from our parish churches; shame indeed if it still clings to the mouldering walls of those great establishments which ought each to be the model of its diocese.'[18] Ten years after the appearance of Jebb's manifesto the looked for improvements were still lacking.

But now the appointment of W. K. Hamilton as Bishop of Salisbury in 1854 brought to the bench of bishops a priest who had been in the forefront of the drive to reform parochial worship when the Oxford Movement was in its infancy. At St Peter's-in-the-East, Oxford, during the 1830s Hamilton had encouraged the use of new hymns, chorales and plainsong tunes well before such innovations appeared elsewhere. He was now able to lead the way in the reform of cathedral music with similar energy. That he had already decided to undertake that role is evident from his paper on *Cathedral Reform* written in the year before his enthronement. Discussing current musical practice in cathedrals there he wrote: 'The whole arrangements of divine service often show slovenliness, and want of order and discipline, and are in strange contrast with the manner in which the services are conducted in some parish churches.'[19] It is impossible to doubt that whatever parish churches Hamilton had in mind when writing those words, Leeds parish church was certainly among them.

What Jebb achieved at Leeds, jointly with what Oakeley had already demonstrated in London, heralded major reforms in the conduct of church services which eventually touched every church and cathedral in the land. And while the title of father of the surpliced parochial choir cannot be denied to Oakeley, that of influential godparent belongs indisputably to Jebb. At a time

---

[17] *Ibid.*, p. 12.

[18] *Edinburgh Review*, vol. 97, p. 166.

[19] *Ibid.*, p. 12.

when upheaval in the musical conduct of services has again become commonplace we should perhaps remind ourselves that, for all their apparent conflict, the policies advanced individually by Oakeley and Jebb proved in practice to be complementary. The flexible system that compromise between them was able to produce has endured for more than a century. Whether the equally contentious music arrangements now being introduced in conjunction with alternative forms of Anglican service will prove as accommodating and durable remains to be seen.

FURTHER READING

Jebb, J., *Three Lectures on the Cathedral Service* (Leeds, 1841)

Rainbow, B., *The Choral Revival in the Anglican Church, 1839–72* (London, 1970; Woodbridge, 2001)

Temperley, N., *The Music of the English Parish Church* (Cambridge, 1979)

In Quires and Places Where They Sing:
Some Historical Aspects of Anglican Church Music
[1995]

To CONTEMPLATE the present state of parochial music in the Anglican Church can prove a dispiriting experience. Instances doubtless come to light where worthy musical standards are vigorously maintained and prized; but these often serve only to highlight the larger number of cases where service music is either neglected or of questionable value.

Even a brief survey of parochial music since the inception of Anglican services at the Reformation reveals that similar musical shortcomings were seldom lacking in the past – to be overcome only when the Church's traditional duty to enlighten as well as evangelise was acknowledged and re-emphasised.

The change from Latin to vernacular forms of service that took place in certain sections of the Western Church early in the sixteenth century was designed to give the people a central role in liturgical worship. This substitution provided Protestantism with one of its most durable characteristics; but the musical consequences that resulted were pronounced and differed considerably from one time and place to another.

Under Luther the new chorale provided German congregations with doctrinal texts married to strong melodies – but without curtailing opportunities elsewhere in the service for a skilful choir to present elaborate settings beyond the powers of the people at large. Under Calvin, on the other hand, metrical versions of the psalms set to stern tunes allowed Genevan congregations to unite their voices in church; but Calvinists were constrained to sing entirely in unison and without what was considered the worldly savour of organ accompaniment. Moreover, Genevan choirs were not permitted to sing to a listening congregation. Where choirs existed at all it was now solely to lead the people's psalmody. Though very different in detail, Luther's and Calvin's musical policies went unquestioned by their respective adherents, swept along as they were by wider aspects of reform. The situation in England was different again.

The English Reformation was not precipitated by a Luther or a Calvin. But a priest who played an important part in the political events heralding it was Thomas Cranmer, then Henry VIII's chaplain. Appointed Archbishop of Canterbury in 1533, Cranmer was to be responsible for producing, in the Book of Common Prayer, an English liturgy in language remarkable for its beauty. Equal care was given under his direction to providing appropriate congregational music for the new rites. The chaste unison setting of Cranmer's *Litany*

(1544) and John Merbecke's simple service music published in the *Common Prayer Noted* (1550) both demonstrate the success of that policy.

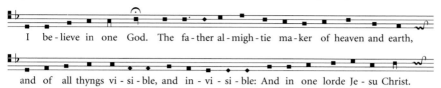

I be - lieve in one God. The fa - ther al - migh - tie ma - ker of heaven and earth,

and of all thyngs vi - si - ble, and in - vi - si - ble: And in one lorde Je - su Christ.

Sadly, the promise of this auspicious beginning was not to be fulfilled.

When Henry VIII died in 1547 the work of reform was still not complete. He was succeeded by Edward VI, then a boy reigning under a regency. Meanwhile religious controversy continued; and in 1552, only three years after it had first appeared, the Book of Common Prayer was substantially revised – thus making obsolete the musical settings Merbecke had so recently provided for it. Yet more devastatingly, a year later with the premature death of Edward VI the throne passed to Mary, daughter of Catherine of Aragon, and England reverted for the five years of her reign to Roman Catholicism.

The confusion and religious turmoil of that troubled decade after 1547 were to rule out the permanent establishment of a recognised form of church service and preclude general acceptance of the way in which it should be conducted musically. And by the time Elizabeth I came to the throne in 1558 well-established customs regulating the conduct of divine service in the past had already begun to be forgotten.

The return at just this time from Geneva of prominent churchmen who had sought refuge there from Marian persecution considerably strengthened Calvinism in this country. Singing of psalms 'after Geneva fashion' now became a popular exercise; and thousands of Londoners would assemble after service at Paul's Cross – a regular public forum adjoining an outdoor pulpit in the cathedral churchyard – to take part. Encouraged by this development, to a small collection of metrical psalms by Thomas Sternhold were now added sundry versions largely produced by English divines in exile. Eventually, in 1562, the entire psalter in verse with associated tunes was published as Sternhold and Hopkins' *Whole Book of Psalms*.

This book contained a number of staunch, durable tunes, versions of which are still in use today and identifiable under the nomenclature *Old 100th*, *Old 104th*, etc; and though the accompanying texts were to be categorised by later critics as 'scandalous doggerel' this collection was not superseded until Tate and Brady's *New Version of the Psalms of David fitted to the tunes used in Churches* appeared in 1696.

Partisan opinion for or against Genevan psalmody has often depended less upon musical or textual considerations than upon individual approval or

To the Reader.

A ſhorte Introduction into the Science of Muſicke, made foꝛ ſuch as are deſirous to haue the knowledge therof, foꝛ the ſinging of theſe Pſalmes.

Oꝛ that the rude & ignoꝛant in Song, may with moꝛe delight deſire, and good wyl be moued and dꝛawen to the godly exerciſe of ſinging of Pſalmes, aſwell in common place of pꝛayer, where altogether with one voyce render thankes & pꝛayſes to God, as pꝛiuatly by them ſelues, oꝛ at home in their houſes : I haue ſet here in the beginning of this boke of pſalmes, an eaſie and moſte playne way and rule, of the oꝛder of the Notes and Kayes of ſinging, whiche commonly is called the ſcale of Muſicke, oꝛ the *Gamma vt.* Wherby (any diligēce geuen therunto) euerye man may in a fewe dayes: yea, in a few houres, eaſely without all payne, & that alſo without ayde oꝛ helpe of any other teacher, attayne to a ſufficient, knowledg, to ſinge any Pſalme contayned in thys Booke, oꝛ any ſuche other playne and eaſy Songes as theſe are.

✠.ii.   Be

Musical preface included in Sternhold and Hopkins' *Whole Book of Psalms* (1562) disapproval of the Calvinistic ethic originally associated with it: for Calvin's followers were led to believe that the pageantry of religion – the beautification of churches, the decent ceremonial of services, the inspirational aid of instrumental music – must all be swept away; moreover, in line with Calvin's policy that nothing but the text of Scripture be admitted in worship, his followers made stern metrical psalmody the sole musical medium of worship.

A later English critic of this implicit thrust toward Puritanism, the eighteenth-century Poet Laureate, Thomas Warton, recklessly claimed by way of explanation that Calvin's original flock had been drawn from 'republican rabble with no relish for elegant externals'. And we may perhaps see in the confrontation between supporters and opponents of the point at issue something akin to class struggle – as defenders and detractors of purely congregational considerations each pressed for supremacy.

Queen Elizabeth's strongly held preference had always been for beauty and solemnity in the conduct of worship. But faced with influential Puritan opposition within the Church, political sagacity made her skilfully framed *Injunctions* of 1559 decree only that 'for the comforting of such that delighteth in music, it may be permitted that in the beginning, or at the end of common prayers, either at morning or evening, there may be sung an Hymn, or such like song'. The loose term 'Hymn' here has always reasonably been taken to include 'Anthem'.

Eventually, relentless Puritan objection saw to it that later versions of the Book of Common Prayer offered little in the way of encouragement to the musically inclined. Indeed, the sole concession made in that direction was to lie in the rubric at morning and evening prayer: *In Quires and Places where they sing, here followeth the Anthem.*

The struggle of many churchmen to escape from the stranglehold of Calvinistic puritanism seemed lost in England with the beheading of Archbishop Laud in 1645 and of King Charles I himself four years later. The Cromwellian Commonwealth that followed saw the total destruction of service music. In cathedral and parish church alike metrical psalmody alone survived. And as John Milton's nephew, John Phillips, pointed out in his *Satyr against Hypocrites* (1655), the sanctimonious were now at pains to be observed devoutly singing psalms Geneva-fashion even in their own homes:

> ... singing with woful noise,
> Like a cracked saint's bell jarring in the steeple,
> Tom Sternhold's wretched prick-song for the people,
> And if the windows gaze upon the street,
> To sing a Psalm they hold it very meet.

The reference there to 'singing with woful noise' calls attention to another displeasing consequence of the long era of metrical psalmody. After 200 years of psalm-singing, contemporary accounts of parochial services regularly spoke with dismay of the people's pitiful attempts to sing in church. And whatever the reputed zeal of those who first sang psalms at Paul's Cross may have been, when the eminent Dr Burney came to describe the psalm-singing congregations of his own day in his *General History of Music* (1789) he roundly declared that the greatest blessing for lovers of music attending a parish church was to find there 'an organ sufficiently powerful to render the voices of the clerk and those who join in his outcry wholly inaudible'.

We must bear in mind that even so late as Burney's day, outside the cathedrals and large urban churches, organs hardly existed at all. Their systematic destruction in churches throughout England during the Civil War – together with stained glass, sculpture and paintings, music books, vestments, and surplices – formed part of the price of Calvinism. But even after popular uprisings at length brought the Puritan regime to an end and Charles II was recalled from exile in May 1660, reparation was slow.

Soon after Charles's return twenty-seven-year-old Samuel Pepys recorded in his *Diary* a visit to the Chapel Royal:

> *8 July, 1660. Lords Day* To Whitehall to chapel ... where I heard very good Musique, the first time that I remember ever to have heard the Organs and singing-men in Surplices in my life.

In a matter of weeks, that is to say, and well before Charles was crowned, sung services in the royal chapel had been restored. Progress in parish churches, however, was very much less speedy. Three months later Pepys was to write:

> *4 November, 1660. Lords Day.* In the morn to our own church [St Olave's, Hart Street,] where Mr Mills [the Rector] did begin to nibble at the Common Prayer by saying 'Glory be to the Father,' &c, after he had read the two psalms. But the people have beene so little used to it that they could not tell what to answer.

That signal event took place in the heart of London. By contrast, the introduction of the Book of Common Prayer in backward rural areas, where illiteracy was common and resources scarce, will be seen to have presented exceptional problems.

Eventually though, the manner of performing services in parish churches generally found the people reciting, not singing, the responses; and, led by the parish clerk, repeating the prose psalms alternately verse-by-verse with the parson. Metrical psalms were still sung at other points in the service, commonly by the process known as 'lining-out'. Designed to enable those who could not read to add their voices, this involved the parish clerk's reading each line of the psalm before the people sang it. Its inevitable effect, of course, was to destroy the sense of what was being sung.

Until the last quarter of the eighteenth century, when church bands were commonly established in rural parishes to make up for the lack of organs, all singing took place unaccompanied – with results, as Dr Burney witnessed, that were invariably painful. Hindsight enables us to see that the vocal incompetence displayed by eighteenth-century congregations in England was due to the almost complete absence since Cranmer's day of musical instruction for children at school. Luther and Calvin had both been careful to equip future congregations in this way.

Systematic music teaching of the kind organised in churches and schools by Guillaume Franc and Loys Bourgeois in Geneva, and by Martin Agricola, Georg Rhau, and many others in Lutheran Germany was not undertaken in this country. The political and theological confusion that followed Henry VIII's break with Rome inhibited such steps. And it was not until the appearance of the *Whole Book of Psalms* in 1562 that an attempt was made to remedy the musical ignorance of a new generation by publishing within it a prefatory *Shorte Introduction into the Science of Musicke, made for such as are desirous to have the knowledge thereof, for the singing of these Psalmes.*

However, this proved to be a bafflingly verbose tract, opening with a promise that 'every man may in a few days, yea in a few hours ... attain to a sufficient knowledge to sing any psalm contained in this book'. The emptiness of that incautious claim was quickly acknowledged when the *Shorte Introduction* was dropped from later editions.

By the end of the seventeenth century the absence of more authoritative effort to remedy the musical incapacity of ordinary folk encouraged rustic musicians to begin advertising their services as itinerant teachers of psalmody. Scornfully described by Sir John Hawkins as 'illiterate professors who travel about the country to teach psalmody by the notes at such rates as the lower sort of people are able to pay', these musical pedlars relied upon the sale of books of psalm-tunes to supplement their fees. The books they sold were usually their own compilations, and included largely plagiarised prefaces summarising the rudiments of music.

In some country parishes the local squire, or a group of the gentry clubbing together, would perhaps engage the services of a psalmody teacher of this sort to instruct the villagers. But such well-intentioned philanthropy often served only to encourage a group of musically ambitious yokels to form themselves into a self-appointed choir for the local church. Nominally under the direction of the local parish clerk but usually defiantly independent, 'cock-and-hen' choirs of this kind would dispose themselves prominently in a hotly defended section of a church gallery, inviting the admiration of

THE
COMPLETE PSALMODIST:
OR THE
ORGANIST'S PARISH-CLERK'S,
AND
PSALM-SINGER'S COMPANION.

CONTAINING

I. A new and complete Introduction to Pfalmody, and mufical Dictionary.

II. Five and Thirty capital ANTHEMS, compofed of SOLOS, FUGUES, and CHORUSSES, after the Cathedral Manner.

III. A complete Set of grave and folemn PSALM TUNES, both ancient and modern: containing near one Hundred different TUNES, properly adapted to the moft fublime Portions of the PSALMS, being proper for Parifh-Clerks, and ufeful to country Congregations.

IV. A Set of DIVINE HYMNS, fuited to the Feafts and Fafts of the Church of England, with feveral excellent CANONS of three and four Parts in one.

The whole fet in SCORE, for one, two, three, four and five VOICES, with the Baffes figured for the ORGAN; principally defigned for the Ufe of COUNTRY CHOIRS.

The SEVENTH EDITION, with large and new ADDITIONS.

By JOHN ARNOLD, Philo Muficæ.

All hallow'd Acts fhould be perform'd with Awe,
And Reverence of Body, Mind, and Heart:
We've Rules to pray; but thofe who never faw
Rules how to fing, how fhould they bear a Part?

T' avoid therefore a difagreeing Noife,
This will unite the Organ and the Voice.

LONDON:
Printed by *G. Bigg*, for *J. Buckland*, *J. F.* and *C. Rivington*, *S. Crowder*, *T. Longman*, and *B. Law*, 1779.

[Price Four Shillings and Six Pence.]

Title-page of a celebrated psalmody collection with musical preface their fellows below and often defying the authority of the parson to discipline them.

John Wesley's *Diary* records that when visiting a Middlesex church he found it necessary to rebuke the unruly Singers there:

> *Sun, Feb. 4, 1750.* – preached at Hayes ... The church was filled ... and all behaved well but the singers, whom I therefore reproved before the congregation, and some of them were ashamed.

Nor were choirs of this sort guilty only of irreverent conduct. Once established they would take upon themselves to sing parts of the service hitherto spoken by the congregation as a whole: the Responses to the Commandments, for instance, or the prose Canticles; they might even elect to mark special occasions with a gimcrack 'Anthem'.

As fledgling Curate of Castle Cary in Somerset, the youthful James Woodforde found himself confronted by such a group of wilful Singers in 1769. As his *Diary* records:

> *Nov. 12, 1769.* I read Prayers and preached this morning at C. Cary Church. I was disturbed this morning at Cary Church by the Singers. I sent my Clerk some time back to the Cary Singers, to desire that they would not sing the Responses in the Communion Service, which they complied with for several Sundays, but this morning after the first Commandment they had the Impudence to sing the Response, and therefore I spoke to them out of my desk, to say and not sing the Responses which they did after, and at other places they sang as usual. The Singers in the Gallery were, John Coleman, the Baker, Jonathan Croker, Willm Pew Junr., Thos Penny, William Ashford, Hooper the Singing Master, James Lucas, Peter, Mr Francis's man, Mr Mellinar's man James, ...

There was a sequel a fortnight later:

> *Nov. 26, 1769.* I read Prayers and preached this morning at C. Cary Church. N.B. No singing this morning the Singers not being at Church, they being highly affronted with me at what I had lately done ...

The Cary Singers had clearly taken themselves off to sing at a church elsewhere – something not unusual then. Without waiting for an invitation or even seeking permission a choir would arrive self-importantly and make their way into the church. Village gossip would have announced their intentions to all but the parson; and there would be an eager crowd to welcome them. Such an occasion would arouse something of the feckless enthusiasm a visit by a pop group might be expected to cause today.

At that time country parsons everywhere had similar tantrums to contend

A late eighteenth-century village choir, the work of an unknown primitive painter, this caricatures the singers with almost Brueghel-like malice; only the youthful flageolet player is spared.

with from time to time; and before the end of the century opportunities for disruptive behaviour in singing galleries became yet more pronounced. Rural churches still unable to afford to install an organ now began to introduce amateur church bands to accompany the singers in their galleries. Players would essentially include a bass instrument – a cello or double-bass (both popularly known for their ubiquity in churches as 'the Lord's Fiddle'). In addition there might be a small selection from among clarinets, violins, or flutes to strengthen the upper vocal parts.

The make-up of these bands was largely decided either by what local talent could muster, or by the range of instruments the churchwardens could be persuaded to purchase. For instance, a very different band recalled by George Eliot in *Scenes of Clerical Life* included a bassoon and two key-bugles, while K. H. Macdermott's study of the subject in *Old Church Gallery Minstrels* mentions in a long list such present-day rarities as serpents, ophicleides, and the vamphorn – a five-foot-long megaphone through which a singer might amplify the bass line.

Perhaps the best known contemporary representation of a church singing gallery in action is Thomas Webster's sympathetic canvas of the choir at Bow Brickhill in Buckinghamshire. Painted about 1840 and preserved at the Victoria and Albert Museum it shows a choir together with a few supporting instruments; and serves to indicate clearly enough the way in which particular voices would group themselves about the player who was doubling their part. It also reveals that, unlike others, this unusually modest choir had no temperamental sopranos: it was left to a handful of boys and girls to sing the psalmtune from memory.

This is a picture contrasting strongly with some earlier portrayals where a less sophisticated artist would often caricature the performers' idiosyncrasies. Indeed, for a modern observer perhaps the most surprising feature of the choir at Bow Brickhill is to find the parish clerk keeping the time with vigorous hand-claps.

Less well-behaved groups of singers – perhaps those at Castle Cary – attracted such fascinated attention from their simple admirers in the nave below that the whole assembly would turn about to stare up at the gallery when singing began. This invariable practice originated the expression 'to face the music' – a saying notable for carrying ominous undertones of trouble ahead. We are left in no doubt that the eighteenth-century singing gallery offered small contribution to the solemnity and sanctity of worship.

The neglect that characterised the musical conduct of Anglican services during the eighteenth century failed to arouse wider dismay because it was no more than a facet of the general disregard for propriety then affecting churchmanship as a whole. Religious energy had long been frowned upon and, purely as a social expedient, the ranks of the clergy were filled by the youngest sons of the gentry with little or no sense of vocation. Under the apathetic control of a careless incumbent, services in rural areas would be held irregularly and conducted hurriedly and insincerely. The church fabric would become neglected, the furnishings uncared for, the altar untended.

Exceptions to this rule certainly existed, but these were the conditions found in very many churches when John Wesley began his 'methodising' drive for reform in 1729 – a movement that seemed at first a dedicated religious Order within the Church of England. As an ordained minister himself, Wesley's original aim was to achieve improvement from within. But as his movement grew nationwide the pull of greater independence became irresistible; and after

1744 Methodism broke away to become a separate sect – if only to allow its new preaching-houses to be registered under the Toleration Act.

It was now that Wesley formally declared his stand upon seemliness in worship. His meeting-houses, he said, might not be ornate or splendid, but neither were they dirty or sordid; those who assembled there had not come just to see and be seen but to worship; those who led the prayers there were careful to avoid a careless, slovenly manner.

> Nor [Southey's *Life of John Wesley* has him saying] are their solemn addresses to God interrupted by the formal drawl of a parish clerk, the screaming of [choir]boys, who bawl out what they neither feel nor understand, or the unreasonable and unmeaning impertinence of a voluntary on the organ. When it is seasonable to sing praise to God, they do it with the spirit, and with the understanding also: not in the miserable, scandalous doggerel of Hopkins and Sternhold, but in psalms and hymns which are both sense and poetry.

In that declaration we find the manifesto of a new concept of a singing congregation – a spontaneous hymn-singing assembly which the new 'personal' hymns of Charles Wesley, Isaac Watts, Toplady and many others were already supplying. Adopted first by the Methodists, then tentatively by a few Evangelicals within the Establishment, the new type of hymn with its simple flowing tune quickly gained popularity for its uplifting appeal.

Aware of the stimulus that hearty singing was affording to Methodist gatherings Bishop Porteus of London addressed the clergy of his diocese in 1790 on the urgent need to reform parochial psalmody in the Established Church. Pointing out in a formal *Charge* that a singing congregation was best created in the schools of the land, Porteus became the first authoritative figure of his day to emphasise this fact, unwittingly repeating the arguments of Luther and Calvin 300 years earlier.

As a result, attempts were now made in many quarters to equip existing schools – mainly small charitable foundations and Sunday schools – to teach singing and music-reading. It was in this way that the school music lesson made its first modest but decisive reappearance in this country following its virtual abandonment at the Reformation. Singing in churches now became less tentative – at least in urban areas where uniformed Charity Children often provided new gallery choirs; but real improvement called for much wider measures.

Many churchgoers, meanwhile, made their first acquaintance with hymn-singing in maintained places of worship such as the Foundling and Magdalen Chapels. There, hymns and anthems drawn from a local *Collection* and sung by a trained choir of inmates, formed regular features of services. Indeed, the attendance (and scale of the offerings) at chapels of this kind largely depended on the attractiveness of the music. As Alexander Pope remarked at the time:

> ... as some to Church repair
> Not for the Doctrine, but the Musick there.

Yet many orthodox churchgoers still held to the Calvinistic view that only scriptural texts should be sung in church; and it was not until 1820 that a Consistory Court ruling made hymn-singing formally permissible in churches. Even then, its adoption was far from general; and opposition was soon to be reinforced by the objections of a rising generation of young clergy who blamed the practice for encouraging and spreading what they regarded as unhealthy Nonconformist *Enthusiasm*.

As the debate for and against hymn-singing persisted, an event occurred that robbed less fundamental questions of their moment and sharply brought to a halt the lackadaisical attitude toward religious matters typical of eighteenth-century thought. In 1833 a group of Oxford Fellows led by John Keble, J. H. Newman and Dr E. B. Pusey, set out to trace historical evidence defining the true nature of the Church and so resist growing Erastian and rationalising trends. Their profound theological findings, published in a series of *Tracts for the Times*, aroused nationwide attention and under the designation of the 'Oxford Movement' began to educate and lead devout opinion.

Though the sister university of Cambridge took a less active role in this field, under the stimulus of Tractarian achievement a society was formed there in 1839 to bring the newly-revived church principles to bear upon the preservation of churches and the ordering of services. To begin with, the participants were all earnest undergraduates – led by John Mason Neale and Benjamin Webb. But as their activities gathered eminent support an Ecclesiological Society was formed with a monthly journal, *The Ecclesiologist*; and they could soon count archbishops, bishops, peers, and Members of Parliament among their patrons.

The pages of *The Ecclesiologist* in its early years are filled with accounts of investigations conducted in country churches where neglect and ignorance had caused harm. Chancels were found in use as lumber rooms or vestries; ancient fonts were used to house floorcloths and scrubbing brushes; altars had been masked by three-decker pulpits and reading-desks. Almost everywhere amidst the dirt and damp, the prominent siting of the pulpit – and corresponding neglect of altar and font – strengthened the popular view that the sermon was far more important than the sacraments.

The Ecclesiologists determined to restore such damaged or distorted features to their original state – so as to secure churches where the liturgy might be solemnly celebrated according to ancient usage. Within that context the topic of church music naturally found mention in the columns of *The Ecclesiologist*; and

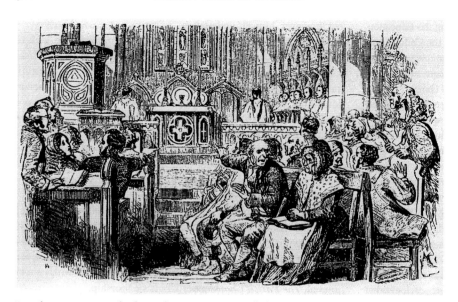

Parishioners astonished at the appearance of their restored parish church. This illustration, from an anonymous anti-Tractarian novel, *St Dorothy's Home* (1866), deliberately overstates the dismay of a congregation on finding the previously neglected chancel reordered and a surpliced choir installed.

in September 1843 a substantial musical article appeared. In it Benjamin Webb regretted that the college chapels of Cambridge should offer so little in the way of musical example – apart from 'a few miserable and effete singers running about from choir to choir, and performing to a crashing and bellowing of organs, the most meagre and washy musick'. In contrast, he announced, a rare demonstration of the true nature of church music was currently to be found in London, and at a far more humble institution – St Mark's College, Chelsea.

That seemingly implausible claim was in fact justified. St Mark's was a recently-founded Church of England teacher-training college. There, daily services were being sung, unaccompanied, by a surpliced choir, with the psalms chanted. Sixteenth-century anthems were sung, and the whole student body joined in both psalms and responses. There was no organ.

The impact of that example upon future choral practice throughout the Church of England was to be remarkable. Further investigation will show how, and why, all this came about.

It has long been a part of the folk-lore of church music that a surpliced choir was first introduced in a parish church in modern times by Dr W. F. Hook, the Vicar of Leeds, in 1841. This is readily disproved. Surpliced choirs are known to have been maintained elsewhere much earlier in the century – for instance, at St James's, Ryde; at St John's, Donaghmore; at Leeds itself, by one of Hook's predecessors; and latterly at Christ Church, Albany Street, Euston; and at Margaret Chapel, Marylebone, in 1839.[1] In all these cases the innovation was due to an individual priest's sense of propriety; and, except in the last instance, the choir's duties were limited to singing metrical psalms and an occasional anthem.

At Margaret Chapel, Marylebone – an unimposing building on the site of the present Church of All Saints, Margaret Street, – the Revd Frederick Oakeley had begun his ministry in 1839 by deliberately removing existing box-pews and a dominant three-decker reading desk. By thus focusing attention on the altar he emphasised his intention to celebrate the services of the Book of Common Prayer with the dignity and reverence of former times. During his tenure this tiny, obscure chapel was recognised as the vital centre of Tractarian observance in London.

From the first, Oakeley determined to introduce chanting and intoning in the services; and soon, with the assistance of Richard Redhead as organist, he mustered a small surpliced choir that sang the psalms and canticles to Anglican chants, Tallis's *Responses*, and various settings of the *Sanctus*. His eventual aim was to have the psalms sung to Gregorian tones; but in the absence of a pointed psalter this was impossible – until he had boldly co-operated with Redhead to compile one himself. Upon its publication in 1843 *Laudes Diurnae* became the first plainchant psalter with English text. All told, simple as it now appears, the music at Margaret Chapel was of an elaboration then unknown in parochial use.

The situation at St Mark's College, Chelsea, was quite different. Founded in 1841 by the National Society [for Promoting the Education of the Poor in the Principles of the Church of England], the College was designed to train teachers for Church Schools. But a unique additional feature of its policy was to prepare every student to teach elementary music and assist the clergy with the running of parochial choirs.

Candidates for admission to St Mark's were not tested for musical ability; but to enable them to meet those requirements special arrangements had been made for their musical and choral training. John Hullah, the organiser of a cel-ebrated and flourishing singing school at London's Exeter Hall was engaged to train the whole student body to sing at sight. And the Revd Thomas Helmore, formerly a priest-vicar at Lichfield Cathedral, was appointed Vice-principal with the responsibility of organising daily choral services and training the stu-dents to take part in them. There were music classes every day. Both were men

---

[1] The circumstances surrounding the introduction of surpliced parochial choirs are exhaustively examined in Bernarr Rainbow, *The Choral Revival in the Anglican Church, 1839–1872* (London, 1970; R/Woodbridge, 2001), to which the reader seeking source references is referred.

of tireless energy. Helmore would say, 'Hullah grinds them, I strop them!'; and pleasing results were soon apparent.

Three years after the College opened, the Principal was able to report to the National Society that though production of a single service had at first required 'very extraordinary and long-continued exertions', it was now found comparatively easy to introduce new anthems and settings as often as required. This was the situation when *The Ecclesiologist* first drew attention to the choral services at St Mark's in 1843.

By that time the musical services at the College were arousing growing attention in London as well as attracting visitors from much further afield. And as the first students to complete their training now left to take up work in church schools attempts to improve musical standards and set up robed choirs followed in churches throughout the land. The stir created by these developments, while not always welcoming, drew further attention to the choral movement; and already a number of publishers – James Burns, John Ollivier and Joseph Masters among them – had begun producing books and service music to meet a new and growing need. Perhaps the most important of these publications was William Dyce's *Order of Daily Service* (1843).

This was a version of Merbecke's *Book of Common Prayer Noted* with the musical settings adjusted to accommodate sundry revisions of Edward VI's Prayer Book since 1550. Dyce was a professional painter but also an estimable musicologist. And the results of a scholarly study he had made into Latin plainchant were recorded in an *Appendix* to the new book. They revealed the feasibility of preparing an English Gregorian psalter without sacrificing the text's natural verbal stresses.

Oakeley's earlier attempt, in his pioneer *Laudes Diurnae*, had associated word and note purely by rule of thumb. The result had regularly produced faulty verbal accentuation. Dyce now showed that, where Latin was concerned, clear rules governed the distribution of long and short syllables at Mediation and Ending according to *quantity*. He thence concluded that when chanting English words the same rules were applicable to differences between accented and unaccented syllables.

Thus, for example, to sing:

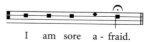

was incorrect. The authentic treatment would be:

This and other similar revelations on Dyce's part opened the way to a sound

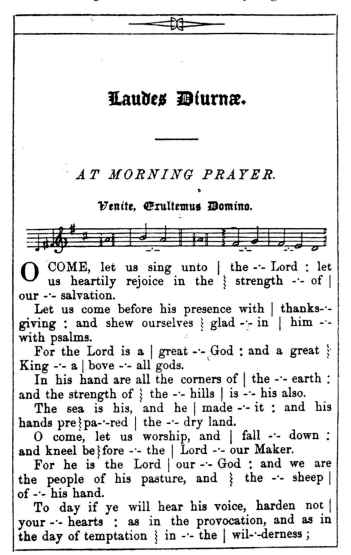

Opening page of Frederick Oakeley's *Laudes Diurnae*. The faulty verbal accentuation that marred this book is already apparent in the first verse.

system of pointing the psalms in English – a task he had not, however, himself undertaken.

At that time Thomas Helmore already recognised the lack of authenticity in existing four-square, barred versions of Psalm Tones – a debased type still found under the erroneous heading 'Gregorian' in many chant books. These he had used only in the absence of something better. On examining Oakeley's *Laudes Diurnae* as a possible alternative he had disliked its faulty verbal accentuation and rejected it. But now, following his discovery of Dyce's book, Helmore began pointing individual psalms himself according to Dyce's theories – next trying them out at St Mark's. In this way, over the years he steadily built up his own pointed version of the psalms. It was to be published in 1849, as *The Psalter Noted*.

Yet more widespread interest in the movement to establish parochial choirs was stimulated in 1845 by the publication of Robert Druitt's *Popular Tract on Church Music, with Remarks on its Moral and Political Importance*. This was followed by the formation of a new Society for Promoting Church Music with its own journal, *The Parish Choir*, under Druitt's editorship.

This paper may be regarded jointly with *The Ecclesiologist* as forming the public voice of the choral movement at that time. Its first number impressed upon readers the folly of leaving the musical part of the church service to chance; subsequent numbers offered advice on many aspects of the church musician's duties and provided free copies of suitable music – ranging from chants and responses to short anthems.

Examination of *The Parish Choir* provides a clear picture of the growth of the movement. Significantly, the part played by Helmore at St Mark's was readily acknowledged in it from the outset. And two years later, in 1848, a leading article emphasised that response in uncompromising terms:

> There is perhaps no institution of modern times which has done so much for the choral music of the Church of England as St. Mark's College, Chelsea.

But besides chronicling the course of the choral movement *The Parish Choir* also served to record the views and recommendations of its leaders and supporters. Central to its own policy was this definition of what it set out to achieve:

> By *Choral Service* is meant that mode of celebrating the public service by both priest and people, in which they sing all portions allotted to each respectively ... [*Parish Choir*, vol. 1, p. 26]

That this was not just an editor's opinion – nor even the view of a small managing committee – can be established by comparing those remarks with a comparable statement published in *The Ecclesiologist* in the same year:

> No music for the common parts of our offices is admissible which cannot be easily sung by all. [*Ecclesiologist*, vol. 5, p. 173]

Whenever *Parish Choir* and *Ecclesiologist* speak with one voice there is little room to doubt the truth of the matter. But there was to be a significant difference between them as to the best way of attaining this particular goal.

The Ecclesiologist, in its uncompromising way, insisted that plainchant provided the ideal medium for devout congregational participation. With that
goal in mind, once Helmore's *Psalter Noted* appeared, in 1849, it was adopted
almost as a party badge by ecclesiologists generally; and J. M. Neale speedily
arranged to join forces with Helmore in compiling a companion volume in *The
Hymnal Noted* (1851).

The Parish Choir, on the other hand, took a more realistic view of the matter.
The editor claimed that it was the merest common sense to avoid forcing upon
people changes they could not comprehend. To attempt a sudden transition
from vulgar hymn tunes to severe and strange Gregorian chants would arouse
a storm of opposition and prejudice. He ventured to ask if those who were so
loudly crying out for Gregorian chanting and nothing else, had not themselves
at some stage gone through the gradual development of musical taste that he
was recommending for the education of churchgoers generally.

In the sequel Robert Druitt's forecast was proved right. Both *The Psalter
Noted*, and *The Hymnal Noted* produced jointly with J. M. Neale, were to be
adopted mainly in churches noted for Tractarianism. Neither book obtained
general, or even wide, use. Indeed, both acquired the taint of party in the inter-
necine struggle between High and Low churchmen that surfaced after J. H.
Newman's secession in 1845 and the establishment of a Roman Catholic arch-
diocese of Westminster five years later. In the disgraceful 'No Popery' riots that
followed, one of the most violent affrays took place at St Barnabas, Pimlico,
where the adoption of *The Psalter Noted* and *The Hymnal Noted* together with
a robed choir underlined the exalted standards of churchmanship that so easily
inflamed mob feeling then.

Moreover, it is revealing to note that the unappealing 'strangeness' of plainchant mentioned by Druitt was to persist in the popular mind well beyond
the end of the century. Unreadiness to accept an unfamiliar, modal repertoire
was apparent even in the comparatively sophisticated musical atmosphere of
the cathedrals at least until the second decade of the present century. The title
alone of one of the Church Music Society's *Occasional Papers*, published in 1912,
says as much:

> *Elizabethan Church Music: A Short Enquiry into the Reasons for its Present
> Unpopularity and Neglect*

By mid-nineteenth century, as churches steadily responded to a new concept of
ordered worship, the movement to establish surpliced chancel choirs gathered
strength. Yet before long it became evident that many of those who had been
persuaded to follow the example of St Mark's College by setting up a robed

choir in their own churches were not adopting the type of choral service demonstrated at the college.

Instead, once a choir was established the tendency was often for it to sing the service while the congregation remained largely silent. The pattern for this as a deliberate practice in a parish church had first appeared at Leeds in 1841. Though not intended as a model for imitation elsewhere the choral services at Leeds appealed especially to those lacking Tractarian conviction. The usage was precisely opposed to that favoured by *The Parish Choir*. There was no plainchant; and singing was left to the choir – a policy incidentally welcomed both by music-lovers and by 'respectable' churchgoers who found communal singing incompatible with gentility.

The circumstances that gave rise to this state of affairs were unusual. As we have noted, a surpliced choir had been introduced at Leeds parish church by Dr. W. F. Hook's predecessor, the Revd Richard Fawcett, in 1818. The singers' fees were paid from the church rates, but after frequent objections at vestry meetings payment was withdrawn in 1833 and the choir was soon disbanded. When Dr Hook arrived to take up his appointment four years later the question of a choir did not arise. He was quite unmusical himself and certainly not a Tractarian sympathiser. In any case, Hook's overriding concern was with the neglected fabric of the church. Finding it too small and incapable of extension he decided to replace it with a new building.

It was only at this stage that a deputation of influential parishioners urged Hook to mark the opening of the new church by introducing daily choral services sung by a new surpliced choir. Hook's personal sense of the dignity of worship persuaded him to agree to the proposal – on condition that the highest standards were allowed to prevail and financial backing was assured.

For advice on future musical policy Hook now turned, not to Thomas Helmore or the editor of *The Parish Choir*, but to John Jebb, the nephew of his longstanding mentor Bishop Jebb of Limerick, and himself a prebendary of Limerick Cathedral. A devoted student of both liturgy and church music, Jebb's viewpoint was yet that of a cathedral dignitary: his attitude was precisely opposed to that of *The Parish Choir* and *The Ecclesiologist*. Hearty singing in the nave he dismissed as 'the roar of the congregation'; the Gregorian tones to his mind were merely 'the product of an age of musical infancy'.

But now, commissioned by Hook to address the townsfolk on the subject, it was Jebb who secured general assent to the introduction of a cathedral-type service, and the project went ahead. James Hill, recently a lay-clerk at Windsor, was engaged to recruit and train the new choir; and before the year was out Dr S. S. Wesley, then at Exeter Cathedral and the most admired church musician of his day, accepted the post of organist.

Although then only thirty-one years old, the ten frustrating years he had spent at Exeter and Hereford had left Wesley brusque, entrenched in his views, and not a little eccentric. If the subject of congregational singing was raised he made no attempt to hide his aversion to it. The use of plainchant equally exasperated him. Defenders of such primitive chants, he scornfully declared, would look a Michaelangelo in the face and tell him Stonehenge was the perfection of architecture.

There can be no doubt that for Leeds townsfolk generally the polished choral services at their splendid new church under S. S. Wesley's direction became a matter for intense pride – a pride other provincial towns were soon to envy while attempting to improve their own musical arrangements. And so, although without another S. S. Wesley to direct their efforts, churches in large towns tended to develop cathedral-type services of their own. Some of them, particularly where a serving organist had been trained as an articled pupil in a cathedral organ-loft, were able to produce praiseworthy results, musically speaking; but the concept of a choral service as one in which priest and people sang 'all portions allotted to each respectively' was contradicted by each success.

As attempts to adopt the Leeds model service spread further afield, failure became more common. Incompetent organists, inadequate choirs, unmusical parsons, interfering churchwardens, untalented composers and opportunistic music publishers, all helped to create travesties of the cathedral service – at first in larger towns, and eventually in remote towns and villages as well. Each failure virtually marked a return to the former regime of services dominated by incompetent choirs – but choirs now moved from west galleries to chancels and clad in surplices.

Twenty years after the introduction of cathedral-type services at Leeds Parish Church, a yet more extravagant form of choral service was introduced in London. In 1862 Benjamin Webb, one of the founders of the Ecclesiological Society, was appointed to the crown living of St Andrew's, Wells Street – a church with a fashionable and wealthy congregation that included many art-lovers and regular patrons of Covent Garden opera. With the moral and financial backing of those parishioners Webb set out to introduce into his church the best sculpture, stained glass, and music available. To help ensure the inclusion of admired examples of contemporary music, in 1863 he engaged the go-ahead and ambitious young Joseph Barnby as his organist.

St Andrew's at that time possessed a large professional, surpliced choir which Barnby forthwith trained to perform his own adaptations of continental motets and masses at choral celebrations of communion. Perhaps his most daring adventure in that line came in 1866 with a performance of Gounod's intense *Messe Solonnelle de Sainte Cécile* (1855) complete with harp obbligato. Despite his former advocacy of the simplicity of Gregorian music, Benjamin Webb now

A High Church congregation, as depicted in *Punch*, the leading humorous paper of the day. This illustration nicely captures the mundane attitude of a fashionable congregation in 1857.

defended the innovation against the charge of impropriety by declaring that 'the best of everything should be offered in God's service.' Following Barnby's boldness it now became usual for other affluent High churches in London to employ continental and Viennese Masses, often with orchestral accompaniment, at communion services.

Made celebrated if not notorious by these events, in 1871 Barnby moved to a new appointment at St Anne's, Soho, where even more lavish musical services were organised, attracting large congregations mainly drawn from outside the parish. One candid observer recorded that beyond 'a quiet hum' during the hymns there was no congregational singing at all at St Anne's. During an anthem people would crane their necks to identify individual soloists; and at its conclusion 'a small stampede' took place as many present left the church before the service was over.

The boundary between choral service and concert-hall performance had by this time grown culpably indistinct. Among the sardonic poor of the neighbourhood St Anne's was derisively known as 'The Sunday Opera'. But other churches were to strain their resources to match its musical splendours.

In dramatic contrast to the lavish musical display at St Anne's, Soho, a very different type of service made its appearance at another church in London in 1864. This time, the service was 'choral' only in the sense that it included noteworthy singing. What made it more remarkable was the complete absence of a choir in the church – apart from the congregation as a whole.

The prototype, indeed the sole true specimen of a genre never quite duplicated elsewhere, was to be found at the church of St Pancras, Euston Road, where Henry Smart became organist in 1864. He had been specifically appointed by the low-church vicar to develop a congregational form of service. This he proceeded systematically to do, adopting an unchanging order of service in which the responses were spoken and the psalms read; but the canticles were sung by all to familiar double chants and the singing of the hymns was acknowledged to be magnificent.

When he went to St Pancras at the age of fifty-one Smart was one of the leading organists of his day. A particularly facile extemporiser, he employed that talent to coax the people to sing – providing on the organ what would now be called a running commentary on the text of each hymn. The rule was that the people sang in unison. That left Smart free to reharmonise the tune so as to illustrate the changing sense and mood of each verse. Congregational hymn-practices of the type introduced in other churches were found unnecessary at St Pancras; the people simply learnt to respond to Smart's stimulating lead at the organ. Before long the whole congregation sang with enthusiasm and evident gratification. An attempt at one stage to introduce a surpliced choir at the church was roundly rejected.

Organists at other churches sought to follow Smart's example; but lacking his performing technique and the flair that enabled him to win over the congregation they were unable to repeat his success. But another reason for their failure was that the organs at their disposal were inadequate for the task.

At St Mark's College, Chelsea, there had been no organ at all. Services were unaccompanied – a circumstance governing the choice of music employed there. But by the 1860s opinions were changing and, where uncommitted churchmen were concerned, the musical splendours found in several 'fashionable' churches made the sedate services at St Mark's fade into pallor. Only in the staunchest of what were beginning to be called 'Anglo-Catholic' circles was loyalty to the original concept of a choral service maintained. Elsewhere the emotional pull exerted by lush music won eager converts. The self-satisfied term 'fully choral service' now came into use to emphasise the distinction.

Despite differences separating them in other respects, all types of service featuring music of any elaboration depended for much of their effect upon the judicious use of a sizeable organ at the hands of a skilful player. From about 1860 there was consequently a great increase in the number of churches installing new organs. The decisive factor for most parishes was, of course, expense.

The cheapest pipe-instrument available was a barrel-organ of the simple kind first introduced in country churches to replace gallery bands. With a few interchangeable barrels and the sexton to turn the handle, the salary of an organist – even if one could be found locally – was spared. Such an instrument was well suited to the needs and means of small communities.

'The Self-Playing Organ' (*c.* 1840),
from George Cruikshank's *Humorous Illustrations*

Later, and up to about 1870, larger and more elaborate barrel-organs were often installed in urban churches. Sometimes they were clockwork-operated. Special barrels could be supplied with a wide variety of tunes, chants, marches, and voluntaries. But these instruments were never without their hazards. One of George Cruikshank's most delightful illustrations depicts the stir, exasperation, and ill-concealed amusement caused when a large clockwork barrel-organ had to be removed during a service because it would not be silenced.

Clearly, no barrel-organ could meet the needs of a 'fully choral' service. And now that many of the grander provincial Town Halls were being supplied with vast new organs for concert use nothing less than a reasonably well equipped two- or three-manual and pedal organ would satisfy the parochial church council in a flourishing industrial town.

This was an important local development – for even some cathedral organs at the time were without full pedalboards; most of them belonged to an age when organ accompaniment was limited to playing from figured basses. When Sir George Smart, organist of the Chapel Royal, was invited to try a modern pedal-organ at the Crystal Palace in 1851 he is said to have refused – because, as he boasted, he had 'never played on a *gridiron*'. It is also significant in this respect that T. A. Walmisley's remarkable *Evening Service* in D minor (*c.* 1855) was one of the very first Anglican settings to have an independent organ part.

The installation or rebuilding and enlarging of church organs – and the consequent growth of a more advanced school of organ-playing – was only one of the developments in church music to take place in mid-century on the tide of growing industrial and commercial prosperity. Another indirect influence stemming from the same source was the amazing number of new churches then being built.

Between 1840 and 1874 more than £25m was raised for the building and restoration of churches. All shades of churchmanship were involved; but for present purposes the impact this expansion made among Broad churchmen is most interesting. As a direct result of the Ecclesiological Society's activities, by mid-century neo-Gothic churches on approved lines had been built in parishes throughout the land. A standard feature of their structure was a deep chancel with facing choir-stalls. It was the mute invitation of those rows of empty stalls, quite as much as external argument, that persuaded many Broad churches to introduce surpliced choirs. However, we are told that a sense of rivalry with neighbouring parishes was not without its influence as well.

Once introduced, a choir's duties in a Broad church were largely undefined. The authorities concerned, disregarding on grounds of churchmanship unwelcome Tractarian admonition, usually settled for an unconscious parody of a 'fully choral service' amounting in most cases to little more than banal settings and anthems written to order for choirs just like their own.

Long before the century ended it was clear that the only realistic medium for congregational participation in church was the strophic hymn with a regularly rhythmic tune repeated verse by verse. Chanting, whether to plainsong melodies, Anglican chants or otherwise, never proved more than tentative – because it lacked regular drive and had no secular counterpart to familiarise it. And since chanting becomes confident only with regular practice it was found to be something best left to choirs, whose weekly rehearsals could strive to perfect it.

As to hymn repertory, there was at this time certainly no shortage of available hymnals. The flood of hymns produced during the eighteenth and nineteenth centuries was at first scattered among scores of sectarian hymnals containing examples of verse and tunes that occasionally touched excellence but more frequently proved regrettable. With the compilation of *Hymns, Ancient*

& Modern in 1861 the Church of England came near to having its own hymnal. As its title foretold, the book brought together examples of plainsong melodies, Lutheran chorales, metrical psalms, eighteenth- and nineteenth-century hymns, together with a few new tunes of a distinctive type, the work of Dykes, Ouseley and Monk. An *Appendix* followed in 1868 in which more than half the tunes were new. Among them were examples by Dykes, Smart, Elvey, Stainer and Barnby overtly reflecting the emotional style of the day.

To particularise: As we have seen, Barnby's admiration for the lush style of Charles Gounod had been responsible for his introducing the *Messe Solennelle* at St Andrew's, Wells Street, in 1866. It was to be no less responsible for the emotional content of Barnby's own hymn tunes. One example. *Cloisters*, provides a notable instance. This tune found a place in the 1868 Appendix to *Hymns, A&M*, and has continued to appeal to romantically susceptible churchgoers ever since.

The pocket-romanticism captured in *Cloisters* often recurs elsewhere. It is salutary, for instance, to investigate how frequently new tunes of the 1860s included what may be called the 'Liebestraum ending':

Some commentators today (perhaps attempting to imitate yesterday's artistic rehabilitation of the Albert Memorial) are inclined to disregard such issues and rate Victorian hymn tunes solely on grounds of popularity. The process involves equating, say, Barnby's swooning *Cloisters* with Goss's forthright *Praise, my soul* and commending both equally. But this is to ignore the opinions of Barnby's professional contemporaries – such as S. S. Wesley and Henry Smart, both of whom deplored his vulgarity. It is also to brush aside Thomas Helmore's outspoken condemnation:

> To me most modern hymn tunes are ... nauseous; and there are some others I utterly abhor, as being so tainted with the natural expression of frivolous, or even corrupt associations, that in their very essence they are wholly unsuitable for divine worship ...

Nor was such outspokenness on Helmore's part limited to the condemnation of voluptuous hymn tunes. He was equally frank on wider questions – such as the partisan stance of some churchgoers over the roles of choir and people in church.

One wonders today whether it was just a lingering puritanic trait in the national character that led protestors to see the choral movement only as a source of confrontation between choir and people. For there were many who maintained that if singing took place in church, all should sing; that a choir only robbed them of that right. Then there were others who insisted that it was only the unmusical who wished to do all the singing. Understandably in such circumstances, the intermediate notion that members of a congregation might benefit – even spiritually – from listening to a capable and well-rehearsed choir, found little sympathy among the musically inept.

Yet in defining the choral service *The Ecclesiologist* had been careful to emphasise that it was just the *common* parts of the liturgy that were to be sung by all. And in addressing the Church Congress in 1867 Thomas Helmore re-emphasised the part listening played in church services:

> I fear [he said] many pious people have not fully realised the fact that it is as possible, and as right (abstractly speaking) to stand before the altar in worship silently, while a choir is raising some solemn or joyous strain to the praise of Almighty God, as it is to stand silent while the Scripture lesson or the Epistle is read.

The point at issue – the choir's role – was a matter that from the outset had set Calvinist and Lutheran at variance. Calvin's choir was never to sing alone. Luther deliberately gave to the choir the duty of stimulating devotion among a listening assembly. Cantors and choir schools were pointedly retained by him. His determination to safeguard the Lutheran church in this way from the musical sterility of Calvinism is acknowledged to have played a major part in developing the Germans as a musical race. It also exemplifies the Church fulfilling its ancient function as educator and enlightener.

That there were not more among the clergy prepared to follow Helmore's outspoken lead on choral issues – whether locally or nationally – seems due to the prevalence in England at the time of a musically uneducated priesthood. It is disconcerting to realise that while ultimate authority for the musical conduct of church services rests with the clergy, when choral services were reintroduced very many parsons showed themselves incapable of singing even the versicles at morning and evening prayer.

In his day Luther had little truck with unmusical clergy. As Henrie Bell's translation of Luther's *Colloquia Mensalia* has it:

> I alwaies loved Musick (said Luther) ... neither should we ordain young fellows to the office of preaching, except before [hand] they have been well exercised and practised in the School of Musick. [Cap. LXVIII]

Circumstances are too different today for direct comparisons with the events outlined here to be profitable. But within the panorama of aspiration and disappointment unfolded in these pages certain details will no doubt strike readers as reminiscent of their own experience. The purpose in making this record has been historical rather than oracular. Yet when old difficulties reappear, it is perhaps as well to recognise within them problems previously pushed to one side in the hope they would disappear. Patently, some of them have not done so.

Rich Source Material

[1998]

Review of Ruth M. Wilson, *Anglican Chant and Chanting in England,
Scotland and America, 1660–1820* (Oxford: Clarendon Press, 1996)

O N HIS FIRST VISIT to London in the 1880s Antonín Dvořák was
taken to attend Evensong at St Paul's Cathedral. After listening somewhat restively to the choir chanting the psalms for the day he whispered to
his escort, 'Why do they keep singing that wretched little tune over and over
again?' More than half a century later church musicians in England would still
recount that discreditable incident as an indictment of the Anglican chant.

For although in its initial post-Reformation form what was to become
known as an Anglican chant had comprised a plainsong *canto fermo* with
added parts above and below it, later opinion found the structure restrictive
and its effect wearisome. Psalm-tone tenors were steadily abandoned. Then,
growing congregational participation in sung services in parish churches and a
popular disposition to sing rather than chant encouraged the use of new chants
dominated by a 'tuneful' treble line. The wider compass involved was welcome
to ambitious sopranos in the nave – though their menfolk could no longer join
in. An illuminating example of this 'improved' form is found in the double
chant that Goss cannibalised from the Adagio in Beethoven's 'Pathétique'
sonata.

As to the history of the Anglican chant prior to that deterioration, the information and sources cited in Scholes and Grove have long been found sufficient.
Indeed, before the publication of the present book, that resource went unchallenged. The appearance of Dr Wilson's consummate treatise has radically
altered the situation.

What we find here is a survey beginning at the crucial point when the return
of King Charles II from exile in 1660 marked both the end of Puritan rule
and the reinstatement of the Common Prayer. But before launching into discussion of purely musical matters Dr Wilson is careful to introduce her readers to the tangle of unresolved debate impeding liturgical revival in 1600. Few
assumptions are made about the general reader's familiarity with the complex contemporary scene. Each step of the way is carefully scanned. Hitherto
arcane political, legal, and liturgical circumstances preceding or delaying each
major musical development are examined. The same policy is pursued in later
sections of the book where the differing situations in England, Scotland and
America are considered. In each case an introductory section explains the historical circumstances and often rigorously defended religious differences to

be resolved before musical innovation became feasible. Not least among this book's many strengths are those explanatory surveys and the rich source material they introduce.

The author reminds us that the traditional manner of performing Divine Service – something formerly taught by example – was largely forgotten during the long hiatus of the Commonwealth. But on Charles' return, aided by the recollections of former precentors, organists and singing men, an acceptable form of choral service was restored surprisingly quickly at Westminster Abbey, the Chapel Royal, and sundry university college chapels. Elsewhere, as new dignitaries, organists, and lay-clerks were appointed or reinstated, fresh choristers mustered and new surplices sewn, the publication of Edward Lowe's authoritative *Short Direction for the Performance of Cathedral Service* in 1661, enabled provincial cathedrals to follow suit.

Meanwhile, surviving part-books and archives had been combed for details of the music formerly in use – most copies of it since destroyed by Cromwellian fanatics. Prominent among the findings were Sarum responsorial and psalm-tone melodies, some of them with contemporary harmonisations.

Much of this recovered material (a good part of it pre-dating the Reformation) was now published anew by such compilers as Lowe, Clifford, and Playford to form the stock-in-trade of most cathedral and collegiate choirs. A number of early chant melodies recovered in that way are reproduced here, together with sundry four-part harmonised settings with verbal underlaying to demonstrate the syllabic and rhythmic treatment of the opening verses of particular psalms or canticles.

At this time, too, among the first new choristers recruited and trained by Henry Cooke for the Chapel Royal were several boys who became competent composers. A number of the youthful chants they composed for the Chapel Royal (without psalm-tone tenors) were widely used elsewhere and became models for other composers. The most durable of them remain in use to this day.

While psalm and canticle represented the most substantial and variable sections of the liturgy to be chanted, versicles and responses (including the Litany) and exhortatory prayers also called for musical recitation – if only because 'in very large Churches it serves to make the voice more audible.' To trace ancient usage surviving documents were further examined. But chanting was not universally welcomed by the clergy. Dr Wilson examines the arguments advanced for and against the practice in several dioceses where it was not to be adopted until well into the 19th century.

Once a pattern had been established and demonstrated in the major cathedrals an ambition to adopt at least some part of the choral service in urban churches began to make itself felt early in the 18th century. The precise meaning of ambiguous rubrics governing what should be 'said or sung' in Divine Service came under eager discussion. The author quotes some characteristic arguments concerning the desirability of sung services in parish churches; and supplies extracts from contemporary hymn collections and chant books revealing the often ambitious material local choirs were being invited to undertake. Evidence confirms that in some cases – perhaps particularly in Yorkshire – not just church choirs, but whole congregations were soon making successful attempts to 'chaunt' parts of the service. Dr Wilson attributes this new competence to the efforts of those independent 'teachers of psalmody' who formed an established feature of the musical scene in England at this time. However, while conceding that the best of these men were successful teachers, one knows from evidence elsewhere that many of their fellows were sadly incompetent.

Amid a diversity of early attempts to develop choral services in parish churches a common pattern at length established itself. Versicles and responses generally remained spoken. Prose canticles and doxologies, not being subject to change, were chanted by rote. The constantly changing prose psalms were usually read, augmented by sung metrical versions, though a few churches chanted them. Additionally, an anthem might mark a special occasion; and where an organ was available, voluntaries were played before and after service.

Such was the form of 'musical' service attempted in the generality of English parish churches during the 18th century. It was next to become the model for imitation in Scotland and the United States of America.

Strangers to Scotland sometimes expect to find that Calvinism permanently destroyed all church music there. Nurtured on hoary tales of grim chapelgoers battling unsuccessfully with Genevan psalm-tunes in compulsorily organless meeting houses, they are surprised to find that, among Episcopalians at least, music's contribution to worship has long been esteemed.

Before examining the Scottish aspect of her topic, Dr Wilson consequently outlines the vicissitudes of episcopacy in Scotland since its re-establishment at the Restoration. Her readers learn that Episcopalian assemblies on the Lord's day initially started with singing a metrical psalm during which 'most of the congregation sat irreverently on their breech, only they were uncovered. Then came a long Sermon, the text of which was no sooner read, but most of the People put on their hats or bonnets ... They rose up at the Doxology, though some thought even that too superstitious.' There was little to promise an upsurge of liturgical decorum in those early days.

Yet before long, modified versions of the English prayer book were in use; and by mid-18th century new chapels were being built – one in Aberdeen reported by an English visitor around 1730 as having 'an organ, the only one I know of, and the service is chanted as in our cathedrals'. That advanced model was to be imitated – though not always smoothly – in Edinburgh, Glasgow,

Inverness, Perth, and many smaller towns before the close of the century. Indeed, by the 1780s St Andrew's Church, Glasgow had eighteen boy choristers and its own published collection of sacred music. Dr Wilson lists no fewer than thirty local Scottish music books of this type published between 1742 and 1817, and reproduces numerous 'chant tunes' of the type used in Scottish Episcopal services.

In America the presence of many longstanding British emigres coupled with the incursion of Scottish Episcopalian refugees fleeing punitive measures that followed the '45 rebellion helps explain the establishment of an independent Protestant Episcopal Church in America with a liturgy of its own. Dr Wilson guides her readers through the complexities heralding those events and then describes the gradual emergence of a repertory of service music for its use. The first of a succession of locally published books containing metrical psalms, responses, anthems and a few chants appeared in 1783. Most of the chants in it were drawn from an earlier Scottish collection. Almost hidden among the indigenous material contained in later books of service music were to be found chants written by Blow and Turner for the Chapel Royal of Charles II.

Venite, Te Deum, and canticles are known to have been chanted in a few Episcopalian churches in America by 1787; and mixed choirs were now established in organ galleries 'to fill the harmonies with bass and treble parts, and give dignity to the performance.' Surpliced choirs with boy trebles are first recorded in the last years of the century.

Listed in an Appendix are some forty early collections of service music published for Episcopalian use. In addition, sundry examples of chant tunes and settings drawn from many sources appear in the text. Most reflect Anglican usage, but sometimes added embellishments or an idiosyncratic organ interlude seem to betray the adventurous spirit of the New World.

Dr Wilson's achievement in researching and writing this boundary-stretching book has produced a valuable companion volume to Ian Spink's recent *Restoration Cathedral Music, 1660–1714* by exhibiting the other side of the same medal. Indeed, this latest addition to the continuing *Oxford Studies in British Church Music* confers a further trophy upon that justifiably acclaimed series.

Index

Classic Texts in Music Education

Edited with introductions by Bernarr Rainbow

The above titles are available separately from Boydell & Brewer

Rainbow's introductions to the complete series of forty-five texts are collected in *Four Centuries of Teaching Manuals, 1518–1932*, with an Introduction by Gordon Cox (Boydell, 2009). The prefaces are:

1 Georg Rhau, *Enchiridion utrisque musica practicae*, 1518

2 Martin Agricola, *Rudimenta musices*, 1539

3 Loys Bourgeois, *The Direct Road to Music* (*Le droict chemin de musique*), 1550 [CTME 4]

4 Bernarr Rainbow and various authors, *English Psalmody Prefaces: Popular Methods of Teaching*, 1562–1835 [CTME 2]

5 William Bathe, *A Briefe Introduction to the Skill of Song*, 1587 [CTME 3]

6 J. C. Pepusch, *A Treatise on Harmony*, 1731

7 J. J. Rousseau, *Project Concerning New Symbols for Music* (*Projet concernant de nouveaux signes*), 1742 [CTME 1]

8 Anne Gunn, *Introduction to Music*, 1803

9 A. F. C. Kollmann, *A New Theory of Musical Harmony*, 1806

10 J. W. Callcott, *A Musical Grammar in Four Parts*, 1806

11 H. G. Nägeli, *Die Pestalozzische Gesangbildungslehre*, 1809

12 H. G. Nägeli, *Gesangbildungslehre*, 1810

13 William Crotch, *Elements of Musical Composition*, 1812 [CTME 16]

14 J. B. Logier, *Companion to the Patent Royal Chiroplast*, 1815

15 P. Galin, *Rationale for a New Way of Teaching Music* (from *Exposition d'une nouvelle méthode*), 1818 [CTME 8]

16 J. Kemp, *The New System of Musical Education*, 1819

17 M. P. (Dorothy Kilner), *The Child's Introduction to Thorough Bass*, 1819

18 Edouard Jue de Berneval, *La musique apprise sans maître*, 1824

19 F. J. Fétis, *Music Explained to the World* (*La musique mise à la portée de tout le monde*), 1830 [CTME 13]

20 William C. Stafford, *A History of Music*, 1830 [CTME 18]

21 William Crotch, *Substance of Several Courses of Lectures on Music*, 1831

22 John Turner, *A Manual of Instruction in Vocal Music*, 1833 [CTME 6]

23 S. Glover, *Scheme for Rendering Psalmody Congregational* together with *The Sol-fa Tune Book*, 1835 [CTME 5]

24 W. E. Hickson, *The Singing Master*, 1836 [CTME 10]

25 A. Rodwell, *The Juvenile Pianist*, 1836

26 Adolph Bernhard Marx, *The Universal School of Music* (*Allgemeine Musiklehre*), 1839 (trans 1853)